DUE DILIGENCE OBLIGATIONS IN INTERNATIONAL HUMAN RIGHTS LAW

With the importance of non-State actors ever increasing, the traditional State-centric approach of international law is being put to the test. In particular, significant accountability lacunae have emerged in the field of human rights protection. To address these challenges, this book makes a case for extraterritorial due diligence obligations of States in international human rights law. It traces back how due diligence obligations evolved on the international plane and develops a general analytical framework making the broad and vague notion of due diligence more approachable. The framework is applied to different fields of international law which provides guidance on how due diligence obligations can be better conceptualized. Drawing inspiration from these developments, the book analyses how extraterritorial human rights due diligence obligations could operate in practice and foster global human rights protection.

MARIA MONNHEIMER is a research assistant at LMU Munich. Prior to this she served as legal clerk to the Federal Ministry of Justice in Berlin and the European Court of Human Rights in Strasbourg. Maria studied law at the University of Heidelberg and University of Cambridge and holds a Ph.D. in Public International Law from LMU Munich.

DUE DILIGENCE OBLIGATIONS IN INTERNATIONAL HUMAN RIGHTS LAW

Maria Monnheimer

Ludwig Maximilian University of Munich

CAMBRIDGE
UNIVERSITY PRESS

University Printing House, Cambridge CB2 8BS, United Kingdom

One Liberty Plaza, 20th Floor, New York, NY 10006, USA

477 Williamstown Road, Port Melbourne, VIC 3207, Australia

314–321, 3rd Floor, Plot 3, Splendor Forum, Jasola District Centre, New Delhi – 110025, India

79 Anson Road, #06-04/06, Singapore 079906

Cambridge University Press is part of the University of Cambridge.

It furthers the University's mission by disseminating knowledge in the pursuit of education, learning, and research at the highest international levels of excellence.

www.cambridge.org
Information on this title: www.cambridge.org/9781108841733
DOI: 10.1017/9781108894784

© Maria Monnheimer 2021

This publication is in copyright. Subject to statutory exception and to the provisions of relevant collective licensing agreements, no reproduction of any part may take place without the written permission of Cambridge University Press.

First published 2021

A catalogue record for this publication is available from the British Library.

Library of Congress Cataloging-in-Publication Data
Names: Monnheimer, Maria, 1988– author.
Title: Due diligence obligations in international human rights law / Maria Monnheimer, Ludwig Maximilian University of Munich.
Description: Cambridge, United Kingdom ; New York, NY : Cambridge University Press, 2020. | Includes bibliographical references and index.
Identifiers: LCCN 2020019030 (print) | LCCN 2020019031 (ebook) | ISBN 9781108841733 (hardback) | ISBN 9781108795265 (paperback) | ISBN 9781108894784 (ebook)
Subjects: LCSH: International law and human rights. | Liability for human rights violations.
Classification: LCC KZ1266 .M66 2020 (print) | LCC KZ1266 (ebook) | DDC 341.4/8–dc23
LC record available at https://lccn.loc.gov/2020019030
LC ebook record available at https://lccn.loc.gov/2020019031

ISBN 978-1-108-84173-3 Hardback

Cambridge University Press has no responsibility for the persistence or accuracy of URLs for external or third-party internet websites referred to in this publication and does not guarantee that any content on such websites is, or will remain, accurate or appropriate.

CONTENTS

Acknowledgments *page* xv
List of Abbreviations xvi

Introduction 1

1 **Why to Analyze State Responsibility for Human Rights Violations: The Flawed Debate on Direct Human Rights Obligations for Non-State Actors** 9

    I. Introductory Remarks 9

    II. Why the Existing Human Rights Regime Cannot Be Construed to Contain Direct Obligations for Non-State Actors 13
        1. Customary International Law 14
        2. General Principles 16
        3. Human Rights Treaties 17
            a. Human Rights Treaties as Living Instruments 18
            b. *Drittwirkung* 23
            c. "Abuse of Rights" Clauses 26
        4. Summary 28

    III. Reasons Speaking for Direct Human Rights Obligations on Behalf of Private Actors 30

    IV. Reasons against Imposing Direct Human Rights Obligations on Non-State Actors 32
        1. Procedural and Definitional Questions 32
            a. Non-State Actors and International Norm Setting 32
            b. Making Non-State Actors Duty Bearers: "Capacity" as an Adequate Yardstick? 34
            c. Shared Accountability between States and Non-State Actors? 37

2. Legitimacy Questions: Non-State Actors and the Balancing of Public Interests   38
3. Abuse Concerns   41
   a. A Chance for States to Neglect Their Own Duties   42
   b. Awarding Corresponding Rights to Non-State Actors   42

V. Conclusion: The Necessity of Exploiting the Full Potential of State Responsibility   43

2 Establishing State Responsibility for Human Rights Violations: Proposal for a Conduct-Based Typology of Human Rights Obligations   47

I. Introductory Remarks   47

II. The Inadequacy of Traditional Human Rights Typologies   48
   1. Three Generations of Human Rights   49
   2. Obligations to Respect, Protect, and Fulfill   51
   3. Positive versus Negative Obligations   52

III. Proposal for a Conduct-Based Typology of Human Rights   54
   1. Positive Human Rights Obligations of Result   55
      a. Preventive Obligations of Result   56
         aa. The Duty to Enact Legislation   56
            (1) Failure to Enact Legislation   58
            (2) Enacting Legislation That Violates Human Rights   60
         bb. The Duty to Establish an Administrative Apparatus   61
      b. Punitive Obligations of Result   63
         aa. The Duty to Establish an Investigative and Judicial Apparatus   63
         bb. The Duty to Create Legal Remedies   64
         cc. The Duty to Investigate Allegations of Human Rights Violations   65
         dd. The Duty to Provide for Specific Criminal Legislation   67
         ee. The Duty to Award Reparations   68
   2. Positive Human Rights Obligations of Diligent Conduct   69
      a. Preventive Obligations of Diligent Conduct   71

           b. Repressive Obligations of Diligent Conduct   71
        3. Positive Obligations of Progressive Realization   74
        4. Margin of Appreciation   75
   IV. Summary   76

3 **The Origins of Due Diligence in International Law   78**
   I. Introductory Remarks   78
   II. Due Diligence in Early Scholarly Writings   78
        1. Grotius's Concept of *Patientia* and *Receptus* Responsibility   79
        2. Pufendorf and the Presumption of Capacities to Prevent   80
        3. Wolff and Vattel: From Responsibility of the Monarch to Responsibility of States   80
        4. Hall and Oppenheim: Reasonable Measures of Prevention and Vicarious Responsibility   81
        5. Summary   82
   III. Due Diligence in Early Jurisprudence   83
        1. The Duty to Protect Foreigners and the Establishment of Claims Commissions   83
        2. The Jurisprudence of the Claims Commissions   84
           a. Preventive Obligations of Due Diligence   85
           b. Repressive Obligations of Due Diligence   86
           c. Due Diligence versus Complicity   87
           d. Responsibility in Case of Civil Insurgency   88
        3. Due Diligence Obligations in Transboundary Cases   89
   IV. Due Diligence within the System of State Responsibility   90
        1. Failed Attempts at Codification   90
        2. The ILC's Work on State Responsibility and the Due Diligence Concept   92
   V. Confusion of Concepts: Distinguishing Due Diligence from Other Responsibility Concepts   92
        1. Actions and Omissions   93
        2. Fault   94
           a. The Role of Fault within the Law on State Responsibility: General Remarks   95
           b. Due Diligence Obligations and Negligence   96

c. Due Diligence as a Standard of Conduct Contained in Primary Norms   97
3. Liability for Acts Not Prohibited by International Law   99
   a. Responsibility versus Liability   99
   b. Draft Articles on Prevention of Transboundary Harm   101
4. Obligations of Conduct and Obligations of Result   102
   a. Ago's Proposal   102
   b. Why the Distinction Matters: The Temporal Dimension of a Breach   103
   c. The ILC's Proposal on Preventive Obligations   105
5. Complicity   106
   a. Complicity in Wrongful Conduct of Other States   107
   b. Complicity in Non-State Conduct   109
      aa. Complicity in Case of Individual Criminal Responsibility   109
      bb. Complicity as Ground for Attribution   110
      cc. Complicity versus Due Diligence: Where the Confusion Comes From   111
         (1) Why the Distinction Is Relevant   112
         (2) Distinction Based on the "Knowledge" Criterion   112

VI. Summary   114

4 The Components of the Due Diligence Standard   116

I. Introductory Remarks   116

II. Knowledge   117
   1. Positive Knowledge   118
   2. Constructive Knowledge   118
      a. An Obligation to Acquire Knowledge   119
      b. Determination by Objective Factors   119

III. Capacities   121
   1. Institutional Capacities   122
   2. Territorial and Financial Capacities   123
      a. Territorial Capacities   124
      b. Technical and Financial Capacities   126
      c. *Force Majeure* / Necessity   127

IV. Reasonableness 128
  1. Elements of Reasonableness under International Law 129
     a. Reasonableness and Proportionality 130
     b. Reasonableness and Rationality 132
     c. Reasonableness and Compliance 133
     d. Reasonableness and Balancing 134
  2. Assessing Reasonableness: Objective versus Subjective Approaches 136
  3. Burden of Proof 137

V. Summary 140

5 Lessons to Be Learned from the Application of Due Diligence Obligations in Other Fields of International Law 142

5.1. Due Diligence Obligations in International Environmental Law 144

I. Introductory Remarks 144

II. Preventive Obligations and the No-Harm Rule 145

III. Knowledge 147
  1. Precautionary Obligations 147
  2. An Obligation to Acquire Knowledge: Environmental Impact Assessments 150
  3. An Obligation to Share Knowledge? Duties to Cooperate 153

IV. Capacities 154
  1. Best Available Technologies 155
  2. Common but Differentiated Responsibilities 156

V. Reasonableness 159
  1. Technological Development 159
  2. Sustainability 159
  3. Objective versus Subjective Standards of Care 160
  4. Burden of Proof 161

VI. Summary 163

5.2. Due Diligence Obligations to Curb Terrorist Activities   167

    I. Introductory Remarks   167

    II. Knowledge   171

    III. Capacity   172
         1. Institutional Capacities   172
         2. Financial and Territorial Capacities   173
             a. Self-Defense against Non-State Actors?   173
             b. The Unwilling or Unable-Standard   177
                 aa. Is There an Obligation to Enhance Capacities?   178
                 bb. Does Inability Justify a Forceful Response by Other States?   179
                 cc. Broadening the Scope of Reasonable Efforts   181

    IV. Summary   183

5.3. Due Diligence Obligations in the Cybersphere   185

    I. Introductory Remarks   185

    II. The Problem of Attribution in the Cybersphere   186

    III. Due Diligence in the Cybersphere   188
         1. Due Diligence Obligations in the Aftermath of a Cyber Incident   189
         2. Preventive Due Diligence Obligations in the Cybersphere   190
             a. Knowledge: The Foreseeability of Harmful Cyber Incidents   190
             b. Reasonable Measures of Prevention   193
             c. Shifting the Burden of Proof?   195
             d. Capacities in the Cybersphere   197

    IV. Summary: Is There Room for Preventive Cyber Obligations?   199

5.4. Summary   202

6 Applying the Due Diligence Framework to the Field of Human Rights Protection 204

I. Introductory Remarks   204

II. Knowledge   204
1. Obtaining Knowledge: The Risk of Excessive Surveillance and Control   206
2. The Knowledge Standard in Human Rights Jurisprudence   208
   a. Information of Human Rights Risks   209
   b. Constellations in Which States Create or Contribute to the Creation of Human Rights Risks   212
      aa. Licensing Procedures   212
      bb. Creation of Risks   213
   c. Consistent Patterns of Human Rights Violations   214
      aa. Frequency of Human Rights Contraventions in the Past   215
      bb. Frequent Human Rights Violations in a Particular Region   215
      cc. Particular Risks for Certain Groups of Individuals   216
   d. Summary   217
3. Human Rights Impact Assessments   218

III. Capacities   220
1. Human Rights Due Diligence Obligations of Developing Countries   222
2. Human Rights Due Diligence Obligations in Times of Economic Crisis   225
3. Human Rights Due Diligence Obligations in Conflict Situations   227
4. Human Rights Obligations Not Dependent on Capacities   231
   a. Nondiscrimination   232
   b. Duties to Monitor and to Inform   233
   c. Duties of Cooperation   236
      aa. Obligations to Seek Assistance   237
      bb. Obligations to Render Assistance: Drawing Inspiration from the "Common but Differentiated Responsibilities" Approach   239
   d. Core Obligations   241
      aa. Nonderogable Rights   242
      bb. Minimum Core Obligations   242

5. Summary   244

IV. Reasonableness   244
   1. Scope of Measures   248
      a. Status of the Right That Is to Be Protected   248
      b. Preventive Obligations: Seriousness of Risk   250
      c. Punitive Obligations: Seriousness of Violation   251
      d. Balancing with Other Human Rights and Public Interests   252
   2. Nature of Measures   254
   3. Conclusion   255

V. Concluding Remarks   256

7 A Case for Extraterritorial Due Diligence Obligations in the Human Rights Context   258

I. Introductory Remarks   258

II. Between Universal Human Rights Protection and the Principle of Non-Intervention: The Tension Underlying Extraterritorial Human Rights Protection   260

III. Jurisdictional Clauses in International Human Rights Regimes   263

IV. Jurisdictional Clauses and State Responsibility   265

V. Negative versus Positive Obligations in Extraterritorial Cases   267
   1. The ECtHR's Perspective   268
   2. The ICJ's Perspective   272

VI. The Underdeveloped Potential of Positive Obligations of Diligent Conduct in Extraterritorial Constellations   274
   1. When Knowledge Can Be Expected in Extraterritorial Constellations   275
      a. Due Diligence Obligations When the Victim is within a State's Jurisdictional Reach   276
      b. Due Diligence Obligations When the Perpetrator is within a State's Jurisdictional Reach   277

2. Reasonable Efforts in Extraterritorial Constellations: Reconciling Positive Obligations with the Principle of Non-Intervention   278
3. Capacities   284

VII. Can There Be an Obligation to Act Extraterritorially? Drawing Inspiration from the "Unwilling or Unable" Standard   284
1. Human Rights as a Common Concern and the Issue of Diverging Capacities   286
2. How Extraterritorial Regulations Based on the Active Personality Principle Could Improve Human Rights Protection   289

VIII. First Steps in the Right Direction: Social and Economic Rights   290

IX. Areas in Which Extraterritorial Due Diligence Obligations Could Be Applied   292
1. Licensing Procedures   292
   a. Foreign Trade Promotion: Drawing Inspiration from Procedural Obligations in Environmental Law   293
   b. Applying the Due Diligence Standard to Arms Transfer Control   296
      aa. International Norms Applicable to Arms Transfer   296
      bb. Human Rights Law and Arms Transfer   297
      cc. Attribution, Complicity, and Aiding and Abetting in the Context of Arms Transfers   299
      dd. Due Diligence Obligations in the Context of Arms Transfers?   300
         (1) The *Tugar* Decision   300
         (2) Knowledge   301
         (3) Capacities   301
         (4) Reasonableness   302
         (5) Impact Assessments   303
      ee. Summary   306
   c. Conclusion   306
2. Regulating Extraterritorial Corporate Conduct   307
   a. Introductory Remarks   307
   b. The French Law on Duty of Care 2017   309

- c. Proposals on Corporate Regulations within the European Union   312
  - aa. EU Directive 2014/95/EU   313
  - bb. EU Flagship Initiative on the Garment Sector   313
- d. The Californian Transparency in Supply Chains Act of 2010   314
- e. The UK Modern Slavery Act of 2015   315
- f. Domestic Proposals on the Regulation of Extraterritorial Corporate Conduct   316
  - aa. Proposal by the German Green Party of 2016 and Coalition Agreement of 2018   316
  - bb. Switzerland: *Konzerninitiative Verantwortung*   318
- g. Conclusion   319

Summary and Outlook   322

Index   327

ACKNOWLEDGMENTS

This book is a revised and abridged version of my doctoral thesis, which I defended at the LMU Faculty of Law in December 2018.

Among the many people who accompanied me on the long way to completing a PhD, the person I am most indebted to is my supervisor *Professor Dr. Christian Walter,* whom I genuinely thank for never pushing me – but for always having sound advice, constructive criticism, and a word of encouragement when it was needed. Without his guidance and support, I could not have completed this work the way I did.

Further thanks are due to my second supervisor *Professor Dr. Rudolf Streinz* for his thorough and favorable report, as well as to *Professor Dr. Jens Kersten* for an interesting and inspiring viva.

To my friends and colleagues at the LMU Chair of Public International Law, *Stefan Herrmann, Stefan Schäferling, Chun-Kyung Paulus Suh,* and *Markus Vordermayer-Riemer,* I am grateful not only for creating an enriching academic environment but even more for making my time in Munich so memorable.

Finally, I offer my heartfelt thanks to *Tom Randall* of Cambridge University Press, who patiently guided me through my publishing journey from the first step to the last and to two anonymous reviewers for their helpful comments and suggestions.

ABBREVIATIONS

ACHR	American Convention on Human Rights
AfComHPR	African Commission of Human and Peoples' Rights
AJIL	American Journal of International Law
a.o.	and others
ASIL	American Society of International Law
AVR	Archiv des Völkerrechts
BIT	bilateral investment treaty
CESCR	Committee on Economic, Social and Cultural Rights
CETS	Council of Europe Treaty Series
CLP	Current Legal Problems
CRC	Committee on the Rights of the Child
DARS	Draft Articles on Responsibility of States for Internationally Wrongful Acts
DRC	Democratic Republic of the Congo
ECHR	European Convention on Human Rights
ECJ	European Court of Justice
EComHR	European Commission of Human Rights
ECOWAS	Economic Community of West African States
ECtHR	European Court of Human Right
EHRLR	European Human Rights Law Review
EJIL	European Journal of International Law
ESIL	European Society of International Law
ETS	European Treaty Series
EU	European Union
GA	General Assembly
GYIL	German Yearbook of International Law
HRC	Human Rights Committee
HRLR	Human Rights Law Review
IAComHR	Inter-American Commission of Human Rights
IACtHR	Inter-American Court of Human Rights
IAEA	International Atomic Energy Agency
ICC	International Criminal Court
ICCPR	International Covenant on Civil and Political Rights

LIST OF ABBREVIATIONS

ICESCR	International Covenant on Economic, Social and Cultural Rights
ICJ	International Court of Justice
ICLQ	International and Comparative Law Quarterly
ICSID	International Centre for Settlement of Investment Disputes
ICTY	International Criminal Tribunal for the former Yugoslavia
ILA	International Law Association
ILC	International Law Commission
ILM	International Legal Materials
IMO	International Maritime Organization
ITLOS	International Tribunal for the Law of the Sea
JILP NYU	Journal of International Law and Politics
LJIL	Leiden Journal of International Law
MJIL	Michigan Journal of International Law
NATO	North Atlantic Treaty Organization
NGO	Nongovernmental Organization
NILR	Netherlands International Law Review
NYIL	Netherlands Yearbook of International Law
OAU	Organisation of African Unity
OECD	Organisation for Economic Cooperation and Development
PCIJ	Permanent Court of International Justice
RdC	Recueil des Cours
RGDIP	Revue Générale de Droit International Public
RIAA	Reports of International Arbitral Awards
TRNC	Turkish Republic of Northern Cyprus
UN	United Nations
UNCITRAL	United Nations Commission on International Trade Law
UNCLOS	United Nations Convention on the Law of the Sea
UNESCO	United Nations Educational, Scientific and Cultural Organisation
UNFCCC	United Nations Framework Convention on Climate Change
UNTS	United Nations Treaty Series
WHO	World Health Organization
WTO	World Trade Organization
ZaöRV	Zeitschrift für ausländisches öffentliches Recht und Völkerrecht

Introduction

There has been much debate in recent years about the role of non-state actors in international law. Whereas their presence is undisputedly acknowledged, their status and legal accountability remain unsettled. In many areas of public international law, harm is now significantly often caused by actors other than states.[1] Terrorist groups threaten the territorial integrity of states; private security companies are involved in armed conflicts; individual hackers initiate cyber-attacks; and multinational corporations cause transboundary environmental harm or business-related human rights violations. Nonetheless, international treaties and customary international law still assign rights and duties almost exclusively to states. Outside of international criminal law, there are but few attempts to establish individual responsibility. On the other hand, state responsibility only arises if an international obligation is breached and that breach is attributable to a state, whereas only the actions of state organs acting in their official capacity may implicate state responsibility and the conduct of private individuals usually does not. Such conduct may be attributed if private citizens act as so-called de facto organs or a state acknowledges their behavior as its own – which occurs rather rarely. The nature of state responsibility is inherently restorative with the primary objective to maintain or restore equilibrium between equal and sovereign states. In sum, there is thus a broad range of private activities that remain below the threshold of attribution. This leads to the somewhat dissatisfying situation that there

---

[1] Philip Alston, "The 'Not-a-Cat' Syndrome: Can the International Human Rights Regime Accommodate Non-State Actors?" in Philip Alston (ed.), *Non-State Actors and Human Rights* (Oxford: Oxford University Press, 2005), pp. 7 ff.; Nehal Bhuta, "The Role International Actors Other Than States Can Play in the New World Order," in Antonio Cassese (ed.), *Realizing Utopia* (Oxford: Oxford University Press, 2012), p. 61; Anja Seibert-Fohr, "Die völkerrechtliche Verantwortlichkeit des Staates für das Handeln von Privaten: Bedarf nach Neuorientierung?" (2013) 73 *ZaöRV* 37–60 at 38 f.

are quite well-defined regulations on what states are expected to do, whereas comprehensive regulations on private conduct are missing from the international scene. With harmful conduct now often stemming from non-state actors, there exists a substantial accountability lacuna.

It thus comes as little surprise that criticism of an outdated state-centric approach of international responsibility is increasing, arguing that the scope of responsibility needs to be expanded so as to include private actors in order to ensure the full and effective implementation of international law – particularly in the field of human rights protection. When compared with other areas of international law, the field of human rights protection indeed shows several peculiarities: Human rights issues rarely arise in a transboundary context as they do not cause immediate effects on another state's territory. Moreover, human rights violations mostly affect individuals and not other states as such, which explains why states are rather reluctant to bring human rights claims before international courts. The logics undergirding the traditional reciprocal nature of state responsibility do not fully apply to the human rights context,[2] which makes gaps in legal protection particularly worrisome. Further concerns stem from the fact that human rights law requires the balancing of various interests and positions. When regulating private conduct, states may protect the human rights of some while simultaneously infringing upon those of others. A state, therefore, cannot be burdened with too-expansive duties to control private conduct, lest it would encroach on the very freedoms it is supposed to protect. Besides, many states lack capacities to effectively prevent and sanction harmful private conduct in the first place, which further calls into question whether the rules on state responsibility could actually foster global human rights protection at all.

For these reasons, the creation of direct human rights obligations for non-state actors is increasingly considered. As we will further explore, however, there is a range of serious concerns speaking against such obligations. While the desirability of greater liability for human rights contraventions caused by harmful private conduct is beyond question, making non-state actors duty bearers under international human rights law would create substantial legal problems; and it does not seem likely that consensus on such duties could be reached in the foreseeable

---

[2] Hélène Tran, *Les Obligations de Vigilance des États Parties à la Convention Européenne des Droits de l'Homme* (Brussels: Bruylant, 2013), para. 32.

future, either. The focus should thus be shifted on how the rules of state responsibility could be adjusted to enhance global human rights protection with regard to harmful private conduct.

That international human rights law requires states not only to refrain from actively committing human rights violations but also to actively protect against contraventions stemming from other sources – including harmful private conduct – is now undisputedly recognized. However, these types of obligations are commonly subsumed under the very broad notion of "positive obligations," whereas substantial concretizations of what these obligations actually entail and how they might be adjusted so as to better address the growing role of non-state actors are absent. In order to enhance the coherence and effectiveness of the rules on state responsibility, it is thus necessary to take a closer look at what states are actually expected to do in order to comply with their positive obligations.

It is in this context that the standard of due diligence could provide substantial guidance on how state responsibility for failure to prevent human rights contraventions by non-state actors might be established and even extended so as to cover constellations that are considered to fall outside the scope of human rights law as it stands today. Concretizing and expanding the reach of positive obligations appears to be a more promising (and more realistic) approach than creating direct human rights obligations for actors other than states.

Due diligence obligations of states[3] have a long history in international law, and while they are mainly associated with the sphere of environmental law today, they originally evolved in the context of alien protection laws and thus within an area of international law that is genuinely concerned with the protection of individuals. Meanwhile, the concept has long transcended its historical origins and is applied in various fields of international law, where it is acknowledged that states not only have a negative obligation to refrain from breaching their international duties through actions of their own officials; they also have a positive obligation to take reasonable measures to prevent harmful activities by non-state actors and to sanction such conduct, should it occur nonetheless.[4] Due

---

[3] Due diligence standards are also applied in a private law context where they describe duties of care on behalf of private actors including multinational corporations.

[4] Cedric Ryngaert, "State Responsibility and Non-State Actors," in Math Noormann et al. (eds.), *Non-State Actors in International Law* (Oxford: Hart, 2015), p. 164; Robert Barnidge, "The Due Diligence Principle Under International Law" (2006) 8 *International Community Law Review* 81–121 at 91 ff.; Riccardo Pisillo-Mazzeschi, "The

diligence obligations are mostly considered a necessary corollary to the concept of state sovereignty in that they oblige states to prevent incidents and activities on their territory that cause harm to other states.[5] Even if harmful private conduct is not attributable to a state, failure to act in a sufficiently diligent manner could give rise to an independent ground for state responsibility.[6] What constitutes diligent measures will vary according to individual circumstances – in particular the likelihood of harm and the extent and seriousness of such harm.[7] It is essential to notice, however, that such duties are not strict obligations of result but rather obligations to employ "best efforts."[8]

It is due to their inherently flexible and broad character that due diligence obligations are often criticized for being too vague and of limited reach.[9] Since the concept would lack any precise content, it could not serve as an adequate basis for state responsibility. Applying flexible standards that are subject to individual circumstances would lead to differing results that would not only undermine the basic principles of fairness but also unduly burden states due to a lack of legal clarity and certainty.[10] As a matter of fact, due diligence is among the most ambiguous terms in international law. It has been referred to

Due Diligence Rule and the Nature of International Responsibility of States" (1992) 35 *GYIL* 9–51 at 22 ff.
[5] François Dubuisson, "Vers un Renforcement des Obligations de Diligence en Matière de Lutte Contre le Terrorisme?" in Karine Christakis-Bannelier et al. (eds.), *Le Droit International Face au Terrorisme* (Paris: Pedone, 2002), p. 142.
[6] Ryngaert, "State Responsibility and Non-State Actors," 181; Seibert-Fohr, "Völkerrechtliche Verantwortlichkeit," 43; Astrid Epiney, *Die völkerrechtliche Verantwortlichkeit von Staaten für rechtswidriges Verhalten im Zusammenhang mit Aktionen Privater* (Baden-Baden: Nomos, 1992), p. 205.
[7] Vincent Chetail, "The Legal Personality of Multinational Corporations, State Responsibility and Due Diligence," in Denis Alland et al. (eds.), *Unity and Diversity of International Law* (Leiden: Martinus Nijhoff, 2014), pp. 125 f.; Pisillo-Mazzeschi, "The Due Diligence Rule," 44.
[8] Seibert-Fohr, "Völkerrechtliche Verantwortlichkeit," 50; Epiney, "Völkerrechtliche Verantwortlichkeit von Staaten," p. 208.
[9] Malgosia Fitzmaurice, "Legitimacy of International Environmental Law" (2017) 77 *ZaöRV* 339–370; Menno Kamminga, "Due Diligence Mania: The Misguided Introduction of an Extraneous Concept into Human Rights Discourse" (2011) Maastricht Faculty of Law Working Paper No. 07, p. 6; Vassilis Tzevelekos, "In Search of Alternative Solutions: Can the State of Origin Be Held Responsible for Investors' Human Rights Abuses That Are Not Attributable to It?" (2010) 35 *Brooklyn Journal of International Law* 155–231 at 199; Danwood Mzikenge Chirwa, "In Search of Philosophical Justifications and Suitable Models for the Horizontal Application of Human Rights" (2008) 8 *African Human Rights Journal* 294–311 at 307.
[10] Fitzmaurice, "Legitimacy of Environmental Law," 364 ff.

as "principle,"[11] "doctrine,"[12] "test,"[13] "concept,"[14] "general principle,"[15] and "obligation,"[16] with the ILC still mostly referring to due diligence as a "standard,"[17] underlying more "specific expressions" in various sub-branches of international law.[18] Already, this brief summary of definition attempts illustrates the great difficulties in assessing what due diligence means in the context of state responsibility.

Against the background of this terminological confusion, this book seeks to explore what due diligence obligations actually entail for states and how state responsibility for failure to comply with them can be established. A comparative analysis of their application in different fields of international law will reveal how the standard was tailored and modified to meet the challenges of each individual field. In a second step, it will be discussed if and to what extent due diligence obligations can be conceptualized or even expanded so as to address the growing problems stemming from harmful private conduct in the human rights context. Assessing their potential will help decide whether the state responsibility regime in human rights law is in need of general reform or whether it can be adjusted so as to effectively confront private human rights contraventions. While some lessons might be drawn from the application of due diligence obligations in other fields of international law, due regard has to be paid to the peculiarities of human rights regimes. Against this

---

[11] Joanna Kulesza, *Due Diligence in International Law* (Leiden: Brill Nijhoff, 2016), p. 11; Ryngaert, "State Responsibility and Non-State Actors," 177; Michael Schmitt, "In Defense of Due Diligence in Cyberspace" (2015) 125 *Yale Law Journal Forum* 68–81 at 69.

[12] Jan Arno Hessbruegge, "The Historical Development of the Doctrines of Attribution and Due Diligence in International Law" (2003) 36 *JILP* 265–306 at 266; Xue Hanqin, *Transboundary Damage in International Law* (Cambridge: Cambridge University Press, 2003), p. 162.

[13] Richard Lillich/John M. Paxman, "State Responsibility for Injuries Caused to Aliens Occasioned by Terrorist Activities" (1977) 26 *The American University Law Review* 217–313 at 269.

[14] Pisillo-Mazzeschi, "The Due Diligence Rule," 44.

[15] Awalou Ouedraogo, "La Due Diligence en Droit International: de la Règle de la Neutralité au Principe Général" (2012) 42 *Revue Générale de Droit* 641–683 at 644; Timo Koivurova, "What Is the Principle of Due Diligence?" in Jarna Petman/Jan Klabbers (eds.), *Nordic Cosmopolitanism* (Leiden: Martinus Nijhoff, 2003), p. 344.

[16] Yakin Ertürk, "The Due Diligence Standard: What Does It Entail for Women's Rights?" in Carin Benninger-Budel (ed.), *Due Diligence and Its Application to Protect Women from Violence* (Leiden: Martinus Nijhoff, 2008), p. 38.

[17] Among many others: ILC, Report of its 46th Session, ILC Yearbook 1994, Volume II, UN Doc. A/49/10, pp. 169 f.

[18] ILA Study Group on Due Diligence, Second Report of July 2016, available at www.ila-hq.org/index.php/study-groups, p. 6.

background, the following analysis will investigate the role due diligence duties could play when it comes to preventing and sanctioning private actions contrary to international human rights law. It will engage critically with arguments that due diligence as a concept is inadequate to meet the challenges imposed by the rise of non-state actors and seeks to reveal unexploited possibilities of how such obligations could contribute to an effective human rights protection.

The debate on direct human rights obligations for non-state actors will serve as a starting point for the analysis. While the creation of such obligations has become an increasingly popular suggestion,[19] the first chapter identifies several substantial but often neglected concerns. Given the fact that direct human rights obligations for non-state actors are neither particularly desirable nor overly realistic, alternative means to address private human rights contraventions need to be explored. However, when analyzing typical categorizations of human rights, it soon becomes clear that they fail to precisely describe what states are required to do. Against this background, a conduct-based typology of human rights obligations is suggested in the second chapter, which will render the broad notion of positive obligations more accessible. As we will see, positive human rights obligations entail both obligations of result as well as obligations of diligent conduct to adequately prevent and sanction private harmful conduct. Yet, not only are obligations of diligent conduct of higher practical relevance, they are also more difficult to narrow down. In order to explore how the rules on state responsibility could be better adjusted in reaction to the increasing importance of private actors, it is thus necessary to elaborate in greater detail on how due diligence obligations might operate in the human rights context.

To this end, the origins of due diligence duties in international law will be retraced in a general but concise manner that concludes with an attempt to classify the status of the principle of due diligence within the state responsibility system in Chapter 3. In order to then compare and contrast how due diligence obligations are applied in different fields of

---

[19] Lee McConnell, *Extracting Accountability from Non-State Actors in International Law* (London: Routledge, 2017), p. 73; David Bilchitz, "The Necessity for a Business and Human Rights Treaty" (2016) 1 *Business and Human Rights Journal* 203–227; Jean Thomas, "Our Rights, but Whose Duties?" in Tsvi Kahana/Anat Scolnicov (eds.), *Boundaries of State, Boundaries of Rights* (Cambridge: Cambridge University Press, 2016), p. 7; Jennifer Moore, "From Nation State to Failed State: International Protection from Human Rights Abuses by Non-State Agents" (1999) 31 *Columbia Human Rights Law Review* 81–121 at 120.

international law, Chapter 4 will conceptualize an analytical framework of the individual components of due diligence obligations. It will help define in a more precise manner the different requirements generally contained in due diligence obligations and identify common problems. It will focus on how the foreseeability threshold can be overcome and how the inherently vague reasonableness standard could be filled with content. In addition to this, it will address the fundamental question of whether diverging capacities are to be taken into consideration or whether uniform standards of diligence apply to all states. Embedded in this analytical framework, the fifth chapter will discuss the application of due diligence duties in different areas of international law that are confronted with similar challenges as the field of human rights protection. This will allow drawing more general conclusions on the character of diligence duties in international law, and more importantly, it will reveal several tests and standards that have been developed to address specific problems such as evidentiary hurdles or diverging capacities. Later on, it will be discussed whether those concepts might provide guidance for the further development of human rights due diligence obligations and could help overcome substantial and procedural hurdles that stand in the way of more effective human rights protection.

With this in mind, the sixth chapter will analyze human rights due diligence along the general framework introduced previously. Narrowing down the broad and vague notion of due diligence to a general analytical framework will help assess more accurately what states are expected to do with regard to harmful private conduct. While thereby contributing to greater legal certainty, the analysis will also reveal severe problems – most notably that powerful non-state actors often operate in states that lack the capacities to effectively control harmful private activities. Accordingly, the final chapter will discuss if and to what extent the concept of human rights due diligence obligations could be adequately applied to extraterritorial constellations and whether states with sufficient resources could be expected to diligently react toward human rights risks beyond their territory. As we will see, a strong case can be made for such extraterritorial due diligence obligations as a viable alternative to directly binding obligations for non-state actors. While due regard has to be paid to the principle of non-intervention and no undue burden should be imposed on any state, there are several constellations in which states could be reasonably expected to exercise due diligence with regard to human rights risks abroad. Even though there still is significant reluctance, some recent examples of state practice implement extraterritorial due diligence frameworks. In contrast to the complicated and possibly fruitless task of creating human rights obligations for a whole new array of actors, expanding the reach of human rights due diligence obligations to extraterritorial constellations could be easily integrated in the existing human rights system and thus presents a more promising way to foster global human rights protection, with the importance of non-state actors ever increasing.

1

Why to Analyze State Responsibility for Human Rights Violations: The Flawed Debate on Direct Human Rights Obligations for Non-State Actors

I. Introductory Remarks

The array of potential human rights abusers is far more fragmented than it used to be. While human rights have traditionally been understood as a means of protection against state abuse, different phenomena have undermined this state-centric approach. Globalization and trade liberalization have just as much increased the role of non-state actors as the outsourcing of traditional state functions, the growing influence of international organizations, and the changing nature of armed conflicts. Many non-state actors now possess significant economic and political power that increases their potential as both perpetrator and protector of human rights at the international stage.[1] This is particularly true for international organizations, powerful non-state armed groups, and multinational corporations, and it is all the more true if those actors operate in states that do not have comprehensive human rights provisions and/or the ability to effectively enforce them.[2]

It thus comes as little surprise that the human rights system is among the areas of international law where direct obligations for non-state

---

[1] Katharina Weilert, "Transnationale Unternehmen im rechtsfreien Raum?" (2009) 69 ZaöRV 883–917 at 884; David Weissbrodt and Muria Kruger, "Human Rights Responsibilities of Businesses as Non-State Actors," in Philip Alston (ed.), *Non-State Actors and Human Rights* (Oxford: Oxford University Press, 2005), p. 317; Nicola Jägers, "The Legal Status of the Multinational Corporation under International Law," in Michael Addo (ed.), *Human Rights Standards and the Responsibility of Transnational Corporations* (The Hague: Kluwer Law, 1999), pp. 260 f.

[2] Manfred Nowak and Karolina Miriam Januszewski, "Non-State Actors and Human Rights," in Math Noormann et al. (eds.), *Non-State Actors in International Law* (Oxford: Hart, 2015), pp. 117, 124; Michael Addo, "Human Rights and Transnational Corporations," in Michael Addo (ed.), *Human Rights Standards and the Responsibility of Transnational Corporations* (The Hague: Kluwer Law, 1999), p. 31.

actors are most vigorously discussed. To focus on state-initiated abuses is often seen as a barrier to the fullest possible implementation of human rights.[3] Consequently, increasingly more authors suggest the imposition of directly binding international obligations upon non-state actors, in particular upon non-state armed groups and business corporations. Despite the fact that an increasingly detailed corpus of human rights has developed at the international stage, significant gaps of protection remain, so they argue, as it does not cover non-state human rights abuses. So far, Article 4 of the Optional Protocol to the Convention of the Rights of the Child is the only treaty provision that explicitly introduces a direct obligation upon non-state actors by urging non-state armed groups not to recruit children or let them participate in hostilities. And even this provision uses "should" instead of "shall," which usually indicates a recommendation rather than a legally binding regulation.[4] Other than that, the African Charter on Human and People's Rights is a single outlier among human rights treaties containing a chapter on individual duties toward the family and society in general,[5] though those provisions are rather impalpable and their legal content remains disputed. It thus is no stretch to say that international human rights instruments generally do not address actors other than states.

To a certain extent, this gap was mitigated by the development of international criminal law in the aftermath of the Second World War. It was the Nuremberg Tribunal which famously recognized that crimes were committed by individual persons and not by states.[6] Criminal provisions that address individuals are now enforceable before the International Criminal Court, but their scope is limited. It only extends to certain crimes codified in the

---

[3] Lee McConnell, *Extracting Accountability from Non-State Actors in International Law* (London: Routledge, 2017), p. 73; Jean Thomas, "Our Rights, but Whose Duties?" in Tsvi Kahana and Anat Scolnicov (eds.), *Boundaries of State, Boundaries of Rights* (Cambridge: Cambridge University Press, 2016), p. 7; Jennifer Moore, "From Nation State to Failed State: International Protection from Human Rights Abuses by Non-State Agents" (1999) 31 *Columbia Human Rights Law Review* 81–121 at 120.

[4] Optional Protocol to the Convention on the Rights of the Child on the Involvement of Children in Armed Conflict, signed on 25 May 2000, entered into force on 12 February 2002, contained in UN Doc. A/RES/54/263.

[5] Chapter II of the African Charter on Human and People's Rights, signed on 27 June 1981, entered into force on 21 October 1986, OAU Doc. CAB/LEG/67/3, 21 ILM 58.

[6] International Military Tribunal (Nuremberg), Judgment of 1 October 1946, reprinted in: 41 AJIL 172–333 at 221.

Rome Statute,[7] leaving many harmful practices beyond the Court's reach. Besides, the Statute exclusively addresses individuals with the Court's mandate equally restricted where the individual responsible for a certain crime cannot be identified or stems from entities such as corporations or armed groups. While making an important contribution to affirming individual responsibility for the most heinous crimes, international criminal law is thus no suitable tool to ensure widespread human rights compliance by non-state actors.

Outside of international criminal law, much of the international discourse on non-state actors has centered around the work of UN Special Rapporteur *John Ruggie* on human rights obligations for business entities, which was finalized (for the time being) by his Guiding Principles on Business and Human Rights in 2011.[8] Prior to that, the most ambitious attempt to expand human rights obligations to private actors had been the Draft Norms on the Responsibilities of Transnational Corporations and Other Business Enterprises with Regard to Human Rights of 2003.[9] The Draft, while recognizing that states had the primary responsibility to respect and promote human rights, suggested that human rights obligations might be directly applicable to non-state actors, at least to transnational corporations and other business enterprises.[10] *Ruggie*, however, rejected the assumption that businesses had any legally binding obligations under existing international law and reemphasized the central role of states for human rights protection.[11]

Understandably enough, there still are complaints that "[i]nternational human rights law simply does not hear the voices of those who are being violated by non-state actors."[12] Any reform of the human rights system, so it is argued, should move away from the central role of states and their due diligence obligations.[13] International human rights law

---

[7] Rome Statute of the ICC, signed on 17 July 1998, entered into force on 1 July 2002, 2187 UNTS 90.
[8] Human Rights Council, John Ruggie, Guiding Principles on Business and Human Rights: Implementing the UN "Protect, Respect and Remedy" Framework, 21 March 2011, UN Doc. A/HRC/17/31.
[9] UN Commission on Human Rights, Sub-Commission on the Promotion and Protection of Human Rights, 26 August 2003, UN Doc. E/CN.4/Sub.2/2003/12/Rev.2.
[10] Ibid., para 1, p. 4.
[11] Human Rights Council, John Ruggie, Protection and Promotion of Human Rights, UN Doc. E/CN.4/2006/97 (2006), paras. 60–61, 79.
[12] Robert McCorquodale, "Overlegalizing Silences: Human Rights and Non-State Actors" (2002) 96 *ASIL Proceedings* 384–388 at 384.
[13] Leigh Payne and Gabriel Pereira, "Corporate Complicity in International Human Rights Violations" (2016) 12 *Annual Review of Law and Social Science* 63–84 at 71.

could only remain relevant and effective if it were to succeed in legally binding the full range of actors capable of violating human rights.[14] Directly binding obligations for non-state actors should be developed, in particular with regard to business corporations,[15] as was reemphasized by a recent statement made by Ecuador to the Human Rights Council on behalf of an entire group of countries strongly supported by many NGOs and calling for a "legally binding instrument framework ... [that] would clarify the obligations of transnational corporations in the field of human rights."[16]

In fact, international law does not prohibit states from entering into agreements that provide for direct international obligations of non-state actors.[17] While they might face enforcement challenges, nothing in international law disallows such agreements per se.[18] As early as 1928, the Permanent Court of International Justice held that "it cannot be disputed that the very object of an international agreement according to the intention of the contracting parties, may be the adoption by the parties of some definite rules creating individual rights and obligations."[19] Principally, states could thus enact an international human rights instrument containing direct obligations for non-state actors. Some authors go even further and argue that such an instrument

---

[14] Erika George, "Expanding the Array of Accountable Actors: Human Rights and Corporate Social Responsibility" (2015) *ASIL Proceedings* 246–248 at 246; David Bilchitz, "A Chasm between 'Is' and 'Ought'?" in Surya Deva and David Bilchitz (eds.), *Human Rights Obligations of Business* (Cambridge: Cambridge University Press, 2013), p. 127; Philip Alston, "The 'Not-a-Cat' Syndrome: Can the International Human Rights Regime Accommodate Non-State Actors?" in Philip Alston (ed.), *Non-State Actors and Human Rights* (Oxford: Oxford University Press, 2005), p. 6; McCorquodale, "Overlegalizing Silences," 388; Moore, "From Nation State to Failed State," 95.

[15] Denis Arnold, "Corporations and Human Rights Obligations" (2016) 1 *Business and Human Rights Journal* 255–275 at 275; Marko Karavias, *Corporate Obligations under International Law* (Oxford: Oxford University Press, 2013), pp. 3f.; Steven Ratner, "Corporations and Human Rights: A Theory of Legal Responsibility" (2001) 111 *Yale Law Journal* 443–545 at 461 ff.; Chris Jochnik, "Confronting the Impunity of Non-State Actors" (1999) 21 *HRQ* 56–79 at 79.

[16] Human Rights Council, 24th Session 2013, Statement on behalf of the African Group, the Arab Group, Pakistan, Sri Lanka, Kyrgyzstan, Cuba, Nicaragua, Bolivia, Venezuela, Peru, and Ecuador, available online at https://www.business-humanrights.org/sites/default/files/media/documents/statement-unhrc-legally-binding.pdf.

[17] See already Hersch Lauterpacht, *The Development of International Law by the Permanent Court of International Justice* (London: Pinter, 1934), p. 51.

[18] McConnell, "Extracting Accountability," pp. 131 ff.; Nadia Bernaz, *Business and Human Rights* (London: Routledge, 2017), p. 100.

[19] PCIJ, Jurisdiction of the Courts of Danzig, Advisory Opinion of 3 March 1928, PCIJ Series B, No. 15, p. 17.

was not even necessary, as existing human rights provisions could already be reinterpreted so as to encompass such obligations.[20]

However, while acknowledging (or creating) directly binding obligations for non-state actors seems to be an unexceptionally popular argument, there are several objections that could and should be raised. Retracing this demurral will underline why it is more promising to focus on how to exploit the full potential of state responsibility when it comes to human rights protection. To set the broader context of this debate, the following section will first briefly discuss whether direct obligations for non-state actors may already be deduced from the existing human rights system for this would render futile any debate on the desirability of new international regulations. In fact, several options are being discussed of how the existing human rights provisions could be reinterpreted so as to contain such direct obligations. While some of these options deserve closer consideration, the following analysis will reveal that it would be too far a stretch to read such obligations into the human rights system as it stands today (II.). This leaves us with the question of whether direct obligations for non-state actors should be established in the future, with several reasons for such an expansion (III.). What might seem desirable and conceptually feasible in theory would yet be overly difficult to put into practice. Several substantial objections (IV.) reinforces that positive obligations on behalf of states are and remain important to ensure effective human rights protection with regard to harmful non-state conduct (V.).

II. Why the Existing Human Rights Regime Cannot Be Construed to Contain Direct Obligations for Non-State Actors

The most far-reaching among the views favoring an expansion of human rights obligations to non-state actors argue that such obligations are already contained in the existing human rights regime. From their point of view, the development of new and specific rules would even be dispensable. When discussing whether such obligations might indeed be derived from the existing human rights system, the different sources of

---

[20] Adam McBeth, *International Economic Actors and Human Rights* (London: Routledge, 2010); Angelika Emmerich-Fritsche, "Zur Verbindlichkeit der Menschenrechte für transnationale Unternehmen" (2007) 45 *AVR* 541–565; Jordan Paust, "Human Rights Responsibilities of Private Corporations" (2002) 35 *Vanderbilt Journal of Transnational Law* 801–825 at 810; Ratner, "Corporations and Human Rights," 469; Jochnik, "Confronting Impunity," 63.

international human rights law have to be distinguished. For each category, separate questions need to be addressed. While it is rather rarely argued that non-state actor obligations arise out of customary norms of international law (1.), general principles (2.) and international treaties (3.) are regularly referred to as potential sources for such legally binding obligations.

1. Customary International Law

Norms under customary international law are formed by common state practice out of a sense of legal obligation.[21] When discussing whether customary international law entails direct human rights obligations for non-state actors, it first needs to be clarified what kind of state practice would form such obligations. For a customary rule of this kind, state practice and *opinio juris* should show that states hold non-state actors accountable for human rights contradictions and that they feel obligated under international law to do so. Individual responsibility for the gravest forms of international crimes is indeed recognized as customary, which indicates that customary international law may generally provide for non-state actor responsibility. However, while it is true that most states have enacted domestic legislation providing for the liability of private actors in case of grave human rights contradictions, there is no indication that they do so out of sense for an international obligation.[22] Most domestic regulations providing for the accountability of private actors take the form of civil or criminal liability sanctioning harmful conduct. While these regulations are commonly imposed by states in order to fulfill their own positive obligations to prevent human rights contraventions by private actors, they do not impose direct human rights obligations upon those actors. Consequently, there are hardly any instances of state practice showing that private actors are being held directly responsible for violating international human rights obligations.[23]

Nonetheless, support for customary human rights obligations is occasionally drawn from the fact that international organizations – as

---

[21] See, for instance, ICJ, North Sea Continental Shelf Cases (*Germany* v. *Denmark/Germany* v. *Netherlands*), Judgment of 20 February 1969, ICJ Reports 1969, 3, para. 77.

[22] McConnell, "Extracting Accountability," p. 78; Karen Weidmann, *Der Beitrag der OECD-Leitsätze für multinationale Unternehmen zum Schutz der Menschenrechte* (Berlin: Duncker & Humblot, 2014), p. 105.

[23] Karavias, "Corporate Obligations," p. 83.

II. DIRECT OBLIGATIONS FOR NON-STATE ACTORS

a distinct category of non-state actors – are increasingly seen to be bound by customary norms.[24] However, the application of international norms, including customary norms, to international organizations is to be explained by the fact that international organizations are jointly set up by states in order to fulfill specified functions[25] and states should not absolve themselves from their obligations by delegating tasks.[26] These assumptions cannot be easily applied to other categories of non-state actors, which neither were created by states nor fulfill delegated tasks. Moreover, it should not be overlooked that recognizing direct customary obligations for non-state actors in general could create fundamental problems of legitimacy.[27] While states may regulate private conduct in their domestic sphere and jurisdiction, direct customary obligations for non-state actors would mean that the conduct of states in its entirety would establish an obligation for all non-state actors, no matter to which state they are linked. This might be recognized within very narrow limits for those particularly grave international crimes that are considered to fall within the ambit of universal jurisdiction, but does not seem very likely to find broader support. With this in mind, the hesitance to acknowledge direct customary obligations for private actors might also be explained by the fact that it is far from clear how this would change the character of customary law itself. In particular, whether the conduct of non-state actors might then become relevant in forming customary international norms and to what extent.[28] Given these conceptual difficulties, it is only rarely argued that customary international law would

---

[24] Notably, the ICJ stated that "[i]nternational organizations are subjects of international law and, as such, are bound by any obligations incumbent upon them under general rules of international law"; see ICJ, Interpretation of the Agreement of 25 March 1951 between the WHO and Egypt, Advisory Opinion of 20 December 1980, ICJ Reports 1980, 73, para. 37; and also ILC, Draft Articles on the Responsibility of International Organizations with Commentaries, ILC Yearbook 2011, Volume II, Commentary to Article 4, para. 2.

[25] McConnell, "Extracting Accountability," p. 65; Cedric Ryngaert, "Imposing International Duties on Non-State Actors and the Legitimacy of International Law," in Math Noortmann and Cedric Ryngaert (eds.), *Non-State Actor Dynamics in International Law* (Farnham: Ashgate, 2010), p. 69; Georges Abi-Saab, "Cours Général de Droit International Public" (1987) 207 RdC VII, p. 82.

[26] Christian Tomuschat, "International Law: Ensuring the Survival of Mankind on the Eve of a New Century" (1999) 281 RdC, p. 129.

[27] Ryngaert, "Imposing International Duties on Non-State Actors," 71 ff.

[28] Cedric Ryngaert, "Non-State Actors in International Humanitarian Law," in Jean d'Aspremont (ed.), *Participants in the International Legal System* (London: Routledge, 2011), p. 289; Stephan Hobe, "Die Zukunft des Völkerrechts im Zeitalter der Globalisierung" (1999) 37 *AVR* 253–282 at 266 f.

impose human rights obligations on non-state actors, and there is hardly any state practice to support such claims either.

2. General Principles

In contrast, general principles of law have occasionally been referred to as a source of directly binding human rights obligations for private actors. General principles are legal principles of a broad and general manner which become part of international law due to their widespread acceptance in domestic legal orders. They are mostly employed to fill regulatory gaps and steer the interpretation of open legal terms.[29] Given their broad and general character, their acknowledgment as general principles of international law does not mean that domestic law is applied at the international stage. It is rather "modes of general legal reasoning"[30] that are transferred to the international level and only insofar as these modes can be reasonably applied.[31] To acknowledge a general principle of international law providing for the human rights accountability of non-state actors, such legal principle would have to exist within the domestic orders of most states and its application at the international level would have to be feasible and appropriate.

In fact, this has been suggested on several occasions, most prominently during the *Kiobel*[32] and the *Exxon Mobil*[33] proceedings in the United States. It was submitted that hardly any domestic jurisdiction would entirely exempt private actors from liability if they cause harm to the rights of others. The vast majority of legal systems would recognize different forms of responsibility including civil and criminal liability. Based on this assumption, it was maintained that there was a general principle of law

---

[29] Malcolm Shaw, *International Law* (Cambridge: Cambridge University Press, 8th ed., 2017), p. 73; Robert Jennings and Arthur Watts (eds.), *Oppenheim's International Law* (London: Longman, 9th ed., 1992), i. 40; Alfred Verdross and Bruno Simma, *Universelles Völkerrecht* (Berlin: Duncker & Humblot, 3rd ed., 1984), p. 389; Wolfgang Friedmann, "The Uses of 'General Principles' in the Development of International Law" (1963) 57 AJIL 279–299 at 287.

[30] James Crawford, *Brownlie's Principles of Public International Law* (Oxford: Oxford University Press, 8th ed., 2012), p. 35; Hugh Thirlway, *The Sources of International Law* (Oxford: Oxford University Press, 2014), p. 104.

[31] Verdross and Simma, "Universelles Völkerrecht," p. 384.

[32] Brief of Amici Curiae, 13 July 2011, Center for Constitutional Rights, International Human Rights Organizations and International Law Experts in Support of Petitioners, US Supreme Court, No. 10–1481, *Ester Kiobel et al. v. Royal Dutch Petroleum Co. et al.*

[33] US Court of Appeals for the District of Columbia Circuit, *John Doe et al. v. Exxon Mobil Corporation*, Judgment No. 09–7125 of 8 July 2011.

II. DIRECT OBLIGATIONS FOR NON-STATE ACTORS

providing for the accountability of private actors for the harm they cause to others.[34] When applied to the international level, this would necessarily mean that non-state actors could be held accountable for violating internationally recognized human rights.[35] If non-state actors were accountable for the violation of domestic regulations at the domestic level, then they should be accountable for the violation of international regulations at the international level. The majority in the *Exxon* case explicitly held that "given that the law of every jurisdiction in the United States and of every civilized nation ... provide that corporations are responsible for their torts, it would create a bizarre anomaly to immunize corporations from liability ... in lawsuits brought for shockingly egregious violations of universally recognized principles of international law."[36] What seems a straightforward conclusion at first glance, however, gravely ignores that domestic liability is not a general legal principle that could be appropriately applied in an international context. Under domestic laws, private actors are accountable for the violation of provisions that directly address them. At the international plane, however, private actors are not directly addressed by human rights provisions, and this gap cannot be adequately filled by general principles. The fact that private actors are bound by domestic provisions that explicitly address them does not allow for the conclusion that they are equally bound by international obligations that do not address them. As we have seen, general principles are no source of detailed and precise regulations; they are meant to fill gaps in international law by providing interpretative guidance.[37] That individuals are held accountable for violating their obligations under domestic law might indicate a general principle that the violation of binding obligations triggers legal consequences, but it cannot create binding obligations where they do not exist.

3. Human Rights Treaties

Far more promising is the approach followed by those scholars who argue that the existing human rights treaties with their detailed provisions could

---

[34] Center for Constitutional Rights et al., Amici Curiae of 13 July 2011, p. 15.
[35] See also: Christine Breining-Kaufmann, "The Legal Matrix of Human Rights and Trade Law," in Thomas Cottier, et al. (eds.), *Human Rights and International Trade* (Oxford: Oxford University Press, 2005), p. 134.
[36] US Court of Appeals for the District of Columbia Circuit, *John Doe et al. v. Exxon Mobil Corporation*, Judgment No. 09-7125 of 8 July 2011, para. 133.
[37] Shaw, "International Law," p. 81; Daragh Murray, *Human Rights Obligations of Non-State Armed Groups* (Oxford: Hart, 2016), p. 90; Thirlway, "Sources of International Law," pp. 102 ff.

be reinterpreted so as to apply to private actors,[38] which would render obsolete the need for a specific agreement. Even though the language of human rights provisions clearly addresses states as the sole duty bearers, it is nevertheless suggested that the reality of international law has changed so significantly that a reinterpretation of the relevant provisions would not only be possible but even indispensable.[39] The broadest attempt of reinterpretation is based on the qualification of human rights treaties as so-called living instruments that are open to adjustments in light of changed circumstances (a.). The concept of *Drittwirkung* is also consulted in order to affirm direct obligations for non-state actors (b.), as have the "abuse of rights" clauses contained in most human rights treaties (c.). Though as we will see, even the most progressive approaches toward interpretation cannot alter the fact that human rights treaties exclusively bind states (d.).

a. Human Rights Treaties as Living Instruments

Human rights treaties are deemed "living instruments" that could and should be dynamically adjusted if changed circumstances so require to ensure the most effective human rights implementation.[40] As early as 1978, the Strasbourg Court found the Convention was "a living instrument which ... must be interpreted in the light of present-day conditions."[41] Considering that the object and purpose of human rights treaties is the effective protection of rights derived from the fundamental human dignity of each individual, the interpretation of human rights treaties should react to new forms of threats.[42] Since significant human

---

[38] David Weissbrodt, "Roles and Responsibilities of Non-State Actors," in Dinah Shelton (ed.), *The Oxford Handbook of International Human Rights Law* (Oxford: Oxford University Press, 2013), p. 727; McBeth, "International Economic Actors"; Emmerich-Fritsche, "Verbindlichkeit der Menschenrechte"; Barbara Frey, "The Legal and Ethical Responsibilities of Transnational Corporations in the Protection of International Human Rights" (1997) 6 *Minnesota Journal of Global Trade* 151–188; Andrew Clapham, *Human Rights in the Private Sphere* (Oxford: Clarendon, 1993); Jordan Paust, "The Other Side of Right: Private Duties under Human Rights Law" (1992) 5 *Harvard Human Rights Journal* 51–63.

[39] Murray, "Non-State Armed Groups," p. 164; Surya Deva, "Business and Human Rights: Time to Move Beyond the Present?" in César Rodríguez-Garavito (ed.), *Business and Human Rights* (Cambridge: Cambridge University Press, 2017), p. 69.

[40] Verdross and Simma, "Universelles Völkerrecht," pp. 498 f; Christoph Grabenwater and Katharina Pabel, *Europäische Menschenrechtskonvention* (München: Beck, 6th ed., 2016), p. 39; Georg Ress, "Supranationaler Menschenrechtsschutz und der Wandel der Staatlichkeit" (2004) 64 *ZaöRV* 621–639 at 628.

[41] ECtHR, *Tyrer* v. *UK*, Judgment of 25 April 1978, Application No. 5856/72, para. 31.

[42] Deva, "Business and Human Rights," 69; Jochnik, "Confronting Impunity," 61.

II. DIRECT OBLIGATIONS FOR NON-STATE ACTORS

rights risks now stem from harmful private conduct, human rights treaties should be reinterpreted so as to cover private actions.

Support for such an expansion is often taken from the Universal Declaration of Human Rights,[43] stating in its Preamble that "every individual and every organ of society ... will strive ... to promote respect for these rights and freedoms and ... to secure their universal and effective recognition and observance."[44] The object and purpose of human rights treaties is thus the universal protection of individual rights with the protection of human dignity at its core that should guide any application of international human rights law and is now read to allow expanding the range of obligations to private actors.[45] Since it was the effective protection of rights and not the allocation of duties to specific actors that characterizes human rights, the source of harmful conduct should not be overemphasized. In order to adjust human rights treaties to present-day conditions, the range of duty bearers should thus be expanded.[46]

Further authority for such progressive interpretations is taken from two ICJ decisions in which the Court elaborated on evolutive means of interpretation.[47] In its *Reparations for Injuries Suffered in the Services of the United Nations* Advisory Opinion, the Court held that even though this was not explicitly provided for in the Charter, certain implied powers had to be recognized if the UN were to effectively fulfill their international tasks. Though no specific provision recognized its legal personality, the creation of responsibilities and functions implied that the UN must actually possess the power to perform those duties.[48] Taking up this

---

[43] Deva, "Business and Human Rights," 69; McBeth, "International Economic Actors," 60; Emmerich-Fritsche, "Verbindlichkeit der Menschenrechte," 558 f.; Weissbrodt and Kruger, "Human Rights Responsibilities," 329 f.; Paust, "Human Rights Responsibilities," 811; Jochnik, "Confronting Impunity," 63; Clapham, "Human Rights in the Private Sphere," p. 96.

[44] Universal Declaration of Human Rights, GA Resolution of 10 December 1948, UN Doc. A/RES/217/(III).

[45] Manisuli Ssenyonjo, *Economic, Social and Cultural Rights in International Law* (Oxford: Hart, 2nd ed., 2016), p. 178; Weissbrodt and Kruger, "Human Rights Responsibilities," 330 f.; Ratner, "Corporations and Human Rights," 472; Clapham, "Human Rights in the Private Sphere," p. 343.

[46] Emmerich-Fritsche, "Verbindlichkeit der Menschenrechte," 560; Clapham, "Human Rights in the Private Sphere," p. 343; Paust, "The Other Side of Right," 62.

[47] Jean-Marie Kamatali, "The New Guiding Principles on Business and Human Rights': Is It Time for an ICJ Advisory Opinion?" (2011) 20 *Cardozo Journal of International and Comparative Law* 437–464 at 460 ff.; Clapham, "Human Rights in the Private Sphere," pp. 99 ff.

[48] ICJ, Reparations for Injuries Suffered in the Services of the UN, Advisory Opinion of 11 April 1949, ICJ Reports 1949, 174, p. 182 f.

argument, it is now stated that if human rights protection was to remain effective, it would be just as necessary to extend the range of duty bearers under international human rights law and acknowledge the capacity of non-state actors.[49] Reference is also made to the ICJ's *Continued Presence of South Africa in Namibia* Advisory Opinion, in which the Court famously stated that "an international instrument has to be interpreted and applied within the framework of the entire legal system prevailing at the time of interpretation,"[50] based upon which it is now suggested that the human rights system has significantly changed, calling for an adjusted interpretation of human rights obligations.[51]

However, when taking a closer look at both decisions, it becomes clear that the matters before the Court cannot support the recognition of direct private obligations under human rights law. In the *Reparations* Advisory Opinion, the Court held that if states founded an international organization and assigned certain duties to that organization, it was in line with the parties' intention to assume that they wanted that organization to have the capacity to actually fulfill its duties. The ICJ found this to arise "by necessary intendment out of the Charter."[52] While it might now be argued that the legal capacity of non-state actors could follow the same logic, the situation that leads to the Advisory Opinion needs to be distinguished from the wording of human rights treaties. Whatever is derived by necessary implication out of an international treaty still has to be in line with its unambiguous wording which is presumed to authentically reflect the intention of the parties.[53] While it is clear that the reality of international law has changed profoundly since the drafting of most human rights treaties, it cannot be readily assumed that it is consistent with their provisions that application should be extended to other actors. Even though the circumstances prevailing at the time should be taken into consideration when interpreting a treaty, such interpretation cannot go beyond the unambiguous language upon which the parties agreed.

---

[49] See, for instance, Andrew Clapham, *Human Rights Obligations of Non-State Actors* (Oxford: Oxford University Press, 2006), pp. 63 ff.

[50] ICJ, Legal Consequences for States of the Continued Presence of South Africa in Namibia Notwithstanding Security Council Resolution 276, Advisory Opinion of 21 June 1971, ICJ Reports 1971, 16, para. 53.

[51] Clapham, "Human Rights in the Private Sphere," p. 99; Emmerich-Fritsche, "Verbindlichkeit der Menschenrechte," 560.

[52] ICJ, Reparations Advisory Opinion, p. 184.

[53] Oliver Dörr, "Article 31," in Oliver Dörr and Kirsten Schmalenbach (eds.), *Vienna Convention on the Law of Treaties. A Commentary* (Berlin: Springer, 2nd ed., 2018), para. 3.

II. DIRECT OBLIGATIONS FOR NON-STATE ACTORS

A similar conclusion is to be drawn when examining the ICJ's reasoning in the *Namibia* Opinion, where the Court found it to be "the primary necessity" to interpret an international instrument "in accordance with the intentions of the parties at the time of its conclusion."[54] Only the fact that the parties had deliberately used evolutionary concepts and open terms allowed the Court to take changed circumstances into account when interpreting those provisions.[55]

While the material content of human rights provisions might generally be subject to new developments, the fact that states are their sole addressees is yet not an ambiguous or evolutionary regulation. Any attempt to read direct obligations into existing human rights treaties met with intense criticism on behalf of many states,[56] which indicates that such expansion is inconsistent with their original intent. Moreover, many international instruments now acknowledge the growing influence of non-state actors but still address states as the only direct duty bearers.[57] With regard to private conduct, those instruments usually impose an obligation upon their member states to provide for the domestic liability of private actors.[58] Consequently, non-state actors are held responsible under corresponding domestic regulations but do not become direct addressees of the international provision in question.[59] The fact that states explicitly regulate the role of non-state actors in certain constellations points out that such obligations could not be read into those treaties which do not contain comparable provisions.

---

[54] ICJ, Namibia Advisory Opinion, para. 53.
[55] Ibid.
[56] See, for instance, the general statements as contained in Human Rights Council, Report of 5 February 2016 on the First Session of the Open-Ended Intergovernmental Working Group on Transnational Corporations and Other Business Enterprises with Respect to Human Rights, UN Doc. A/HRC/31/50, para. 26; and Report of 4 January 2017 on the Second Session, UN Doc. A/HRC/34/47, paras. 10 ff.
[57] Carlos Lopez, "Human Rights Legal Liability for Business Enterprises," in Surya Deva and David Bilchitz (eds.), *Building a Treaty on Business and Human Rights* (Cambridge: Cambridge University Press, 2017), p. 307.
[58] See, among many others, Art. 10 I of the European Convention on the Prevention of Terrorism, entered into force on 16 May 2005, 196 CETS 2005; Art. 2 of the Convention on Combating Bribery of Foreign Public Officials in International Business Transactions, signed on 17 December 1997, entered into force on 15 February 1999, 37 ILM 1; Art. 4 II c) of the Basel Convention on the Control of Transboundary Movements of Hazardous Wastes and their Disposal, signed on 22 March 1989, entered into force 5 May 1992, 1673 UNTS 57.
[59] Cedric Ryngaert, "Non-State Actors: Carving out a Space in a State-Centred International Legal System" (2016) 63 *NILR* 183–195 at 191; Karavias, "Corporate Obligations," pp. 58 f.

That the dynamic approach toward interpretation is of limited reach was also recognized by the Strasbourg Court itself when it held that "the Court cannot, by means of an evolutive interpretation, derive from [the Convention and its Protocols] a right that was not included therein at the outset."[60] Even though evolutive methods of interpretation might thus allow for the adjustment of agreed-upon rights and provisions, they cannot create new forms of obligations – neither with regard to the material content of human rights treaties through the creation of new rights nor with regard to the formal content of human rights treaties through the creation of new categories of duty bearers.

This is even further underlined by one of the few instances in which an international human rights body was confronted with a claim against a non-state party, namely an application lodged against the OAU before the African Commission. Without entering into any substantial debate, the Commission declared the communication inadmissible since the OAU was neither a state nor a party to the African Charter on Human and Peoples' Rights.[61] Notably, the Commission thus seems to imply that human rights claims were inadmissible not only since the OAU was not a member of the Charter but also since it lacked state quality.

On top of that, simply expanding the range of duty bearers under existing human rights treaties would create substantial legal uncertainty. While some provisions in human rights treaties could rather easily be applied to non-state actors, others clearly have states as their sole addresses.[62] When looking at the ICCPR, for instance, it might be simple to agree that non-state actors should respect the right to life as enshrined in Article 6 or refrain from engaging in slavery as prohibited by Article 8. But how should non-state actors ensure the right to vote as enshrined in Article 25 (b) or take steps to ensure the equality of rights of spouses as demanded by Article 23 No. 4? It does not take more than these few examples to illustrate that merely declaring existing human rights treaties applicable to private actors would lead to legal uncertainty. Neither potential perpetrators nor potential victims could assess which rights

---

[60] ECtHR, *Johnston and Others v. Ireland*, Plenary Judgment of 18 December 1986, Application No. 9697/82, para. 53.

[61] AfComHPR, *Mohammed El-Nekheily v. OAU*, Decision of 17–26 October 1988, Communication No. 12/88.

[62] Blair Kanis, "Business, Human Rights, and Due Diligence. An Approach for Contractual Integration," in Jena Martin and Karen Bravo (eds.), *The Business and Human Rights Landscape* (Cambridge: Cambridge University Press, 2015), pp. 415 f.; Anne Peters, *Jenseits der Menschenrechte* (Tübingen: Mohr Siebeck, 2014), p. 98; Karavias, "Corporate Obligations," p. 166; Ratner, "Corporations and Human Rights," 492 ff.

were applicable and to what extent. Even if such reinterpretation of human rights treaties was conceptually feasible, it would thus create new problems that, in the end, might even prove detrimental to their effective enforcement.

While human rights treaties are living instruments and have to be interpreted in light of changed circumstances, dynamic approaches to interpretation thus cannot fundamentally alter the legal system undergirding human rights protection. Interpretation might be adjusted to new threats or changing social expectations by widening or limiting the catalog of duties that member states are expected to adhere to. Yet, it cannot be adjusted so as to impose obligations upon different categories of actors, in particular if such readjustment is obviously inconsistent with the unambiguous wording of a treaty and repeatedly repudiated by state parties.

b. *Drittwirkung*

Next to these evolutive approaches toward interpretation, the concept of *Drittwirkung* has occasionally been referred to in order to establish that non-state actors are bound by international human rights.[63] The *Drittwirkung*-model has mainly evolved in the German constitutional order and describes how and to what extent human rights are applicable to private relationships. Several authors have employed this concept to argue that binding obligations on non-state actors could be derived from the existing positive human rights obligations by "necessary implication." International law, so it is argued, could only require states to ensure that non-state actors do not violate human rights, if those non-state actors were themselves bound to comply with such requirements in the first place.[64] Such a conclusion, however, is based on a misconception of both the notion of *Drittwirkung* and the concept of positive obligations.

Acknowledging positive obligations does not imply that states and non-state actors have exactly the same obligations, with only the former being directly enforceable. The purpose of positive obligations is to ensure that states protect the rights enshrined in human rights instruments against any

---

[63] See, for instance, Nowak and Januszewski, "Non-State Actors and Human Rights," 142 f.; Bilchitz, "Chasm between 'Is' and 'Ought,'" 111 f.; McBeth, "International Economic Actors," 59.

[64] Bilchitz, "Chasm between 'Is' and 'Ought,'" 111 f.; Vincent Chetail, "The Legal Personality of Multinational Corporations, State Responsibility and Due Diligence," in Denis Alland et al. (eds.), *Unity and Diversity of International Law* (Leiden: Martinus Nijhoff, 2014), p. 127; Nowak and Januszewski, "Non-State Actors and Human Rights," 142 f.; see also McBeth, "International Economic Actors," 59.

threats, no matter where they stem from, including harmful conduct by other individuals. It is, however, the state that is ultimately responsible under human rights law for harm caused by private conduct. This responsibility does not arise from the attribution of non-state actor conduct to the state but rather arises from its very own obligation to take preventive measures. While such obligations on behalf of the state might have far-reaching consequences for the rights and duties of non-state actors under domestic law,[65] they do not imply that non-state actors themselves have legally binding international obligations.[66]

This becomes even clearer when considering how the concept of *Drittwirkung* actually operates at the domestic level. International human rights law, as well as constitutional human rights provisions, obligate states to ensure widest-possible human rights protection, also with regard to threats posed by private actors or external events. To this aim, states may enact domestic legislation regulating the conduct of private actors, which ultimately serves the purpose of human rights protection. For instance, states have a positive obligation to protect the right to life of their citizens. Among the central instruments to fulfill this obligation is the adoption of criminal provisions sanctioning manslaughter committed by private individuals. The long-term aspiration of such obligations is indeed the protection of the right to life and thus the protection of a human right. Introducing criminal provisions, however, does not render private individuals the guarantors of human rights protection. They are bound by the criminal provision in question, which necessarily has a narrowly defined scope of application in contrast to the broad human rights provisions entailing various different responsibilities. The same holds true for civil law provisions. States may use human rights as a guide for interpretation, even in a civil law context and particularly where private law provisions contain broad and open terms. Yet, the impact of human rights on private law will remain an indirect one and does not impose direct human rights obligations upon private actors.[67] Such direct obligations are recognized

---

[65] See, for instance, Angelika Nussberger, "Die EMRK und das Privatrecht" (2016) 80 *Rabels Zeitschrift für ausländisches und internationales Privatrecht* 817–850 on the ECHR's influence on domestic civil law.

[66] Ryngaert, "Non-State Actors," 191; Karavias, "Corporate Obligations," 44; Eric de Brabandere, "Non-State Actors and Human Rights," in Jean d'Aspremont (ed.), *Participants in the International Legal System* (London: Routledge, 2011), pp.271 f.

[67] See German Federal Constitutional Court, Judgment of 12 December 1957, 1 BvR 207/56 (Lüth), BVerfGE 7, 192 (205 f.) and also Ralf Brinktrine, "The Horizontal Effect of Human Rights in German Constitutional Law" (2001) 4 *EHRLR* 421–432; August Reinisch, "The Changing International Legal Framework for Dealing with Non-State Actors," in

II. DIRECT OBLIGATIONS FOR NON-STATE ACTORS

only in those constitutional orders in which human rights duties are explicitly and unambiguously imposed upon private actors.[68]

The same logic applies at the international level, where no human rights provision directly addresses non-state actors. That states have the positive obligation to regulate harmful conduct by non-state actors does not render the latter guarantors for the respective human rights provision.[69] This was comprehensively summarized by the Human Rights Committee, which stated that the obligations contained in the ICCPR "do not, as such, have direct horizontal effects as a matter of international law. The Covenant cannot be viewed as a substitute for domestic criminal or civil law."[70] In a similar manner, the IACtHR held in its Advisory Opinion on the rights of undocumented migrants that "the obligation to respect and ensure human rights ... has effects on relations between individuals" but that "it is the State that determines the laws that regulate the relations between individuals ... [and] must also ensure that human rights are respected in these private relationships between third parties." Ultimately, it is only the state that "may be responsible for the violation of those rights."[71] The ECOWAS Community Court also found that

> international bodies rely essentially on treaties to which States are parties as the principal subject of international law. As a matter of fact, the international regime of human rights imposes obligations on States. All mechanisms established thereof are directed to the engagement of State responsibility for its commitment or failure towards those international instruments. ... [F]or the dispute between individuals on alleged violation of human rights ... [it is] only when at the national level, there is no appropriate and effective forum for seeking redress against individuals, that the victim of such offences may bring an action

---

Philip Alston (ed.), *Non-State Actors and Human Rights* (Oxford: Oxford University Press, 2005), p. 70.

[68] To a certain extent, this is done by Art. 8 II, III of the South African Constitution of 4 February 1997, available online at www.gov.za/documents/constitution/constitution-republic-south-africa-1996-1.

[69] Grabenwater and Pabel, "Europäische Menschenrechtskonvention," p. 160; Eric de Brabandere, "Human Rights and Transnational Corporations. The Limits of Direct Corporate Responsibility" (2010) 4 *Human Rights & International Legal Discourse* 66–88 at 74; Constantin Köster, *Die völkerrechtliche Verantwortlichkeit privater (multinationaler) Unternehmen für Menschenrechtsverletzungen* (Berlin: Duncker & Humblot, 2010), p. 79.

[70] Human Rights Committee, General Comment No. 31 on the Nature of the General Legal Obligation Imposed on States Parties to the Covenant, 26 May 2004, UN Doc CCPR/C/21/Rev.1/Add.13, para. 8.

[71] IACtHR, Advisory Opinion OC-18/03 requested by the United Mexican States on Juridical Condition and Rights of Undocumented Migrants, 17 September 2003, Series A, No. 18, paras. 146–147.

before an international court, not against the individuals, rather against the signatory State for failure to ensure the protection and respect for the human rights allegedly violated.[72]

In sum, neither the concept of *Drittwirkung* nor the recognition of positive obligations could thus be construed so as to assign direct human rights obligations to private actors under international law. While positive obligations require states to actively regulate private conduct and the *Drittwirkung* concept obliges courts and state authorities to let human rights provisions guide their interpretation of private law norms, neither one of these concepts creates directly binding human rights obligations for private actors.

c. "Abuse of Rights" Clauses

However, it has also been suggested that "abuse of rights" clauses could be read as containing human rights obligations that directly address private actors.[73] In fact, "abuse of rights" clauses are incorporated in most human rights treaties. Article 5 of the Covenant on Civil and Political Rights, for instance, prescribes that nothing in the present Covenant "may be interpreted as implying for any State, group or person any right to engage in any activity or perform any act aimed at the destruction of any of the rights and freedoms recognized herein or at their limitation to a greater extent than is provided for in the present Covenant."[74] While the status and purpose of such clauses remain disputed, several authors have suggested that they could be construed so as to impose a legal obligation upon private actors not to violate human rights.[75] A recent ICSID award has further animated this debate. The Tribunal had to deal with a complaint lodged by the Spanish company *Urbaser* against the Argentine Republic. *Urbaser* had been granted

---

[72] ECOWAS Court of Justice, *Peter David v. Ralph Uwechue*, Decision of 11 June 2010, ECW/CCJ/RUL/03/10 reaffirmed by ECOWAS Court of Justice, *SERAP v. Nigeria*, Decision of 10 December 2010, ECW/CCJ/APP/07/10.

[73] Emmerich-Fritsche, "Verbindlichkeit der Menschenrechte," 562; Jordan Paust, "The Reality of Private Rights, Duties, and Participation in the International Process" (2004) 25 *MJIL* 1229–1249 at 1243; Moore, "From Nation State to Failed State," 119; Frey, "Legal and Ethical Responsibilities," 163.

[74] Similar provisions can be found in Art. 5 of the ICESCR, Art. 29 of the ACHR; Art. 17 of the ECHR.

[75] See already Marc-André Eissen, "La Convention et les Devoirs de l'Individu," in Travaux du Colloque de Strasbourg, *La Protection Internationale des Droits de l'Homme dans le Cadre Européen* (Paris: Dalloz, 1960), 167–194; Dean Spielmann, *L'Effet Potentiel de la Convention Européenne des Droit des l'Homme entre Personnes Privées* (Brussels: Bruylant, 1995), p. 36.

a concession to provide water and sewage services that – according to the allegations raised by the company – could later not be put into operation due to ongoing administrative problems that intensified in the aftermath of the Argentine financial crisis. Argentina claimed the concession contract had to be terminated due to *Urbaser*'s mismanagement and its manifest failure to expand the sewage network within a reasonable period of time. Besides, Argentina raised a counterclaim claiming that *Urbaser*'s failure to provide for the agreed-upon investments amounted to a violation of the human right to water. When interpreting the relevant provisions of the Bilateral Investment Treaty, the Tribunal found such counterclaims could be based on alleged human rights violations since the relevant BIT encompassed a clause determining the law applicable to investment disputes to include any other treaty in force between the parties, as well as the general principles of international law.

In investigating the merits of Argentina's claim, the Tribunal then wrote a remarkable passage establishing that international human rights treaties could be interpreted so as to impose direct obligations upon non-state actors. Explicitly relying on "abuse of rights" clauses, the Tribunal concluded that human rights treaties had to be read as assigning obligations to both public and private parties. Generally speaking, companies could therefore not rely on their rights ensured by investment treaties if they would thereby destroy the human rights of others.[76] What was at stake in these proceedings, however, was the human right to water, and the Tribunal found this particular right to be exclusively applicable to states. Companies were not obliged to provide contractually required services under international human rights law.[77] Even though Argentina's claim exclusively relied on the right to water and further considerations were thus unnecessary, the Tribunal stressed that if a negative obligation to refrain from human rights violations had been challenged, it would have considered such obligations to be directly applicable to private companies: "an obligation to abstain, like a prohibition to commit acts violating human rights ... can be of immediate application, not only upon States, but equally to individuals and other private parties."[78]

In spite of the Tribunal's firm statement, however, it seems equivocal whether human rights obligations for private actors might

---

[76] ICSID, *Urbaser S.A. and Others v. The Argentine Republic*, Award of 8 December 2016, Case No. ARB/07/26, paras. 1196–1199.
[77] *Urbaser S.A. and Others v. The Argentine Republic*, paras. 1208 ff.
[78] *Urbaser S.A. and Others v. The Argentine Republic*, para. 1210.

actually be derived from "abuse of rights" clauses. While they stipulate that individuals should not purposely misuse their human rights to destroy those of others, there is hardly any indication that they were meant to create direct obligations. Systematically, such clauses are rather an instrument of forfeiture removing harmful conduct from the scope of protection of the respective human rights norm. While they thus restrict the invocation of human rights under certain circumstances, they do not impose independent obligations upon individuals.[79] An examination of the preparatory works to the relevant human rights instruments reveals that such clauses were mainly intended to have protective character. In particular, with regard to political rights and freedoms, they should ensure that such rights and freedoms would not be abused to destroy democracy and the rule of law and thereby the very foundation of political freedom and participation itself.[80] Commonly, they are deemed an element of militant democracy protecting against individuals who try to destroy human rights regimes by purposely misusing the freedoms they offer.[81] In practice, abuse of rights clauses are thus employed to deny individuals protection if they engage in activities that aim at destroying the respective human rights system itself,[82] though they have never been employed to establish individual responsibility for violating the human rights of others.[83]

4. Summary

To summarize the previous sections, none of the approaches arguing in favor of an expansive interpretation of existing human

---

[79] Karavias, "Corporate Obligations," p. 28 f.
[80] Council of Europe, *Collected Edition of the "Travaux Préparatoires" of the ECHR*, volume I (The Hague: Martinus Nijhoff, 1975), p. 192.
[81] Manfred Nowak, *UN Covenant on Civil and Political Rights. A Commentary* (Kehl: N.P. Engel, 2nd ed., 2005), Commentary to Article 5, para. 7; Hannes Cannie and Dirk Voorhoof, "The Abuse Clause and Freedom of Expression in the ECHR" (2011) 29 *Netherlands Quarterly of Human Rights* 54–83 at 56 f.; Katja Wiesbrock, *Internationaler Schutz der Menschenrechte vor Verletzungen durch Private* (Berlin: Arno Spitz, 1999), p. 39.
[82] ECtHR, *Lawless v. Ireland* (No. 3), Judgment of 1 July 1961, Application No. 332/57, para. 7; and in greater detail, Ulrich Karpenstein and Franz Mayer, *Konvention zum Schutz der Menschenrechte und Grundfreiheiten. Kommentar* (München: Beck, 2nd ed., 2015), Commentary to Article 17, para. 2.
[83] Weidmann, "OECD-Leitsätze," p. 99; Kirsten Schmalenbach, "Multinationale Unternehmen und Menschenrechte" (2001) 39 *AVR* 57–81 at 66.

II. DIRECT OBLIGATIONS FOR NON-STATE ACTORS

rights obligations yields convincing arguments. It is undeniably true that the object and purpose of human rights treaties lie in the most effective protection of human rights. This necessarily implies that such rights have to be interpreted in light of changed circumstances lest they become irrelevant and ineffective. Nonetheless, even the most progressive methods of interpretation cannot extend the applicability of a treaty to a whole new array of actors. The majority of states have so far repudiated any attempt to expand human rights obligations to private actors and the jurisprudence of international human rights bodies does not support such an expansion either.

Against this background, there is a rather broad consensus that the international human rights regime as it stands today does not contain legally binding obligations for actors other than states. The only constellations in which such obligations are increasingly accepted are international organizations and territorial non-state armed groups. If states assign human rights sensitive tasks to international organizations, it is now commonly assumed that these organizations are bound to at least abide by customary human rights norms. Moreover, if non-state armed groups have brought substantial parts of territory under their control and thereby entirely replaced state authorities, they find themselves in a position of vertical authority toward individuals equivalent to the position traditionally filled by states.[84] Apart from these peculiar situations, however, direct obligations are not acknowledged under the current human rights system. Reinterpreting its provisions not only is inconsistent with their explicit wording; it would also undermine legal certainty, as neither the scope of applicable provisions nor the respective accountability mechanisms could be identified. International regulations thus should not be lightly presumed to contain legally binding obligations for new categories of actors.

If the existing human rights system does not allow for reinterpretation, the next step to be discussed is whether the accountability of non-state actors should be addressed by a revised convention and what reasons speak for so expansive an approach.

---

[84] In greater detail, see Murray, "Non-State Armed Groups," pp. 164 f.; Katharine Fortin, "The Application of Human Rights Law to Everyday Civilian Life under Rebel Control" (2016) 63 *NILR* 161–181 at 179.

III. Reasons Speaking for Direct Human Rights Obligations on Behalf of Private Actors

As already indicated, the growing influence of powerful non-state actors has reinforced existing problems in the field of human rights protection and created new ones. Against this background, there are indeed several good reasons speaking for a direct application of human rights provisions to certain categories of non-state actors. A first argument in favor is that non-state actors enjoy increasingly more rights under international law and that they even have the capacity to enforce them. This is particularly true for multinational corporations, which profit from certain human rights and additional protection through investment treaties. The enjoyment of such rights, so the argument runs, should be accompanied by corresponding responsibilities.[85] Some large multinational corporations indeed have budgets far exceeding those of the countries they operate in. They are free to choose where they invest and thereby impose massive economic pressure restricting the regulatory options for the governments concerned. Eventually, the implementation of human rights law is hindered where it is most needed: in weak states that lack the financial and institutional capacities or the political willingness to fully implement international protection schemes.[86] In this context, the privatization of core public activities gives further grounds for concern, since it involves non-state entities in human rights-sensitive functions historically carried out by state organs.[87] Some authors thus advance the argument that the status of multinational corporations already is akin to that of states,

---

[85] David Bilchitz, "The Necessity for a Business and Human Rights Treaty" (2016) 1 *Business and Human Rights Journal* 203–227 at 214 f.; Uta Kohl, "Corporate Human Rights Accountability" (2014) 63 *ICLQ* 665–697 at 694 f.; Kamatali, "Guiding Principles on Business and Human Rights," 461; Peter Muchlinski, "Multinational Enterprises as Actors in International Law, in Math Noortmann and Cedric Ryngaert (eds.), *Non-State Actor Dynamics in International Law* (Farnham: Ashgate, 2010), p. 35; McCorquodale, "Overlegalizing Silences," 387.

[86] Alexandra Popova, "Business and Human Rights after Ruggie's Mandate," in Jena Martin and Karen Bravo (eds.), *The Business and Human Rights Landscape* (Cambridge: Cambridge University Press, 2016), p. 120; Daniel Augenstein and David Kinley, "Beyond the 100 Acre Wood: In Which International Human Rights Law Finds New Ways to Tame Global Corporate Power" (2014) Sydney Law School Legal Studies Paper No. 14/90, p. 9; Weilert, "Transnationale Unternehmen," 883 f.; Kamatali, "Guiding Principles on Business and Human Rights," 446; Kimberly Gregalis Granatino, "Corporate Responsibility Now" (1999) 23 *Suffolk Transnational Law Review* 191–226 at 199 ff.

[87] Antenor Hallo de Wolf, *Reconciling Privatization with Human Rights* (Antwerpen: Intersentia, 2012), p. 683; Reinisch, "Changing International Legal Framework," 75 f.;

III. DIRECT HUMAN RIGHTS OBLIGATIONS

which would justify imposing direct human rights obligations upon them.[88] Moreover, it is undeniably true that it makes no difference from a victim's perspective whether the harmful conduct originally stems from a state organ or was carried out by a private actor.[89] The harmful consequences are just the same. If states as the primary addressees of human rights norms are unwilling or unable to live up to their obligations to effectively prevent or at least adequately sanction harmful conduct by other actors, it may become necessary to expand the range of duty bearers in order to ensure effective implementation.[90] Considering the growing potential of non-state actors to cause adverse effects on the enjoyment of human rights and the inability of many states to address those effects, direct obligations for non-state actors are increasingly endorsed as a viable policy option.

Though, as we will see, there are several serious objections to making non-state actors duty bearers under international human rights law. In 2014, the Human Rights Council installed an intergovernmental working group to elaborate on an international legally binding instrument on the human rights activities of corporations and business enterprises.[91] So far, however, the working group has only produced rather general reports. Its first comprehensive proposal as published in September 2017 and revised in July 2019[92] does not contain any far-reaching suggestions going

---

Wesley Cragg, "Human Rights and Business Ethics: Fashioning a New Social Contract" (2000) 27 *Journal of Business Ethics* 205–214 at 209.

[88] Arnold, "Corporations and Human Rights," 266; Florian Wettstein, *Multinational Corporations and Global Justice: Human Rights Obligations of a Quasi-Governmental Institution* (Stanford: Stanford University Press, 2009), p. 207; Emmerich-Fritsche, "Verbindlichkeit der Menschenrechte," 541; Reinisch, "Changing International Legal Framework," 75; Ratner, "Corporations and Human Rights," 65.

[89] Surya Deva, "Scope of the Proposed Business and Human Rights Treaty," in Surya Deva and David Bilchitz (eds.), *Building a Treaty on Business and Human Rights* (Cambridge: Cambridge University Press, 2017), p. 158; Clapham, "Human Rights Obligations of Non-State Actors," p. 35; Sigrun Skogly, "Economic and Social Human Rights, Private Actors and International Obligations," in Michael Addo (ed.), *Human Rights Standards and the Responsibility of Transnational Corporations* (The Hague: Kluwer Law, 1999), p. 239.

[90] David Jason Karp, *Responsibility for Human Rights. Transnational Corporations in Imperfect States* (Cambridge: Cambridge University Press, 2014), p. 102.

[91] UN Human Rights Council, Resolution No. 26/9 of 14 July 2014, Elaboration of an International Legally Binding Instrument on Transnational Corporations and Other Business Enterprises with Respect to Human Rights, UN Doc. A/HRC/RES/26/9.

[92] Elements for the Draft Legally Binding Instrument on Transnational Corporations and other Business Enterprises With Respect to Human Rights of 29 September 2017 and the revised version of 16 July 2019, available online at www.ohchr.org/en/hrbodies/hrc/wgtranscorp/pages/igwgontnc.aspx.

beyond the legal status quo. While this is often attributed to a lack of political will, it might also indicate that there are more serious objections that need to be taken into consideration before binding business corporations to international human rights law. The following section will problematize these concerns and show that exploiting the full potential of the rules on state responsibility is a more promising way to address gaps in human rights protection with regard to harmful private conduct.

IV. Reasons against Imposing Direct Human Rights Obligations on Non-State Actors

That private actors can have adverse impacts on the enjoyment of human rights is beyond question, and it is equally irrefutable that some categories of non-state actors – such as powerful business entities – have created substantial human rights risks that are not adequately addressed. At first glance, creating direct international obligations for non-state actors might thus seem an attractive solution, and yet this approach entails risks that are often overlooked. The following section will address these concerns, which may roughly be categorized in objections relating to procedural and definitional matters (1.), objections relating to legitimacy concerns (2.), and finally the potential for abuse (3.).

1. Procedural and Definitional Questions

The first category of objections comprises several procedural and definitional questions. All of them illustrate the difficulties in drafting a legally binding human rights instrument for non-state actors.

a. Non-State Actors and International Norm Setting

As we have seen earlier, such instrument could significantly alter the norm-setting procedure of international law. In any legal order, it is among the most fundamental questions who may legitimately create legal duties. Whereas duties in the domestic sphere are established through institutionalized decision-making procedures, norm setting at the international stage is less coherent. International norms are either created by international treaties that are negotiated and ratified among states or by customary rules that result from state practice and the willingness of states to accept such rules as legally binding. Non-State actors are not involved in those procedures, except for international organizations that may enter into treaties. It thus needs to be examined how

IV. IMPOSING DIRECT HUMAN RIGHTS OBLIGATIONS

international norms may even legitimately impose duties upon non-state actors and how acknowledging non-state actors as duty bearers would change the setting of international norms. Indisputably, states may exercise their territorial or personal jurisdiction and regulate the conduct of non-state actors acting on their territory or having their nationality. Outside of their jurisdiction, however, states have very limited means to control private conduct. With regard to an international human rights instrument for non-state actors, several fundamental questions necessarily arise: Would all non-state actors be bound or only those actors that are jurisdictionally linked to the ratifying states? Could non-state actors themselves become parties to the respective treaty? And would the treaty establish international accountability mechanisms or allow for a concept such as universal jurisdiction to enforce the treaty's provisions?

It does not take more than these few questions to indicate the conceptual difficulties a treaty framework would face if it were to impose direct human rights obligations upon non-state actors. To assume that some states could create binding obligations for non-state actors to which they have no jurisdictional link would create fundamental problems of legitimacy and most likely face firm opposition by other states. So far, universal jurisdiction is limited to the most heinous and atrocious crimes and even then, states are rather reluctant to exercise it.[93] The two remaining options, therefore, are that only those non-state actors would be bound that are jurisdictionally linked to a ratifying state or that non-state actors themselves enter into such agreement. The first option – and the one pursued in the first draft of the international working group[94] – would not fundamentally alter the status quo since the establishment and enforcement of human rights obligations would still depend on states adding little to the existing framework of positive obligations. Given the substantial opposition on behalf of many governments, it seems rather doubtful whether a substantial number of states would even ratify such an instrument. Alternatively, non-state actors could join an international agreement and submit themselves to the jurisdiction of corresponding enforcement mechanisms.[95] However,

---

[93] McConnell, "Extracting Accountability," p. 103; Cedric Ryngaert, *Jurisdiction in International Law* (Oxford: Oxford University Press, 2015), p. 130.
[94] Elements for the Draft Legally Binding Instrument on Transnational Corporations and other Business Enterprises with respect to Human Rights 2017, pp. 7 ff.
[95] Manfred Nowak, "The Need for a World Court of Human Rights" (2007) 7 *HRLR* 251–259 at 256 f.; Ssenyonjo, "Economic, Social and Cultural Rights," pp. 660 ff.; McBeth, "International Economic Actors," 320 f.

considering the competitive disadvantages such ratification would imply, it seems even less likely they would voluntarily assume far-reaching international obligations, in particular if it is not settled how corresponding accountability mechanisms would operate in practice.[96] Moreover, allowing private actors to become parties to international treaties would necessarily prompt a debate on whether they could or should then also participate in the treaty's drafting. Giving private actors a more active role in international decision-making would alter their legal status at the international plane adding up to the concerns already indicated previously, most notably whether private actors would then also be bound by customary norms and change international norm setting in general.

Before drafting an international agreement, such jurisdictional issues would need to be addressed. While these concerns do not object direct obligations for non-state actors per se, it seems probable that the only way to create such an instrument would consist in binding non-state actors within the jurisdiction of the treaty's member states, which would not add much to existing human rights frameworks.

b. Making Non-State Actors Duty Bearers: "Capacity" as an Adequate Yardstick?

In addition to this, a non-state actor human rights instrument would have to clearly define which categories of non-state actors could and should be bound by its provisions and which human rights obligations could even be adequately applied.[97] Non-State actors are still being labeled as the broadest possible category comprising all actors that are not states,[98] even though there are myriads of different kinds of non-state actors: individuals just as much as international organizations or multinational businesses. Those different categories of non-state actors not

---

[96] Robert Blitt, "Beyond Ruggie's Guiding Principles on Business and Human Rights" (2012) 48 *Texas International Law Journal* 33–62 at 55; and the comprehensive summary of statements to the Guiding Principles on behalf of multinational corporations in: Susan Ariel Aaronson and Ian Higham, "Re-Righting Business: John Ruggie and the Struggle to Develop International Human Rights Standards for International Firms" (2013) 35 *HRQ* 333–364 at 353 ff.

[97] Ralph Steinhardt, "Corporate Responsibility and the International Law of Human Rights," in Philip Alston (ed.), *Non-State Actors and Human Rights* (Oxford: Oxford University Press, 2005), pp. 215 ff.

[98] Noemi Gal-Or, "Observations on the Desirability of an Enhanced International Legal Status of the Non-State Actor," in Math Noortmann and Cedric Ryngaert (eds.), *Non-State Actor Dynamics in International Law* (Farnham: Ashgate, 2010), p. 130; Alston, "The 'Not-a-Cat' Syndrome," 3.

IV. IMPOSING DIRECT HUMAN RIGHTS OBLIGATIONS

only greatly vary regarding their capacities and resources; they are also engaged in substantially different activities, which makes it difficult to assess which categories of human rights they are likely to affect. This is even true when comparing seemingly coherent groups such as business corporations. Whereas resource-exploiting corporations are more likely to infringe upon basic human rights such as the right to life or protection of the home, internet corporations might be more likely to infringe upon privacy rights or the right to freedom of expression. Against this backdrop, different approaches might be necessary to address the specific human rights issues related to different business activities.

While it is rarely argued that all non-state actors including private individuals should be bound by the entire range of human rights provisions, compliance is demanded from "powerful" non-state actors. Even when focusing on one category of "powerful" non-state actors, such as business corporations, however, it would be necessary to define whether any kind of business entity should be bound by human rights obligations or only corporations of a certain size. While it is indeed occasionally argued that all businesses irrespective of their size and sphere of activity should be bound by human rights provisions,[99] most authors submit that only some forms of business entities should become duty bearers. In this context, "capacity" is the most often referred to threshold criterion for acquiring international obligations.[100] If non-state actors have sufficient capacities to adversely affect human rights, so the argument goes, then they should be held accountable irrespective of whether they are acknowledged as subjects of international law or not.[101] On the surface, this seems to be an attractive argument: if non-state actors are powerful enough to violate human rights at large scale, imposing corresponding obligations upon them seems justified. And if they have the capacities to actively protect and foster the enjoyment of human rights, they should

---

[99] Arvind Ganesan, "Towards a Business and Human Rights Treaty," in Dorothée Baumann-Pauly and Justine Nolan (eds.), *Business and Human Rights* (London: Routledge, 2016), p. 74; Bilchitz, "Business and Human Rights Treaty," 221.

[100] Deva, "Business and Human Rights," 69; Florian Wettstein, "From Side Show to Main Act: Can Business and Human Rights Save Corporate Responsibility?" in Dorothée Baumann-Pauly and Justine Nolan (eds.), *Business and Human Rights* (London: Routledge, 2016), p. 85; Math Noortmann and Cedric Ryngaert, "Non-State Actors: Law-Takers or Law-Makers? Is that the Question," in Math Noortmann and Cedric Ryngaert (eds.), *Non-State Actor Dynamics in International Law* (Farnham: Ashgate, 2010), p. 197; Jochnik, "Confronting Impunity," 77.

[101] Deva, "Business and Human Rights," 69; see also Karp, "Transnational Corporations in Imperfect States," pp. 89 ff.

adhere to positive obligations as well.[102] What seems desirable from a policy standpoint, however, might still prove difficult to apply to legal practice. First of all, taking capacity as a threshold for binding obligations would introduce new evidentiary burdens upon the victims of human rights violations. Not only would they have to establish the violation itself; they would also have to show that the non-state actor's capacity is sufficient enough to be bound by human rights obligations. And how exactly should capacity be defined? Would it be sufficient to show that a given non-state actor was capable of infringing upon the human right at stake in the case at hand? Or that it was capable of infringing upon a greater number of different human rights provisions? And how extensive capacities should be for being qualified as human rights duty bearer? Would financial capacities be an adequate yardstick or the number of persons involved in an organization or could even powerful individuals be seen as having sufficient capacities? And what would happen if the legal or institutional structures of non-state actors are dissolved and they lose their capacity entirely?

There are no simple answers to these questions. Yet they illustrate that capacity cannot serve as an adequate yardstick for imposing directly binding international obligations. If a human rights convention would directly bind all actors that have sufficient capacity to infringe upon the convention, a clear definition of "sufficient capacity" is indispensable.[103] Also, it would have to be regulated how cases should be handled if corporate non-state actors lose their capacity, either through bankruptcy or because they are dissolved. Otherwise, it would have to be decided on a case-by-case basis whether the respective non-state actor had sufficient capacities leading to unnecessary legal uncertainty and procedural burdens upon the victims. It should not be neglected that non-state actors, including business corporations, enjoy human rights protection themselves. They are equally entitled to legal certainty, which means that any provision imposing far-reaching obligations upon them has to be accurate and precise. Vague and general obligations with legal consequences that are not foreseeable would potentially infringe upon the own human rights of the non-state actors concerned.[104] So far, it is hard to see how a definition of non-state actors as duty bearers could be phrased in a workable way, taking all those open questions into account.

---

[102] Stepan Wood, "The Case for Leverage-Based Corporate Human Rights Responsibility" (2012) 22 *Business Ethics Quarterly* 63–98 at 76 f.

[103] See also Carlos Vázquez, "Direct vs. Indirect Obligations of Corporations under International Law" (2004) 43 *Columbia Journal of Transnational Law* 927–959 at 946.

[104] Christian Tomuschat, *Human Rights. Between Idealism and Realism* (Oxford: Oxford University Press, 3rd ed., 2014), p. 130.

c. Shared Accountability between States and Non-State Actors?

Even if it were possible to find an adequate and precise definition of what kind of non-state actors should be bound by human rights, it would still be necessary to regulate the exact accountability relationship between states and non-state actors.[105] Qualifying states as the only guarantors of human rights has one advantage that need not be neglected: duty bearers can be easily identified. For the victim, it is clear against whom to bring a judicial claim. With non-state actors, such legal certainty does not exist. Would states still have some sort of back-up accountability if the accountability of non-state actors could not be established or if non-state actors lack the resources necessary to provide for adequate compensation? Such difficulties in establishing a clear accountability relationship among various duty bearers have been described as a problem of overinclusion.[106] Ruggie rightly warned that to place on multinational corporations the same duties as those already imposed on states would cause "endless strategic gaming" between states and corporations. To avoid that states try shifting their responsibility to corporations and vice versa, it would be necessary to clearly define who bears primary responsibility for human rights violations.[107] Particularly difficult to address would be those constellations in which non-state actors cause human rights harm but acted in pursuance of legislative provisions or governmental orders. This is, for instance, well-illustrated by the controversial role played by Vodafone during the Arab Spring movement in Egypt. At the Egyptian government's request, Vodafone cut its mobile services with the government using the services to issue calls against the demonstrators and mobilize government support.[108] Still more recently,

---

[105] Jean d'Aspremont et al., "Sharing Responsibility between Non-State Actors and States in International Law" (2015) 62 *NILR* 49–67; Wouter Vandenhole, "Obligations and Responsibility in a Plural and Diverse Duty-bearer Human Rights Regime," in Wouter Vandenhole (ed.), *Challenging Territoriality in Human Rights Law* (London: Routledge, 2015), p. 133.

[106] John Knox, "Horizontal Human Rights Law" (2008) 102 *AJIL* 1–47 at 41.

[107] John Ruggie, "Business and Human Rights: The Evolving International Agenda" (2007) 101 *AJIL* 819–840 at 826.

[108] See, for a detailed analysis, Andrew Hoffmann, "Vodafone Egypt and the Arab Spring: When Government and Business Collide," William Davidson Institute Case Study No. 1-429-417, University of Michigan, 27 February 2015, available online at https://erb.umich.edu/2015/03/02/vodafone-egypt-and-the-arab-spring-when-government-and-business-collide/.

the government of Pakistan called upon Facebook and Twitter to help identify blasphemers who may await the death penalty when prosecuted in Pakistan.[109] These few examples already indicate how difficult the relationship between states and corporations could turn out in a human rights context. Should Vodafone or Facebook be seen as primarily responsible for possible human rights violations? Or could they use the governmental orders as a defense for non-compliance with international human rights norms? Could it be expected from corporations to protect human rights even if they thereby violate explicit governmental orders and even if this might endanger their future economic activities in that country? And who has the ultimate authority to decide in which scenario a corporation is complicit in governmental human rights violations and in which scenario a corporation does not comply with unwanted government provisions under the pretense of securing human rights?

This final question leads us to another category of objections that goes beyond mere procedural and definitional difficulties. Human rights protection comprises more than just refraining from causing harm. It requires the careful balancing of different human rights and public interests, and in many cases, conflicting aims will have to be reconciled. As we will see, non-state actors have neither the political legitimacy nor the resources to adequately fulfill this balancing task.

2. *Legitimacy Questions: Non-State Actors and the Balancing of Public Interests*

It is commonplace that the protection of human rights goes beyond the mere duty to refrain from direct human rights violations. States are also required to take active protective and preventive measures and to create an environment in which human rights are promoted and respected. In order to do so, finding an adequate balance between various human rights and public interests is indispensable. Even the mere negative obligation not to infringe upon human rights requires weighing up competing rights and interests. Protecting one individual's right might easily infringe upon the rights of another. Individual rights might also come into conflict with various public interests. Infringing upon human rights might be necessary and also

---

[109] *The Guardian* of 17 March 2017, "Pakistan Asks Facebook and Twitter to Help Identify Blasphemers," available online at www.theguardian.com/world/2017/mar/17/pakistan-asks-facebook-twitter-help-identify-blasphemers.

IV. IMPOSING DIRECT HUMAN RIGHTS OBLIGATIONS

justified to protect other rights or to achieve legitimate public goals. This balancing of rights and interests shapes societies in a normative manner and is among the very fundamental functions underlying human rights protection. Notwithstanding, the need for achieving an adequate balance between conflicting rights and interests is often neglected in the debate on direct human rights obligations for non-state actors. Some authors suggest that private actors could simply have recourse to well-established balancing principles such as proportionality tests,[110] and the risk of inadequate results should not be overstated, as affected individuals could easily raise counterclaims to protect their interests.[111]

Bringing competing human rights and public interests into a suitable balance, however, is not a task that non-state actors could adequately fulfill because they lack the legitimacy and the resources to do so. First of all, finding such a balance requires the ability to even assess which different interests are at stake. While conflicting rights and interests might be voiced in the political decision-making process, non-state actors do not adhere to transparent decision-making procedures. Neither do they have access to as much information as states in order to make substantial assessments. And even where this could be mitigated – through mandatory impact assessments and corresponding participatory options – private actors would still lack the legitimacy to weigh rights and interests against each other. Private actors are not in a position to decide which infringements might be justified and which right or interest should prevail over another. It is the state that has the political legitimacy to make those decisions. Not only are state organs institutionally (and ideally democratically) legitimized; they are also best equipped to assess competing interests and find proportional solutions. Even more importantly, states are mere duty bearers and not protected by human rights themselves. They are thus in a position to solve conflicts between rights and interests from a neutral perspective. Moreover, it is the state that has a monopoly on the use of force to ensure and enforce the protection of human rights.[112] None of this applies to non-state actors. In contrast to states, private actors are entitled to enjoy human rights protection

---

[110] Ratner, "Corporations and Human Rights," 514 f.; Addo, "Human Rights and Transnational Corporations," 30.
[111] Clapham, "Human Rights Obligations of Non-State Actors," p. 526.
[112] Josef Isensee, "Die heikle Weltherrschaft der Menschenrechte," in Marten Breuer et al. (eds.), *Der Staat im Recht* (Berlin: Duncker & Humblot, 2013), p. 1089.

themselves.[113] They do not act neutrally in the public interest but pursue their own private interests and that they do so is a legitimate exercise of their personal freedom.[114] Even if the notion of corporate social responsibility is gaining increasing acceptance, it would contravene the fundamental notions of private freedom and autonomy to impose upon non-state actors an obligation to purely act in the public interest and serve common goods.[115]

In fact, there are two sides to this problem and both are worrying in equal measure. Since private actors – including corporations – enjoy human rights protection themselves, they cannot be required to act in a neutral manner and to exclusively pursue public interests. Even more importantly, however, they are not in a position in which they could legitimately solve conflicts between different rights and interests. If private actors were the guarantors of human rights, it would also be for private actors to define the material content of human rights provisions and to decide whether an infringement would be justified or not. For instance, obliging Facebook to erase comments and posts that infringe upon personal human rights also means that it would be left to Facebook to decide which comments are protected under freedom of speech and which are not. Facebook, however, is not politically legitimized to make such an assessment, and its decision may not necessarily be neutral but also guided by business interests, such as ensuring advertising revenues arising from popular but controversial posts. It would thus be necessary to clearly define who would be competent to review the human rights balancing carried out by non-state actors.[116]

Overall, non-state actors are thus ill-equipped to weigh conflicting human rights and interests against each other. Finding an adequate balance is a difficult task, requiring political legitimacy and sufficient resources. Human rights obligations go beyond individual protection; they also shape and normatively structure public life in general, which is why they can be adequately fulfilled only by those entities that represent all

---

[113] Institut de Droit International, "Droits de l'Homme et Droit International Privé: Rapporteur Jürgen Basedow" (2016) 77 *Annuaire de l'Institut de Droit International* 391–453 at 404; Karavias, "Corporate Obligations," p. 197; Ratner, "Corporations and Human Rights," 513.
[114] Nien-Hê Hsieh, "Should Business Have Human Rights Obligations?" (2015) 14 *Journal of Human Rights* 218–236 at 230.
[115] Olivier de Schutter, *International Human Rights Law* (Cambridge: Cambridge University Press, 2nd ed., 2014), p. 465.
[116] On this matter, see also Gavin Anderson, "Rights and the Art of Boundary Maintenance" (1997) 60 *Modern Law Review* 120–132 at 129 f.

segments of society.[117] It is not up to single private actors to define social standards, and it would be undemocratic for them to do so if transparency and public access to their decision-making process could not be guaranteed. Any international instrument providing for the accountability of private actors, therefore, should not allow those actors to take over the role traditionally played by states. They should not become human rights guarantors in the sense that they would be responsible for human rights protection in a broader sense and could decide how conflicts between rights and interests are to be solved. This would create substantial problems of legitimacy, as private actors are not in a position to make normative legal decisions, and it would also impose a disproportionate burden upon these private actors. Binding them by broad human rights obligations of unforeseeable scope would potentially infringe upon their own rights and freedoms. For these reasons, it would be necessary to narrowly tailor the obligations of private entities and precisely define how infringements by non-state actors could be justified and for what reasons.[118]

Furthermore, simply declaring international human rights law applicable to non-state actors would not only negligently ignore these serious concerns but also create a situation in which states and non-state actors could both misuse their new position.

3. Abuse Concerns

Directly binding human rights obligations could easily be abused by states and non-state actors alike, which, in the long run, would impair the situation they were supposed to improve. The potential for such abuse is twofold. On the one hand, states could be inclined to neglect their own protective duties with regard to human rights, since they could easily shift responsibilities to private actors. They might even instrumentalize private human rights accountability in order to persecute opponents under the pretense that these opponents violate their human rights obligations (a.). On the other hand, imposing human rights obligations upon non-state actors would presuppose giving them the means to actually realize these obligations, which could have unwelcome side effects (b.)

---

[117] Vázquez, "Direct vs. Indirect Obligations," 946; and in a similar manner: Sigrun Skogly, "Regulatory Obligations in a Complex World," in Surya Deva and David Bilchitz (eds.), *Building a Treaty on Business and Human Rights* (Cambridge: Cambridge University Press, 2017), p. 336.
[118] See also Peters, "Jenseits der Menschenrechte," p. 97.

a. A Chance for States to Neglect Their Own Duties

While it is undisputedly true that the human rights performance of many states is far from satisfactory, there are reasons to be concerned with letting states off the hook by imposing obligations upon other actors instead of enforcing state compliance more vigorously. The accountability of other actors can easily be exploited as a feeble excuse not to comply with one's own human rights provisions.[119] It even seems likely that such accountability would lower the incentives for states to increase resources in order to improve their own human rights record.[120] This further underlines how important it would be to clearly define the accountability relationship between states and private actors and to emphasize that states would still bear primary responsibility under international human rights law even if other obligations were to be imposed.

In addition to this, there is a substantial risk that states would misuse direct human rights obligations for non-state actors in order to regulate and persecute non-state actors under the pretense of ensuring their compliance with human rights provisions.[121] Reproaching non-state actors for having violated their human rights obligations could easily be abused to give domestic enforcement measures or criminal prosecution greater legitimacy. It would thus be necessary that any international instrument containing such obligations for private actors would include distinct enforcement mechanisms and international review options.

b. Awarding Corresponding Rights to Non-State Actors

The potential of abuse does not rest with states alone. It is an often evaded fact that for non-state actors to have human rights obligations, corresponding rights to actually fulfill these obligations would have to be awarded.[122] In particular, with regard to corporate activities, even positive obligations on behalf of businesses are increasingly promoted.[123] The

---

[119] Lopez, "Human Rights Legal Liability," 310.
[120] Graham Markiewicz, "The Logical Next Step: Motivations on the Formation of a Business and Human Rights Treaty" (2017) 26 *Minnesota Journal of International Law* 63–80 at 78; Sigrun Skogly, "Extraterritorial Obligations and the Obligation to Protect" (2016) 47 *NYIL* 217–244 at 242.
[121] Knox, "Horizontal Human Rights Law," 20.
[122] Hugh Thirlway, "The Role of Non-State Actors" (2017) 64 *NILR* 141–153 at 149.
[123] Deva, "Business and Human Rights," 69; Ssenyonjo, "Economic, Social and Cultural Rights," 178; George Brenkert, "Business, Respect, and Human Rights," in Jean Martin and Karen Bravo (eds.), *The Business and Human Rights Landscape* (Cambridge: Cambridge University Press, 2015), p. 156; Radu Mares, "Respect Human Rights: Concept and Convergence," in Robert Bird et al. (eds.), *Law, Business and Human*

problems related thereto are easily illustrated when considering the right to life as an example. It is simple to agree that corporations should be under an obligation not to kill anyone. If, however, corporations were to have additional positive obligations to actively protect the life and physical integrity of their employees, they would rely on corresponding rights to hire security personnel or even arm such personnel. Fulfilling positive obligations generally requires sufficient resources to take protective and preventive measures. If the entire range of human rights obligations should be extended to non-state actors, they would need adequate resources to fulfill them. Before imposing direct obligations upon non-state actors, it would thus be necessary to discuss whether awarding further resources to private actors would not bear the risk of even more severe human rights violations.

This reemphasizes that non-state actors are ill-equipped to take over the balancing of rights and interests necessary to implement the entire human rights framework. Corporations are established for economic purposes and aim at maximizing private profits. It is incompatible with this purpose to impose on corporations the duty to enhance specific developments and build a society in which human rights are respected.[124] The shaping of social structures is a task that cannot be adequately and legitimately performed by actors which ultimately seek to enhance their own economic benefits. The private nature of corporate interests imposes too high a risk of substantial human rights abuses,[125] particularly if this is accompanied by significantly increased powers and resources.

V. Conclusion: The Necessity of Exploiting the Full Potential of State Responsibility

Summarizing the above said, one might be tempted to draw an overly pessimistic picture of the future role non-state actors could play within the human rights context. And yet, none of the arguments brought forward is supposed to imply that private entities should not be held responsible for the harm they cause. The matter is rather whether it is

---

Rights. Bridging the Gap (Cheltenham: Edward Elgar, 2014), pp. 14 ff.; McBeth, "International Economic Actors," 79; Granatino, "Corporate Responsibility," 219.

[124] See, for a similar argument, Ratner, "Corporations and Human Rights," 518.

[125] John Douglas Bishop, "The Limits of Corporate Human Rights Obligations and the Rights of For-Profit Corporations" (2012) 22 *Business Ethics Quarterly* 119–144 at 139.

useful and desirable to achieve this by imposing direct human rights obligations under international law.

While the creation of such obligations has drawn substantial attraction among legal scholars, it should not be overlooked that the role of non-state actors remains substantially different from the role of states and there are good reasons to uphold these differences. As we have seen, non-state actors lack the resources and the legitimacy to administer the central role of states in the human rights context. Any human rights obligations for private actors would have to be narrowly tailored and precisely defined. It will be for states to determine which actors should be bound by such provisions and what the substantial content of this instrument could look like. Given the great procedural and definitional difficulties, as well as the substantial reluctance on behalf of many states to engage in further regulatory efforts on this matter,[126] it does not seem very likely that such an international instrument and corresponding enforcement mechanisms will be drafted in the foreseeable future.

The success of such an instrument, though, would be highly dependent on effective enforcement mechanisms. In particular, the need of corporations to survive in the market suggests that they would only comply with norms in their economic interest and where such norms are not inherently beneficial only to the extent that they are backed up with economic sanctions. Thus, it is highly unlikely that direct international obligations imposed on non-state actors would be efficient if they were not accompanied by specific coercive enforcement mechanisms.[127] Even less likely could it be expected that human rights bodies expand their jurisdictional scope. Taking into account that existing human rights institutions are already reluctant to deal with human rights complaints against international organizations, even though those organizations are set up and controlled by states, it seems not very likely that they would be willing to extend their jurisdiction to entirely private actors.[128] In sum, it thus

---

[126] See the general statements as contained in Human Rights Council, Report of 5 February 2016 on the First Session of the Open-Ended Intergovernmental Working Group on Transnational Corporations and Other Business Enterprises with Respect to Human Rights, UN Doc. A/HRC/31/50, para. 26; and Report of 4 January 2017 on the Second Session, UN Doc. A/HRC/34/47, paras. 10 ff.

[127] Lee McConnell, "Assessing the Feasibility of a Business and Human Rights Treaty" (2017) 66 *ICLQ* 143–180 at 180; Lopez, "Human Rights Legal Liability," 315 f.; de Brabandere, "Human Rights and Transnational Corporations," 87; Weilert, "Transnationale Unternehmen," 912; Frey, "Legal and Ethical Responsibilities," 164.

[128] Reinisch, "Changing International Legal Framework," 85.

V. CONCLUSION

does not appear very realistic that an international agreement on binding human rights obligations for non-state actors will be drafted in the foreseeable future and that it could be enforced through effective international mechanisms.

And even if consensus on such an agreement could be reached, it would still be necessary to carefully consider the proper role for non-state actors in the human rights sphere. As we have seen, they lack both the legitimacy and the resources to be bound by the entire human rights framework. When acknowledging that non-state actors cannot be simply put in the position of human rights duty bearers under international law, it becomes clear that the role of states is and remains crucial.[129] Even if an international instrument containing obligations for non-state actors could be agreed upon, the scope and enforceability of such an instrument would still be contingent on state support. It need not be neglected either that international agreements tend to represent the lowest common denominator. They often are of broad and general nature,[130] while many domestic legal regimes already possess rather detailed approaches to deal with non-state human rights risks. Drafting general international human rights norms for private actors thus entails as a further risk the displacement of existing comprehensive human rights strategies at the domestic level.[131]

Taking all of this into consideration, it seems justified and even necessary to focus on how the rules on state responsibility could be more effectively applied in the context of human rights protection.[132] This is not to say that international treaties on the role of non-state actors should be given up entirely. Given the uncertainty of whether any

---

[129] Costas Douzinas, *Human Rights and Empire: The Political Philosophy of Cosmopolitanism* (London: Routledge, 2007), p. 231; David Kinley and Junko Tadaki, "From Talk to Walk: The Emergence of Human Rights Responsibilities for Corporations" (2004) 44 *Virginia Journal of International Law* 931–1023 at 1021.

[130] Markiewicz, "The Logical Next Step," 80. For a proposal of a broad framework agreement, see Penelope Simons, "The Value-Added of a Treaty to Regulate Transnational Corporations and Other Business Enterprises," in Surya Deva and David Bilchitz (eds.), *Building a Treaty on Business and Human Rights* (Cambridge: Cambridge University Press, 2017), pp. 71 ff.

[131] Tomuschat, "Human Rights," p. 132; Cedric Ryngaert, "State Responsibility and Non-State Actors," in Math Noortmann et al. (eds.), *Non-State Actors in International Law* (Oxford: Hart, 2015), p. 180.

[132] Lopez, "Human Rights Legal Liability," 317; Hurst Hannum, "Reinvigorating Human Rights for the Twenty-First Century" (2016) 16 *HRLR* 409–451 at 430; Samantha Besson, "The Bearers of Human Rights' Duties and Responsibilities for Human Rights: A Quiet (R)evolution?" (2015) 32 *Social Philosophy and Policy* 244–268 at 267.

effective and adequate obligations will be imposed upon non-state actors in the near future, however, it is worth investigating how state responsibility for human rights contraventions can be better conceptualized to tackle the growing human rights risks posed by non-state actors.

2

Establishing State Responsibility for Human Rights Violations: Proposal for a Conduct-Based Typology of Human Rights Obligations

I. Introductory Remarks

Even though there are good reasons to focus on state responsibility for human rights violations, the development of international human rights law has caused significant changes to the historical order of international law, affecting its most basic structures, including the laws on state responsibility. Signs of those changes become visible in a variety of legal concepts, such as *ius cogens* norms; *erga omnes* obligations; the common heritage of mankind; the responsibility to protect; or the recognition of individual criminal responsibility. These concepts all have in common that human rights are increasingly recognized as shared values of the entire international community. How individuals are treated within domestic orders has become an international concern that qualifies the traditional interstate order to a significant extent.[1] The law on state responsibility – regulating the legal consequences of an internationally wrongful act – is among those areas that are most closely linked to this interstate reciprocal conception of international law. Its original purpose was the restoration of equilibrium between sovereign states, including compensation for transboundary harm.[2] Human rights law, with its individualized focus, does not fit in this traditional structure.[3]

---

[1] Among many others, see Olivier de Schutter, *International Human Rights Law* (Cambridge: Cambridge University Press, 2nd ed., 2014), p. 113.
[2] Most notably, Dionisio Anzilotti, "La Responsabilité Internationale des États à Raison des Dommages Soufferts par des Étrangers" (1906) 13 *RGDIP* 5–29 at 13 ff.; Ian Brownlie, *The System of the Law of Nations. Part I. State Responsibility* (Oxford: Clarendon, 1983), p. 22.
[3] Louis Henkins, "International Law: Politics, Values and Functions" (1989) 216 *RcD* 253; Frédéric Mégret, "Nature of Obligations," in Daniel Moeckli et al. (eds.), *International Human Rights Law* (Oxford: Oxford University Press, 2nd ed., 2014), p. 99.

What distinguishes the field of human rights protection quite distinctively from other areas of international law is the absence of transboundary risks. While human rights violations may theoretically trigger refugee crises or civil wars and thereby develop into cross-border problems, human rights protection primarily concerns the relationship between a state and its citizens. Occasionally, human rights law is even qualified as a "field of functional specialization,"[4] to which the established rules on state responsibility could not be applied at all since only distinct regimes are capable of addressing its peculiarities.[5] While this approach did not find substantial support, the field of human rights protection has still given grounds for a vast amount of different typologies aiming at the categorization of human rights obligations. The following section will introduce the most popular of these typologies while focusing on how they conceptualize state responsibility for human rights violations. While providing for a better understanding of the historical development of different types of human rights, none of these approaches satisfactorily establishes when state responsibility for human rights violations arises, which also explains why the potential of the rules on state responsibility is still underdeveloped in the human rights context, in particular with regard to the harmful conduct of non-state actors.

II. The Inadequacy of Traditional Human Rights Typologies

Human rights have been categorized along different generations (1.); as negative versus positive forms of obligations (2.); and within the respect, protect, and fulfill framework (3.). Interestingly however, most of these attempts are of a rather descriptive character. Surprisingly little writings discuss how state responsibility for human rights violations is to be established and how the rules on state responsibility could contribute to more effective human rights protection. Most typologies employ rather broad categories and do not describe what states are actually required to do to comply with international human rights norms. Only when it is sufficiently clearly defined what concrete conduct is expected of states and how different types of obligations relate to each other can state responsibility for human rights violations be narrowed down. This

---

[4] ILC, Fragmentation of International Law: Difficulties Arising from the Diversification and Expansion of International Law, Report of April 13, 2006, UN Doc. A/CN.4/L.682, para. 129.
[5] See, for further reference, Christian Tomuschat, *Human Rights: Between Idealism and Realism* (Oxford: Oxford University Press, 3rd ed., 2014), p. 318.

task is all the more difficult when it comes to positive obligations and the duty to regulate private actors. The scope of positive obligations is particularly broad and their exact content unclear, rendering it all the more difficult to define under which circumstances states may be held responsible for a lack of compliance. Clarifying the exact content of these obligations could help ensure that human rights risks stemming from non-state conduct are mitigated more effectively. Against this background, the following section aims to reevaluate the main categorizations of human rights while focusing on what these concepts tell us about state responsibility for human rights violations.

1. Three Generations of Human Rights

One of the first attempts to specify different kinds of human rights violations is the categorization of human rights belonging to the first, second, and third generation (or dimension).[6] First-generation human rights are civil and political rights, whereas economic, social, and cultural rights form part of the second generation. This distinction is mainly reflected by the adoption of two different International Covenants, each addressing one of the categories. Third-generation human rights were not discussed until a later stage and include rights of a collective nature, such as the right to a clean environment or the right to democracy and good governance.[7] When it comes to state responsibility, some scholars suggest that different generations of human rights also trigger different forms of obligations. While human rights of the first generation are understood to entail precise and justiciable obligations, those of the second and third generation are considered vague or as not imposing any concrete obligations at all.[8] Human rights of the first generation are deemed strictly binding and prescriptive, in contrast to the rather missionary and direction-setting character associated with the second and third generation.[9] Some authors even went so far as to

---

[6] First introduced by Karel Vasak, "A 30-Year Struggle. The Sustained Efforts to Give Force of Law to the Universal Declaration of Human Rights" (1977) *The UNESCO Courier* 29–32 at 29.
[7] On the historical development, see Tomuschat, *Human Rights*, p. 136 ff.
[8] For an overview of this debate, see Mirja Trilsch, *Die Justiziabilität wirtschaftlicher, sozialer und kultureller Recht im innerstaatlichen Recht* (Heidelberg: Springer, 2012), pp. 12 ff.
[9] For an overview, see Philip Alston and Gerard Quinn, "The Nature and Scope of States Parties' Obligations under the ICSECR" (1987) 9 *HRQ* 156–229 at 159 f.; Craig Scott, "The Interdependence and Permeability of Human Rights Norms: Towards a Partial Fusion of

argue that human rights of the first generation imposed only negative obligations upon states, whereas the second and third generations imposed only positive obligations.[10]

When it comes to identifying different forms of human rights obligations, however, the categorization along generations does not prove very fruitful. Deciding which generation best classifies a human rights provision does not help deduce what exactly states are obliged to do or prohibited from doing, and when a breach of the respective human rights obligations can be assumed. The simple distinction between first-generation human rights with a negative connotation and second- or third-generation human rights with a positive one does not adequately reflect the respective human rights provisions. In fact, each human rights provision contains various forms of obligations. Human rights provisions of the first generation impose different forms of sub-obligations, and the same holds true for second- and third-generation rights. Take, for instance, the right to life as a human right belonging to the first generation. It clearly contains a negative duty obliging the state to refrain from illegitimately taking the life of individuals. Yet the right to life was also among the first human rights in the context of which international human rights bodies have recognized positive obligations on behalf of the state, requiring active steps in order to ensure that harm stemming from third parties is prevented. Conversely, the right to food as a human right of the second generation indeed contains a strong positive element in the sense that states are required to take positive steps to ensure adequate food supply. On the other hand, it also contains negative obligations, in that states are obliged to refrain from hindering access to available food. Hence, it cannot be assumed that a certain generation entails only certain forms of obligations.[11] Even without diving into a more specific analysis on different forms of human rights obligations, it is clear that each right, no matter the generation, contains various forms of obligations.[12] While the categorization along different generations of human rights helps reconstruct their historical development, it thus proves of little assistance

---

the International Covenants on Human Rights" (1989) 27 *Osgoode Hall Law Journal* 769–878 at 833.
[10] See, for instance, Vasak, "A 30-Year Struggle," 29.
[11] Patrick Macklem, *The Sovereignty of Human Rights* (Oxford: Oxford University Press, 2015), pp. 58 ff.
[12] Aoife Nolan et al., "The Justiciability of Social and Economic Rights" (2007) Center for Human Rights and Global Justice, Working Paper No. 15, p. 9; Scott, "Interdependence and Permeability of Human Rights," 835.

to understand the manner in which states are expected to carry out their obligations.[13]

2. Obligations to Respect, Protect, and Fulfill

Next to the categorization of human rights along different generations, it is most common to differentiate between human rights obligations to respect, protect, and fulfill. This tripartite typology was originally proposed by Shue – though with a slightly different terminology[14] – and soon became popular among human rights bodies and scholars. It was first cited by the Special Rapporteur on the Right to Food[15] and is still frequently referred to by the CESCR.[16] Shue's categorization is the first to recognize that different forms of sub-obligations are entailed in a single human rights provision, making it more conducive to distinguish between different forms of obligations rather than different forms of rights. His framework differentiates between obligations to respect human rights, which means that states should not infringe upon human rights through the conduct of their own organs, obligations to protect human rights that require states to take active steps to prevent harm stemming from third parties, and obligations to fulfill instructing states to work toward the broadest possible realization of human rights. Violations of those different forms of obligations could occur individually or in various combinations.[17] The protection of a single human right thus requires the fulfillment of a variety of different duties.

Apart from this important conceptual assumption, though, Shue's categorization is mostly descriptive in the sense that it does not delve into the exact actions required of states.[18] To assume that states are under an obligation to facilitate and promote the enjoyment of human rights,

---

[13] Riccardo Pisillo-Mazzeschi, "Responsabilité de l'État pour Violation des Obligations Positives Relatives aux Droit de l'Homme" (2008) 333 *RdC* 187–506 at 237.

[14] Henry Shue, *Basic Rights: Subsistence, Affluence and US Foreign Policy* (Princeton: Princeton University Press, 1980), p. 52.

[15] Economic and Social Council, Report on the Right to Adequate Food as a Human Right by Special Rapporteur Asbjørn Eide of 7 July 1987, UN Doc. E/CN.4/Sub.2/1987/23, p. 24.

[16] Among many others, see CESCR, General Comment No. 12, UN Doc. E/C.12/1999/5 (1999), para. 15.

[17] Eibe Riebel et al., "The Development of Economic, Social, and Cultural Rights in International Law," in Eibe Riebel et al. (eds.), *Economic, Social, and Cultural Rights: Contemporary Issues and Challenges* (Oxford: Oxford University Press, 2014), p. 20.

[18] Olivier de Schutter (ed.), *Economic, Social and Cultural Rights as Human Rights* (Cheltenham: Edward Elgar, 2013), pp. xiii ff.

for instance, does not provide any concrete insights on what course of conduct actually is required of states and under which circumstances states may be held responsible for failure to comply with that obligation.[19] Although the framework of obligations to respect, protect, and fulfill is thus important, insofar as it recognizes that one single human right entails different forms of obligations, the categories employed by Shue are not precise enough to provide any concrete measure to determine state responsibility for human rights violations.

3. Positive versus Negative Obligations

Next to Shue's framework, the differentiation between positive and negative forms of human rights obligations is probably the most popular approach to portraying state responsibility for human rights violations. The broad distinction between positive and negative obligations is applicable to any international obligation: negative obligations are those obligations that require states to refrain from doing something, whereas positive obligations are those obligations that instruct states to actively perform.

In the human rights context, states should take active steps in order to ensure that private conduct does not interfere with human rights and that such conduct is adequately sanctioned if it nonetheless occurs. That human rights instruments entail such positive obligations has meanwhile been acknowledged by all major human rights bodies. The very wording employed by most human rights treaties – instructing states to "ensure" the protected rights – suggests the dual requirement to refrain from actively violating human rights, on the one hand, and to prevent external violations, on the other. Through the application of positive obligations human rights instruments influence and shape private relationships because states will often be required to create binding obligations for non-state actors – for instance, by establishing criminal and civil liability in respect of conduct that contravenes human rights. This position is well accentuated by the Human Rights Committee, stating that "the positive obligations of States Parties to ensure Covenant rights will only be fully discharged if individuals are protected by the State, not just against violations of Covenant rights by its agents, but also against acts committed by private persons or entities that would impair the enjoyment of

---

[19] Ida Elisabeth Koch, "The Justiciability of Indivisible Rights" (2003) 72 *Nordic Journal of International Law* 3–39 at 10.

II. INADEQUACY OF TRADITIONAL HUMAN RIGHTS 53

Covenant rights."[20] The Strasbourg Court has further developed the concept of positive obligations, in particular with regard to the right to life, famously stating that states have a duty "to take appropriate steps to safeguard the lives of those within [their] jurisdiction" and to "do all that could be reasonably expected of them to avoid a real and imminent risk to life of which they have or ought to have knowledge."[21] More recently, several soft law instruments have continued to stress the significance of positive human rights obligations The UN Guiding Principles on Business and Human Rights specify that "States must protect against human rights abuse within their territory and/or jurisdiction by third parties,"[22] and the Maastricht Principles postulate that "States must take necessary measures to ensure that non-state actors which they are in a position to regulate ... do not nullify or impair the enjoyment of economic, social and cultural rights."[23]

Occasionally, positive obligations have even been qualified as the only suitable measure to determine state responsibility for human rights risks caused by non-state actors.[24] In spite of this broad recognition, however, the mere qualification as positive or negative does not provide us with concrete information on which conduct is exactly expected of states and when a violation of the respective human rights provision occurs. The notion of positive obligations merely indicates that states have to take some form of positive steps. Yet it does not provide any further guidance, neither on the concrete form of positive conduct that is to be taken nor on the manner and time in which it is to be fulfilled.[25] Not surprisingly, the category of positive obligations comprises a wide range of different forms of obligations to regulate private conduct.[26] When taking a closer look at

---

[20] HRC, General Comment No. 31 on the Nature of the General Legal Obligation Imposed on States Parties to the Covenant, 26 May 2004, UN Doc CCPR/C/21/Rev.1/Add.13, para. 8.

[21] ECtHR, *Osman v. UK*, Grand Chamber Judgment of 28 October 1998, Application No. 23452/94, paras. 115 f.

[22] Human Rights Council, Guiding Principles on Business and Human Rights, Report of John Ruggie, 21 March 2011, UN Doc A/HRC/17/31, Principle 1.

[23] Maastricht Principles on Extraterritorial Obligations of States in the Field of Economic, Social and Cultural Rights, 28 September 2011, published with commentaries in 34 *HRQ* 1084–1169, Principle 24.

[24] See, for instance, Menno Kamminga, "Due Diligence Mania: The Misguided Introduction of an Extraneous Concept into Human Rights Discourse" (2011) Maastricht Faculty of Law Working Paper No. 07, p. 6.

[25] See also Pisillo-Mazzeschi, "Responsabilité de l'État," 194 and 298.

[26] Alastair Mowbray, *The Development of Positive Obligations under the ECHR by the European Court of Human Rights* (Oxford: Hart, 2004), p. 2; Samantha Besson, "Les

human rights treaties and jurisprudence, one can deduce a variety of positive steps that states are expected to take. To name but few, this includes the positive obligation to have and maintain capable administrative and judicial institutions, to enact and implement adequate legislative frameworks, to establish decent reparation mechanisms, and to take steps toward the progressive realization of social and economic rights. Moreover, positive obligations do not exist with regard to private conduct alone. States are also under an obligation to ensure that the conduct of their organs does not have any undesired side effects and to take suitable precautionary measures.[27]

The notion of positive obligations thus clearly comprises different obligations that vary greatly in content and character. Only some positive obligations exist with regard to the conduct of non-state actors. And only some positive obligations require states to take reasonable measures, while others are rather result oriented. Not every positive obligation is thus an obligation of due diligence, which is why the concept of positive obligations is broader than the notion of due diligence. The duty to take diligent steps to prevent and sanction harmful private conduct is rather a subform of the positive obligation to protect human rights. With this in mind, the next section aims at defining more precisely which concrete obligations can be identified in international human rights instruments. It helps to understand how exactly state responsibility can be established for human rights violations and how the notion of due diligence might operate in the field of human rights protection.

III. Proposal for a Conduct-Based Typology of Human Rights

As we have seen, none of the traditional typologies of international human rights helps identify the material content of positive human rights obligations that would be necessary to establish state responsibility. The following section therefore aims at unfolding a typology of positive human rights obligations that is based on the concrete course of conduct

---

Obligations de Protection des Droits Fondamentaux. Un Essai en Dogmatique Comparative" (2003) 1 *Revue de Droit Suisse* 49–96 at 63; Georg Ress, "The Duty to Protect and to Ensure Human Rights under the ECHR," in Eckart Klein (ed.), *The Duty to Protect and to Ensure Human Rights* (Berlin: Arno Spitz, 2000), p. 177.

[27] See, for instance, ECtHR, *McCann and Others* v. *UK*, Grand Chamber Judgment of 27 September 1995, Application No. 18984/91, paras. 202–214; ECtHR, *Andronicou and Constantinou* v. *Cyprus*, Judgment of 9 October 1997, Application No. 25052/94, para. 185.

III. CONDUCT-BASED TYPOLOGY OF HUMAN RIGHTS 55

that is expected of states.[28] Only if the conduct required of states is described as concisely as possible is it feasible to define under which circumstances failure to comply with positive obligations might be ascertained. It is thus necessary to resolve the broad notion of positive obligations into the various forms of positive measures states are required to take. To this end, the following section is dedicated to an analysis of different forms of human rights obligations that can be deduced from international jurisprudence. Anatomizing these different kinds of obligations will provide a basis on which to discuss how the rules on state responsibility could be adjusted so as to better address human rights risks stemming from private conduct.

When analyzing international human rights jurisprudence with a focus on the concrete actions that are expected of states, three broad categories of positive human rights obligations can be distinguished: positive obligations of result, positive obligations of diligent conduct, and positive obligations of progressive realization.

1. Positive Human Rights Obligations of Result

It is a common mistake to assume that positive obligations could be equated with obligations of diligent conduct.[29] On the contrary, human rights treaties contain several obligations that require states to take positive steps but have to be characterized as immediate obligations of result in the sense that mere failure to take such steps could amount to a violation of the respective human rights provision. From a victim's perspective, such obligations of result are easier to establish since complete failure to achieve a required result is easier to show than failure to act with sufficient diligence. The common misperception that positive human rights obligations would only entail obligations of diligent

---

[28] For a similar proposal based on the type of conduct that is expected under human rights provisions, see Pisillo-Mazzeschi, "Responsabilité de l'État"; for a typology of positive obligations categorized along individual human rights provisions, see Mowbray, "Positive Obligations."

[29] Dinah Shelton and Ariel Gould, "Positive and Negative Obligations," in Dinah Shelton (ed.), *The Oxford Handbook on International Human Rights Law* (Oxford: Oxford University Press, 2013), p. 577; Sandra Stahl, *Schutzpflichten im Völkerrecht* (Heidelberg: Springer, 2012), pp.192 f.; Mzikenge Danwood Chirwa, "The Doctrine of State Responsibility as a Potential Means of Holding Private Actors Accountable for Human Rights" (2004) 5 *Melbourne Journal of International Law* 1–36 at 14; Cordula Dröge, *Positive Verpflichtungen der Staaten in der EMRK* (Heidelberg: Springer, 2003), p. 293.

conduct presumably results from the fact that positive human rights obligations generally serve the prevention and sanctioning of human rights contraventions by third parties. In almost all cases, failure to do so will be established based on the circumstances of an individual case, and the foreseeability of the concrete human rights contradiction will have to be taken into consideration, as will the reasonably available means. Since states are under no obligation to guarantee the non-occurrence of human rights violations, duties of prevention are usually seen as obligations of diligent conduct. In most scenarios, it is thus necessary to show that states failed to exercise due diligence in order to establish their responsibility. Yet, international human rights law also imposes upon states obligations of immediate result to prevent and sanction human rights contradictions as to which preventive and punitive obligations of result can be distinguished.

a. Preventive Obligations of Result

Preventive obligations of result oblige states to establish and maintain suitable legislative and institutional frameworks of human rights protection. These obligations present rather broad "core obligations," creating an environment in which human rights contradictions are generally prevented.

aa. The Duty to Enact Legislation Among the most fundamental obligations contained in international human rights instruments is the obligation to adopt adequate legislation that incorporates human rights guarantees into domestic law.[30] This obligation is somewhat at odds with the traditional understanding that it lies entirely within the discretion of states as to how they ensure compliance with international obligations. In contrast to traditional inter-state treaties, however, human rights regimes aspire to ensure the protection and enforcement of individual rights, which may only be effectively put to practice when human rights guarantees are translated into domestic provisions. While states still enjoy a margin of appreciation, most international human rights regimes place a strong emphasis on protection through legislative means.[31] Illustrative of this is

---

[30] Dimitris Xenos, *The Positive Obligations of the State under the ECHR* (London: Routledge, 2012), p. 107.

[31] Laurens Lavrysen, "Protection by the Law: The Positive Obligation to Develop a Legal Framework to Adequately Protect ECHR Rights," in Yves Haeck and Eva Brems (eds.), *Human Rights and Civil Liberties in the 21st Century* (Dordrecht: Springer, 2014); Osita Mba, "Positive Obligations under the African Charter on Human and Peoples' Rights" (2009) 35 *Commonwealth Law Bulletin* 215–249 at 230.

III. CONDUCT-BASED TYPOLOGY OF HUMAN RIGHTS

Article 2 (II) of the ICCPR, stating that states should adopt domestic laws to give effect to all rights recognized in the Covenant with similar provisions found in Article 2 (I) of the European and Article 4 (I) of the American Convention. In spite of this clear preference for legislative protection, however, the ECtHR held that the Convention would not lay down "for the Contracting States any given manner for ensuring within their internal law the effective implementation of any provisions of the Convention,"[32] so a lack of domestic laws prohibiting any violation of the Convention would not per se amount to a Convention breach.[33] The Human Rights Committee, even though it repeatedly called upon member states "to take appropriate measures to ensure the direct application of the provisions of the Covenant into domestic law," also acknowledged that direct applicability was not formally required.[34] There is thus no obligation to literally integrate human rights treaties into domestic law or to make their provisions directly applicable before domestic courts.

Notwithstanding, the non-existence of domestic legislation can suffice to breach international human rights provisions. The IACtHR stressed that if the right to reply as enshrined in Article 14 I of the Convention was not yet enforceable under domestic law, states parties were under an obligation to adopt legislative measures to give effect to the provision.[35] Both the ECtHR and the IACtHR further held that with regard to severe human rights obligations, providing for civil liability could be insufficient, requiring criminal law provisions to effectively protect the right in question.[36] Though there is no obligation to make human rights treaties directly applicable, there thus is an obligation to enact domestic legislation that effectively ensures the substance of international human rights provisions.[37] Even where the Covenant was not directly applicable, so the Human Rights Committee emphasized, states parties had "nevertheless

---

[32] ECtHR, *Swedish Engine Drivers' Union* v. *Sweden*, Judgment of 6 February 1976, Application No. 5614/72, para. 50.

[33] ECtHR, *Ireland* v. *UK*, Plenary Judgment of 18 January 1978, Application No. 5310/71, para. 240.

[34] HRC, Concluding Observations on Denmark of 18 November 1996, UN Doc. CCPR/C/79/Add.68, para. 17.

[35] IACtHR, Advisory Opinion of 29 August 1986 on the Enforceability of the Right to Reply or Correction, Series A, No. 7, OC-7/85, para. 35, No. 2 B.

[36] ECtHR, *X and Y* v. *Netherlands*, Judgment of 26 March 1985, Application No. 8978/80, para. 27; ECtHR, *Calvelli and Ciglio* v. *Italy*, Grand Chamber Judgment of 17 January 2002, Application No. 32967/96, para. 51; IACtHR, *Albán-Cornejo* v. *Ecuador*, Judgment of 22 November 2007, Series C, No. 171, para. 135.

[37] Tomuschat, "Human Rights," p. 174; Walter Kälin and Jörg Künzli, *Universeller Menschenrechtsschutz* (Basel: Helbing Lichtenhahn, 3rd ed., 2013), para. 543.

accepted the legal obligation to make the provisions of the Covenant effective" and to that extent it was "an obligation ... to adopt appropriate measures to give [them] legal effect."[38] Among others, the Committee thus regularly criticized the United Kingdom, claiming that unwritten rights would fall short of the international standard of protection and the absence of a constitutional Bill of Rights would impede the Covenant's implementation.[39]

The obligation to provide for adequate human rights legislation thus is an obligation of result and not one of due diligence. The mere failure to pass appropriate legislation may constitute a violation of international provisions. The Human Rights Committee plainly stated that member states to the ICCPR were obliged to adopt domestic legislation, ensuring conformity with the Covenant. This obligation was "unqualified and of immediate effect" and included both the abolition of legislation contrary to the Covenant and the enactment of legislation, introducing its rights into domestic law.[40] In general, legislative obligations might thus be violated in two ways: On the one hand, states may violate human rights by completely failing to enact adequate legislation. On the other hand, states may violate human rights by enacting legislation that is incompatible with their international obligations.

(1) Failure to Enact Legislation That the duty to enact adequate human rights legislation constitutes an obligation of result is best illustrated by those cases in which the absence of domestic legislation was qualified as human rights violation on its own. Even though an obligation to take legislative steps is recognized, however, the exact content of such steps cannot be deduced from international provisions.[41] Whether a certain piece of domestic legislation is adequate remains subject to a due diligence standard, and a clear differentiation between both forms of obligation is often hard to draw.

Such a fine line is well-exemplified by the case of *X and Y*, in which the ECtHR found the Netherlands responsible for a lack of domestic criminal legislation penalizing the sexual abuse of mentally handicapped

---

[38] HRC, *Roberts v. Barbados*, Decision of 1 June 1992, Communication No. 504/1992, UN Doc. CCPR/C/51/D/504/1992, para. 6.3.
[39] See the Committee's considerations before the enactment of the British Human Rights Act in 1998, for instance: HRC, Concluding Observations on the UK of 27 July 1995, UN Doc. CCPR/C/79/Add.55, para. 9.
[40] HRC, General Comment No. 31, paras. 13 f.
[41] Kälin/Künzli, "Universeller Menschenrechtsschutz," para. 543.

persons.[42] At first glance, this could be qualified as a failure to comply with the positive obligation of result to enact any legislation at all. However, since the Dutch Criminal Code did contain provisions criminalizing sexual assault in general, it might also be seen as a failure to enact legislation with adequate diligence, since sexual assault was criminalized but in an insufficient manner. A more conclusive example for legislative obligations of result is the *Mikulić* case, in which the Court found the absence of any domestic procedure enabling the applicant to have the paternity of her alleged father established equaled a violation of Croatia's positive obligation under Article 8.[43] The mere failure to have human rights legislation in place thus amounted to a violation of the respective human rights provision, irrespective of any further actions on behalf of the state. In a similar manner, the IACtHR recognized legislative positive obligations of result. It found that states were under an obligation to ensure legal protection, for instance, of the right to life, which included inter alia a concrete obligation to regulate the use of lethal force by members of the State security forces[44] implying that the complete absence of such legislation would violate the right to life. Furthermore, in a case involving the *Awas Tingni* Community, the Court found that Nicaragua had violated the Convention since it had not adopted any domestic legal measures regulating the titling of indigenous community lands.[45] Here, again, it was the complete failure to enact legislation that amounted to a violation of the Convention.

While there is thus an obligation of result requiring states to provide for legislative protection, it is yet important to bear in mind that this does not extend to an obligation to regulate in detail every possible human rights infringement that might theoretically occur. When it comes to enacting human rights legislation, states still enjoy a margin of appreciation as to the details of such regulations.[46] Caution is thus called for with regard to the scope of legislative positive obligations. No doubt there is a broad and general obligation to provide for legislative human rights

---

[42] ECtHR, *X and Y v. Netherlands*, Judgment of 26 March 1985, Application No. 8978/80, para. 27.
[43] ECtHR, *Mikulić v. Croatia*, Judgment of 7 February 2002, Application No. 53176/99, paras. 64 ff.
[44] IACtHR, *Montero-Aranguren et al. (Detention Center of Catia) v. Venezuela*, Judgment of 5 July 2006, Series C, No. 150, para. 75.
[45] IACtHR, *The Mayagna (Sumo) Awas Tingni Community v. Nicaragua*, Judgment of 31 August 2001, Series C, No. 79, paras. 135–137.
[46] See, for instance, ECtHR, *Rees v. UK*, Plenary Judgment of 17 October 1986, Application No. 9532/81, para. 44.

protection. This is an obligation of result insofar as the mere failure to provide for sufficient legislation may give rise to a breach of the respective human rights instrument. Notwithstanding, this obligation does not extend to an all-comprising obligation to painstakingly regulate any human rights contradiction that could possibly occur. The lack of appropriate legislation must in itself contravene human rights provisions, whereas mere "adverse consequences" of a failure to regulate do not attract the responsibility of the respective state.[47]

It may thus be summarized that the duty to enact legislation is among the most fundamental of positive obligations. It requires states to incorporate human rights into their domestic legal order, which constitutes an obligation of result, as the mere failure to enact legislation may amount to a human rights violation in itself. States are obliged to guarantee in a domestic context the substance of international human rights provisions though direct applicability of international norms is no prerequisite. If states do not enact any human rights legislation at all, this alone might constitute a failure to comply with their international human rights obligations. Where states have enacted some form of human rights, however, they have fulfilled this obligation of result, and the question of whether they still fall short of international standards becomes one of whether the legislation is sufficiently diligent to ensure effective protection. Different forms of human rights obligations are thus closely intertwined, which is even more apparent when considering that – next to the obligation of positively enacting legislation – states are also obliged to refrain from enacting legislation that contravenes human rights provisions.

(2) Enacting Legislation That Violates Human Rights It was occasionally brought forward that a piece of legislation could not in itself infringe upon human rights, and violations of international provision would only occur where legislation was applied to concrete cases.[48] On several occasions, however, human rights bodies held that domestic legislation could in itself violate protected rights. The ECtHR found in its *Klass* judgment on surveillance measures that "the mere existence of the legislation itself" amounted to a violation of the Convention.[49] In like manner, the

---

[47] EComHR, *Tugar* v. *Italy*, Decision of 18 October 1995, Application No. 22869/93.
[48] See, for instance, the arguments submitted by the German government in ECtHR, *Klass and Others* v. *Germany*, Plenary Judgment of 6 September 1978, Application No. 5029/71, paras. 30 f.
[49] ECtHR, *Klass and Others* v. *Germany*, Plenary Judgment of 6 September 1978, Application No. 5029/71, para. 41.

IACtHR consistently argues that legislation as such can violate the Convention, regardless of whether it is enforced in a particular case[50] – a position confirmed by the African Commission on Human and Peoples' Rights[51] and the Human Rights Committee.[52]

The fact that enacting legislation contrary to human rights provisions constitutes a human rights violation also illustrates how different forms of obligations overlap. On the one hand, states are obliged to enact legislation protecting human rights. As we have seen, this is an obligation of immediate result. By enacting legislation that adversely affects human rights, on the other hand, states contradict human rights through the conduct of their legislative organs, thereby violating their negative duties. While there is an obligation to enact criminal legislation that deters and sanctions grave human rights violations, states may also violate their obligation by enacting criminal legislation that is so wide that it unduly infringes upon individual freedoms.[53] It is not always easy to distinguish which exact part of an obligation was violated in an individual case. Notwithstanding, it can be summarized that international human rights regimes contain a positive obligation of result to enact domestic laws that ensure the substantial protection of internationally recognized human rights. This obligation of result constitutes a very general core obligation to take legislative steps. If states have not enacted any form of human rights protection, they thereby violate their international obligations. The adequateness and effectiveness of domestic provisions, however, are subject to a due diligence standard. If states have human rights legislation in some form, they might violate their human rights obligations only if that legislation is not sufficiently diligent.

bb. The Duty to Establish an Administrative Apparatus States are further obliged to establish and maintain an administrative apparatus that is capable of implementing human rights provisions and prevent

---

[50] IACtHR, *Rafael Ivan Suarez Rosero* v. *Ecuador*, Judgment of 12 November 1997, Series C, No. 35, para. 98; IACtHR, *Castillo Petruzzi and Others* v. *Peru*, Judgment of 30 May 1999, Series C, No. 52, para. 110; The Last Temptation of Christ (*Olmedo-Busos and Others* v. *Chile*), Judgment of 5 February 2001, Series C, No. 73, para. 88.

[51] AfComHPR, *The Constitutional Rights Project (in respect of Zamani Lakwot and six others)* v. *Nigeria*, Decision of 22 March 1995, Communication No. 87/93; AfComHPR, *Purohit and Moore* v. *The Gambia*, Decision of 29 May 2003, Communication 241/2001.

[52] HRC, *Rodríguez* v. *Uruguay*, Decision of 19 July 1994, Communication No. 322/1988, UN Doc. CCPR/C/51/D/322/1988, para. 12.4.

[53] With reference to a so-called principle of "minimum penal law"; IACtHR, *Kimel* v. *Argentina*, Judgment of 2 May 2008, Series C, No. 177, para. 77.

contraventions.[54] While such an apparatus ultimately aims at preventing human rights violations, it still forms an obligation of immediate result. A state that does not maintain administrative capacities may thereby alone violate its human rights obligations. As we will see, however, different forms of obligations overlap also with regard to a state's administrative apparatus. In fact, the character of this obligation is twofold: the obligation to possess an administrative framework that is generally capable of preventing human rights violations is an obligation of result with the consequence that a state which does not maintain an adequate apparatus thereby falls short of international standards. In contrast, the obligation to employ this apparatus to take preventive or repressive measures in particular cases is an obligation of due diligence.

This differentiated approach is clearly mirrored in the ECtHR's *Osman* case. The Court first drew the general conclusion that Article 2 of the Convention required states not only to refrain from taking lives but also to take "appropriate steps to safeguard ... lives." It then went on to declare that this positive obligation entailed several sub-obligations, inter alia an obligation to "take preventive operational measures to protect an individual whose life is at risk."[55] Failure to implement a law-enforcement machinery could in itself amount to a violation of the Convention. This was even further accentuated by the Court's *Perk* case, in which it held that a state's obligation to protect the right to life "implique le devoir primordial d'assurer le droit à la vie en mettant en place un cadre juridique et administratif propre à dissuader de commettre des atteintes contre la personne et s'appuyant sur un mécanisme d'application conçu pour en prévenir, réprimer et sanctionner les violations."[56] Likewise, the Inter-American Court recognized an obligation to "organize the governmental apparatus and, in general, all the structures through which public power is exercised, so that they are capable of juridically ensuring the free and full enjoyment of human rights."[57] Notably, the obligation to establish a preventive framework cannot be excluded by outsourcing public functions to private institutions. The positive obligation to maintain an adequate administrative and

---

[54] Xenos, "Positive Obligations," p. 110.
[55] ECtHR, *Osman* v. *UK*, Grand Chamber Judgment of 28 October 1998, Application No. 23452/94, para. 115.
[56] ECtHR, *Perk and Others* v. *Turkey*, Judgment of 28 March 2006, Application No. 50739/99, para. 54.
[57] IACtHR, *Godínez-Cruz* v. *Honduras*, Judgment of 20 January 1989, Series C, No. 5, para. 175.

judicial apparatus is not curbed if public functions are carried out by private institutions.[58]

There is thus an independent obligation to have an administrative apparatus in place that is generally capable of implementing human rights legislation and of taking preventive measures to deter human rights abuses.[59] The mere failure to establish such an apparatus could suffice to establish a state's responsibility under the respective human rights treaty, underlying its character as an immediate obligation of result.

b. Punitive Obligations of Result

Next to these preventive obligations of result, states are also expected to sanction human rights if they occur in spite of preventive measures. A broad and general obligation of result can be derived from international human rights law instructing states to establish and maintain an investigative and judicial framework that is generally capable of sanctioning human rights contradictions.

aa. The Duty to Establish an Investigative and Judicial Apparatus

States are obliged to establish and maintain an apparatus that is capable of investigating alleged human rights violations and sanctioning conduct that contravenes human rights.[60] In contrast to an administrative apparatus, the main purpose of which is implementing human rights provisions and preventing violations thereof, a judicial apparatus should be established to investigate and prosecute human rights violations if they have occurred in spite of preventive efforts. Likewise, however, the obligation to erect such an apparatus is an obligation of result, meaning that its absence alone might amount to a violation of human rights law. When laying out the positive obligations contained in the right to life, the Strasbourg Court emphasized the necessity not only of a preventive apparatus but also of a law-enforcement machinery to sanction conduct that contradicts the Convention.[61] That the establishment of an

---

[58] See, for instance, ECtHR, *Calvelli and Ciglio* v. *Italy*, Grand Chamber Judgment of 17 January 2002, Application No. 32967/96, para. 49; IACtHR, *Ximenes-Lopes* v. *Brazil*, Judgment of 4 July 2006, Series C, No. 149, para. 85.

[59] Laurens Lavrysen, "Positive Obligations in the Jurisprudence of the IACHR" (2014) 7 *Inter-American and European Human Rights Journal* 94–115 at 100.

[60] ECtHR, *Güleç* v. *Turkey*, Judgment of 27 July 1998, Application No. 21593/93, para. 77; HRC, General Comment No. 31 (Fn. 20), para. 15.

[61] ECtHR, *Osman* v. *UK*, Grand Chamber Judgment of 28 October 1998, Application No. 23452/94, para. 115.

investigatory apparatus is an independent obligation is further illustrated by the ECtHR's *Mahmut Kaya* case, in which the Court found that even though Turkey had adequate criminal legislation in place, systemic defects "undermined the effectiveness of the protection afforded by criminal law in the south-east region."[62] Rather than relying on a failure to diligently investigate the particular case at hand, the Court thus based its finding on the ongoing systemic failures of the Turkish investigatory apparatus. In like manner, the Court held Italy responsible for an unreasonably long duration of legal proceedings and explicitly based this finding on the fact that there was "a continuing situation," which amounted to "a practice that is incompatible with the Convention."[63] The Court thus clearly referred to general and systemic deficiencies within the judicial apparatus in order to establish a state's failure to comply with its obligations under the Convention, indicating that there is indeed an obligation of result to establish such an apparatus, independent of the circumstances of individual cases.

bb. The Duty to Create Legal Remedies Another obligation of result is the positive obligation to create remedies for victims of human rights violations. Inter alia, the right to remedy is recognized in Article 2 (III) lit. a) of the ICCPR, Article 25 of the ACHR, and Article 13 of the ECHR, and the nonexistence of any domestic remedies might present a human rights violation in itself.[64] The Human Rights Committee, for instance, argued that the adoption of amnesty laws in itself prevented Uruguay from discharging its responsibility to provide effective remedies to the victims of human rights abuses.[65] Obviously, this obligation would be meaningless if it was not accompanied by an obligation to ensure court access to have human rights claims examined. The Strasbourg Court thus confirmed that everyone had "a right to have any claim relating to his civil rights and obligations brought before a court or tribunal."[66]

---

[62] ECtHR, *Mahmut Kaya* v. *Turkey*, Judgment of 28 March 2000, Application No. 22535/93, paras. 96 ff.
[63] ECtHR, *Bottazzi* v. *Italy*, Grand Chamber Judgment of 28 July 1999, Application No. 34884/97, para. 22.
[64] de Schutter, "International Human Rights Law," p. 813; Kälin/Künzli, "Universeller Menschenrechtsschutz," para. 544; Dröge, "Positive Verpflichtungen," p. 313.
[65] HRC, *Rodríguez* v. *Uruguay*, Decision of 19 July 1994, Communication No. 322/1988, UN Doc. CCPR/C/51/D/322/1988, para. 12.4.
[66] ECtHR, *Golder* v. *UK*, Plenary Judgment of 21 February 1975, Application No. 4451/70, para. 36; see also *Airey* v. *Ireland*, Judgment of 9 October 1979, Application No. 6289/73, para. 25.

Similarly, the IACtHR held that the mere "inexistence of an effective recourse against the violation of the rights recognized by the Convention constitutes a transgression of the Convention."[67] Notwithstanding, the obligation to create legal remedies shows yet again how closely different forms of human rights obligations are intertwined. If states fail to establish any remedy mechanism within their domestic order, they thereby fail to meet an obligation of result. If mechanisms are created, however, their adequateness and effectiveness are subject to due diligence standards.

cc. **The Duty to Investigate Allegations of Human Rights Violations** Apart from the creation of remedies, states are also obliged to undertake investigations if well-founded allegations of human rights violations are raised.[68] These investigatory obligations are triggered by any allegation which does not entirely lack a plausible and substantial foundation.[69] The duty to initiate investigations is an obligation of result insofar as complete failure to investigate well-founded allegations might in itself breach human rights provisions. Insufficient resources cannot justify a state's failure to comply with this obligation.[70] This was confirmed by the Human Rights Committee, which argued that "failure by a State Party to investigate allegations of violations could in and of itself give rise to a separate breach of the Covenant."[71] Failure to investigate may even cause a reversal of the burden of proof supporting a victim's claim brought forward against a state.[72] Nonetheless, the duty to investigate does not amount to a duty to sanction in a particular manner or to even sanction at all; it merely requires states to undertake some form of effective investigations.[73] There is no obligation of result to carry out

---

[67] IACtHR, *The Mayagna (Sumo) Awas Tingni Community* v. *Nicaragua*, Judgment of 31 August 2001, Series C, No. 79, para. 113.
[68] IACtHR, *Myrna Mack Chang* v. *Guatemala*, Judgment of 25 November 2003, Series C, No. 101, para. 156.
[69] de Schutter, "International Human Rights Law," p. 813; Kälin/Künzli, "Universeller Menschenrechtsschutz," para. 545.
[70] ECtHR, *Ahmet Özkan and Others* v. *Turkey*, Judgment of 6 April 2004, Application No. 21689/93, para. 319.
[71] HRC, *Irene Bleier Lewenhoff and Rosa Valino de Bleier* v. *Uruguay*, Decision of 29 March 1982, Communication No. 30/1978, para. 13.3; General Comment No. 31, para. 15.
[72] AfComHPR, *Amnesty International and Others* v. *Sudan*, Decision of 15 November 1999, Communication Nos. 48/90, 50/91, 52/91, 89/93, para. 52.
[73] ECtHR, *Perez* v. *France*, Grand Chamber Judgment of 12 February 2004, Application No. 47287/99, para. 70; ECtHR, *Giuliani and Gaggio* v. *Italy*, Grand Chamber Judgment of 24 March 2011, Application No. 23458/02, para. 306.

investigations in a specific way or to guarantee a certain outcome of such investigations.[74]

However, if states do not investigate substantial allegations at all, this suffices to establish a violation of the respective human rights provision. While resource constraints may affect the circumstances under which investigations can be carried out, all human rights institutions have confirmed that the duty to undertake investigations is an obligation that has to be fulfilled regardless of state's individual capacities, which further underlines that this obligation is one of result.[75] Moreover, while states enjoy a margin of appreciation in determining the manner in which they investigate alleged violations, international human rights bodies have established certain minimum requirements for such investigations and may thus be considered as forming part of the investigatory obligation of result.[76] States are required to investigate independently and without relying upon the initiative of individual victims. Once well-founded allegations of human rights violations have been made, the investigations' progress should be driven forward by the authorities.[77] It has to be carried out by institutionally independent organs that thoroughly collect all relevant evidence.[78] All of these obligations might be classified as obligations of result in the sense that failure to comply with one of these minimum requirements would in itself violate the positive obligation to investigate. When it comes to those minimum requirements, states are thus not granted any leeway: they have to be fulfilled for a state to comply with its human rights obligations. This was clearly

---

[74] *Kelly and Others v. UK*, Judgment of 4 May 2001, Application No. 30054/96, para. 96.

[75] See, notably, Commission on Human Rights, Civil and Political Rights, Including the Questions of Disappearances and Summary Executions. Extrajudicial, Summary or Arbitrary Execution, Report by Special Rapporteur Philip Alston, UN Doc. E/CN.4/2006/53 (8 March 2006), para. 36.

[76] See also, for a comprehensive summary of the case law on investigatory obligations in the ECtHR's case law, Mowbray, "Positive Obligations," pp. 37 ff.; and in the IACtHR's case law, Lavrysen, "Positive Obligations," 107 ff.

[77] ECtHR, *Ergi v. Turkey*, Judgment of 28 July 1998, Application No. 23818/94, para. 82; *Kelly and Others v. UK*, Judgment of 4 May 2001, Application No. 30054/96, para. 94; IACtHR, *Velásquez Rodríguez v. Honduras*, Judgment of 29 July 1988, Series C, No. 4, para. 177.

[78] See, among many others, ECtHR, *McCann and Others v. UK*, Grand Chamber Judgment of 27 September 1995, Application No. 18984/91, para. 161; *Ergi v. Turkey*, Judgment of 28 July 1998, Application No. 23818/94, paras. 83 ff.; *McKerr v. UK*, Judgment of 4 May 2001, Application No. 28883/95, para. 111; AfComHPR, *Amnesty International and Others v. Sudan*, Decision of 15 November 1999, Communication Nos. 48/90, 50/91, 52/91, 89/93, para. 51; IACtHR, *Five Pensioners v. Peru (Torres Benvenuto and Others v. Peru)*, Judgment of 28 February 2003, Series C, No. 98, para. 136.

underlined by the Strasbourg Court's *Al-Skeini* decision in which it emphasized that, whatever mode of investigation was employed in a particular case, the authorities had to engage in investigations of their own motion.[79] The obligation to independently initiate investigatory proceedings is thus clearly removed from the particular mode of investigations, which is subject to a due diligence standard. Apart from these generally recognized requirements, however, it is once again important to emphasize that the obligation of result does not provide any further guarantee with regard to the content of investigatory proceedings: "The nature and degree of scrutiny ... depends on the circumstances of the particular case ... [and] it is not possible to reduce the variety of situations which might occur to a bare check-list of acts of investigation."[80] That investigations have to be carried out in an adequate and effective manner is thus an obligation subject to the due diligence standard, which leaves states substantial discretion in determining reasonable means.

dd. The Duty to Provide for Specific Criminal Legislation Some of the specific human rights instruments contain explicit provisions requiring member states to punish individual perpetrators.[81] Many of these provisions can be seen as imposing an obligation of result to enact domestic criminal legislation penalizing specific forms of harmful conduct. The Genocide Convention,[82] for instance, stipulates in its Article 3 that genocide, as well as any form of incitement to or complicity in genocide, will be punishable acts, which is complemented by Article 6, requiring persons charged with any of the acts enumerated to be tried by a competent tribunal.

All respective treaties contain an explicit obligation to enact criminal legislation with rather specific content. Not to enact respective legislation

---

[79] ECtHR, *Al-Skeini and Others* v. *UK*, Grand Chamber Judgment of 7 July 2011, Application No. 55721/07, para. 165.
[80] ECtHR, *Velikova* v. *Bulgaria*, Judgment of 18 May 2000, Application No. 41488/98, para. 80.
[81] Among others, see International Convention on the Elimination of All Forms of Racial Discrimination, signed on 7 March 1966, entered into force 4 January 1969, 660 UNTS 195; Convention against Torture and Other Cruel, Inhuman or Degrading Treatment or Punishment, signed on 10 December 1984, entered into force 26 June 1987, 1465 UNTS 85; International Convention for the Protection of All Persons from Enforced Disappearances, signed on 20 December 2006, entered into force 23 December 2010, 2716 UNTS 3.
[82] Convention on the Prevention and Punishment of the Crime of Genocide, signed on 9 December 1948, entered into force 12 January 1951, 78 UNTS 277.

would have to be considered as non-compliance with the treaty regime in question. Those obligations therefore constitute obligations of result to put domestic criminal legislation in place. It is yet again important to consider that these provisions do not contain an obligation to guarantee a certain outcome or certain sanctions. In contrast, criminal sanctions in individual cases may only be imposed after investigations, and proceedings have been carried out in a diligent manner.

ee. The Duty to Award Reparations Finally, there is now a growing consensus that states are under an additional obligation to award adequate reparations for human rights violations. This constitutes an obligation of result in the sense that states are obliged to establish reparation mechanisms, and complete failure to do so would trigger international responsibility.

With regard to the Covenant, the right to reparations was confirmed by the Human Rights Committee stating that the Covenant "generally entails appropriate compensation."[83] Likewise, the International Court of Justice found in its Advisory Opinion dealing with Israel's activities on Palestinian territory that Israel was under an obligation to make adequate reparations to those adversely affected by the construction work, thereby confirming an individual claim to reparations.[84] The African Commission has recognized an independent right to reparations in a decision involving the activities of the Zimbabwe African National Union Patriotic Front, in which it held that state responsibility under the Charter could arise where states did not take the necessary steps to provide the victims of human rights violations with reparations.[85] The importance attached to adequate reparations is also apparent in Article 41 ECHR and Article 63 I ACHR, which allow the regional human rights courts to directly afford satisfaction to injured individuals. Again, however, it is important to differentiate that the obligation of result merely comprises the obligation to have some form of reparation mechanisms in place. It does not extend to the amount of reparations – the determination of which is an obligation of diligent conduct.

In sum, there is thus a broad range of positive human rights obligations that need to be qualified as obligations of result. The mere failure to

---

[83] HRC, General Comment No. 31, para. 16.
[84] ICJ, Legal Consequences of the Construction of a Wall in the Occupied Palestinian Territory, Advisory Opinion of 9 July 2004, ICJ Reports 2004, 136, para. 152.
[85] AfComHPR, *Zimbabwe Human Rights NGO Forum v. Zimbabwe*, Decision of 15 May 2006, Communication No. 245/02, EX.CL/322 (X), para. 143.

III. CONDUCT-BASED TYPOLOGY OF HUMAN RIGHTS 69

adopt human rights legislation; to establish and maintain an administrative, investigative, and judicial apparatus capable of preventing and sanctioning human rights violations; and the mere failure to provide for legal remedies and a reparation mechanism might all amount to a human rights violation irrespective of the circumstances of an individual case. However, all these obligations are rather broad and general. They constitute "core obligations," which states are expected to fulfill in order to create an environment in which human rights contradictions are generally prevented and sanctioned. It is yet important to bear in mind that most states have at least some human rights protection in place and thus are rarely held responsible for complete failure to comply with their obligations of result unless human rights violations clearly stem from systemic deficiencies. In most scenarios, human rights violations arise where protection mechanisms are improperly applied. In such cases, state responsibility may be established for failure to act in a sufficiently diligent manner. In a next step, it is thus necessary to explore which obligations of diligent conduct might be derived from international human rights regimes.

2. Positive Human Rights Obligations of Diligent Conduct

In principal, obligations of diligent conduct accompany and complement the obligations of result just mentioned. Not only are states under an obligation to create and maintain administrative and judicial capacities; they should also make use of these capacities in a diligent manner.[86] While the positive obligations of result indicated previously aim at creating a framework in which human rights are generally recognized and fostered, positive obligations of diligent conduct are closely linked to individual cases.[87] In contrast to positive obligations of result, however, obligations of diligent conduct do not require states to realize a well-defined result. States are merely obliged to employ the reasonable means at their disposal if they have a knowledge of specific human rights risks.

The *Velásquez* case before the Inter-American Court presents a landmark decision recognizing obligations of diligent conduct under international human rights law. The case involved the forceful

---
[86] See, for a similar argument, Xenos, "Positive Obligations," pp. 116 f.
[87] IACtHR, *Case of the Pueblo Bello Massacre* v. *Colombia*, Judgment of 31 January 2006, Series C, No. 140, para. 142.

disappearance of Manfredo Velásquez in Honduras and mainly dealt with the question of whether Honduras was to be held responsible, even though it could not be confirmed with certainty that state agents had carried out the kidnapping. The Court famously stated that "an illegal act which violates human rights and which is initially not directly imputable to a State (for example, because it is the act of a private person or because the person responsible has not been identified) can lead to international responsibility of the State, not because of the act itself, but because of the lack of due diligence to prevent the violation or to respond to it."[88] Following the *Velásquez* judgment, the IACtHR has substantially advanced its jurisprudence on the obligations of states to take diligent affirmative steps.[89] Later on, the Human Rights Committee in its General Comment No. 31 also recognized that the ICCPR obliges states to "exercise due diligence to prevent, punish, investigate or redress" the harm caused by private actors.[90] A similar approach was taken by the African Commission of Human and Peoples' Rights, which explicitly referred to the *Velásquez* judgment holding that

> the established standard of due diligence ... provides a way to measure whether a State has acted with sufficient effort and political will to fulfil its human rights obligations. ... A failure to exercise due diligence to prevent or remedy violations, or failure to apprehend the individuals committing human rights violations gives rise to State responsibility even if committed by private individuals.[91]

There thus is broad consensus that human rights instruments contain obligations of diligent conduct. As we have seen already, it is often difficult to determine which specific form of obligation was violated in a given scenario, and most often, state responsibility will be based on a combination of different violations. Notwithstanding, the next section will seek to identify those distinct forms of obligations that constitute obligations of diligent conduct. Here as well, a distinction can be drawn between preventive and repressive obligations.

---

[88] IACtHR, *Velásquez Rodríguez v. Honduras*, Judgment of 29 July 1988, Series C, No. 4, para. 172.
[89] Thomas Antkowiak and Alejandra Gonza, *The American Convention on Human Rights* (New York: Oxford University Press, 2017), p. 19.
[90] HRC, General Comment No. 31, para. 8.
[91] AfComHPR, *Zimbabwe Human Rights NGO Forum v. Zimbabwe*, Decision of 15 May 2006, Communication No. 245/2002, EX.CL/322 (X), paras. 146 f.

a. Preventive Obligations of Diligent Conduct

On the preventive side, states are first and foremost obliged to employ due diligence when fulfilling their preventive obligations of result. This means that they are bound to diligently implement their human rights legislation and to ensure their administrative apparatus takes diligent steps to prevent human rights violations. All human rights bodies confirmed that merely fulfilling positive obligations of result was insufficient to ensure effective human rights protection: "the obligation to ensure the free and full exercise of human rights is not fulfilled by the existence of a legal system designed to make it possible to comply with this obligation – it also requires the government to conduct itself so as to effectively ensure the free and full exercise of human rights."[92]

Next to this obligation to ensure that administrative and judicial capacities are employed in a diligent manner, states are also expected to take preventive steps if they obtain knowledge of specific human rights risks.[93] In contrast to positive obligations of result, obligations of diligence cannot be predetermined but are dependent on the particular circumstances at hand. Moreover, they are only triggered if there is a concrete risk of human rights risks contradictions. This was underlined by the Strasbourg Court in its *Taïs* case, where it held that "pour qu'il y ait obligation positive, il doit être établi que les autorités savaient ou auraient dû savoir sur le moment qu'un individu donné était menacé de manière réelle et immédiate."[94] It is thus clear that in order to establish state responsibility for non-compliance with such obligation, it is not sufficient to show that human rights contradictions eventually occurred. It is rather necessary to establish that the state in question failed to apply diligent measures, even though it had knowledge of a particular risk. Those due diligence obligations cannot be delegated, even where the state outsources functions to other actors, its obligations to exercise due diligence remain the same.[95]

b. Repressive Obligations of Diligent Conduct

With regard to repressive obligations – that is, the obligations that arise after harmful conduct has occurred – three general duties can be

---

[92] IACtHR, *Velásquez Rodríguez* v. *Honduras*, Judgment of 29 July 1988, Series C, No. 4, para. 167.
[93] ECtHR, *Mahmut Kaya* v. *Turkey*, Judgment of 28 March 2000, Application No. 22535/93, para. 101.
[94] ECtHR, *Taïs* v. *France*, Judgment of 1 June 2006, Application No. 39922/03, para. 97.
[95] Report of Special Rapporteur Yakin Ertürk, The Due Diligence Standard as a Tool for the Elimination of Violence against Women, UN Doc. E/CN.4/2006/61, para. 34.

distinguished: the duty to carry out investigations, the duty to award reparations, and the duty to punish the perpetrators. As we have seen, these obligations contain obligations of result in the sense that states are required to have an investigative and judicial apparatus in place and domestic legislation providing for remedies and compensation. The respective obligations of diligent conduct imply that states should make sure that such investigations are carried out in an adequate manner.[96] As we have seen, the duty to investigate does not extend to an obligation to reach a certain outcome; it "is not an obligation of result, but of means"[97] to carry out investigations in a diligent manner. Although there is thus a wide margin of appreciation with regard to concrete investigations, severe human rights violations might call for diligent sanctioning.

As we have seen, several human rights treaties contain explicit provisions mandating states to provide for domestic criminal legislation. While the enactment of such legislation constitutes an obligation of result, the application of these provisions to individual cases is an obligation of diligent conduct. Even though the general international human rights treaties do not prescribe an explicit duty to sanction, several tribunals and institutions have derived such obligations from the "respect and ensure" framework. The Inter-American Court held that the obligation to effectively ensure human rights encompassed the duty "to impose an appropriate punishment and to ensure the victim adequate compensation."[98] Likewise, the Human Rights Committee stated that "those found guilty must be held responsible."[99] The ECtHR on several occasions found civil-law remedies unsuitable in case of particularly grave human rights violations. Where fundamental values were at stake, effective deterrence could only be achieved through criminal-law provisions,[100] indicating that there is an obligation to sanction in case of severe human rights violations. Notwithstanding, the duty to punish perpetrators is only recognized for particularly grave human rights violations. This is easily explained, given the fact that any criminal

---

[96] IACtHR, *Case of the Xákmok Kásek Indigenous Community* v. *Paraguay*, Judgment of 24 August 2010, Series C, No. 214, para. 141.
[97] ECtHR, *Kelly and Others* v. *UK*, Judgment of 4 May 2001, Application No. 30054/96, para. 96.
[98] IACtHR, *Velásquez Rodríguez* v. *Honduras*, Judgment of 29 July 1988, Series C, No. 4, para. 174.
[99] HRC, General Comment No. 7 on the Prohibition of Torture or Cruel, Inhuman or Degrading Treatment or Punishment, UN Doc. HRI/GEN/1/Rev.1 (1982), para. 1.
[100] ECtHR, *X and Y* v. *Netherlands*, Judgment of 26 March 1985, Application No. 8978/80, para. 27.

punishment interferes with the human rights of the perpetrator. Wherever satisfaction and deterrence can be adequately achieved through civil or administrative law provisions, imposing criminal liability would be disproportionate.[101]

In general, it is therefore not an easy task to classify the duty to sanction perpetrators within our framework of human rights obligations. On the one hand, the duty to sanction presents a repressive form of obligation, as it only arises when human rights obligations have already occurred. On the other hand, human rights bodies have constantly emphasized that the duty to sanction forms part of states' preventive obligations, given the deterrent effect of criminal penalties.[102] This twofold purpose is clearly mirrored in the different elements of the duty to sanction. While there is an obligation of result to enact respective criminal provisions with a deterrent effect, the duty to apply those provisions to specific cases is an obligation of diligent conduct. There is no obligation of result to reach a certain outcome, which is also why there is no individual right for victims to have their perpetrators sanctioned in a specific manner.[103]

In sum, there are thus preventive and repressive obligations of diligent conduct. In order to comply with their human rights obligations, it is not sufficient for states to pass protective legislation and establish an administrative and judicial framework. It is equally necessary and maybe even more important to ensure that diligent steps are undertaken to protect human rights in any given circumstance. This includes the obligation to apply human rights legislation in a diligent manner, to take diligent steps to prevent human rights contraventions, and to diligently carry out investigations and impose sanctions. Next to positive obligations of result and of diligent conduct, in particular, the International Covenant on Economic, Social, and Cultural Rights has introduced yet another distinct category of positive obligations – so-called obligations of progressive realization.

---

[101] Dominic Steiger, "Menschenrechtliche Bestrafungspflichten," in Marten Breuer et al. (eds.), *Der Staat im Recht* (Berlin: Duncker & Humblot, 2013), p. 1332; Anja Seibert-Fohr, *Prosecuting Serious Human Rights Violations* (Oxford: Oxford University Press, 2009), p. 199.

[102] Among many others, see IACtHR, *Villagrán Morales and Others* v. *Guatemala*, Judgment of 26 May 2001, Series C, No 77, para. 100; ECtHR, *Mahmut Kaya* v. *Turkey*, Judgment of 28 March 2000, Application No. 22535/93, para. 85.

[103] In other words, ECtHR, *M.S.S.* v. *Belgium and Greece*, Grand Chamber Judgment of 21 January 2011, Application No. 30696/09, para. 289.

3. Positive Obligations of Progressive Realization

Some human rights instruments, most notably the ICESCR, impose upon states a form of obligations that has become known as "duties of progressive realization."[104] The Covenant's preparatory documents illustrate that these obligations were expressly understood as obligations to continuously take action in contrast to obligations of achieving immediate results.[105] There has been much debate on their content and nature,[106] with some scholars even arguing that they would be of merely declaratory nature and could not have any legally binding force at all.[107] The Committee views obligations of progressive realization as a distinct category of human rights obligations. On the one hand, they have obvious similarities with due diligence obligations in that they require adequate efforts and not the realization of immediate results. One the other hand, they have a distinct character insofar as they require ongoing gradual efforts over a long period of time.[108] Most rights enshrined in the Covenant are rights, the realization of which is much dependent on the general conditions within a state. They require broader policy strategies compared to most civil and political rights. Ensuring the right to food and water of the entire population, for instance, makes it necessary for the state to coordinate efforts and develop long-term coherent strategies. In particular, within the jurisprudence of the IACtHR, duties of progressive realization also overlap with "traditional" human rights. On several occasions did the Court find that the right to life contained obligations of progressive realization as well and that states were obliged to generate "minimum living conditions that are compatible with the dignity of the human person" by taking "positive, concrete measures geared toward fulfillment of the right to a decent life."[109] This broad understanding of the right to life underlines that obligations of progressive realization are

---

[104] See also Convention on the Protection of the Rights of the Child; Inter-American Charter on Human Rights and its San Salvador Protocol; European Social Charter.
[105] UN Doc. E/CN.4/SR.270, p. 11.
[106] See further Lilian Chenwi and Danwood Chirwa, "Direct Protection of Economic, Social and Cultural Rights in International Law," in Danwood Chriwa and Lilian Chenwi (eds.), *The Protection of Economic, Social and Cultural Rights in Africa* (Cambridge: Cambridge University Press, 2016), p. 48; Manisuli Ssenyonjo, *Economic, Social and Cultural Rights in International Law* (Oxford: Hart, 2nd ed., 2016), p. 7.
[107] See notably the criticism brought forward by the US government and the respective quotes contained in UN Doc. A/40/C.3/SR.36 (1985).
[108] CESCR, General Comment No. 3, para. 9.
[109] IACtHR, *Yakye Axa Indigenous Community* v. *Paraguay*, Judgment of 17 June 2005, Series C, No. 125, paras. 161 f.

not a distinct ICESCR feature but may be deduced from other human rights provisions. A clear-cut distinction between civil and political rights, on the one hand, and economic and social rights, on the other, is therefore difficult to draw, which further underlines that different human rights obligations are intertwined to a significant extent.[110]

Obligations of progressive realization thus contain elements of both obligations of diligent conduct, as they require best efforts on behalf of the state, and obligations of result, as these efforts must be targeted toward a defined result.[111]

4. Margin of Appreciation

Considering the various different forms of obligations imposed upon states under international human rights law calls for an examination of another distinct human rights feature, and that is the so-called margin of appreciation. Generally, international law does not grant states any leeway to adjust their international obligations to domestic circumstances. The protection of human rights, however, is inextricably linked with the basic structures and values of each community. As we have seen, the balancing of different rights and interests is a normative task and might well produce different results in different communities. It is against this background that some international human rights bodies, most notably the Strasbourg Court, have recognized that international human rights regimes do not require absolutely uniform implementation.[112] States and domestic courts generally enjoy a certain margin of appreciation when it comes to the way in which human rights obligations are implemented, since they are better suited to adequately take local peculiarities into account.[113] Such margin is particularly wide where morally or culturally sensitive issues are at stake. In those constellations, the Court will pay great deference to the policy choices of states and exercise only limited judicial review.[114] In order to assess whether states have complied with

---

[110] Aoife Nolan, "Addressing Economic and Social Rights Violations by Actors" (2009) 9 HRLR 225–255 at 253.
[111] Ssenyonjo, *Economic, Social and Cultural Rights*, p. 31
[112] See, for instance, ECtHR, *Sunday Times* v. *UK* (No. 1), Plenary Judgment of 26 April 1979, Application No. 6538/74, para. 61.
[113] Mégret, "Nature of Obligations," 104; Andrew Legg, *The Margin of Appreciation in International Human Rights Law* (Oxford: Oxford University Press, 2012), p. 58.
[114] Mónika Ambrus, "The European Court of Human Rights and Standards of Proof," in Lukasz Gruszczynski and Wouter Werner (eds.), *Deference in International Courts and Tribunals* (Oxford: Oxford University Press, 2014), pp. 236, 240 f.

their various forms of positive human rights obligations, it is thus necessary to remain mindful that compliance does not require uniform implementation but may be achieved in accordance with local peculiarities. This is particularly relevant with regard to obligations of diligent conduct, which go beyond broad core obligations and assess specific human rights risks.

IV. Summary

When categorizing positive human rights obligations along the conduct that is required of states, three forms of obligations can be identified: positive obligations of result, positive obligations of diligent conduct, and positive obligations of progressive realization. Each category contains various subforms of obligations. In contrast to traditional typologies, this categorization helps better comprehend what exactly states are required to do under international human rights treaties and when state responsibility for failure to meet these requirements might be established. Obligations of result impose upon states the obligation to immediately realize a given result. Typical human rights obligations of result are the obligation to enact legislation and to put in place an administrative and judicial apparatus capable of preventing human rights violations and imposing adequate sanctions. In contrast, obligations of diligent conduct require states to employ best efforts to ensure that this legislative and administrative apparatus is applied in a diligent manner to individual cases. Finally, obligations of progressive realization instruct states to develop cohesive strategies to realize protected rights.

A clear distinction between those different forms of obligations is rather difficult, and often enough, a violation will arise out of the combination of different state actions and omissions. Notwithstanding, it is important to consider that violating obligations of result is relatively straightforward – state responsibility is engaged as soon as the desired result is not achieved – whereas state responsibility for failure to act with due diligence is far more difficult to establish. It is thus hardly surprising that state responsibility is rather rarely based on the violation of obligations of result alone. Most states have enacted some form of human rights legislation and possess administrative and judicial structures. Human rights issues are more likely to arise when these frameworks do not function properly. To derive the concrete content of due diligence obligations, however, is a far more difficult undertaking. While this section has given a first overview of different human rights obligations of diligent

IV. SUMMARY

conduct, it is thus necessary to explore in greater detail how the due diligence standard might be applied in the human rights sphere, in particular with regard to human rights contraventions by non-state actors.

With this in mind, the following section will retrace the origins of due diligence obligations in international law. Even though such obligations are most often associated with the sphere of environmental protection, they first evolved within the context of alien protection laws and thus within an area of international law that is genuinely concerned with the protection of individuals. Taking this as a starting point, we will analyze how the concept of due diligence fits within the system of state responsibility. Comparing and contrasting due diligence obligations with other forms of state responsibility will help deduce their distinct features. Once the individual components of the due diligence standard will be identified, the concrete application of due diligence standards to different fields of international law will be examined more closely. This will provide guidance on how the standard might be fruitfully applied in the human rights context.

3

The Origins of Due Diligence in International Law

I. Introductory Remarks

In order to evaluate which role the concept of due diligence could play within the law of state responsibility, it is helpful to retrace its origins in international law. When it comes to harm caused by private actors, scholarly writings have long employed due diligence as a standard against which to measure the responsibility of states (II.). Later on, the standard significantly progressed in the context of alien protection laws. In particular, the jurisprudence of so-called Claims Commissions generated several precedents that still provide important guidance on how due diligence obligations might operate in practice (III.). In general, however, the development of the law on state responsibility has followed a rocky path. The ILC's codification project was among the longest and most complex projects the Commission has ever undertaken, which also affected the conception of due diligence. There is a great variety of concepts on different forms of state responsibility which occasionally overlap or even contradict each other. Against this backdrop, the final part of this chapter will retrace how due diligence standards were integrated into the state responsibility system (IV). Comparing and contrasting due diligence obligations with other forms of responsibility will help identify the distinct components of due diligence (V.).

II. Due Diligence in Early Scholarly Writings

Originally, the concept of due diligence stems back to domestic civil law.[1] Both common and civil law systems recognize duties of diligent conduct.

---

[1] On the historical development, see Jan Arno Hessbruegge, "The Historical Development of the Doctrines of Attribution and Due Diligence in International Law" (2003) 36 *JILP* 265–306;

II. DUE DILIGENCE IN EARLY SCHOLARLY WRITINGS

Such duties are based on the legal premise that individuals have to exercise reasonable care to ensure that their actions and omissions may not result in foreseeable injuries to others. In domestic civil law, a duty of care may arise, in particular, if an individual creates or maintains a source of potential harm. In such cases, a heightened level of care is expected, since that individual is most able to evaluate the seriousness of risks and control their sources. While state responsibility has a unique character[2] and the *ratio* of domestic due diligence duties cannot simply be transferred to the international level, some assumptions have yet significantly influenced the debate on state responsibility. Even where private actions cannot be directly attributed, it is still the state that is best equipped to control risks originating from its territory.

The relationship between the state as a collective entity on the one hand and the individual on the other has long been subject to scholarly debate in international law. Many writers have elaborated on the circumstances under which states may be held responsible for wrongful private conduct. In ancient legal systems, the relationship between the collective and the individual had been quite different than it is today. Up until the early Middle Ages, most legal systems were based on a notion of collective responsibility, in which the members of a community could be held responsible for the acts of any other member.[3] Those concepts of collective responsibility faded only gradually and were finally replaced in the absolutist states of the seventeenth century, where state responsibility equaled the fault of the sovereign. It is in this historical setting that early legal scholars started to examine international responsibility as a legal matter between states, including international responsibility for harmful private conduct.

1. *Grotius's Concept of* Patientia *and* Receptus *Responsibility*

For Grotius, international responsibility corresponded with the responsibility of the sovereign as a natural person. In general, private actions could not attract state responsibility, since such responsibility would only be triggered by wrongful acts of the sovereign. They could only implicate

---

Jonathan Bonnitcha and Robert McCorquodale, "The Concept of 'Due Diligence' in the UN Guiding Principles on Business and Human Rights" (2017) 28 *EJIL* 899–919 at 902 ff.

[2] Robert Barnidge, *Non-State Actors and Terrorism. Applying the Law of State Responsibility and the Due Diligence Principle* (The Hague: TMC Asser, 2008), p. 56.

[3] Adolf Jess, *Politische Handlungen Privater gegen das Ausland und das Völkerrecht* (Breslau: M&H Marcus, 1923), p. 11; Heinrich Kipp, *Völkerordnung und Völkerrecht im Mittelalter* (Köln: Deutsche Glocke, 1950), pp. 68 ff.

state responsibility based on the principles of either *patientia* or *receptus*. Responsibility based on *patientia* would arise if a sovereign knew of a crime to be committed by an individual but failed to prevent it, even if measures of prevention were available.[4] Responsibility based on *receptus* would arise if a sovereign failed to adequately punish the wrongdoer after a wrongful act had been committed.[5] While Grotius did not apply modern categories of state responsibility – and his conception was close to individual responsibility based on negligence or malice – his principles of *patientia* and *receptus* still laid an important foundation for our understanding of due diligence as an element of state responsibility. The failure to take preventive measures in view of a known risk and the failure to adequately react to harm still lie at the core of international due diligence standards.

2. Pufendorf and the Presumption of Capacities to Prevent

Pufendorf later endorsed Grotius's categories and rejected strict state responsibility for the conduct of private citizens. He was the first to argue that such liability would make necessary intense state control over the private sphere, inevitably resulting in an undesired interference with civil liberties. Nevertheless, Pufendorf recognized that individual conduct had the potential of causing significant harm, which required some form of action on behalf of states. In trying to solve this conflict, he proposed a presumption of state responsibility. Unless proven otherwise, it should be assumed that the sovereign had been able to prevent wrongful private conduct.[6] Even though he rejected the notion of strict liability, he thus argued in favor of some form of guarantee on behalf of the sovereign while acknowledging for the first time the difficulties of finding an adequate balance between the need to control harmful private conduct and the need to protect civil liberties.

3. Wolff and Vattel: From Responsibility of the Monarch to Responsibility of States

With the decline of absolutism, notions of state responsibility started to change. Fault of the monarch as a natural person was no longer seen as adequate grounds for state responsibility. Wolff and Vattel were among

---

[4] Hugo Grotius, De Jure *Belli Ac Pacis 1646*, translated by F. W. Kelsey (New York: William Hein & Co, 1995), vol. II, chapter XVII, § XX, 523.
[5] Grotius, *De Jure Belli Ac Pacis 1646*, vol. II, chapter XXI, § III, 526.
[6] Samuel Pufendorf, *De Jure Naturae et Gentium, Libri Octo 1688*, translated by C. H. and W. A. Oldfather (Oxford: Clarendon, 1934), 1304.

the first scholars to speak of the responsibility of nations as abstract entities. They recognized that the state was a subject very different from individual persons which made it impossible to transfer the mechanisms of individual responsibility without any form of adjustment. Consequently, Wolff and Vattel also shifted their focus away from notions of negligence and malice and rather found state responsibility established where states noticed and supported harmful private conduct. Wolff argued that states had a duty to prevent such conduct even though it could not be attributed unless the sovereign clearly assented.[7] In Vattel's eyes, the responsibility of a state for private actions was established "when, by its manners, and by the maxims of its government it accustoms and authorises its citizens indiscriminately to plunder and maltreat foreigners [or] to make inroads into the neighbouring countries,"[8] thus recognizing state responsibility for private conduct only where the state positively encouraged or endorsed wrongs committed by its citizens.

4. Hall and Oppenheim: Reasonable Measures of Prevention and Vicarious Responsibility

Later on, Hall and Oppenheim most prominently dealt with state responsibility for private conduct. Following Wolff and Vattel, Hall found the connection between private persons and the state not close enough to allow for the general attribution of private actions to the state. Instead, he argued that a state could "be held responsible for such of them as it may reasonably be expected to have knowledge of and to prevent."[9] With the standard of reasonableness, Hall introduced an important notion that still is crucial to modern standards of due diligence. He suggested that it was "impossible to maintain that a government must be provided with the most efficient means that can be devised for performing its international duties" but that it could be reasonably expected of each state to make the best effort that was compatible with its national institutions, provided it could "be

---

[7] Christian J. Wolff, *Jus Gentium Methodo Scientifica Pertractatum 1749*, translated by J. H. Drake (Oxford: Clarendon, 1934), p. 161.
[8] Emmerich de Vattel, *The Law of Nations or the Principles of Natural Law applied to the Conduct and to the Affairs of Nations and of Sovereigns 1758*, translated by Joseph Chitty (Philadelphia: T. & J. W. Johnson, 1854), book II, ch. VI, § 78, p. 163.
[9] William Edward Hall, *A Treatise on International Law* (Oxford: Clarendon, 4th ed., 1895), p. 227.

described as well ordered to an average extent."[10] Hall thereby introduced two important parameters that remain relevant to the modern concept of due diligence: knowledge on the part of states as a preconditional element of responsibility and the capacity to even take preventive measures.

Oppenheim added a novel element to this concept by distinguishing between two different forms of responsibility: original and vicarious responsibility. Original responsibility of the state would arise either out of an attributable wrongful act or out of the state's failure to prevent harm. However, if states had acted diligently and harm occurred nevertheless, recourse should be taken to an indirect form of vicarious responsibility.[11] Only original responsibility would lead to full responsibility on behalf of the state including an obligation to make reparations, while vicarious responsibility would merely require the state to punish the wrongdoer.[12] Some of Oppenheim's suggestions still form part of modern due diligence standards. Even though the idea of indirect or vicarious responsibility is expressly rejected by tribunals and scholars alike,[13] the duty of states to bring private perpetrators to justice and carry out proceedings in a diligent manner forms part of its due diligence obligations under international law. What other scholars rejected was not so much the reasoning behind Oppenheim's concept but rather the phrasing as "indirect responsibility," with its misleading connotation that the state would not be the immediate bearer of responsibility. It is rather commonly recognized that the state's own failure to adequately react to harmful private conduct leads to international responsibility.[14]

5. Summary

When summarizing this very brief outline of the scholarly debate on state responsibility for private conduct, it becomes clear that how states may be held responsible for harm caused by their citizens has preoccupied generations of international legal scholars. Hardly ever did modern legal

---

[10] Hall, *A Treatise on International Law*, p. 230.
[11] Lassa Oppenheim, *International Law – A Treatise, Volume I: Peace* (London: Longmans, Green, and Co, 1905), p. 200.
[12] Oppenheim, *International Law*, § 165, pp. 211 f.
[13] ILC, Fourth Report on State Responsibility by Special Rapporteur Robert Ago, UN Doc. A/CN.4/264 and Add. 1 (1972), p. 100.
[14] See, for instance, Heinrich Triepel, *Völkerrecht und Landesrecht* (Leipzig: Hirschfeld, 1899), p.334; and later ILC, Fourth Report on State Responsibility by Special Rapporteur Robert Ago, UN Doc. A/CN.4/264 and Add. 1 (1972), p. 100.

authors support absolute forms of responsibility, holding the state accountable for any private conduct. States merely had a duty to prevent wrongful private conduct and to punish such conduct, should it occur nonetheless. Relatively early, it was recognized that this form of responsibility depended on a state's ability to foresee harmful conduct and prevent it by employing reasonable means. In spite of this seemingly broad consensus, the components of due diligence obligations were yet difficult to narrow down, which becomes clear when having a closer look at the first instances in which such obligations were applied to international legal practice.

III. Due Diligence in Early Jurisprudence

Early state practice and jurisprudence soon revealed both the potential of a concept as flexible as due diligence as well as the challenges related to its practical application. Explicitly, the due diligence standard was first mentioned in the *Alabama Arbitration* of 1872. Later on, the concept became a prominent part of alien protection laws which were applied and advanced by so-called Claims Commissions (1.) The protection of foreigners was thus the first area of international law in which due diligence obligations were broadly acknowledged (2.). While the Claims Commissions mainly dealt with how foreigners were treated within a particular state, the concept of due diligence quickly spread to transboundary cases as well (3.).

1. The Duty to Protect Foreigners and the Establishment of Claims Commissions

With growing travel and trade activities, states became increasingly interested in the adequate protection of their nationals in foreign countries. Soon, it was suggested that states had an international obligation to take reasonable measures for the protection of aliens on their territory. In the late nineteenth and early twentieth century, such duties were included in a growing number of bilateral treaties and became the substance of various legal actions. So-called Claims Commissions were set up to adjudicate claims by foreign citizens. Duties of diligent conduct also formed part of the Institut's de Droit International resolution[15] on the "Responsabilité internationale des États à raison

---

[15] The Resolution can be found at www.justitiaetpace.org/idiF/resolutionsF/1927_lau_05_fr.pdf.

des dommages causés sur leur territoire à la personne et aux biens des étrangers" of 1927[16] and the "Harvard Draft Articles on the Responsibility of States for Damage Done in Their Territory to the Person or Property of Foreigners" of 1929.[17] Draft Article 11 states that "[a] state is responsible if an injury to an alien results from an act of an individual or from mob violence, if the state has failed to exercise due diligence to prevent such injury." Though neither of the drafts was transformed into a binding legal instrument, the preparatory works reveal how international consensus emerged with regard to international standards of care. The duty to adequately protect foreigners was so widely accepted that alien protection law became the first area of international law in which it was commonly recognized that states had a duty to take reasonable measures in order to prevent and sanction harmful conduct on their territory. This is further underlined by the fact that, later on, the work of the International Law Commission on the topic of state responsibility was initially limited to state responsibility for injuries caused to foreign citizens,[18] even though the Commission had a wider mandate from the start.[19] State practice and international jurisprudence on the protection of foreigners thus present the first comprehensive source to be consulted when analyzing how due diligence obligations operate in practice.

2. The Jurisprudence of the Claims Commissions

Above all, the Claims Commissions differentiated between preventive and repressive obligations. States had obligations to prevent harm to foreigners, as well as to sanction such harmful conduct if it occurred nonetheless.

---

[16] Art. 3 reads: "L'Etat n'est pas responsable, en ce qui concerne les faits dommageables commis par des particuliers, que lorsque le dommage résulte du fait qu'il aurait omis de prendre les mesures auxquelles, d'après les circonstances, il convenait normalement de recourir pour prévenir ou réprimer de tells faits."

[17] The Draft Articles are reprinted in: 23 AJIL, Supplement on the Codification of International Law, 133–218.

[18] See, for instance, ILC, Second Report on the Responsibility of the State for Injuries Caused in its Territory to the Person or Property of Aliens by Special Rapporteur F.V. García Amador, UN Doc. A/CN.4/106 (1957).

[19] The GA requested the Commission to undertake the codification of the general principles of international law governing state responsibility, Resolution No. 799 (VIII) of 1 December 1953, UN Doc. A/2589, 52.

a. Preventive Obligations of Due Diligence

Even then, it was recognized that the preventive duties of states contained two different elements: First, states had a duty to ensure a permanent legislative and administrative framework providing for effective implementation of their international duties.[20] Second, states had a complementary duty to ensure that, in practice, this general framework would be applied in a sufficiently diligent manner. The US-Panama Claims Commission, for instance, found that states may only be held responsible under international law if "*either* their behaviour in connection with the particular occurrence; *or* a general failure to comply with their duty to maintain order, to prevent crime or to punish criminals"[21] was established.

Notably, early case law already drew a distinction between both obligations: the duty to establish and maintain a legislative and administrative framework was qualified as a strict form of obligation.[22] If states did not establish an adequate framework ensuring that, on their territory, conditions prevailed that guaranteed the safety of persons, this failure alone constituted a breach of their international obligations.[23] The same could not be said of the obligation to apply this framework in connection with a particular occurrence. In that case, a state could be held responsible only if it did not act in a sufficiently diligent manner. Illustrative of this nuanced approach is the *Wipperman* case, in which it was held that for private acts, states were not responsible under international law "as long as reasonable diligence is used in attempting to prevent the occurrence or recurrence of such wrongs."[24] When it came to determining what constituted diligent measures, however, the Claims Commissions were soon confronted with several procedural and substantial hurdles. While they generally acknowledged that duties of diligence existed under alien protection laws, they were hesitant to hold states responsible for

---

[20] Paul Schoen, *Die völkerrechtliche Haftung der Staaten aus unerlaubten Handlungen* (Breslau: J. U. Kern, 1917), p.72.

[21] United States/Panama General Claims Commission, *Walter A. Noyes (US) v. Panama*, Decision of 22 May 1933, RIAA VI 308 (311), emphasis added.

[22] Riccardo Pisillo-Mazzeschi, "The Due Diligence Rule and the Nature of the International Responsibility of States" (1992) 35 *GYIL* 9–51 at 27.

[23] ILC, Second Report on the Responsibility of the State for Injuries Caused in its Territory to the Person or Property of Aliens by Special Rapporteur F.V. García Amador, UN Doc. A/CN.4/106 (1957), p. 106.

[24] The Wipperman Case, *USA v. Venezuela*, 5 December 1885, reprinted in John Bassett Moore, *History and Digest of the International Arbitrations to which the US has been a Party* (Washington, DC: Government Printing Office, 1898), volume III, 3041.

insufficient preventive steps and typically showed great deference toward domestic policies.[25] Most claims before the Commissions thus dealt with a failure to adequately react once harm had already occurred.

b. Repressive Obligations of Due Diligence

Here again, the Commissions differentiated between a general obligation to establish and maintain an administrative and judicial apparatus capable of investigating and sanctioning harmful conduct and an obligation to apply this apparatus in a diligent manner. Albeit the Commissions tended to be more willing to find a violation of repressive obligations, they still followed a rather cautious approach. In the *Wipperman* case, the Tribunal held that it would be contrary to international law if "a government should show indifference with reference to the punishment of the guilty authors of such outrages" but that no failure on behalf of the state could be established as long as "an honest and serious purpose is manifested to punish the perpetrators."[26] While states were principally given generous leeway in defining what an "honest and serious purpose" amounted to, the Commissions yet conveyed several objective categories to assess whether states had adequately investigated harmful conduct. If claims were not properly examined by a fair and impartial court, for instance, the host state's responsibility for failure to comply with its due diligence obligations could be triggered.[27] Indicators for an improper examination were overly inadequate punishments of guilty individuals,[28] an inexcusable delay in judicial proceedings,[29] or negligently letting guilty individuals escape.[30] Notably, however, the Commissions often held that only an inordinate degree of judicial impropriety would attract

---

[25] See, for instance, United States/Mexico Claims Commission, *L.F.H. Neer and Pauline Neer (US)* v. *United Mexican States*, Decision of 15 October 1926, RIAA IV 60; United States/Mexico Claims Commission, *Laura Mecham (US)* v. *United Mexican States*, Decision of 2 April 1929, RIAA IV 443.

[26] The Wipperman Case, USA v. Venezuela, 5 December 1885, reprinted in John Bassett Moore, *History and Digest of the International Arbitrations to Which the US Has Been a Party* (Washington, DC: Government Printing Office, 1898–1906), volume III, 3041.

[27] Sweden/Venezuela General Claims Commission, Bovallins and Hedlund Case, Decision of 10 March 1903, RIAA X 768 (768 f.).

[28] *Settlement of the Claims of Mrs. Charles Renton, of Ella Miller Renton and of the Estate of Jacob Baiz (US)* v. *Honduras*, reprinted in: US Department of States, *Papers Relating to the Foreign Relations of the US* (Washington, DC: Government Printing Office, 1904), p. 363.

[29] United States/Mexico General Claims Commission, *Laura M.B. Janes et al (US)* v. *United Mexican States*, Decision of 16 November 1925, RIAA IV 82 (86).

[30] United States/Mexico General Claims Commission, *Laura M.B. Janes et al (US)* v. *United Mexican States*, Decision of 16 November 1925, RIAA IV 82 (86).

state responsibility. While being generally more lenient compared to the hurdles for establishing a failure to take preventive measures, the Commissions still set rather high thresholds for establishing a failure to exercise repressive due diligence.

c. Due Diligence versus Complicity

Faced with procedural challenges in establishing a lack of diligence, some applicants before the Commissions submitted that violating the obligation to prosecute harmful conduct amounted to active complicity. If states purposely refrained from punishing an individual perpetrator, this would constitute an approval that would allow holding the state directly responsible. The Swedish-Venezuelan Claims Commission, for instance, found Venezuela responsible for the actions of several insurgents who were not properly prosecuted: "[The Government] tacitly approves their conduct, and according to the principles recognized by public law makes itself responsible for all the acts done by them."[31] In other cases, state complicity in private actions was derived from pardoning the perpetrators or from the refusal to award appropriate reparations.[32] States would become complicit either by explicitly endorsing harmful private conduct or "by an implied ... approval in the negligent failure to prevent the injury, or to investigate the case, or to punish the guilty individual."[33] Complicity was thus employed as an instrument to hold states directly responsible for harmful private conduct circumventing the difficulties of establishing a lack of diligence. In general, however, this approach did not gain sufficient acceptance neither among legal scholars nor in the practice of states and tribunals: "it is not permissible to treat this derivative and remote liability not as an attenuate form of responsibility, but as just as serious as if the Government had perpetrated the killing with its own hands."[34] At the Hague Codification Conference of 1930, the majority of states rejected the idea that failure to exercise due diligence would

---

[31] Sweden/Venezuela General Claims Commission, Bollavins and Hedlund Cases, Decision of 10 March 1903, RIAA X, 768 (769).

[32] Great Britain/Colombia Claims Commission, Case of Cotesworth and Powell, reprinted in John Bassett Moore, *History and Digest of the International Arbitrations to Which the US Has Been a Party* (Washington: Government Printing Office, 1898), volume II, 2082.

[33] Edwin Borchard, *The Diplomatic Protection of Citizens Abroad 1915* (reprinted New York: Kraus, 1970), p. 217.

[34] United States/Mexico General Claims Commission, *Laura M.B. Janes et al. (US)* v. *United Mexican States*, Decision of 16 November 1925, RIAA IV 82 (87).

render states the accomplice of the offender.[35] Failure to exercise due diligence thus remained the central point of reference when establishing state responsibility for private actions.

d. Responsibility in Case of Civil Insurgency

Since civil insurgencies tended to cause particularly significant harm, some applicants before the Commissions rejected the notion of due diligence and argued in favor of strict liability on behalf of states if such insurgencies occurred. In principle, however, the same general standards were applied by the Commissions. States were not considered liable for civil revolts in which their organs did not participate. Responsibility could only be invoked for failure to exercise preventive due diligence or to adequately react by suppressing the revolt.[36] The mere fact that civil unrest took place on numerous or even regular occasions did not justify the supposition that states had employed generally deficient means of prevention,[37] in particular when taking into account the suddenness of attacks and limited capacities to effectively fight violent internal opposition. Only where increased risks of attacks on foreigners were known to a state – for instance, because physical attacks had already occurred on a regular basis – were intensified measures of protection required.[38] With solid indications of future attacks often lacking, state responsibility for civil revolts was yet difficult to assign. In sum, the Claims Commissions thus argued that the scale and nature of harmful individual conduct did not affect the general obligation of states to establish an adequate administrative and judicial framework and to diligently employ it. There was no absolute form of responsibility with regard to insurgencies within a state's territory, but the degree of diligence could vary depending on the circumstances.

---

[35] See among many others the Statement by the Swiss Government as contained in Preparatory Committee of the Conference for the Codification of International Law, League of Nations Document V Legal 1929.V3, reprinted in Shabtai Rosenne (ed.), *League of Nations Conference for the Codification of International Law* (Dobbs Ferry: Oceana, 1972),663.

[36] See with extensive references to the relevant state practice: Borchard, "Diplomatic Protection," p. 224 f.

[37] Borchard, "Diplomatic Protection," p. 243.

[38] The Wipperman Case, *USA* v. *Venezuela*, 5 December 1885, reprinted in John Bassett Moore, *History and Digest of the International Arbitrations to Which the US Has Been a Party* (Washington, DC: Government Printing Office, 1898–1906), volume III, 3042.

3. Due Diligence Obligations in Transboundary Cases

While the first area in which due diligence obligations were widely applied was thus the field of alien protection laws, similar obligations were soon recognized in transboundary cases.[39] Even though states generally exerted exclusive sovereignty over their national territory, they had an obligation to ensure that this territory was not used to cause harm to other sovereign states. As arbitrator Huber famously phrased in the Island of Palmas case: "Territorial sovereignty ... involves the exclusive right to display the activities of a State. This right has a corollary duty: the obligation to protect within the territory the rights of other States, in particular their right to integrity and inviolability."[40] Following the Alabama Arbitration, international jurisprudence soon acknowledged that such duty was not only an obligation not to infringe upon the rights of other states through the conduct of state organs but also to diligently prevent such infringement by private actors. In the British Claims in the Spanish Zone of Morocco case of 1925, states were found to have a duty to take all reasonable measures in order to prevent and sanction military harm by non-state actors. Even where internal unrest was not attributable, a state "peut être néanmoins responsable de ce que les autorités font ou ne font pas, pour parer, dans la mesure possible, aux suites."[41] According to the Tribunal, these obligations were not significantly different from those established in the context of alien protection laws. They consisted of an obligation to diligently prevent harmful private conduct and to diligently sanction such conduct, should it occur nonetheless. In like manner, obligations to diligently prevent harmful conduct with transboundary effects would not constitute an absolute form of responsibility of the state for any conduct occurring on its territory. As the Swiss government stated in the *Aggression contre la Légation de Roumaine à Berne* case, "ni l'obligation de prévention ni celle de punition n'ont un charactère absolu ... L'Etat doit faire preuve de 'due diligence'; il n'est pas tenu d'empêcher n'importe quel incident d'une manière absolue, ce qui serait matériellement impossible."[42] There is thus no principal difference between the concept of due diligence as developed in the field of alien protection and due diligence as applied in transboundary constellations.

---

[39] Pisillo-Mazzeschi, "The Due Diligence Rule," 22 ff.
[40] Island of Palmas Case (*Netherlands* v. *USA*), Arbitral Award of 4 April 1928, RIAA II 829 (839).
[41] Permanent Court of Arbitration, Réclamations Britanniques dans la Zone Espagnol du Maroc (*Great Britain* v. *Spain*), Decision of 1 May 1925, RIAA II 615 (642, 656ff.).
[42] Legal Service of the Swiss Federal Council, Agression contre la Légation de Roumaine à Berne (1959) *Annuaire Suisse de Droit International*, p. 225.

This is why due diligence was soon considered a general standard of state responsibility.[43] As early as 1887, the US Supreme Court held that "the law of nations requires every national government to use 'due diligence' to prevent a wrong being done within its own dominion to another nation ..., or to the people thereof."[44] Irrespective of the specific content of international obligations, due diligence thus became the accustomed standard against which to measure the conduct of states toward private actions.

IV. Due Diligence within the System of State Responsibility

In spite of this early recognition in jurisprudence and scholarly writings, the contours of due diligence are still unclear. Several attempts to codify due diligence obligations in various fields of international law have failed (1.), and the role and function of due diligence within the framework of the law on state responsibility remain unsettled (2.).

1. Failed Attempts at Codification

A rather broad consensus on preventive and repressive due diligence obligations could not prevent various attempts to codify these emerging norms from failing.[45] Obligations of diligent conduct to protect foreigners and their property were intensely debated at The Hague Codification Conference of 1930. Next to the jurisprudence of the Claims Commissions, the documents prepared for the Conference are the main source of relevant state practice at the time and the original drafts contained ample references to the due diligence concept. The preparatory committees submitted several so-called bases for discussion, number 10 and 17 of which are particularly relevant. Number 10 stipulated that states may be responsible for damage suffered by foreigners if "the executive power" failed to "show such diligence ... as, having regard to the circumstances and the status of the person concerned, could be expected from a civilized State." Number 17 repeated that exact formula with regard to the damage caused to foreigners or their property by

---

[43] Bonnitcha and McCorquodale, "The Concept of Due Diligence," 905.
[44] US Supreme Court, *United States* v. *Arjona*, Judgment of 7 March 1887, 120 US 479 (7 S. Ct. 628, 30 L.Ed. 728).
[45] On the historical developments, Richard Lillich, "The Current Status of the Law of State Responsibility for Injuries to Aliens," in Richard Lillich (ed.), *International Law of State Responsibility for Injuries to Aliens* (Charlottesville: Virginia University Press, 1983), pp. 5 ff.

private individuals.[46] Eventually, however, the explicit due diligence reference was eliminated in favor of a formulation referring to "such measures as in the circumstances should normally have been taken."[47] Yet, even this general and vague phrasing failed to be adopted and the Conference could not agree upon an international convention dealing with the responsibility of states for damage to foreigners occurring on their territory.

In spite of broad consensus on the existence of such obligations, there was still significant disagreement on how to precisely define international due diligence standards. Whether there should be an objective minimum standard or whether states were merely required not to treat foreigners worse in comparison to their own citizens was subject to a particularly animated controversy. The Alabama Arbitration found that lower domestic standards of care could not justify failure to take diligent measures.[48] A range of states, however, objected to automatically applying this assumption to non-transboundary constellations. Under certain circumstances, so they argued, states were required to provide wider protection to foreigners. Other states fiercely objected, arguing that states were merely required to provide for the same amount of protection to foreigners than that which they afforded to their own nationals.[49] The latter group contended that foreigners voluntarily took up the risk of traveling and doing business in a foreign country. They should inform themselves about potential risks and adjust their behavior accordingly. This vigorous debate is but one example of how the seemingly simple and straightforward concept of due diligence was difficult to fill with actual content. Agreement could not be reached on how to clearly define the standard. Against this background, it comes as little surprise that early codification attempts could not be brought to a successful end, and similar controversies have later accompanied the ILC's codification work.

---

[46] League of Nations Publication LN Doc. C/75/M/69 (1929), pp. 67 and 69, respectively.

[47] 4 Acts of the Conference for the Codification of International Law 143 (Third Committee of the League of Nations), LN Doc. C/351(c)M/145(c) (1930), p. 175.

[48] Alabama Claims (*USA* v. *Great Britain*), Award of 14 September 1872, reprinted in John Bassett Moore, *History and Digest of the International Arbitrations to Which the US Has Been a Party* (Washington: Government Printing Office, 1898), volume I, chapter XIV: The Geneva Arbitration, 495–682 at 656.

[49] See the summary of this debate by ILC, Fourth Report on State Responsibility by Special Rapporteur Robert Ago, UN Doc. A/CN.4/264 and Add. 1 (1972), pp. 108 f.

2. The ILC's Work on State Responsibility and the Due Diligence Concept

The 2001 Articles on State Responsibility[50] regulate neither the direct international responsibility of non-state actors nor the responsibility of states for entirely private conduct. Initially, the Draft Articles had contained a clause expressly stating that "the conduct of a private individual or group of individuals, acting in that capacity, is not considered to be an act of State in international law."[51] With this clause abandoned in the final version, the Articles now do not comment on the responsibility of states for entirely private conduct if it falls out of the regime of attribution.

As is well known, the Articles are generally based on a fundamental distinction between primary and secondary norms. Primary norms define the material content of international obligations, whereas secondary norms regulate the legal consequences that arise once a primary norm was breached.[52] Even though the Articles merely regulate secondary norms to the exclusion of primary norms, the codification process on state responsibility has been among the longest and most complex projects the Commission has ever undertaken. It thus is hardly surprising that the notion of due diligence is often confused and intermingled with other concepts of state responsibility. In order to explore how international due diligence obligations are applied, it is yet necessary to identify as precisely as possible what the standard entails and how it might be distinguished from other responsibility concepts. With this in mind, the following section will trace back those steps in the development of the law on state responsibility, which had an impact on the concept of due diligence to better pinpoint what due diligence entails in international law.

V. Confusion of Concepts: Distinguishing Due Diligence from Other Responsibility Concepts

As mentioned previously, the debate on state responsibility has been complicated and protracted. Quite a number of key issues were

---

[50] ILC, Draft Articles on Responsibility of States for Internationally Wrongful Acts with Commentaries, ILC Yearbook 2001, volume II, part II.
[51] ILC, Fourth Report on State Responsibility by Special Rapporteur Robert Ago, ILC Yearbook 1972, Volume II 126, UN Doc. A/CN.4/264 and Add.1, para 146.
[52] ILC, Report of its 32nd Session, ILC Yearbook 1980, volume II, part II, p. 27, para. 23.

controversial for a long time, and several contested issues significantly affected the understanding of due diligence, which gave ground for substantial confusion. Part of this confusion stems from the fact that, in order to determine international responsibility, reference is often made to terms and categories employed in domestic law. International responsibility, though, is a unique form of responsibility, which is why the transfer of domestic concepts without adequate adjustment contributes to a lack of clarity. Against this backdrop, the next section aims to distinguish due diligence from other concepts of state responsibility. By identifying the concept's unique characteristics, the contours and prerequisites of what constitutes a failure to exercise due diligence will become more approachable.

The proper role of fault within the system of state responsibility has accompanied the ILC's codification work for a significant period of time. With regard to due diligence obligations, this debate is yet ongoing, in particular with due diligence often being equated with omissions and negligence. Therefore, the differentiation between actions and omissions should be clarified first (1.) to show how fault in general and negligence in particular relate to the standard of due diligence (2.). In a second step, the ILC's work on different forms of state responsibility will be expounded. In particular, the concept of liability for harms arising out of acts not prohibited by international law (3.) clarifies the standard of due diligence, which might become even more apparent when the ILC's categorization of obligations of conduct versus obligations of result is recalled (4.). Finally, due diligence needs to be distinguished from the concept of complicity (5.), with which it is regularly confused. Considering these different concepts will help identify the distinctive features of due diligence in international law (6.).

1. Actions and Omissions

The debate surrounding the proper role for fault within the law of state responsibility included several suggestions to distinguish between wrongful state commissions on the one hand and omissions on the other. For our purpose, this distinction is highly relevant, insofar as it seems a popular assumption that failure to exercise due diligence exclusively manifests itself in the form of wrongful omissions.

In general, state responsibility for omissions presupposes a legal duty to act. In the absence of primary norms instructing states to a certain course of conduct, responsibility for omissions cannot be established.[53] And indeed, obligations of diligent conduct are generally seen as imposing upon states a duty to employ best efforts to achieve a certain result, which might consist of either positively bringing about a desired result or preventing an undesired result from occurring. This has tempted several authors to argue that due diligence obligations were always breached by omission.[54] On closer inspection, however, such distinction seems superfluous.[55] Legal responsibility may even arise out of a combination of actions and omissions[56] and whether state conduct was commissive or omissive is often difficult to tell.[57] It is usually comprised of a variety of different actions and omissions on behalf of individual state organs. The same holds true for obligations of diligent conduct. They can be breached by complete failure to take any steps whatsoever but also by taking active steps that turn out to be inadequate or by a combination of both forms. Nothing is gained, therefore, by drawing an artificial line between commissions and omissions. To claim that obligations of due diligence may only be violated through omissions gratuitously limits their scope of application. Notwithstanding, the equation of due diligence obligations with omissions is still lingering with respect to the proper role for fault in the laws on state responsibility.

2. Fault

As mentioned previously, due diligence is not expressly mentioned in the ILC's Articles, which is deemed a logical consequence of their primarily objective character. The decision for an objective approach brought an end to a long-lasting debate as to whether state responsibility required subjective elements or not. The Articles now stipulate that states are responsible under international law if a primary international obligation is breached and that breach is attributable to a state. Additional subjective

---

[53] Franck Latty, "Actions and Omissions," in James Crawford et al. (eds.), *The Law of International Responsibility* (Oxford: Oxford University Press, 2010), pp. 357 f.

[54] See, for instance, Roberto Ago, "Le Délit International" (1939) 68 *RdC* 419–545 at 501; Pisillo-Mazzeschi, "The Due Diligence Rule," 23 f.; Sarah Heathcote, "State Omissions and Due Diligence," in Karine Bannelier et al. (eds.), *The ICJ and the Evolution of International Law* (London: Routledge, 2012), p. 309.

[55] James Crawford, *State Responsibility* (Cambridge: Cambridge University Press, 2013), p. 217; Ian Brownlie, *System of the Law of Nations. State Responsibility* (Oxford: Clarendon, 1983), p. 43.

[56] ILC DARS, Commentary to Article 2, para. 4.

[57] Monica Hakimi, "State Bystander Responsibility" (2010) 21 *EJIL* 341–385 at 354.

elements such as intent or negligence are not principally required[58] and may only become relevant where primary obligations involve subjective components.[59] Now widely accepted, this approach had originally been vigorously disputed. For a long time, many scholars had supported the idea that state responsibility entailed intent or negligence on behalf of a state.[60] When it comes to due diligence, relics of this dispute are still to be detected, which is why this seemingly settled question deserves further remarks.

a. The Role of Fault within the Law on State Responsibility: General Remarks

It was Anzilotti who first delivered a substantiated and very complex reasoning as to why the state as an abstract entity was not able to form a will and could not act with intent. He famously stated that "au sens psychologique du mot, il n'y a pas de volonté propre de l'État."[61] Intent or negligence as inherently subjective categories could not be reasonably applied to the state as an artificial entity. Soon, the validity of his argument was challenged by several scholars, arguing that since the state could not act but through its organs, intent or negligence on behalf of those organs should be attributed to the state.[62] Responding to such criticisms, Anzilotti's argument as to the logical difficulty in conceiving subjective fault of states shifted toward focusing on procedural difficulties, considering complex state structures and exclusive territorial control: "La preuve d'une intention ... est toujours très difficile à rapporter. En droit international, cette preuve devient presque impossible à faire, en raison de l'existence du contrôle territorial exclusif exercé par le défendeur."[63] Due to a state's exclusive control over its territory, obtaining evidentiary material is extremely difficult, and the fact that states act

---

[58] Brigitte Stern, "The Elements of an Internationally Wrongful Act," in James Crawford et al. (eds.), *The Law of International Responsibility* (Oxford: Oxford University Press, 2010), p. 209; André Nollkaemper, "Concurrence between Individual Responsibility and State Responsibility in International Law" (2003) 52 *ICLQ* 615–640 at 617.

[59] ILC, DARS, Commentary to Article 2, para. 3.

[60] Among many others, William Edward Hall, *A Treatise on International Law* (Oxford: Clarendon, 2nd ed., 1884), § 65, para. 193; Lassa Oppenheim, *International Law – A Treatise* (London: Longmans, Greens and Co, 2nd ed., 1912), § 154, p. 212.

[61] Dionisio Anzilotti, "La Responsabilité Internationale des États à Raison des Dommages Soufferts par des Étrangers" (1906) 13 *RGDIP* 285–309 at 287.

[62] See, for instance, Ago, "Le Délit International," 486.

[63] Denis Lévy, "La Responsabilité pour Omission et la Responsabilité pour Risque en Droit International Public" (1961) 65 *RGDIP* 744–764 at 750.

through collective actions of several organs makes it an even greater challenge to determine subjective fault. The unique character of state responsibility thus explains why subjective fault was relinquished as an independent element of the secondary norms of state responsibility.

b. Due Diligence Obligations and Negligence

A much different picture emerges when looking at due diligence obligations. Duties of diligent conduct cannot be assessed on objective criteria alone. Subjective factors – such as knowledge of a risk or calculating and evaluating such risk – play a most significant role. Against this background, it is often argued that at least in case of diligence obligations, state responsibility does entail subjective elements in the form of negligence on behalf of state officials.[64]

The early ILC Special Rapporteurs often referred to notions of fault or negligence when elaborating on state responsibility for private conduct.[65] Not surprisingly, the debate on whether failure to exercise due diligence presupposes negligence (*culpa*) was present in the ICJ's Corfu Channel case as well. Some of the dissenting judges felt urged to emphasize that subjective negligence on behalf of Albania would have to be established which – in their view – the majority opinion had not done in an adequate manner.[66] In fact, the majority had not elaborated on any subjective requirements, which was seen by many observers as support for an objective approach toward state responsibility, even in the context of due diligence obligations.[67]

And, indeed, the assumption that only wrongful omissions required fault raises at least two points of criticism: first, it is arduous to determine whether a given state action is commissive or omissive, as we have already seen.[68] State conduct is formed within complex administrative

---

[64] See, for instance, Charles de Visscher, *La Responsabilités des États* (Leiden: Brill, 1924), p. 92; Manuel García-Mora, *International Responsibility for Hostile Acts of Private Persons against Foreign States* (The Hague: Martinus Nijhoff, 1962), p. 16.

[65] Among others, see ILC, Sixth Report on International Responsibility by Special Rapporteur F.V. García-Amador, UN Doc. A/CN.4/134 and Add. 1 (1961), p. 47.

[66] ICJ, The Corfu Channel Case (*UK* v. *Albania*), Judgment of 9 April 1949, ICJ Reports 1949, 4, Dissenting Opinion by Judge Krylov stating on p. 72 that "[i]n order to found the responsibility of the State recourse must be had to the notion of culpa" and Dissenting Opinion by Judge ad hoc Ečer stating on p. 127 that "the responsibility of a State assumes either dolus or culpa on its part."

[67] Il Yung Chung, *Legal Problems Involved in the Corfu Channel Incident* (Geneva: Droz and Minard, 1959), pp. 166 f.; Lévy, "Responsabilité pour Omission," 747 f.

[68] Brownlie, "System of the Law of Nations," p. 43.

structures and myriads of separate commissions and omissions. It seems arbitrary to make the requirement of fault dependent on whether a given state conduct leans more toward commission or toward omission. Second, omissive behavior – while often deemed a lesser grave breach of international law – could trigger consequences just as harmful as those caused by positive action[69] and might even be intended as a gesture of disrespect for the rights and interests concerned. From a victim state's perspective, it thus seems equally random to impose higher procedural burdens (namely the duty to demonstrate fault).

c. Due Diligence as a Standard of Conduct Contained in Primary Norms

Next to these rather procedural concerns, there is an even more substantial objection to treating lack of diligence and negligence as equivalent for such equating derives from a common misconception: due diligence is not in itself a secondary subjective requirement of state responsibility but rather the objective content of an international obligation.[70] The international obligation is to act in an overall diligent manner. This is not the same as invoking state responsibility by finding a breach of primary obligations and demonstrating that – on secondary level – this breach was brought about by negligent conduct. This unfortunate misconception is reinforced by a confusion of terminology commonly employed in the context of due diligence obligations. The Inter-American Human Rights Institutions, for instance, often explicitly use the term "negligence" when elaborating on due diligence obligations.[71]

However, state responsibility for failure to act diligently does not require that one or several state officials acted with negligence in the sense of subjective fault on behalf of a natural person. Failure to act diligently may arise out of general or systematic deficiencies, which are completely detached from individual intentions.[72] Various state actions may only combinedly constitute a breach of diligence obligations. While negligence on behalf of individual state organs could evince and confirm failure on behalf of a state to comply with its due diligence obligations, it

---

[69] Astrid Epiney, Die völkerrechtliche Verantwortlichkeit von Staaten für rechtswidriges Verhalten im Zusammenhang mit Aktionen Privater (Baden-Baden: Nomos, 1992), p. 81.
[70] Maurice Bourquin, "Règles Générales du Droit de la Paix" (1931) 35 *RdC* 1–232 at 218.
[71] See, for instance, IAComHR, *Maria da Penha Maia Fernandes* v. *Brazil*, Report No. 54/01, Decision of 16 April 2001, para. 56, speaking of "a general pattern of negligence."
[72] Pisillo-Mazzeschi, "The Due Diligence Rule," 42; Jiménez de Aréchaga and Tanzi, "International State Responsibility," 350.

is not a precondition thereof.[73] To classify this under the framework of primary versus secondary obligations: due diligence duties are in principal primary obligations imposing duties of a material content to act in a diligent manner.[74] What constitutes a diligent manner is to be objectively derived from the international obligation in question and should not be confused with what constitutes negligent behavior on behalf of a state organ.[75] The IACtHR has rightly pointed out that "rules that take psychological factors into account in establishing individual culpability" could not be applied to states and that "the intention or motivation of the agent who has violated the rights recognized by the Convention is irrelevant – the violation can be established even if the identity of the individual perpetrators is unknown."[76] In a similar manner, the European Commission on Human Rights held that "'responsibility' does not necessarily require any 'guilt' on behalf of the State."[77] There is thus no need for installing a separate regime of state responsibility for due diligence obligations. Though any primary obligation under international law may contain specific subjective elements,[78] different forms of secondary obligations requiring fault in some cases but not in others do not exist.

A first conclusion to be drawn is thus that due diligence obligations do not require negligence on behalf of individual state organs. While the concept of due diligence indisputably contains subjective elements, evaluating whether a state as an abstract entity has failed to act diligently does not correspond with negligence on behalf of natural persons. Failure to exercise due diligence may only arise out of an overall evaluation of a state's activities. For the same reason, failure to exercise due diligence should not be equated with wrongful omissions either, due to the fact that state conduct may only combinedly result in a manifest failure to adhere to the diligence required.

Notwithstanding, the uncertainty surrounding fault, negligence, omissions, and commissions shaped the ILC's work to a significant extent,

---

[73] Joanna Kulesza, *Due Diligence in International Law* (Leiden: Brill Nijhoff, 2016), p. 263.
[74] Barnidge, "Non-State Actors and Terrorism," p. 62; René Lefeber, *Transboundary Environmental Interference and the Origin of State Liability* (The Hague: Kluwer Law, 1996), p. 62.
[75] Epiney, "Völkerrechtliche Verantwortlichkeit," pp. 80 f.
[76] IACtHR, *Velásquez Rodríguez v. Honduras*, Judgment of 29 July 1988, Series C, No. 4, para. 173.
[77] EComHR, *Ireland v. UK*, Report of the Commission of 25 January 1976, Application No. 5310/71, p. 383.
[78] See also ILC DARS, Commentary to Article 2, para. 3.

V. CONFUSION OF CONCEPTS

resulting in several concepts on different forms of responsibility and different forms of obligations, both of which affected the notion of due diligence. In order to identify components of an international due diligence standard, it is thus necessary to briefly recall the ILC's work on state responsibility for acts not prohibited by international law and – more fundamentally – its differentiation between obligations of result and conduct.

3. Liability for Acts Not Prohibited by International Law

Diligence obligations were of central importance to the ILC's work on liability for acts not prohibited by international law. In the 1970s, the ILC launched a twofold plan for its future work on state responsibility to simultaneously work on two topics the Commission considered necessary to be treated separately. The Special Rapporteur on state responsibility exclusively focused on wrongful acts, which were defined as acts illicit under international law while a second Special Rapporteur dealt with harmful consequences arising out of acts not prima facie prohibited. From the start, the latter concept was linked to environmental hazards[79] and commonly referred to as responsibility for risk.[80] The Commission yet avoided to exclusively focus on environmental law and set a more general context when starting to work on the subject. Distinguishing between those different forms of responsibility, so it argued, was necessary insofar as the amount of compensation payable for a lawful act was less than for a wrongful act. In any event, states would be more willing to pay compensation for lawful acts instead of confessing to any wrongdoing,[81] making it easier for the victim state to obtain compensation.[82] Introducing less grave forms of responsibility would thus help ensure compliance and effective reparation mechanisms.

a. Responsibility versus Liability

Stemming from this twofold approach is a differentiation between "responsibility" and "liability" in the ILC's terminology. Initially used

---

[79] Yearbook of the ILC 1980, volume II, p. 24, para. 4.
[80] Yearbook of the ILC 1969, volume II, p. 233, para. 83.
[81] Michael Akehurst, "International Liability for Injurious Consequences Arising out of Acts Not Prohibited by International Law" (1985) 16 *NYIL* 3–16 at 14 f.
[82] ILC, Third Report on International Liability for Injurious Consequences Arising Out of Acts Not Prohibited by International Law by Special Rapporteur Pemmaraju Sreenivasa Rao, UN Doc. A/CN.4/510 (2000), para. 31.

interchangeably, the Draft Articles on State Responsibility no longer make any reference to "liability,"[83] though the term is widely used in the Draft Articles on Prevention of Transboundary Harm[84] and the Draft Principles on the Allocation of Loss.[85] The distinction between both forms of accountability was meant to be as follows: state responsibility would arise following a breach of a primary obligation under international law, irrespective of whether this breach caused any material damage. In contrast, state liability would arise following the causation of material damage, where the causal conduct was not specifically prohibited.

Neither the terminology nor the substantial arguments for this twofold approach, though, have come to be widely accepted. They were even deemed "fundamentally misconceived"[86] and have been criticized for various reasons. To start with, the ILC's terminological distinction is not commonly reflected in the language of international treaties. They often refer to responsibility, as far as substantial obligations are concerned, and liability, where it comes to the legal consequences of a - breach.[87] Other treaties make use of the term *liability* to describe obligations in private law that states are supposed to instigate in their domestic orders.[88] Treating liability and responsibility as two distinct concepts of state responsibility is thus not adequately reflected in state practice, at least where terminology is concerned. The same holds true when looking at the substantial reasons for a distinction between state responsibility for unlawful acts and for acts not prohibited by international law. This content-based differentiation sparked even more intense criticism. Several scholars argued that such a distinction was not only useless but also failed to adequately represent relevant state practice and case law.[89] Drawing such artificial distinctions could not make any

---

[83] The term is still occasionally referred to in the Commentaries.
[84] ILC, Draft Articles on the Prevention of Transboundary Harm from Hazardous Activities with Commentaries, ILC Yearbook 2001. volume II, part II.
[85] ILC, Draft Principles on the Allocation of Loss in the Case of Transboundary Harm arising out of Hazardous Activities with Commentaries, ILC Yearbook 2006, volume II, part II.
[86] Brownlie, "System of the Law of Nations," p. 50.
[87] This approach is inter alia followed by Article 139 of the UN Convention on the Law of the Sea, signed on 10 December 1982, entered into force on 14 November 1994, 1833 UNTS 3.
[88] See, for instance, Vienna Convention on Civil Liability for Nuclear Damage, signed on 21 May 1963, entered into force on 12 November 1977, 1063 UNTS 266.
[89] See, for instance, Brownlie, "System of the Law of Nations," p. 50.

meaningful contribution to an effective system of state responsibility. Emphasis should rather be led on the enforceability of preventive obligations.[90] If preventive due diligence obligations fit in the context of primary and secondary obligations in the sense that there are primary obligations requiring states to take diligent measures of prevention and failure to do so triggers the secondary obligations as enshrined in the Draft Articles, then there is indeed little need for a separate regime of responsibility. States are entitled to develop primary rules containing almost any substantial obligation they find suitable. They are not hindered to agree upon rules that make the causation of harm an integral part of the primary obligation. To generally distinguish between lawful and unlawful activities for the purposes of establishing state responsibility seems misconceived.[91]

b. Draft Articles on Prevention of Transboundary Harm

This might explain why the twofold approach is no longer a priority on the ILC's agenda. The work on the responsibility of states for acts not prohibited by international law became an integral part of the Draft Articles on Prevention of Transboundary Harm. Those Articles elaborate on the standard of care that is expected of states where they undertake activities with the potential of causing significant transboundary harm and include substantial considerations of the due diligence standard. It is important to notice, however, that the Articles no longer insist on a differentiation between activities that are prohibited or not. They rather emphasize the importance of preventive obligations as compared to obligations to repair and focus on how to effectively ensure compliance with duties to diligently prevent transboundary harm.[92] The original idea of two entirely separate regimes of state responsibility is thus no longer pursued. In contrast, a further dogmatic differentiation between obligations of conduct and obligations of result and its underlying assumptions had a significant impact on the understanding of due diligence obligations and deserves closer consideration.

---

[90] Alan Boyle, "State Responsibility and International Liability for Injurious Consequences of Acts Not Prohibited by International Law: A Necessary Distinction?" (1990) 39 *ICLQ* 1–26 at 24.

[91] ILC, Third Report on International Liability for Injurious Consequences Arising out of Acts Not Prohibited by International Law Special Rapporteur Pemmaraju Sreenivasa Rao, UN Doc. A/CN.4/510 (2000), para. 28.

[92] ILC, Draft Articles on the Prevention of Transboundary Harm from Hazardous Activities with Commentaries, ILC Yearbook 2001, volume II, part II, General Commentary, para. 2.

4. Obligations of Conduct and Obligations of Result

The differentiation between obligations of conduct and obligations of result originally stems from civil law tradition: an obligation of conduct requires endeavoring to realize a given result but not – in the strict meaning of the term – to actually achieve it. In contrast, obligations of result impose a duty to accomplish a desired result with responsibility automatically engaged if the result is not reached. "L'obligation de résultat est une obligation de 'réussir', alors que l'obligation de due diligence est une obligation de 's'efforcer.'"[93] At first glance, obligations to exercise due diligence thus seem to fit perfectly in the category of obligations of conduct, and yet the ILC drafts took a different path.

a. Ago's Proposal

Special Rapporteur Ago was the first to address obligations of conduct. In his Draft, however, the differentiation between obligations of conduct and obligations of result is a slightly different one. Ago developed three different categories: obligations to perform a particular conduct, obligations to achieve a specific result, and obligations to prevent an apprehended event with obligations of conduct being obligations that instruct states to a very precise course of action.[94] Ago's obligations of conduct thus require states to take very specific actions, leaving little or no margin to decide which means are most appropriate. In his categories, obligations of conduct are thus different from obligations of due diligence, which he intended to fall under Article 23 of his draft, covering the distinct category of obligations "to prevent a given event."[95] This distinction had long-term consequences for the notion of due diligence in international law. Traditionally, responsibility for failure to exercise due diligence corresponded with failure to employ a desired conduct. In Ago's proposal, however, the emphasis of due diligence obligations

[93] Riccardo Pisillo-Mazzeschi, "Responsabilité de l'État pour Violation des Obligations Positives Relatives aux Droit de l'Homme" (2008) 333 RdC, 187–506 at 284; Jean Combacau, "Obligations de Résulat et Obligations de Comportement: Quelques Questions et pas de Réponse," in Daniel Bardonnet (ed.), Le Droit International, Unité et Diversité (Paris: Pedone, 1981), p. 196; Constantin Economides, "Content of the Obligation: Obligations of Means and Obligations of Result," in James Crawford et al. (eds.), The Law of International Responsibility (Oxford: Oxford University Press, 2010), p. 377.
[94] ILC, Sixth Report on State Responsibility by Special Rapporteur Robert Ago, UN Doc. A/CN.4/302 (1977), pp. 4 ff.
[95] ILC, Seventh Report on State Responsibility Special Rapporteur Robert Ago, UN Doc. A/CN.4/307 (1978), pp. 32 ff.

was laid on the event to be prevented. It is not surprising that Ago's complex approach sparked criticism by scholars[96] and national governments, many of which raised their doubts on such a "subtle academic distinction between obligations."[97] In spite of justified criticism, however, it need not be neglected that such content-based distinction of obligations is helpful when describing the precise course of action that is expected of states.

b. Why the Distinction Matters: The Temporal Dimension of a Breach

To define the character of an international obligation is much more than a subtle academic distinction. It even is of crucial importance when identifying the temporal dimension of a breach[98] – in particular, the exact moment in which an international obligation is violated, which triggers the rights of other states to engage in legitimate responses such as countermeasures or claims for compensation. While this might be done easily with obligations of result – where the obligation is breached as soon as the desired result is not achieved – things are less clear-cut when it comes to Ago's obligations of conduct or obligations to prevent. Crawford later argued that while an obligation to prevent might only be violated if the undesired event actually occurs, an obligation of conduct could be breached by failure to apply the course of conduct prescribed by the obligation. In his view, obligations of due diligence were a subform of obligations of conduct rather than obligations to prevent. An obligation of due diligence would thus be contravened due to failure to exercise due diligence, regardless of whether the apprehended event occurs or not.[99] And yet it is far from clear where to draw the line between obligations of conduct and obligations to prevent. Many authors do not even take up this subtle distinction and merely refer to obligations of conduct as opposed to obligations of result. Even where the distinction is drawn, it is difficult to differentiate between both forms of obligations, as many areas in which diligence obligations are applied have a strong

---

[96] Brownlie, "System of the Law of Nations," p. 241; Pierre-Marie Dupuy, "Reviewing the Difficulties of Codification: On Ago's Classification of Obligations of Means and Obligations of Result in Relation to State Responsibility" (1999) 10 *EJIL* 371–385 at 377.
[97] ILC, State Responsibility – Comments and Observations Received by Governments, UN Doc. A/CN.4/488 (1998), Comment to Article 20 by Denmark on behalf of the Nordic Countries, p. 123; Comment to Article 20 by Germany, pp. 123 f.
[98] Economides, "Content of the Obligation," p. 377.
[99] Crawford, "State Responsibility," p. 227.

preventive connotation – the duty to diligently prevent environmental harm or the duty to diligently prevent terrorist activities, for instance. Determining the temporal dimension of an internationally wrongful act is thus of crucial importance when it comes to establishing state responsibility, which is also mirrored in several ICJ decisions that involved preventive obligations.

Defining the exact moment in which an international obligation is breached was among the core issues the ICJ addressed in its Genocide Convention case of 2007. The Court found that the Convention required states to take active steps in preventing genocide and that

> [i]t is at the time when commission of the prohibited act ... begins that the breach of an obligation of prevention occurs.... However, if neither genocide nor any of the other acts listed in Article III of the Convention are ultimately carried out, then a State that omitted to act when it could have done so cannot be held responsible a posteriori, since the event did not happen which, under the rule set out above, must occur for there to be a violation of the obligation to prevent.[100]

A similar distinction had already been drawn by the Court in the Gabčíkovo-Nagymaros Project case, where it held that preparatory actions "are not to be confused with the act or offence itself" and could not be qualified as wrongful acts themselves.[101] How the Court understood the obligations contained in the Genocide Convention is thus very close to Ago's obligations to prevent. Ultimately, this reading of obligations to prevent rather resembles obligations of result, though in a negative manner. The obligation is breached if the unwelcome result is not prevented.[102]

While the Court's cautious judgment has to be read with the exceptionally grave nature of genocide in mind, it still prompted criticism for applying preventive obligations in a way that stymies their effective enforcement. Though the Court had decidedly rejected the idea that a preventive obligation "only come[s] into being when perpetration of genocide commences" and would rather "arise at the instant that the

---

[100] ICJ, Case Concerning the Application of the Convention on the Prevention and Punishment of the Crime of Genocide (*Bosnia and Herzegovina* v. *Serbia and Montenegro*), Judgment of 26 February 2007, ICJ Reports 2007, 43, paras. 221 f.

[101] ICJ, Case Concerning the Gabčíkovo-Nagymaros Project (*Hungary* v. *Slovakia*), Judgment of 25 September 1997, ICJ Reports 1997, 7, para. 79.

[102] Rüdiger Wolfrum, "Obligations of Result versus Obligations of Conduct," in Mahnoush Arsanjani et al. (eds.), *Looking to the Future* (Leiden: Martinus Nijhoff, 2011), p. 381.

State learns of, or should normally have learned of, the existence of a serious risk that genocide will be committed," states could only be held responsible where genocide actually occurred.[103] Essentially, this means that states could be acting contrary to their international obligations – possibly even for a long period of time – and still could not be held responsible until after harm actually occurred. Potentially affected states would be left with no means to sanction ongoing failure to take preventive measures downright contradicting the very purpose of prevention.

c. The ILC's Proposal on Preventive Obligations

Obviously, the main purpose of preventive obligations is to prevent an unwelcome event from occurring. If states are not held liable until such an event eventually occurs, preventive obligations would not stimulate compliance. Potential victim states would be barred from sanctioning even ongoing failure to take preventive steps.

The ILC's final draft, though, is more or less silent on the categorization of different types of obligations. The Articles in their final version make no mention of obligations of conduct or obligations of result. The distinction is only addressed in the commentary to Article 12, acknowledging that such twofold classification is helpful to determine whether an obligation was breached, but does not consider the distinction as bearing any "specific or direct consequences as far as the present articles are concerned."[104] Article 14 of the final draft provides further insight into the temporal dimension of an internationally wrongful act. The commentary explains that the existence and duration of a breach are primarily determined by the specific content of each individual obligation. Paragraph 3 of Article 14 supports – at least in parts – Ago's original proposal by stating that obligations to prevent are violated only where the apprehended event has actually materialized. Notwithstanding, the Commentary reemphasizes that to differentiate between mere preparatory acts and actual wrongful acts was a matter of "judgment and degree" impossible "to determine in advance by the use of any particular formula."[105] Summarizing these arguments, there is thus no a priori classification of international obligations based on their character, which would determine in a general manner when and how a breach occurs. Given that "obligations of conduct and result do not

---

[103] ICJ, Genocide Convention Case, para. 431.
[104] ILC DARS, Commentary to Article 12, para. 11.
[105] ILC DARS, Commentary to Article 14, para. 13.

present a dichotomy but rather a spectrum,"[106] finding abstract categories that comprise any form of obligations is a futile task. It seems more auspicious to consider the concrete content of each obligation in order to determine the legal consequences of a breach. While the ICJ and the ILC both seem to assume that responsibility for failure to comply with preventive obligations could only be established if the harmful event was not prevented, much criticism has been voiced against this position, as it basically deprives other states from taking action before they suffer from harm. Countermeasures and other responses are only justified if failure to take preventive steps in itself amounts to an internationally wrongful act. When analyzing the application of due diligence obligations in various fields of international law, how and when a breach of such an obligation can be established and how sufficient compliance with preventive obligations can be ensured is thus an important aspect to consider.

5. Complicity

A final differentiation that needs to be made is the one between failure to exercise due diligence and complicity, two concepts confused already by the Claims Commissions[107] and subject to even further misconception in recent debates. Complicity is itself a controversially discussed concept of state responsibility but found its way in the ILC's final draft, where Article 16 provides for responsibility based on aiding and abetting another state in the commission of an internationally wrongful act. It has been recognized as forming part of customary international law on several occasions.[108] Complicity is characterized by an "essentially derivative nature"[109] in that it establishes responsibility by tying the conduct of an accomplice actor to the wrongful act committed by a principal actor. Albeit the accomplice is held responsible for its own wrongful contribution, the principal's wrongful conduct has to be established beforehand. To differentiate between complicity and failure to exercise due diligence, however, has proved complicated with respect to both complicity in state conduct (a.) and complicity in non-state conduct (b.).

[106] Crawford, "State Responsibility," p. 223.
[107] See Chapter 3, III, 2, c.
[108] See, notably, ICJ, Genocide Convention Case, para. 420.
[109] Miles Jackson, *Complicity in International Law* (Oxford: Oxford University Press, 2015), p. 127.

a. Complicity in Wrongful Conduct of Other States

The ICJ's Corfu Channel case is often cited as the first decision on the concept of due diligence in modern international jurisprudence. Often forgotten in this context is the fact that – among other issues – the Court was actually confronted with the question on how to draw the line between state conduct amounting to complicity and state failure to take diligent measures. In its memorial, the United Kingdom had firmly claimed that "[t]he responsibility of Albania rests, firstly, upon a *direct complicity* in the existence of the minefield which is created by her knowledge of it, whether or not she laid it or connived in its actual laying."[110] Failure to exercise due diligence serves more as a backup claim in that the responsibility of Albania secondly "rests upon a failure ... to discharge an imperative international duty to notify the existence of this dangerous minefield."[111] In the course of the proceedings, the United Kingdom made several substantive attempts to establish Albania's complicity in the laying of the minefield by referring to strong ties between the governments of Albania and Yugoslavia, with the latter allegedly being responsible for the minefield's creation. Interestingly, however, the British memorial only rarely uses the term complicity explicitly but rather refers to "knowledge or connivance." Accountability for complicity thus seems to be derived from mere positive knowledge. As we will see later on, it is particularly this line of reasoning – the equation of acquiescence in another actor's wrongful conduct with complicity – where the concepts of complicity and due diligence most strikingly overlap.

It is well known, however, that – at least with regard to Albania's alleged complicity – the Court did not follow the arguments brought forward by the United Kingdom. Why it refrained from doing so becomes clearer when examining two of the major procedural and evidentiary obstacles related to the concept of complicity: the necessary involvement of third parties and the establishment of intent and knowledge as inherently subjective elements.

First, the derivative nature of complicity requires wrongful conduct of the principal agent in order to hold the accomplice accountable. A successful claim based on complicity inevitably implicates

---

[110] ICJ, Corfu Channel Case, Part II, Documents of the Written Proceedings, Memorial submitted by the UK, para. 94, emphasis added.
[111] Ibid.

a conclusive statement on the principal's responsibility.[112] In particular, in proceedings before the ICJ, this is a delicate proposition to make – for it is among the most fundamental principles of the Court's Statute that it abstains from resolving disputes between states that have not consented to the Court's jurisdiction.[113] Being barred from ruling on Yugoslavia's responsibility might have been an important incentive for the Court to focus on Albania's failure to exercise due diligence, which could well be considered regardless of Yugoslavia's alleged involvement.

Second, the subjective criteria of knowledge and intent are further hurdles to raising a successful complicity claim. Mere knowledge on behalf of the accomplice state is generally deemed insufficient as is already apparent from the Claims Commissions' jurisprudence.[114] The ICJ did not reach a definite conclusion on whether even specific intent was necessary to establish complicity in its *Genocide Convention* case. It did rule, however, that "the conduct of an organ or a person furnishing aid or assistance ... cannot be treated as complicity ... unless *at the least* that organ or person acted knowingly, that is to say, in particular, was aware of the specific intent ... of the principal perpetrator,"[115] which could only be inferred from the accomplice having "full knowledge of the facts."[116] In any case – whether complicity presupposes positive knowledge or intent – both elements call for evidence on inherently subjective components. As we will see later on, it is one of the procedural "advantages" of due diligence that claims can be based on constructive knowledge.

In spite of these procedural and evidentiary burdens, however, the fact that complicity of one state in another state's wrongful conduct principally constitutes an independent ground for the latter state's responsibility is undisputed. The same cannot be said of complicity in non-state conduct.

---

[112] Olivier Corten and Pierre Klein, "The Limits of Complicity as a Ground for Responsibility," in Karin Bannelier et al. (eds.), *The ICJ and the Evolution of International Law* (London: Routledge, 2012), p. 322.

[113] See Article 36 of the Statute and the Court's interpretation thereof in – for instance – Case of the Monetary Gold Removed from Rome in 1943 (*Italy* v. *France, UK, USA*), Judgment (Preliminary Question) of 15 June 1954, ICJ Reports 1954, 19, p. 32; Case Concerning East Timor (*Portugal* v. *Australia*), Judgment of 30 June 1995, ICJ Reports 1995, 90, paras. 34 f.

[114] See Chapter 3, III, 2, c.

[115] ICJ, Genocide Convention Case, para. 421, emphasis added.

[116] ICJ, Genocide Convention Case, para. 432.

b. Complicity in Non-State Conduct

While complicity was initially applied only to situations in which one subject of international law willfully assisted another, it is now also engaged in constellations involving non-state actors, even though the latter are not qualified as subjects of international law. Particularly, the derivative character of the complicity concept, however, renders the application to such scenarios problematic.

aa. Complicity in Case of Individual Criminal Responsibility In the Genocide Convention case, the ICJ consulted Article 16 of the ILC Draft when discussing the responsibility of Serbia and Montenegro for the conduct of the military forces of the Republic of Srpska – technically a non-state actor. The Court was yet reluctant to elaborate on whether the concept of complicity was generally applicable to the assistance of non-state actors. It simply employed complicity as an independent ground for attributing the Srpska forces' conduct,[117] whereas the systematic foundation for this reasoning remained unclear. That the judgment hardly shed any light on the derivative character of complicity was also due to its particular legal context: the Court expounded on Serbia's complicity in those acts of the Srpska forces, which amounted to genocide. Genocide, however, is among the international crimes for which individuals can be held accountable under international law. Even though the case did not concern complicity by one state in the wrongful acts of another, it still concerned the complicity of Serbia in behavior that – while committed by non-state actors – was criminalized as a matter of international law. Outside of international criminal law, however, direct obligations on behalf of non-state actors have not been recognized. Principally, there is thus no wrongful act for a state to be complicit in.

Notwithstanding, the Court's reasoning was followed by several incidents in which either direct reference to Article 16 was made or accountability was established on the basis of complicity in non-state actions – most often, where states aided or abetted non-state actors in their wrongful conduct when this assistance did not amount to effective control and hence failed to satisfy the ordinary criteria for attribution. With generally high standards for attribution, using the concept of complicity is thus another attempt to broaden the scope of state responsibility for harmful private conduct. Since this is among the key purposes of the due diligence concept as well, it becomes even clearer why both concepts are so closely

---
[117] ICJ, Genocide Convention Case, paras. 419 ff.

intertwined. In contrast to due diligence obligations, however, complicity was often engaged as an alternative way to attribute non-state conduct to a state.

bb. Complicity as Ground for Attribution Reference to the terms and language of complicity was made on several occasions, in particular with the "overall control" test developed by the ICTY. When the Court elaborated on the relationship between paramilitary groups and Serbian state organs, it pointed to financial or operational support that does not meet the effective control threshold but is akin to aiding and abetting.[118] The standard of "overall control" thus resembles complicity to a notable extent. Notwithstanding, a systematic difference between those approaches should not be omitted: whereas both take state support for private actions as a starting point, the original purpose of complicity is to establish the responsibility of the accomplice for its supportive actions, in addition to the principal's responsibility. In contrast, the "overall control" standard seeks to attribute non-state conduct on the basis that it was supported or facilitated by a state. Complicity traditionally produces at least two subjects responsible for committing a wrong, whereas overall control makes the controlling state the single bearer of international responsibility.

A similar approach is followed by the IACtHR, which found attributable conduct where the state was accused of "support or toleration of infringement of the rights."[119] The Court blamed wrongful private conduct on states, where state involvement did not amount to effective control but still took the form of active support. It even explicitly held that these rules on attribution formed *lex specialis* to the principles of state responsibility as laid out in the ILC's draft.[120] At least the IACtHR has thus also recognized a complicit relationship to allow for attribution. The general standards for attribution have become equally relaxed in the context of counterterrorism efforts.[121] In light of

---

[118] ITCY, Trial Chamber, *Prosecutor* v. *Kordić and Cerkez*, Judgment of 26 February 2001, IT-95-14/2, para. 115.
[119] IACtHR, *Case of the White Van, Paniagua Morales et al.* v. *Guatemala*, Judgment of 8 March 1988, Series C, No. 37, para. 91; IACtHR, *Case of the Mapiripán Massacre, 49 Victims and Their Next Kin* v. *Colombia*, Judgment of 15 September 2005, Series C, No. 134, para. 120.
[120] IACtHR, *Case of the Mapiripán Massacre, 49 Victims and Their Next Kin* v. *Colombia*, Judgment of 15 September 2005, Series C, No. 134, para. 107.
[121] Helmut Philipp Aust, *Complicity and the Law of State Responsibility* (Cambridge: Cambridge University Press, 2011), pp. 120 ff.

devastating attacks, due diligence was considered inadequate to reflect a state's wrongdoing – in particular where the role of states is insofar aggravated, as it is not limited to lack of preventive action but takes on a more active form. How the concepts of complicity and due diligence have become intertwined in the context of counterterrorism efforts will be discussed later on.[122] For now, it will suffice to begin by summarizing the main reasons for which both concepts are so difficult to differentiate.

cc. Complicity versus Due Diligence: Where the Confusion Comes From
The concept of complicity in non-state conduct and the concept of due diligence are both set in the same context: due to high thresholds of attribution, many forms of state involvement in harmful private activities are not covered by the rules on state responsibility, as laid out in the Draft Articles. While due diligence has long been accepted as grounds for responsibility where states failed to take adequate preventive measures, complicity only came into play where states took a more active stance toward harmful non-state conduct. Active support and more intense forms of involvement, so the argument goes, were graver violations of international law and should not be treated the same as mere failure to diligently prevent.[123] As we have seen, this has tempted several authors to argue that a new secondary norm has developed, providing for attribution if states knowingly support or facilitate harmful private conduct.[124]

Yet complicity and due diligence are not mutually exclusive alternatives. In fact, where a successful claim of complicity is raised, this necessarily entails a simultaneous violation of due diligence obligations.[125] A state that actively participated in an internationally wrongful act logically failed to diligently prevent this act from occurring.[126] In both the Corfu Channel and the Genocide Convention case, the applicant party first accused the respondent of being complicit in wrongful conduct, while failure to prevent that conduct was used as

---

[122] See Chapter 5.2, III, 2, b.
[123] Daniele Amoroso, "Moving towards Complicity as a Criterion of Attribution of Private Conducts" (2011) 24 *Leiden Journal of International Law* 989–1007 at 992.
[124] Amoroso, "Complicity as a Criterion of Attribution," 990; Eduardo Savarese, "Issues of Attribution to States of Private Acts: Between the Concept of De Facto Organs and Complicity" (2006) 15 *Italian Yearbook of International Law Online* 111–133 at 111 ff.
[125] Corten and Klein, "Limits of Complicity," 333; Kimberley Trapp, *State Responsibility for International Terrorism* (Oxford: Oxford University Press, 2011), p. 144.
[126] Jackson, "Complicity in International Law," p. 131.

a substitute argument, indicating that the latter is, as a minus, entailed in the former. Recent state practice and scholarly debates have further complicated a distinction through the concept of acquiescence. In particular, where states were confronted with risks posed by terrorist groups on their territory, complete failure to take preventive measures – and thus entirely omissive conduct – has been qualified as complicity. Where states completely refrained from taking any preventive steps even in spite of a grave risk for potentially devastating harm, attributing the conduct and thereby making the state the immediate bearer of responsibility seems justified in the eyes of many observers.[127]

(1) Why the Distinction Is Relevant It is even more difficult to distinguish the failure to exercise due diligence and complicity through acquiescence. And, yet, the distinction remains important: As we have seen, complicity is used to render non-state conduct attributable. Consequently, any harm caused is seen as harm caused directly by the complicit state. In contrast, where a state is held responsible for failure to exercise due diligence, the wrongful conduct is not attributed. Qualifying conduct as complicity therefore not only carries greater symbolic weight but also has a significant impact on the amount of reparations likely to be awarded.[128] In order to shed some light on how to distinguish responsibility for complicity from responsibility for failure to exercise due diligence, it is thus necessary to discuss parameters that separate one concept from the other. As indicated previously, this is first and foremost the criterion of knowledge.

(2) Distinction Based on the "Knowledge" Criterion Both the concept of complicity and the concept of due diligence contain subjective elements. What is distinctive about the concept of complicity, however, is that the subjective element in the form of *willful* aiding and abetting needs to be positively established. For state conduct to be qualified as complicity, it is indispensable that accomplice states have at least positive knowledge of the principal's actions.[129] In contrast, failure to exercise due diligence can be assumed, as soon as a state should have known of harmful conduct.[130] In the *Genocide Convention* decision, the ICJ

---

[127] See in greater detail in Chapter 5.3, III, 2, b.
[128] Vladyslav Lanovoy, *Complicity and Its Limits in the Law of International Responsibility* (Oxford: Hart, 2016), pp. 323 f.
[129] Jackson, "Complicity in International Law," pp. 159 f.
[130] Kimberley Trapp, "Of Dissonance and Silence: State Responsibility in the Bosnia Genocide Case" (2015) 62 *NILR* 243–257 at 252.

V. CONFUSION OF CONCEPTS

considered it sufficient for a breach of the duty to prevent that "even though it had no certainty ... the State was aware, or should have been aware, of the serious danger that acts of genocide would be committed."[131] Complicity would always presuppose "some *positive action* be undertaken to furnish aid or assistance."[132] Plainly opposing this verdict, some authors argue that where states intentionally omitted what they are supposed to do, they would become complicit in the harm they failed to prevent.[133] When (and if at all) a state's failure to respond to a known risk becomes so grave as to impute complicity rather than mere failure to prevent is open to debate and will be taken up in the substantial analysis of due diligence in the context of counterterrorism efforts and human rights protection.

For the moment, it suffices to summarize that complicity was originally designed to hold states accountable for aiding and abetting other actors in conduct that is illicit under international law. Increasingly, the concept is now applied when states actively support improper private actions where an important differentiation needs to be drawn: holding states responsible on the basis of complicity is consistent with the traditional concept where states become complicit in non-state conduct that is wrongful under international law – namely in international crimes. Complicity is yet frequently referred to in situations where states actively support harmful private conduct, even though this conduct is not in itself regulated by international law. In those constellations, complicity is most often considered to allow for the attribution of the wrongful conduct to the state, as due diligence standards are deemed ill-equipped to cover graver forms of state involvement – in particular, willful support or tolerance of harmful activities.[134] This categorization has become increasingly flawed in recent scholarly debate. Some authors argue that foreseeability of harm – actually a distinct component of the due diligence standard – should suffice to accuse a state of complicity.[135] Even mere acquiescence, so they maintain, could amount to complicity where the omission was willful – though whether a corresponding rule of customary international law has emerged seems doubtful. The ICJ, in particular, remains reluctant to find states responsible of complicity.

---

[131] ICJ, Genocide Convention Case, para. 432.
[132] ICJ, Genocide Convention Case, para. 432.
[133] See, for instance, Jackson, "Complicity in International Law," pp. 210 f.
[134] Jackson, "Complicity in International Law," p. 197.
[135] See, for instance, Lanovoy, "Complicity and Its Limits," p. 100.

VI. Summary

Although due diligence was initially among the central issues of the codification process on state responsibility, it has not made its way into the final draft. Partly, this is due to the fact that the ILC refrained from regulating state responsibility for entirely private conduct. Moreover and more importantly, defining a standard as flexible and broad as the due diligence standard comes with enormous dogmatic difficulties. While due diligence obligations are applied in various fields of international law, there is no consensus on what the standard actually entails.

By distinguishing it from similar concepts of state responsibility, the foregoing section has helped narrow down the distinct features of an international due diligence standard. It revealed that failure to meet due diligence obligations might stem from omissive as well as commissive conduct, or even a combination of both forms. Besides, state responsibility based on failure to exercise due diligence does not presuppose negligence on behalf of states. Content-wise, the most significant overlap exists between the concepts of due diligence and complicity, since both are employed as alternative means to establish state responsibility, where the high thresholds of attribution are not met in case of harmful private conduct. While complicity had originally been equated with active aiding or abetting, it is increasingly applied where states remain inactive toward well-known risks of illicit private actions. However, the procedural hurdles for establishing positive knowledge and deliberate passivity are particularly high, which is why recourse is often taken to the due diligence standard, the prerequisites of which are easier to prove. Most importantly, meeting the constructive knowledge threshold is sufficient to establish state responsibility based on failure to exercise due diligence. There are thus distinct features distinguishing the due diligence standard from the concept of complicity.

With respect to the ILC's dogmatic work, the twofold approach separating different forms of responsibility is no longer pursued by the Commission. Due diligence obligations are thus not limited to acts not prohibited by international law but may arise in any area of international law. The attempt to differentiate between various forms of obligations has not entered the final draft either. While a categorical approach toward different forms of obligations might indeed hinder an effective implementation, separating obligations of conduct from obligations of result helps to detect when and how an international obligation is breached. When determining whether a state has breached its international obligations, it is indispensable to analyze as precisely as possible what that state was actually required to do. It is exactly at this point that the vague concept of due diligence has its shortcomings. To a certain extent, this lack of legal clarity is inherent in a notion as broad and flexible as due diligence. Notwithstanding, concretizing the elements of due diligence in a more precise manner is not an entirely desperate undertaking. While the standard of due diligence depends on the circumstances of each individual case, it still entails common components, which can be outlined in a general manner. The following section will take a closer look at those components in order to more precisely describe what an international standard of due diligence entails.

4

The Components of the Due Diligence Standard

I. Introductory Remarks

Step by step, the application of due diligence duties expanded over various areas of international law.[1] However, given the fact that the different sub-branches of international law greatly vary, there is no uniform diligence: "The due diligence principle means, or at least can be construed to mean, everything to everyone and nothing to no one."[2] And, yet, early state practice and jurisprudence reveal the character of due diligence as a general standard against which to measure state conduct. Entailed in this standard are the duty to diligently prevent harm and the duty to diligently sanction harm, should it occur nonetheless.[3] And while due diligence standards develop a distinct character when applied to particular fields of international law, they still encompass prevalent characteristics.[4] Analyzing these common features will reveal both general problems inherent in due diligence obligations as well as their

---

[1] ILA Study Group on Due Diligence in International Law, First Report of 7 March 2014, available online at www.ila-hq.org/index.php/study-groups; and on the historical development, Sarah Heathcote, "State Omissions and Due Diligence," in Karine Bannelier et al. (eds.), *The ICJ and the Evolution of International Law* (London: Routledge, 2012), pp. 305 f.; Joanna Bourke-Martignoni, "The History and Development of the Due Diligence Standard in International Law and Its Role in the Protection of Women against Violence," in Carin Benninger-Budel (ed.), *Due Diligence and Its Application to Protect Women from Violence* (Leiden: Martinus Nijhoff, 2008), p. 49.

[2] Robert Barnidge, *Non-State Actors and Terrorism. Applying the Law of State Responsibility and the Due Diligence Principle* (The Hague: TMC Asser, 2008), p. 139.

[3] Awalou Ouedraogo, "La Due Diligence en Droit International: De la Règle de la Neutralité au Principe Général" (2012) 42 *Revue Générale de Droit* 641–683 at 681 f.

[4] ILA Study Group on Due Diligence, Second Report of July 2016, available online at www.ila-hq.org/index.php/study-groups, p. 47.

potential for enhancing the effectiveness of state responsibility. To this end, the following section draws a general framework of due diligence obligations that will render the vague notion of due diligence more approachable. Later on, the application of due diligence duties in several branches of international law will be analyzed along this analytical framework in order to identify specific problems. Finding similarities and differences will help evaluate the general potential of due diligence obligations as a concept of state responsibility and provide guidance for their application in the field of human rights protection.

As we have seen, due diligence obligations commonly entail that once a state has knowledge of a certain risk, it is under an obligation to employ all reasonable means at its disposal to prevent harm or to mitigate its consequences. Three major components can be derived from this concise definition: The first is knowledge, which is often referred to as *foreseeability*. A state may only be held accountable for failure to exercise due diligence if it knew or ought to have known of harmful conduct. How knowledge as an inherently subjective concept may be established and what problems could arise in relation hereto shall be considered first (II.). The second is capacities: states are merely obliged to take such measures as their resources allow for. Whether the same standard of care applies to all states irrespective of their individual situation or whether diverging administrative, technical, and financial capacities should be taken into account are thus addressed next (III.). The third is reasonableness: what factors determine what a reasonable course of action consists of and whether this standard is to be determined in an objective or a subjective manner gives ground for further debate (IV.). In this context, the procedural aspects of due diligence, namely the allocation of the burden of proof, also require some remarks.

II. Knowledge

Failure to exercise due diligence may only be established if states had knowledge of a certain risk of harm. As we have seen already, the proof of knowledge as an inherently *subjective element* involves procedural difficulties that are particularly hard to overcome.[5] This is already the case when establishing knowledge of one single individual, but it is all the more difficult where a multitude of actors is involved. As state action is composed of a plurality of acts, establishing positive state knowledge is an arduous task.

---

[5] See Chapter 3, V, 2, and 5.

1. Positive Knowledge

In order to establish positive knowledge on behalf of a state, it is not only necessary to identify which actors were involved and to what extent overall knowledge of the relevant circumstances also needs to be shown – a difficult task, which is even further complicated by the exclusivity of territorial control hindering the applicant state in international proceedings from obtaining information about the decision-making process within another state's administration. Against this background, positive knowledge is hardly ever affirmed in international proceedings. Among the few exceptions are scenarios in which the harmful event has already occurred, and states are expected to diligently mitigate the consequences. This includes scenarios in which the harmful event was directly reported to state organs, or happened in their presence, or was of such massive scale that it could not have remained unnoticed.[6] Other than that, however, establishing positive knowledge presents a procedural hurdle that is rarely overcome.

2. Constructive Knowledge

However, states may also breach their due diligence obligations if they ought to have known of harmful activities, which is commonly described as foreseeability.[7] Due to their exclusive territorial sovereignty, states are best equipped to identify risks stemming from their territory. Imposing an obligation to acquire knowledge of such risks does not put an improper strain on states either, given the fact that they have superior knowledge and access to relevant information.[8] It is for this reason that states are expected to identify "reasonably discoverable threats"[9] and assess the potential for harm arising out of perilous activities on their territory.

---

[6] Illustrative of those exceptions are, for instance, Mexico/United States General Claims Commission, *Thomas O. Youmans (US) v. United Mexican States*, Decision of 23 November 1926, RIAA IV 110 (113); Mexico/Great Britain Claims Commission, Mexico City Bombardment Claims, Decision of 15 February 1930, reprinted in: 25 AJIL at 769.

[7] Mexico/United States General Claims Commission, *Louise O. Canahl (US) v. United Mexican States*, Decision of 15 October 1928, RIAA IV 389 (389); Committee Against Torture, General Comment No. 2 on the Implementation of Article 2 by States Parties, UN Doc. CAT/C/GC/2 (2008), para. 28.

[8] See also Kristen Boon, "Are Control Tests Fit for the Future? The Slippage Problem in Attribution Doctrine," (2014) 15 *Melbourne Journal of International Law* 330–377 at 369 ff.

[9] Kimberley Trapp, *State Responsibility for International Terrorism* (Oxford: Oxford University Press, 2011), p. 66.

II. KNOWLEDGE

a. An Obligation to Acquire Knowledge

To a certain extent, the constructive knowledge threshold thus entails an obligation to actively acquire knowledge and to monitor potentially harmful activities on a state's territory.[10] Judge Azevedo's opinion to the Corfu Channel case, for instance, elaborates in greater detail on Albania's obligation to place lookout posts at those spots on the coast, which were most suitable to monitor the area,[11] hinting at a concrete obligation to acquire knowledge. However, while establishing constructive knowledge is generally deemed easier than establishing positive knowledge, no clear-cut parameter indicates under which circumstances states are expected to obtain knowledge of potentially harmful events. The threshold for constructive knowledge is mostly contingent on the circumstances of each individual case. Notwithstanding, the following section will illustrate that several common elements can be derived from state practice and international jurisprudence.

b. Determination by Objective Factors

First, it is important to notice that the mere fact of a risk emanating from a state's territory is not sufficient to show that this state had positive or constructive knowledge, and it does not generally shift the burden of proof either.[12] There is, however, a clear tendency to define the ought-to-have-known threshold on the basis of objective criteria – in particular, the likelihood and seriousness of potential harm.[13] Remote or unforeseeable consequences do not suffice to meet the constructive knowledge threshold.[14] However, international concern expressed with regard to a certain risk might well increase the level of awareness that is expected of

---

[10] ILA Study Group on Due Diligence, Second Report of July 2016, p. 12; Rashida Manjoo, "State Responsibility to Act with Due Diligence in the Elimination of Violence against Women" (2013) 2 *International Human Rights Law Review* 240–265 at 246.

[11] ICJ, The Corfu Channel Case (*UK v. Albania*), Judgment of 9 April 1949, ICJ Reports 1949, 4, Dissenting Opinion by Judge Azevedo, p. 93.

[12] ICJ, Corfu Channel Case, p. 18; see, however, p. 44 of the Separate Opinion by Judge Alvarez, where he states that "every State is considered as having known, or as having a duty to have known, of prejudicial acts committed in parts of its territory where local authorities are installed; . . . [this is] the consequence of its sovereignty. If the State alleges that it was unaware of these acts . . . it must prove that this was the case."

[13] Mexico/United States General Claims Commission, *The Home Insurance Company (US) v. United Mexican States*, Decision of 31 March 1926, RIAA IV 48 (52), para 17.

[14] See, for instance, Arbitral Tribunal (Great Britain/United States), *Home Frontier and Foreign Missionary Society of the United Brethren in Christ (US) v. Great Britain*, Decision of 18 December 1920, RIAA VI 42 (43).

states.[15] If warnings had been issued or information on potential risks was prevalent and easily available, states will generally be expected to obtain knowledge.[16] Already the Alabama Arbitration Tribunal found Britain obliged to take diligent preventive steps, as repeated warnings had been notified.[17] Where factual circumstances show a significant risk or the international community alerted to such, states may thus not claim ignorance of the facts.[18] The ICJ held in the Corfu Channel case: "From all the facts and observations mentioned above, the Court draws the conclusion that the laying of the minefield ... could not have been accomplished without the knowledge of the Albanian Government."[19] Notably, the Court relied on objective criteria alone – such as the location of look-out posts Albania had near to the Channel – and did not elaborate on the subjective knowledge of Albanian state organs. In like manner, the Court found in the Genocide Convention case that the factual circumstances were such that "the Belgrade authorities ... could hardly have been unaware of the serious risk."[20] Even in the absence of proof of positive knowledge, it is thus sufficient to show objective criteria that allow for the conclusion that the state at least ought to have known of the risk in question. The ICJ expressly recognized the difficulties a state may face in producing evidence on circumstances on another state's territory. While refusing to shift the burden of proof, the Court nonetheless allows for "a more liberal recourse to inferences of fact and circumstantial evidence" as long as "*no room* for reasonable doubt" remains.[21]

Summing up the previous notes, the knowledge element is easier to establish in the context of due diligence obligations compared to other concepts of state responsibility. Unlike complicity, which presupposes positive knowledge on behalf of the state, it is sufficient to affirm

---

[15] Trapp, "State Responsibility for International Terrorism," p. 69.
[16] Joachim Wolf, *Die Haftung der Staaten für Privatpersonen nach Völkerrecht* (Berlin: Duncker & Humblot, 1997), p. 242.
[17] Alabama Claims (*USA* v. *Great Britain*), Award of 14 September 1872, reprinted in John Bassett Moore, *History and Digest of the International Arbitrations to Which the US Has Been a Party* (Washington, DC: Government Printing Office, 1898), volume I, chapter XIV: The Geneva Arbitration, 495–682 at 655.
[18] Joachim Wolf, "Die gegenwärtige Entwicklung der Lehre über die völkerrechtliche Verantwortlichkeit der Staaten" (1983) 43 *ZaöRV* 481–536 at 524.
[19] ICJ, Corfu Channel Case, p. 22.
[20] ICJ, Case concerning the Application of the Convention on the Prevention and Punishment of the Crime of Genocide (*Bosnia and Herzegovina* v. *Serbia and Montenegro*), Judgment of 26 February 2007, ICJ Reports 2007, 43, para. 436.
[21] ICJ, Corfu Channel Case, p. 18; see, for a more detailed analysis, Mojtaba Kazazi, *Burden of Proof and Relates Issues* (The Hague: Kluwer Law, 1996), pp. 86 f.

constructive knowledge. While there is no general presumption for constructive knowledge based on territorial control alone, the evidentiary approach toward constructive knowledge is much more lenient. Constructive knowledge can be derived from objective circumstances or the fact that warnings and information have been distributed. Though states are not required to have all-comprising knowledge, they are expected to monitor risks and to acquire knowledge of harmful conduct on their territory. The procedural hurdles for establishing constructive knowledge, therefore, are relatively lower compared to positive knowledge. How its threshold is applied to different fields of international law will be discussed in greater detail in the following chapter.

III. Capacities

More controversial is the question of whether a state's capacity has to be taken into account when determining the standard of care, or rather, a uniform standard has to apply to all states. The problem of capacities stems from the legal principle of *ad impossibilia nemo tenetur*, meaning that no one has to perform the impossible.[22] When defining standards of care, the degree of diligence should not exceed the actual capacities of states.[23] While the threshold of knowledge predetermines whether there even is an obligation of diligent conduct in the first place, questions of incapacity shape the specific standard of care once such an obligation is found to exist. In domestic law, standards of care are usually based on what could be reasonably expected of the average person in a given situation. Yet, this assumption cannot be transferred to the field of public international law without adjustment. Between citizens of a state, there is at least a certain minimum commonality of means. In contrast, the administrative, financial, and technical capabilities of states significantly vary. There is no average state that could serve as an adequate yardstick in order to determine international standards of care. So how do varying capacities alter the standard of due diligence? May a state claim that it did not have an adequate institutional framework or sufficient financial and technical means to effectively control private conduct? Do developing

---

[22] See, for an explicit reference to this principle, Mixed Commission established under the Convention concluded between the United States of America and Mexico, *Case of Salvador Prats v. USA*, Decision of 4 July 1868, Opinions of the Commissioners, RIAA XXIX 187 (196).

[23] Cedric Ryngaert, "State Responsibility and Non-State Actors," in Math Noortmann et al. (eds.), *Non-State Actors in International Law* (Oxford: Hart, 2015), p. 181.

countries generally have to adhere to lower standards of care than industrial countries? And, are states under an obligation to actively enhance their capacities or to seek international assistance in order to fulfill their obligations?

Given these many controversial questions, it comes as little surprise that discrepant capacities were vigorously discussed already in early due diligence jurisprudence. In the Alabama Arbitration, the United States argued that the degree of diligence should be proportionate to the "dignity and strength of the power which is to exercise it."[24] A position later followed by several arbitral decisions and even included in international treaties.[25] From the start, however, important distinctions were drawn between different forms of capacities. The Alabama Arbitration Tribunal expressly stated that the British government could not be absolved from its responsibility with regard to deficiencies in domestic law,[26] which marks an important contrast: in determining adequate standards of care, institutional capacity (1.) on the one hand and territorial and financial resources (2.) on the other have to be treated separately.

1. Institutional Capacities

As we have seen earlier, the duty to establish and maintain an institutional framework enabling states to prevent and mitigate harm forms an important element of states' obligation to protect.[27] It was even considered an obligation of result in the sense that failure to acquire institutional capabilities would in itself amount to a violation of the international norm in question.[28] In general, inadequate administrative frameworks or insufficient domestic regulations cannot justify noncompliance with international obligations.[29] A lack of preventive

---

[24] Alabama Claims, pp. 572 f.
[25] For instance, see Convention XIII of 18 October 1907 concerning the Rights and Duties of Neutral Powers in Naval War, entered into force 26 January 1910, reprinted in 2 AJIL Supplement, 202–216.
[26] Alabama Claims, p. 656.
[27] See Chapter 3, III, 2, a.
[28] See, for instance, Riccardo Pisillo-Mazzeschi, "The Due Diligence Rule and the Nature of the International Responsibility of States" (1992) 35 *GYIL* 9–51 at 35, calling it "an 'absolute' obligation."
[29] ILA Study Group on Due Diligence, Second Report of July 2016, pp. 19 f.; and already Edwin Borchard, *The Diplomatic Protection of Citizens Abroad* 1915 (reprinted New York: Kraus, 1970), p. 214; Maurice Bourquin, "Crimes et Délits Contre la Sûreté des États Étrangers" (1927) 16 *RdC* 117–246 at 238.

regulations or institutions in domestic law does not lower the degree of diligence, either. Consequently, little deference to less developed states was paid with respect to institutional capacities.[30] States are under an obligation to establish and maintain a legal and administrative framework that provides for the effective implementation of their international obligations. Any deference to insufficient institutional capacities would create an incentive for states to exonerate themselves from their international duties by decreasing institutional capacities. Discouraging such evasion was clearly the approach followed by the Alabama Arbitration, which later found ample support by other Claims Commissions.[31]

Having in place a legislative and institutional framework to prevent harmful activities, however, is a matter quite different from having the capacity to put that institutional capacity into actual practice.[32] With regard to the territorial, financial, and technical capabilities of states, the drawing of definite conclusions proves less simple.

2. Territorial and Financial Capacities

Whether a dearth of territorial and/or financial capacities should affect the standard of care was a question raised yet not settled by the Claims Commissions and has been controversial ever since. Many scholars suggest that resources should be a relevant parameter in determining the required degree of diligence.[33] Particularly notable is Judge Krylov's dissenting opinion to the Corfu Channel decision, in which he argued that the scarce resources of Albania should be taken into account when delineating the expected standard of care. Even if Albania knew of potential threats, it would have been unable to

---

[30] Astrid Epiney, *Die völkerrechtliche Verantwortlichkeit von Staaten für rechtswidriges Verhalten im Zusammenhang mit Aktionen Privater* (Baden-Baden: Nomos, 1992), pp. 224 f.
[31] See, among many others, Mexico/United States General Claims Commission, *L. F. H. Neer and Pauline Neer (US) v. United Mexican States*, Decision of 15 October 1926, RIAA IV 60 (62).
[32] Trapp, "State Responsibility for International Terrorism," p. 71.
[33] See, for instance, Yoshifumi Tanaka, "Obligations and Liability of Sponsoring States concerning Activities in the Area" (2013) 60 *NILR* 205–230 at 211; Xue Hanqin, *Transboundary Damage in International Law* (Cambridge: Cambridge University Press, 2003), p. 164; Eduardo Jiménez de Aréchaga and Attila Tanzi, "International State Responsibility," in Mohammed Bedjaoui (ed.), *International Law: Achievements and Prospects* (Dordrecht: Martinus Nijhoff, 1991), p. 360.

effectively eliminate the source of harm.[34] In a similar manner, Special Rapporteur *García-Amador* was in favor of taking into account "the physical possibility of preventing ... with resources available to the State."[35] Indirectly, the issue of discrepant capacities was addressed in the ICJ's US Diplomatic and Consular Staff in Tehran judgment as well. The Court held Iran responsible for not intervening during the first phase of attacks since "the failure ... to take such steps was due to more than ... lack of appropriate means,"[36] implying that a lack of such means could indeed excuse a state's tardiness. In its Genocide Convention case, the ICJ further explained that states had a duty to employ "all means reasonably available to them" and "all measures ... which were within its powers."[37] It even qualified capacity as one of the predominant parameters when assessing whether a state had acted with due diligence.[38] Principally, varying capacities of states are thus relevant to the degree of due diligence. To what extent deference should be paid to lacking resources, however, is still subject to debate. In this context, an even finer distinction might be drawn between territorial capacities on the one hand and technical and financial capacities on the other.

a. Territorial Capacities

In the historical context of alien protection laws, impaired territorial capacities were concerned on a regular basis. Legal claims mostly revolved around the question of if and how far states could be held responsible for events occurring on parts of their territory that they did not fully control. Territorial capacities were often limited due to hardly accessible and sparsely populated terrain, strenuous climatic conditions, or sheer distance to government authorities. The inability of states to effectively oversee every remote part of their territory was soon taken into consideration when determining the degree of diligence that could be expected.

Some Commissions rejected an adjusted standard of care.[39] Other decisions, however, show greater willingness to take a dearth of territorial

---

[34] ICJ, Corfu Channel Case, Dissenting Opinion of Judge Krylov, p. 72.
[35] ILC, Sixth Report on International Responsibility by Special Rapporteur F. V. García-Amador, UN Doc A/CN.4/134 and Add. 1 (1961), Draft Article 7, Paragraph II, p. 47.
[36] ICJ, Case Concerning US Diplomatic and Consular Staff in Tehran (*USA* v. *Iran*), Judgment of 24 May 1980, ICJ Reports 1980, 3, para. 63.
[37] ICJ, Genocide Convention Case, para. 430.
[38] Ibid.
[39] See, for instance, Mexico/United States General Claims Commission, *Mrs. Elmer Elsworth Mead (US)* v. *United Mexican States*, Decision of 29 October 1930, RIAA IV 653 (654 f.).

III. CAPACITIES

capacity into account. In the *Buckingham* case, the Commission found that "no Government of a country, of the immense extent of the Mexican Republic ... can be expected to furnish adequate military protection to all the isolated [areas] scattered over the territory."[40] This is in line with the Arbitral Tribunal's decision in the *Home Frontier* case, confirming that, under the due diligence standard, there was no need to ensure an "omnipresence of forces."[41] Notwithstanding, a heightened standard of care was expected in areas where conflicts and tensions frequently occurred. If states knew of elevated security risks in a specific part of their territory, they were obliged to allocate intensified means of prevention.[42]

Given these many controversies, it is hardly surprising that territorial capacities were such a vigorously disputed issue before the Claims Commissions and remain controversial to this day. In its *Genocide Convention* case, the ICJ held that "capacity itself depends, among other things, on the geographical distance of the State concerned from the scene of the events."[43] Already in the Nicaragua judgment had the Court reached the conclusion that – due to geographical difficulties – Nicaragua had been unable to stop arms trading in remote border regions.[44] A similar approach was followed in the Armed Activities on the Territory of the Congo judgment, concluding that the Congolese government had not breached its due diligence obligations with respect to insurgent activities in an inaccessible area without government institutions.[45] The absence of effective territorial authority thus shapes the degree of diligence required of states without absolving them from their international duties. In particular, where harmful activities regularly occur, states are expected to make an effort to (re-)establish control.[46] Notably, this also implies that wherever states control territory – whether legally or not – they are bound by due diligence obligations.

---

[40] Great Britain/Mexico Claims Commission, *Leonor Buckingham v. United Mexican States*, Decision of 3 August 1931, RIAA V 286 (288).
[41] Arbitral Tribunal (Great Britain/US), *Home Frontier and Foreign Missionary Society of the United Brethren in Christ (US) v. Great Britain*, Decision of 18 December 1920, RIAA VI 42 (44).
[42] See, for instance, Mexico/United States General Claims Commission, *J. J. Boyd (US) v. United Mexican States*, Decision of 12 October 1928, RIAA IV 380 (380).
[43] ICJ, Genocide Convention Case, para 430.
[44] ICJ, Military and Paramilitary Activities in and against Nicaragua, para 147.
[45] ICJ, Armed Activities on the Territory of the Congo (*DR of the Congo* v. *Uganda*), Judgment of 19 December 2005, ICJ Reports 2005, 168, para. 301.
[46] Trapp, "State Responsibility for International Terrorism," p. 75.

b. Technical and Financial Capacities

Next to territorial capacities, the availability of technical and financial resources is an even more disputed parameter. Territorial capacity is inseparably linked to the question of whether states are able to effectively control a course of events at all. If, ultimately, a state has no authority over an area, regulating private conduct in that area shifts beyond its capabilities. A different scenario arises where states could theoretically take measures of prevention but fail to do so due to a lack of expertise and/or financial means. Such capacity problems emerge in all areas of international law but particularly so in fields interlinked with rapid technological developments – such as cyber or environmental law. Preventive measures in such areas require technical expertise and financial resources to an extent that many states neither possess nor have access to. Therefore, it is crucial to determine whether international standards of care depend on a state's financial capacities and whether states may deny responsibility if they claim to lack sufficient means. In this context, further difficulties arise when evaluating the allocation of resources if a state has to meet several obligations at the same time but lacks sufficient means to fulfill them all. Demanding a specific allocation and prioritization could well present too intrusive an interference with the domestic policy choices of a sovereign state.

There are thus good reasons to consider financial and technical shortcomings, and many authors suggest adjusting the degree of diligence with regard to a state's resources.[47] Paying too great deference to lacking capacities yet is delicate. It provides little incentive for states to enhance their abilities. It does, however, provide great incentive for non-state actors to carry out harmful activities on the territory of resource-lacking states knowing that they do not have to fear excessive control and regulation. Allocating too much weight to insufficient capacities could thus stymie effective implementation. Therefore, it is often argued that lacking financial and technical resources should be considered but not exempt states from their international obligations.[48]

---

[47] ILA Study Group on Due Diligence, Second Report of July 2016, pp. 13 ff.; Sandra Stahl, *Schutzpflichten im Völkerrecht* (Heidelberg: Springer, 2012), p. 322; Trapp, "State Responsibility for International Terrorism," p. 85; Jan Arno Hessbruegge, "Human Rights Violations Arising from Conduct of Non-State Actors" (2005) 11 *Buffalo Human Rights Law Review* 21–88 at 85; Epiney, "Völkerrechtliche Verantwortlichkeit," pp. 254 f.

[48] See, for instance, Joanna Kulesza, *Due Diligence in International Law* (Leiden and Boston: Brill Nijhoff, 2016), p. 260; Trapp, "State Responsibility for International Terrorism," p. 75; Hessbruegge, "Human Rights Violations," 85.

In spite of such general consensus that capacities are relevant to delineating international standards of care, many practical questions remain unsettled. When discussing the application of due diligence obligations in various fields of international law in the following chapters, capacity issues will thus play a prominent part of the analysis: if states have a duty to expand their resources and to what extent (particularly if adequate technical and financial solutions are theoretically available elsewhere), if industrial states have a duty to deliver technical and financial assistance to less-developed states, and if resource-lacking states are required to ask for support in the event that they cannot provide adequate protection themselves. Different answers and solutions will be addressed when considering the application of due diligence obligations in different areas of international law.[49]

c. *Force Majeure* / Necessity

Before turning to reasonableness as the third component of due diligence, a clarifying remark needs to be made. The question of whether insufficient capacities alter international standards is sometimes confused with circumstances that preclude wrongfulness – in particular, the concept of *force majeure*.[50] Widely recognized as forming part of customary international law,[51] *force majeure* was applied in both interstate disputes and disputes between states and private persons. The ILC Draft Articles define it as an "irresistible force or an unforeseen event" beyond the control of states making it "materially impossible ... to perform the obligation." The defense of *force majeure*, therefore, does not extinguish the primary obligation in question; it merely suspends that obligation for a limited period of time. As with all circumstances precluding wrongfulness, *force majeure* requires high standards to be met:[52] With its threshold of material impossibility, it is not sufficient to show that performing an international obligation is unusually burdensome.[53]

---

[49] See Chapter 5.
[50] See, for instance, Kulesza, "Due Diligence," p. 265.
[51] See already: PCIJ, Brazilian Loans Case (*France* v. *Brazil*), Judgment of 12 July 1929, PCIJ Series A, No. 21), and Serbian Loans Case (*France* v. *Kingdom of the Serbs, Croats and Slovenes*), Judgment of 12 July 1929, PCIJ Series A, No. 20).
[52] Malcolm Shaw, *International Law* (Cambridge: Cambridge University Press, 8th ed., 2017), p. 603.
[53] Case concerning the difference between New Zealand and France regarding the interpretation or application of two agreements concluded on 9 July 1986 between the two States and which related to the problems arising from the Rainbow Warrior Affair (*New Zealand* v. *France*), Decision of 30 April 1990, RIAA XX 215 (253).

Economic difficulties accordingly fail to qualify as *force majeure*,[54] which takes us back to the question of diverging capacities in the due diligence concept.

Both concepts relate to the fundamental question of how to handle situations in which states are not able to perform their international obligations, and yet they are not identical. *Force majeure* is a legal defense available for states to justify the non-performance of an international obligation due to irresistible, unpredictable, and external circumstances and ensued despite their best efforts to comply.[55] The standard of due diligence, in contrast, focuses on how to determine what those best efforts are and in how far capacities might play a role in the process of determination. In this context, considering capacities is not about justifying contraventions of an international obligation; it is about altering the very content of that obligation in light of diverging capacities. The concept of *force majeure* and the issue of capacities thus operate on different levels. Whereas the former is an exceptional justification of conduct contrary to international obligations, the latter deals with the potentially diverging content of such obligations.

We will thus now turn to the final component of due diligence standards: Once states have knowledge of a risk, they are expected to take *reasonable* measures. This prerequisite of reasonableness gets easily entangled with the issue of capacities with both concepts overlapping to a considerable extent. Notwithstanding, the standard of reasonableness goes beyond the issue of capacities and thus deserves closer consideration on its own.

IV. Reasonableness

Under the standard of due diligence, states are expected to employ reasonable measures. Mainly in two instances, the notion of reasonableness becomes relevant: First, it determines the constructive knowledge threshold as states are expected to acquire knowledge of *reasonably* assessable threats. Second, it determines what state reaction is expected in view of a given risk, as states are merely required to take

---

[54] PCIJ, Brazilian Loans Case (*France* v. *Brazil*), Judgment of 12 July 1929, PCIJ Series A, No. 21), and Serbian Loans Case (*France* v. *Kingdom of the Serbs, Croats and Slovenes*), Judgment of 12 July 1929, PCIJ Series A, No. 20).

[55] Shaw, "International Law," p. 603; James Crawford, *State Responsibility. The General Part* (Cambridge: Cambridge University Press, 2013), p. 295.

reasonable preventive and punitive steps. In both instances, however, reasonable is a broad and inherently dynamic term. What is reasonable under some circumstances might not be reasonable under others. And even under the same circumstances, what seems reasonable to one state might not seem reasonable to another. Its vagueness makes it particularly hard to fill the standard of reasonableness with actual content. In a first step, the elements of an international reasonable standard will thus be identified to enrich the concept with legal substance and meaning (1.). The standard's inherent subjectiveness poses particular procedural difficulties, most importantly as to whether reasonable standards of care are defined in an objective manner through international practice and jurisprudence or whether they are derived from standards of care commonly employed by states in their domestic affairs (2.). Finally, how the burden of proof is allocated when it comes to establishing the unreasonableness of state conduct deserves some closing remarks (3.).

1. Elements of Reasonableness under International Law

Reasonableness as a standard is found in all branches and fields of law. Inter alia, it is applied to evaluate the actions of persons and institutions but also the content of judgments, legislation, and theoretical views. In spite of its broad scope of application, there is yet profound ambiguity in legal debate and jurisprudence when it comes to defining it. In international law, "reasonable" is sometimes listed as an explicit component of international norms but was applied by international tribunals, even despite its absence from the actual wording of an international norm.[56] Generally, the standard of reasonableness is highly subjective and content-specific:[57] "what is reasonable and equitable in any given case must depend on its circumstances"[58] and what is reasonable in view of a certain risk may well be unreasonable in view of another.[59] Reasonable is thus both, relative in the sense that it might

---

[56] See, for instance, ECtHR, Case Relating to Certain Aspects of the Laws on the Use of Languages in Education in Belgium, Plenary Judgment of 23 July 1968, Applications Nos. 1474/62 a.o., p. 34, para. 10.
[57] Federico Ortino, "Investment Treaties, Sustainable Development and Reasonableness Review: A Case against Strict Proportionality Balancing" (2017) 30 *LJIL* 71-91 at 87; T. R. Hickman, "The Reasonableness Principle: Reassessing Its Place in the Public Sphere" (2004) 63 *Cambridge Law Journal* 166-198 at 166.
[58] ICJ, Continental Shelf (*Tunisia* v. *Libyan Arab Jamahiriya*), Judgment of 24 February 1982, ICJ Reports 1982, 18, para. 72.
[59] Monica Hakimi, "State Bystander Responsibility" (2010) 21 *EJIL* 341-385 at 373.

mean different things to different parties and temporary in the sense that its content might change over time.[60]

Some have even suggested that reasonableness could not be described in an objective manner at all.[61] Any such attempt would go beyond the law since legal categories could not cover concepts as subjective as the reasonableness standard. It would "implique une évaluation qui échappe à vrai dire au droit."[62] Though while it may not be possible to fill the standard of reasonableness with accurate and definite content, it could at least be identified how the standard and its normative connotation operate in international proceedings.[63] While flexibly allowing for deference toward a state's choice of means, state efforts are evaluated in light of the concrete regulatory aims of an obligation. Taking this as a starting point, the next section consults international jurisprudence and scholarly debates in order to identify the elements of an international standard of reasonableness.

a. Reasonableness and Proportionality

First, the notion of reasonableness is often compared to the notion of proportionality, as both concepts serve similar purposes.[64] The framework of proportionality is employed to assess the adequacy of administrative or legislative decisions as well.[65] While proportionality tests stem mostly from the tradition of continental administrative law, the reasonableness standard is of common law origin. To a certain extent, the notion of proportionality is much akin to that of reasonableness, and both standards will often yield the same results. In most cases, a lack of

---

[60] Olivier Corten, "The Notion of 'Reasonable' in International Law: Legal Discourse, Reason and Contradictions" (1999) 48 *ICLQ* 613–625 at 623.
[61] See, for instance, Jean Salmon, "Les Notions à Contenu Variable en Droit International Public," in Chaïm Perelman and Raymond vander Elst (eds.), *Les Notions à Contenu Variable en Droit* (Brussels: Bruylant, 1984), p. 265.
[62] Jean Salmon, "Le Fait dans l'Application du Droit International" (1982) 175 *RdC* 257–414 at 306.
[63] Corten, "The Notion of Reasonable," 614.
[64] See, for instance, Katharine Young, "Proportionality, Reasonableness, and Economic and Social Rights," in Vicki Jackson and Mark Tushnet (eds.), *Proportionality: New Frontiers, New Challenges* (Cambridge: Cambridge University Press 2017), pp. 248–272; Asier Garrido-Muñoz, "Managing Uncertainty: The International Court of Justice, 'Objective Reasonableness' and the Judicial Function" (2017) 30 *LJIL* 457–474 at 467 ff.
[65] See, for a comprehensive overview on the various forms of proportionality test in international law, Michael Newton and Larry May, *Proportionality in International Law* (Oxford: Oxford University Press, 2014).

IV. REASONABLENESS

reasonableness will be considered disproportional and the other way around.[66]

Notwithstanding, several important distinctions can be drawn. Despite all similarities, the concepts of proportionality and reasonableness are applied in slightly different contexts. While proportionality is applied to assess state conduct in a single instance, due diligence obligations to employ reasonable means entail overall state conduct toward a certain risk. Consequently, proportionality tests usually include an inquiry into the necessity of a measure and a call for the application of the least-restrictive alternative. In assessing proportionality, the availability of a less-intrusive option is thus an important parameter.[67] Tests of reasonableness, in contrast, are often deemed less restraining.[68] The mere fact that different means had been available does not render state conduct unreasonable. This is in line with the jurisprudence of the Claims Commissions, which tended to show great deference to a state's choice of means when applying preventive or punitive obligations of diligent conduct. Unreasonableness was only found where state conduct proved manifestly deficient. The Commissions did not find themselves competent to assess whether more effective alternative means had been available[69] and thus did not apply strict tests of proportionality. Traces of this cautious approach can still be found in contemporary case law. "Unreasonable" is occasionally equated with arbitrary, capricious, or absurd,[70] indicating that "mere" disproportionality would not meet such standard. In more recent jurisprudence, as well, the

---

[66] Jan Wouters and Sanderijn Duquet, "The Principle of Reasonableness in Global Administrative Law" (2013) Jean Monnet Working Paper Series 12/13, p. 28; Aharon Barak, *Proportionality* (Cambridge: Cambridge University Press, 2012), p. 378.

[67] Yutaka Arai-Takahashi, "Proportionality," in Dinah Shelton (ed.), *The Oxford Handbook of International Human Rights Law* (Oxford: Oxford University Press, 2013), p. 452; Barak, "Proportionality," p. 317; Michael Krugmann, *Der Grundsatz der Verhältnismäßigkeit im Völkerrecht* (Berlin: Duncker & Humblot, 2004), pp. 68 ff.

[68] See in particular: *House of Lords, R. v. Secretary of State for the Home Department*, ex parte Daly, 23 May 2001, 2001 UKHL 26, Opinion by Lord Steyn, para. 27; and also: Giacinto della Cananea, "Reasonableness in Administrative Law," in Giorgio Bongiovanni et al. (eds.), *Reasonableness and Law* (Heidelberg: Springer, 2009), p. 304.

[69] See, for instance, United States/Mexico General Claims Commission, *L. F. H. Neer and Pauline Neer (US) v. United Mexican States*, Decision of 15 October 1926, RIAA IV 60, para. 5; United States/Mexico General Claims Commission, *Laura Mecham (US) v. United Mexican States*, Decision of 2 April 1929, RIAA IV, 443.

[70] See, for instance, the arguments brought forward by the Japanese government in ICJ, *Whaling in the Antarctic (Australia v. Japan, New Zealand intervening)*, Judgment of 31 March 2014, ICJ Reports, 2014, 226; Counter-Memorial of Japan of 9 March 2012, in particular paras. 7.16 and 7.24.

conduct of state organs was considered unreasonable only if it had been systematically "flawed and deficient."[71] In the *Frontier* investment dispute, for instance, the Tribunal explicitly hold that even if "in the eyes of an outside observer, such as an international tribunal, [the decisions seems] 'wrong,'" this would not lead to state responsibility as long as the decision is "reasonably tenable."[72] The standard of reasonableness can thus be considered less strict than the standard of proportionality. Further guidance on the standard's substance is yet needed to pinpoint its legal character.

The ICJ's jurisprudence has tended to draw comparisons so broad and general that they hardly help define the standard of reasonableness at all. In its Preah Vihear case, the Court held that the principle of ordinary meaning in the context of treaty interpretation should not apply where a purely literal interpretation would lead to "something unreasonable or absurd."[73] Hence, what is absurd cannot be considered reasonable – a definition that lacks any concrete content. However, the Court then went one to argue that "the case of a contradiction would clearly come under that head."[74] While still being rather vague, one important element might be derived from this decision: logical cogency forms an inherent element of the standard of reasonableness.

b. Reasonableness and Rationality

It is for this reason that the notion of reasonableness is sometimes compared or even equated with the notion of rationality, though these concepts also need to be distinguished. Rationality is an inherent part of reasonableness but not the other way around: "[t]he reasonable is, of course, also rational – but the 'merely rational' is not always reasonable."[75] The concept of reasonableness is accompanied by notions of morality,[76] whereas "merely rational agents lack a sense of justice."[77]

---

[71] UNCITRAL, *Frontier Petroleum Services Ltd. v. Czech Republic*, Final Award of 12 November 2010, para. 435.
[72] Ibid., para. 273.
[73] ICJ, Temple of Preah Vihear (*Cambodia v. Thailand*), Judgment (Preliminary Objections) of 26 May 1961, ICJ Reports 1961, 17 (33).
[74] Ibid.
[75] Georg Henrik von Wright, "Images of Science and Forms of Rationality," in Georg Henrik von Wright (ed.), *The Tree of Knowledge* (Leiden: Brill, 1993), p. 173; Anashri Pillay, "Reviewing Reasonableness: An Appropriate Standard for Evaluating State Action and Inaction?" (2005) 122 *South African Law Journal* 419–440 at 420 f.
[76] James W. Boettcher, "What Is Reasonableness?" (2004) 30 *Philosophy & Social Criticism* 597–621 at 603.
[77] John Rawls, *Political Liberalism* (New York: Columbia Press, 1993), p. 52.

Though not identical, rationality nevertheless forms an important element of reasonableness. Even where Courts and Tribunals refrained from moral evaluations, references to the rationality or irrationality of arguments are commonly found. The Strasbourg Court, for instance, held that provisions of domestic law had to be "sufficiently accessible" and uncertainty resulting from inconsistent action could violate the Convention.[78] Logical incoherence, contradictions, or erroneous assumptions are indicators for an unreasonable response.[79] Vice versa, reasonable responses are ideally based on scientific evidence.[80]

States are expected to support their choice of means by finding empirical evidence, for instance, through employing statistics and collecting information on best practices.[81] "Traditions or general assumptions" are insufficient to justify measures where governments cannot provide any "science-based evidence."[82] Even where discretion is awarded to domestic policy choices, states are thus required to provide sufficient evidence for their legislative strategies. As a first conclusion, it might thus be summarized that the standard of reasonableness requires at least a rational response on behalf of states.

c. Reasonableness and Compliance

A second element of the standard of reasonableness that is relatively easy to identify is the requirement of compliance with other obligations. The standard of due diligence is usually described as what a "good government" would or should have done under the circumstances at hand. Most importantly, this implies that states are to take preventive measures only within the framework of legally available means. The preventive measures they opt for should not contravene other

---

[78] ECtHR, *Broniowski v. Poland*, Grand Chamber Judgment of 22 June 2004, Application No. 31443/96, para. 147, 151.
[79] Claire Brighton, "Unravelling Reasonableness: A Question of Treaty Interpretation" (2014) 32 *Australian Yearbook of International Law* 125–134 at 132.
[80] Alberto Artosi, "Reasonableness, Common Sense, and Science," in Giorgio Bongiovanni et al. (eds.), *Reasonableness and Law* (Heidelberg: Springer, 2009), p. 74.
[81] Among others, see ECtHR, *Hatton and Others v. The United Kingdom*, Grand Chamber Judgment of 8 July 2003, Application No. 36022/97, para. 125; UN Economic and Social Council, The Due Diligence Standard as a Tool for the Elimination of Violence against Women, Report of Special Rapporteur Yakin Ertürk, UN Doc. E/CN.4/2006/61, para. 37.
[82] ECtHR, *Bayev v. Russia*, Judgment of 20 June 2017, Application No. 67667/09 a.o., paras. 68, 69, 78.

international obligations.[83] This was unambiguously emphasized by the ICJ holding that in pursuing its diligence obligations, "every State may only act within the limits permitted by international law."[84] Since the requirements of due diligence in one field of international law may well conflict with the requirements in another, compliance is an important aspect of reasonableness demanding closer consideration when analyzing the application of due diligence in specific areas of international law.

d. Reasonableness and Balancing

Other authors have qualified the balancing of interests as the very essence of reasonableness. The "existence of a plurality of factors," which had to be evaluated "in respect of their relevance to a common focus of concern,"[85] should be addressed by resorting to a standard of reasonableness. A reasonable response would thus require that all potentially relevant aspects are considered and a balance is struck between them in accordance with their "relative weight or importance."[86]

Among others, the International Tribunal on the Law of the Sea engages in such balancing and stresses that, in assessing reasonableness, the balancing of interests was the most important "guiding criterion"[87] and drew up a list of factors that should be taken into account when evaluating reasonableness. This view has found ample support in the ILC's considerations on preventive obligations, which also identified several components of reasonableness: the likelihood that a certain risk results in harm, the scope of such harm, and the importance of the rights and interests involved.[88] All of these factors leave room for interpretation rendering the balancing exercise highly dependent on the circumstances of each individual case. It thus comes as little surprise that significant deference is usually paid toward a state's assessment of reasonable measures. When it comes to the balancing of interests, human rights bodies,

---

[83] Anja Seibert-Fohr, "Die völkerrechtliche Verantwortung des Staats für das Handeln von Privaten: Bedarf nach Neuorientierung?" (2013) 73 *ZaöRV* 37–60 at 52.
[84] ICJ, Genocide Convention Case, para. 430.
[85] Neil MacCormick, *Rhetoric and the Rule of Law. A Theory of Legal Reasoning* (Oxford: Oxford University Press, 2005), p. 173; see also Barak, "Proportionality," p. 374.
[86] MacCormick, "Rhetoric and the Rule of Law," p. 168.
[87] ITLOS, Monte Confurco (*Seychelles* v. *France*), Case No. 6, Judgment of 18 December 2000, para. 71 f.
[88] ILC, Draft Articles on Prevention of Transboundary Harm from Hazardous Activities with Commentaries, ILC Yearbook 2001, Volume II, Part II, Commentary to Article 3, paras. 11 ff.

in particular, have awarded wide discretion to states – often referred to as the margin of appreciation doctrine.[89] It is the balancing of individual rights and public interests, where this doctrine has its most prominent place. It is applied to all constellations in which states are expected to find an adequate balance between conflicting interests. Not only does this include constellations in which states have to assess a proportional application of human rights but also when assessing the reasonableness of preventive measures.

In spite of this wide margin of appreciation, however, the balancing exercise of states has been put to a reasonableness review by international courts and tribunals. Abstract tests and categories can provide guidance for the balancing of rights and interests and thereby contribute to greater legal certainty. How the balancing exercise is put to practice and what factors shape reasonable equilibrium between conflicting rights and interests will thus be taken up again when analyzing the application of due diligence in different fields of international law.

Summarizing the previous discussion, at least three general components of an international standard of reasonableness can be identified: a reasonable response cannot be irrational, it cannot violate any other international obligations, and it requires the balancing of the affected rights and interests. A positive definition of what is reasonable, however, seems impossible to reach. What the standard entails can only be approached through negative definitions by identifying the factors that render a state's course of action unreasonable. Often, it is criticized that the vagueness inherent in the notion of reasonableness would make its application arbitrary. States would have little clarity on what is required of them in order to comply with their international obligations.[90] Since reasonableness is always assessed in accordance with the circumstances of each individual case, it is indeed hard to predict the relevant criteria beforehand.[91] An uncertain standard renders it also more difficult for a damaged state to demonstrate a failure to exercise due diligence. This brings us to the procedural side of the notion of reasonableness and the question of whether the degree of diligence is determined in an objective or subjective manner and how the burden of proof is allocated.

---

[89] Yuval Shany, "Toward a General Margin of Appreciation Doctrine in International Law" (2006) 16 *EJIL* 907–940.

[90] See, for instance, Malgosia Fitzmaurice, "Legitimacy of International Environmental Law." (2017) 77 *ZaöRV* 339–370 at 364 ff.

[91] Stephen Tully, "Objective Reasonability as a Standard for International Judicial Review" (2015) 6 *Journal of International Dispute Settlement* 546–567 at 552.

2. Assessing Reasonableness: Objective versus Subjective Approaches

The normative character of reasonableness makes it all the more important to decide how the standard is practically assessed – in particular, whether states are obliged to apply such standards of care as they usually apply in their own affairs (*diligentia quam in suis*) or whether adherence is required to common and internationally defined standards.

In general, state practice and international jurisprudence seem to favor an objective approach. The Claims Commissions already stressed that even though states may sovereignly decide on how to treat foreigners on their territory, they are not allowed to fall short of a "minimum standard *required by international law*"[92] and that "the propriety of governmental acts should be put to *the test of international standards.*"[93] In the Alabama Arbitration, the United States supported an objective standard, whereas Great Britain claimed it was merely obliged to act with *diligentia quam in suis*. The United States' memorial determined the required standard of care as a "diligence proportioned to the magnitude of the subject and to the dignity and strength of the power which is to exercise it,"[94] whereas the standard proposed by Great Britain, as "such care as Governments ordinarily employ in their domestic concerns"[95] was vigorously rejected.[96] As is well known, the Tribunal sided with the American submissions and rejected Britain's reliance on domestic standards.[97] In like manner, the Swiss government later emphasized that "l'obligation de prévention ... ne se réalise que dans le cadre d'un standard général."[98] In the British Claims in the Spanish Zone of Morocco case, however, arbitrator Max Huber advocated the *diligentia quam in suis*-standard as being the only standard compatible with the principle of non-interference in the domestic affairs of states: "Cette règle conforme au principe primordial de l'indépendance des États dans leurs affaires

---

[92] Mexico/United States General Claims Commission, *A. L. Harkrader (US)* v. *United Mexican States*, Decision of 3 October 1928, RIAA IV 371 (373); Mexico/United States General Claims Commission, *H. G. Venable (US)* v. *United Mexican States*, Decision of 8 July 1927, RIAA IV 219 (229), emphasis added.
[93] Mexico/United States General Claims Commission, *L. F. H. Neer and Pauline Neer (US)* v. *United Mexican States*, Decision of 15 October 1926, RIAA IV 60 (61), emphasis added.
[94] Alabama Claims, pp. 572 f.
[95] Ibid., p. 612.
[96] Ibid., p. 613.
[97] Ibid., p. 656.
[98] Legal Service of the Swiss Federal Council, Agression contre la Légation de Roumaine à Berne, *Annuaire Suisse de Droit International* 1959, p. 225.

intérieures, offre en fait aux États, pour leurs ressortissants, le degré de sécurité auquel ils peuvent raisonnablement s'attendre."[99]

On closer inspection, though, the *diligentia quam in suis* standard is an inadequate yardstick for international diligence standards. If states could define international standards by reference to their internal practice, domestic law would predetermine the content of international obligations. Generally, however, international law does not recognize contradictory domestic norms as justification for noncompliance with international commitments – for doing so would severely hinder the effective implementation of international law.[100] For the same reasons, a lack of institutional capacity does not alter the required degree of diligence as we have seen already. There is thus a broad consensus that the degree of diligence has to be determined on the basis of an objective international standard:[101] "the 'due diligence' is nothing more nor less than the reasonable measures of prevention which a well-administered government could be expected to exercise under similar circumstances."[102] Notwithstanding, objective standards also need to find the middle ground: On the one hand, standards of care should not be so rigid and expansive that a majority of states are not in the position to fulfill them. On the other hand, they should not be too soft and bendable, lest they stymie an effective implementation. It will thus be analyzed for each area of international law how such objective approaches are developed and to what extent deference can be paid toward a state's own margin of appreciation.

3. Burden of Proof

The objective-subjective division is equally relevant to the evidentiary standards for proving a breach of due diligence obligations. With due diligence duties containing a certain margin of appreciation, it is principally easier for the damaged state to establish the breach of an obligation

---

[99] Permanent Court of Arbitration, Réclamations Britanniques dans la Zone Espagnol du Maroc (*Great Britain* v. *Spain*), Decision of 1 May 1925, RIAA II 615 (644).

[100] Enzo Cannizzaro, "Margin of Appreciation and Reasonableness in the ICJ's Decision in the Whaling Case" (2016) 27 *EJIL* 1061–1069 at 1068; Epiney, "Völkerrechtliche Verantwortlichkeit," p. 246.

[101] ILA Study Group on Due Diligence, Second Report of July 2016, p. 6; Boon, "Control Tests," 367; Seibert-Fohr, "Völkerrechtliche Verantwortlichkeit," 50 f.; Pisillo-Mazzeschi, "The Due Diligence Rule," 44; Wolf, "Völkerrechtliche Verantwortlichkeit," 523.

[102] Alwyn Freeman, "Responsibility of States for Unlawful Acts of Their Armed Forces" (1955) 33 RdC, II, 263–415 at 227 f.

of result for which it is sufficient to demonstrate whether the desired result was reached or not. To substantiate the breach of a due diligence obligation, however, the damaged state has to show that the respondent state knew or should have known of a risk and that its response thereto was manifestly inadequate.[103] Such evidence is difficult to produce: "in a great many cases it will be extremely difficult to establish beyond any doubt the omission or the absence of suppressive or punitive measures ..., the evidence of negative facts can hardly be given in an absolutely convincing manner."[104] Not surprisingly, the standard of proof in cases involving due diligence obligations is subject to a controversial debate. Only the most basic elements of such evidentiary standard meet with general approval, such as the obligation to substantiate the alleged breach of a due diligence obligation: "the want of due diligence must be made a part of the claimant's case and be established by competent evidence."[105] What constitutes competent evidence, however, is still vigorously discussed in modern jurisprudence, and three major procedural obstacles regularly occur: the inherent vagueness of the diligence standard, the exclusivity of territorial control, and the complexity of a state's administrative structures.

Even when codified in treaty law, due diligence obligations usually involve general language and broad legal terms. Their content is specific to particular facts and circumstances leaving ample room for interpretation. As we have seen, state parties to a dispute involving diligence standards apply different criteria when interpreting their duties or arrive at different conclusions, even when applying the same criteria. There is an undeniable degree of subjectivity when determining what is foreseeable or what is reasonable in an individual case. At the domestic level, duties of diligent conduct are phrased in the same vague and general language. Here, however, domestic courts are competent to deal with such ambiguity and to fill open terms with actual legal content. At the international level though, the concretization of diligence duties mainly evolves within an ongoing conversation between affected state

---

[103] Ricardo Pisillo-Mazzeschi, "Responsabilité de l'État Pour Violations des Obligations Positives Relatives aux Droits de l'Homme" (2008) 333 RdC 187–506 at 287; and already Borchard, "Diplomatic Protection," p. 217.

[104] Great Britain/Mexico General Claims Commissions, Mexico City Bombardment Claims, Decision of 15 February 1930, RIAA V 76 (80).

[105] UK/Venezuela Mixed Claims Commission, Aroa Mines Case, Decision of 13 February 1903, RIAA IX 402 (442); Mexico/United States General Claims Commission, *Lina Balderas de Díaz (United Mexican States)* v. *USA*, Decision of 16 November 1926, RIAA IV 106 (108).

parties.[106] The standard of care is reargued on a case-by-case basis, which creates legal uncertainty on both ends. On the one hand, it is difficult for states to assess beforehand which conduct is lawful and which is not. On the other hand, it is equally difficult for the damaged state to initiate proceedings where suitable precedents are absent. As we have seen, however, the standard of reasonable care is assessable through negative definitions. Several common factors and categories help identify what a reasonable response consists of. Albeit inherently flexible, the substantial content of due diligence obligations is thus fairly approachable.

Notwithstanding, even if adequate criteria can be agreed upon in international proceedings, the exclusivity of territorial control may further hamper the applicant's ability to give evidence. It is particularly difficult to retrace a course of events that entirely took place on another state's territory and to establish that more appropriate means had been available. In a great many cases, the applicant will not have access to the information it requires to produce such evidence.[107] If the respondent state did not take any measures whatsoever, it is still relatively uncomplicated to show a breach: "a strong *prima facie* evidence can be assumed to exist in these cases in which the [respondent] does not show any evidence as to action taken by the authorities."[108]

Procedurally far more difficult are those constellations in which the preventive measures taken by the respondent state are deemed inadequate by the applicant. Even where significant damage occurred, the respondent state's responsibility is not automatically triggered: "The mere fact that an alien has suffered at the hands of private persons an aggression ... does not make a government liable for damages under international law. There must be shown *special circumstances* from which the responsibility of the authorities arises."[109] The applicant has to show in a substantiated manner if and why the measures of the respondent state were not diligent enough.

---

[106] Barnidge, "Non-State Actors and Terrorism," pp. 158 f.
[107] Markus Benzing, *Das Beweisrecht vor internationalen Gerichten und Schiedsgerichten in zwischenstaatlichen Streitigkeiten* (Heidelberg: Springer, 2010), p. 691; Joachim Wolf, "Zurechnungsfragen bei Handlungen von Privatpersonen" (1985) 45 *ZaöRV* 232–264 at 236.
[108] Mexico/UK Claims Commission, Mexico City Bombardment Claims, Decision No. 12 of 15 February 1930, reprinted in 25 AJIL at 769, para. 6; and more recently, ICSID, *Wena Hotels Limited* v. *Arab Republic of Egypt*, Case No. ARB/98/4, Award of 8 December 2000, paras. 89–95.
[109] Panama/United States General Claims Commission, *Walter A. Noyes (US)* v. *Panama*, Decision of 22 May 1933, RIAA VI 308 (311), emphasis added.

On the other hand, however, the respondent state may not claim that harm would have occurred anyway, even if it had employed reasonable measures, as it could never be entirely excluded that "the combined efforts of several States, each complying with its obligation to prevent, might have achieved the result."[110] For the applicant, it is not mandatory to establish that the undesired event could certainly have been prevented since states have a general duty to employ all means "which could have had a real prospect of altering the outcome or mitigating the harm."[111]

To a certain extent, the difficulties of producing evidence are further mitigated by the fact that – even though the ICJ adheres to rather high thresholds for attributing private conduct to states – the Court does accept a somewhat lower standard with respect to due diligence duties.[112] Most notably in the *Genocide Convention* case, the Court rejected the attribution of non-state actions, despite close ties to the Serbian government, but found that Serbia had breached its obligation to prevent, as it had the "capacity to influence effectively,"[113] which clearly presents a lower threshold.

In sum, it becomes clear that due diligence duties cannot be defined in a manner as objective as obligations of result. Elements such as knowledge and reasonableness have a distinctively subjective connotation. Nonetheless, state practice tends to favor an objective international standard as opposed to *diligentia quam in suis*. Even where the ICJ allows for a "more liberal recourse to inferences of fact and circumstantial evidence,"[114] evidentiary hurdles yet remain. When analyzing the application of due diligence in specific areas of international law, how evidence issues are handled by states and international tribunals is thus another issue worth considering.

V. Summary

It is the broadness of the due diligence concept that permits its application to substantially different situations. Such flexibility comes with important advantages. Static legal provisions can never fully account for ever-changing social necessities and circumstances. Broad and

---

[110] ICJ, Genocide Convention Case, para. 430.
[111] ECtHR, *Opuz* v. *Turkey*, Judgment of 9 June 2009, Application No. 33401/02, para. 136.
[112] Benzing, "Beweisrecht vor internationalen Gerichten," p. 692.
[113] ICJ, Genocide Convention Case, para. 430.
[114] ICJ, Corfu Channel Case, p. 18.

V. SUMMARY

flexible concepts help adapt legal norms to such new constellations, thereby ensuring their endurance and effectiveness,[115] which is all the more relevant on the international plane. Norms of international law tend to be even broader and more general than domestic norms, as they often represent the lowest common denominator of international negotiations. They are also apt to be more static, as the procedures for changes and amendments are complicated and lengthy. Against this backdrop, flexible concepts of state responsibility ensure that norms of international law remain applicable, even where circumstances change. On the other hand, however, they are less tangible, and establishing their breach is challenging in international proceedings.

In any event, the main conclusion that is to be drawn from analyzing the different components of due diligence is that the standard is context-specific.[116] Its potential can be fully accounted for only when analyzing its application to different fields of international law. The next chapter thus considers how due diligence obligations operate in various areas of international law. Assessing how they are put to practice will help identify solutions for conceptual and procedural difficulties and thereby provide guidance on how the standard may be adequately applied to human rights protection.

---

[115] Robert Barnidge, "The Due Diligence Principle under International Law" (2006) 8 *International Community Law Review* 81–121 at 121.

[116] Awalou Ouedraogo, "La Neutralité et l'Emergence du Concept de Due Diligence en Droit International. L'Affaire Alabama Revisitée" (2013) 13 *Journal of the History of International Law* 307–346 at 308.

5

Lessons to Be Learned from the Application of Due Diligence Obligations in Other Fields of International Law

While it is beyond the scope of this book to analyze each and every instance in which due diligence obligations have been applied on the international plane, the following section will illustrate how such obligations have evolved in various fields of international law. As we have seen in the previous chapter, due diligence obligations are context specific, which is why their regulatory potential is best illustrated with regard to specific problems and challenges. Analyzing how due diligence obligations are adjusted so as to meet the peculiarities of different areas of law will reveal several dogmatic and practical efforts to overcome substantial and procedural hurdles. Later on, we will explore whether some of these concepts could also be fruitfully applied to the human rights sphere. The following section will therefore focus on three areas of international law that face challenges, similar to that of human rights law. How due diligence obligations have evolved in those areas will provide guidance on how the standard might contribute to more effective human rights protection.

The first part of this chapter will focus on environmental protection as the field of international law in which due diligence obligations have been most frequently applied. The early recognition of an obligation to diligently prevent environmental harm has paved the way for increasingly specific due diligence obligations. Similar to the field of human rights protection, a strong emphasis on prevention has evolved in environmental law, and some inspiration might be drawn from the way in which preventive obligations have become more concrete and substantiated in light of environmental risks. The development of independent procedural obligations, in particular, could also enhance global human rights protection. Besides, the problem of varying capacities has been of great concern to environmental due diligence generating several concepts, such as the idea of common but differentiated responsibilities, that might provide guidance on how to handle diverging capacities in the human rights context.

The second part of this chapter will analyze the changes and developments due diligence obligations have undergone with regard to counterterrorism laws. With international efforts to combat terrorist groups ever increasing, the obligation of states to diligently react to security threats on their territories has gained significant importance. In particular, the inability of some states to effectively combat terrorist threats prompted a debate on how an adequate due diligence standard could look like eventually culminating in a so-called unwilling or unable test. While cooperative mechanisms have also been strengthened in the wake of terrorist threats, support is increasing for a right to intervene where states manifestly fail to adhere to international diligence standards of terrorism prevention. How other states could and should react toward insufficient capacities equally concerns human rights law, which is why reconstructing the "unwilling or unable" test might prove fruitful for the human rights context as well.

Finally, the chapter's third part will address the rather recent development of cybersecurity due diligence obligations. Shaped by rapid technological developments, the cyber context challenges many traditional legal concepts, and yet, it might still teach a lesson for the future of human rights law. Most notably, preventive obligations with regard to cyberthreats entail the risk of inadequate surveillance and control, which is also relevant to the constructive knowledge threshold in human rights law.

In sum, analyzing how due diligence standards evolved in these three fields of international law could provide substantial guidance on how the specific challenges of due diligence obligations in the human rights field should be addressed.

5.1

Due Diligence Obligations in International Environmental Law

I. Introductory Remarks

In international environmental law, due diligence obligations are of particular importance. Transboundary environmental harm potentially has long-term negative effects on the territory of other states; it may adversely affect human health and cause severe resource shortages which is likely to result in high political and economic costs for the affected state. At the same time, damage to the environment is particularly often caused by private companies.[1] It is hardly surprising, therefore, that environmental law soon witnessed the rise of due diligence obligations.[2] As far back as 1912, *Oppenheim* summarized that "a State, in spite of its territorial supremacy, is not allowed to alter the natural conditions of its own territory to the disadvantage of the natural conditions of the territory of a neighbouring State."[3]

Early case law began with the famous Trail Smelter case involving environmental harm on US territory that had been caused by a private company residing in Canada. The Tribunal's renowned conclusion laid groundwork for environmental diligence duties: "under the principles of international law ... no State has the right to use or permit the use of its territory in such a manner as to cause injury ... in or to the territory of another or the properties or persons therein, when the case is of serious

---

[1] Günther Handl, "State Liability for Accidental Transnational Environmental Damage by Private Persons" (1980) 74 *AJIL* 525–565 at 525; Xue Hanqin, *Transboundary Damage in International Law* (Cambridge: Cambridge University Press, 2003), p. 327.

[2] Otto Kimminich, "Völkerrechtliche Haftung für das Handeln Privater im Bereich des internationalen Umweltschutzes" (1984) 22 *AVR* 241–282 at 267.

[3] Lassa Oppenheim, *International Law, A Treatise* (London: Longmans, Green & Co, 2nd ed., 1912), § 127, p. 182.

consequence and the injury is established by clear and convincing evidence."[4] A proposition that would later bolster the ICJ's reasoning in the Corfu Channel case acknowledging that a state was obliged "not to allow knowingly its territory to be used for acts contrary to the rights of other States."[5] While concern continues to be raised by several authors arguing that such supposedly customary obligation was not adequately reflected in state practice,[6] the Court's assumption is inextricably linked to the fundamental concept of the sovereign equality of states: "The proposition that no State may disregard the rights and interests of its neighbours is an offspring of conceptual reasoning ... [which] could not be invalidated by evidence pointing to manifold departures from the conduct required."[7]

II. Preventive Obligations and the No-Harm Rule

Against this background, it is now widely recognized that while the discretionary use of its territory does indeed form an essential part of a state's sovereignty, states are also obliged "to ensure that activities within their jurisdiction or control do not cause damage to the environment of other States."[8] The duty not to cause transboundary environmental harm is probably the most fundamental element of contemporary international environmental law.[9] As we have seen, this so-called no-harm rule directly flows from the principles of state sovereignty and non-interference and has

---

[4] The Trail Smelter Case (*USA* v. *Canada*), Arbitral Award of 16 April 1938 and 11 March 1941, RIAA III 1905 (1965).
[5] ICJ, Corfu Channel Case (*Albania* v. *UK*), Judgment of 9 April 1949, ICJ Reports 1949, 4 (22).
[6] John Knox, "The Myth and Reality of Transboundary Impact Assessment" (2002) 96 *AJIL* 291–319 at 291; Daniel Bodansky, "Customary (and Not So Customary) International Environmental Law" (1995) 3 *Indiana Journal of Global Legal Studies* 105–120 at 116.
[7] Christian Tomuschat, "Obligations Arising for States without or against Their Will" (1993) 241 RdC 195–374 at 295.
[8] Rio Declaration on Environment and Development, 12 August 1992, UN Doc A/CONF.151/26, Article 2; ICJ, Gabčíkovo-Nagymaros Project (*Hungary* v. *Slovakia*), Judgment of 25 September 1997, ICJ Reports 1997, 7, para. 53; ICJ, Legality of the Threat or Use of Nuclear Weapons, Advisory Opinion of 8 July 1996, ICJ Reports 1996, 226, para. 29.
[9] Rebecca Bratspies, "State Responsibility for Human-Induced Environmental Disasters" (2012) 55 *GYIL* 175–216 at 179; Wolfgang Durner, *Common Goods. Statusprinzipien von Umweltgütern im Völkerrecht* (Baden-Baden: Nomos, 2001), p. 61; Riccardo Pisillo-Mazzeschi, "Forms of International Responsibility for Environmental Harm," in Francesco Francioni and Tullio Scovazzi (eds.), *International Responsibility for Environmental Harm* (London: Graham & Trotman, 1991), p. 15.

been confirmed by countless arbitral and judicial decisions.[10] It was included in the Stockholm[11] and Rio Declarations,[12] and meanwhile, forms part of several international treaties.[13]

Similar to early due diligence obligations of alien protection, the environmental no-harm rule is twofold: States have a duty not to cause transboundary environmental harm through their own conduct and to ensure that such conduct is not caused through the actions of private individuals. In addition to this, they are expected to take reasonable measures to mitigate harm should it occur nonetheless. In the context of environmental protection, however, a strong emphasis has always been laid on preventive measures, mainly because environmental damage has long-term adverse effects that are often irreversible.[14] While the environmental precedents before the ICJ and other tribunals mostly dealt with cases in which harm had already materialized, they still advanced the development and concretization of preventive obligations. Already in the Gabčíkovo-Nagymaros Project judgment had the Court found that "in the field of environmental protection, vigilance and prevention are required on account of the often irreversible character of damage to the environment."[15] In the Pulp Mills case, the ICJ then recognized the principle of prevention as part of customary international law.[16]

Under this principle, states are obliged to prevent activities on their territory from causing transboundary harm.[17] If a state knows that

---

[10] Among others, see ICJ, Corfu Channel Case, p. 22; Affaire du Lac Lanoux (*France v. Spain*), Arbitral Award of 16 November 1957, XII RIAA 281; ICJ, Gabčíkovo-Nagymaros Project, para. 53; ICJ, Pulp Mills on the River Uruguay (*Argentina v. Uruguay*), Judgment of 20 April 2010, ICJ Reports 2010, 14, para. 193.

[11] Stockholm Declaration on the Human Environment, 16 June 1972, UN Doc. A/CONF.48/14/Rev. 1, Principle 21.

[12] Rio Declaration on Environment and Development, Principle 2.

[13] That is, Art. 194 II of the UNCLOS, signed on 10 December 1982, entered into force on 16 November 1994, 1833 UNTS 3; Art. 3 of the Convention on Biological Diversity, signed on 5 June 1992, entered into force on 29 December 1993, 1760 UNTS 79.

[14] Alexandre Kiss, "Present Limits to the Enforcement of State Responsibility for Environmental Damage," in Francesco Francioni and Tullio Scovazzi (eds.), *International Responsibility for Environmental Harm* (London: Graham & Trotman, 1991), p. 12.

[15] ICJ, Gabčíkovo-Nagymaros Project, p. 78.

[16] ICJ, Pulp Mills, para. 101.

[17] Ibid. Arbitration Regarding the Iron Rhine Railway (*Belgium v. The Netherlands*), Arbitral Award of 24 May 2005, XXVII RIAA 35, para. 59; and also Patricia Birnie et al., *International Law and the Environment* (Oxford: Oxford University Press, 3rd ed., 2009), p. 143.

certain activities involve the risk of significant transboundary harm, it has to employ preventive means even if the activities are carried out by private actors. Such duties of prevention found their way in many multilateral treaties prescribing that member states should take "appropriate measures,"[18] "necessary measures,"[19] or "practicable steps"[20] to minimize environmental risks. How to concretize independent preventive duties and whether these obligations might be enforceable even before harm actually occurs has become a main concern for environmental law. To identify the substantial content of such preventive obligations, the individual components of the due diligence standard will now be considered with a specific focus on the peculiarities of environmental protection.

III. Knowledge

As we have seen, effective prevention was soon declared a major goal of environmental law though concretizing preventive due diligence obligation proved an arduous task. Environmental risks are complex and little predictable. Even scientific research often fails to produce conclusive results making it difficult to meet the constructive knowledge threshold with regard to environmental hazards. On the other hand, however, environmental harm can be particularly grave and devastating. It is in this context that the so-called precautionary approach emerged and altered the constructive knowledge criterion for environmental due diligence.

1. Precautionary Obligations

The ILC's Draft Articles on Prevention of Transboundary Harm deal in great detail with the obligations of states to regulate hazardous activities and point out that the duty to prevent harm applies even in the absence of compelling scientific evidence.[21] Preventive steps are thus required even

---

[18] Art. 2 (I), Vienna Convention for the Protection of the Ozone Layer, signed on 22 March 1985, entered into force 22 September 1988, 1513 UNTS 293.
[19] Art. 194 (I), UNCLOS.
[20] Art. 1, London Convention on the Prevention of Marine Pollution by Dumping of Wastes and Other Matters, signed 13 November 1972, entered into force 30 August 1975, 1046 UNTS 120.
[21] ILC Draft Articles on Prevention of Transboundary Harm from Hazardous Activities with Commentaries, ILC Yearbook 2001, UN Doc. A/56/10 Commentary to Article 3, para. 14.

148   DUE DILIGENCE OBLIGATIONS IN INTERNATIONAL LAW

where knowledge of certain risks is still fragmentary. By the ITLOS, this so-called precautionary principle was recognized as forming part of customary international law.[22]

The inconclusiveness of scientific evidence on the character and magnitude of environmental risks is indeed the most problematic characteristic of environmental law. Often enough, the actual significance of such risks and the suitability of measures to address them are disputed even within the scientific expert community.[23] On the other hand, environmental disasters not only produce substantial economic costs; they also affect health and living conditions in a particularly severe manner and may even result in permanent damage.[24] It is against this background that the precautionary principle was included in several declarations and raised in many proceedings,[25] though its customary status remains contested.[26] Skepticism mostly derives from the fear that requiring precautionary measures would lead to excessive regulations infringing upon personal autonomy and entrepreneurial freedom.

In many ways, however, the principle of prevention and the principle of precaution are inextricably linked. Preventive measures are always

---

[22] ITLOS, Responsibilities and Obligations of States Sponsoring Persons and Entities with Respect to Activities in the Area, Advisory Opinion of 1 February 2011, ITLOS Case No. 17, ITLOS Reports 2011, 10, para. 131; and already ITLOS, Southern Bluefin Tuna Cases (*New Zealand* v. *Japan, Australia* v. *Japan*), Order of 27 August 1999, ITLOS Reports 1999, 274, para. 80.

[23] Mónika Ambrus et al., "Risk and International Law," in Mónika Ambrus et al. (eds.), *Risk and the Regulation of Uncertainty in International Law* (Oxford: Oxford University Press, 2017), pp. 4 f.; Bernard Reber, *Precautionary Principle, Pluralism and Deliberation* (London: Wiley, 2016), pp. 122 ff.; Nicolas de Sadeleer, "The Precautionary Principle as a Device for Greater Environmental Protection" (2009) 18 *Review of European Community & International Environmental Law* 3–10.

[24] Daniel Steel, *Philosophy and the Precautionary Principle* (Cambridge: Cambridge University Press, 2014), pp. 73 ff.

[25] See, for instance, the submissions made on behalf of Ireland in ITLOS, The Mox Plant Case (*Ireland* v. *UK*), Order of 3 December 2001, ITLOS Case No. 10, para. 71; WTO Appellate Body, EC Measures Concerning Meat and Meat Products (Hormones) (*European Communities* v. *USA*), Report of 16 January 1998, WT/DS26/AB/R, para. 16; and also Rio Declaration on Environment and Development, Principle 15; Art. 3 III of the UN Framework Convention on Climate Change, signed on 9 May 1992, entered into force on 21 March 1994, 1771 UNTS 107.

[26] Yoshifumi Tanaka, "Reflections on Time Elements in the International Law of the Environment" (2013) 73 *ZaöRV* 139–175 at 167; Mónika Ambrus, "The Precautionary Principle and a Fair Allocation of the Burden of Proof in International Environmental Law" (2012) 21 *Review of European, Comparative & International Environmental Law* 259–270 at 259; Joakim Zander, *The Application of the Precautionary Principle in Practice* (Cambridge: Cambridge University Press, 2010), p. 73.

III. KNOWLEDGE

employed to address future risks and inevitably entail a degree of uncertainty as to whether and how these risks might actually materialize.[27] The precautionary principle simply extends the principle of prevention by lowering the constructive knowledge threshold in relation to the seriousness of potential harm.[28] One essential parameter for the degree of diligence necessary to address certain environmental risks is the gravity of those risks, which is determined not only by the likelihood of harm but also its severity.[29] The more acute potential harm could be, the more extensive prevention is required. The magnitude of potential harm is thus as important a factor as the statistical frequency of its actual occurrence.[30]

At least the principle of prevention undisputedly forms part of customary international law on the environment. When acknowledging that both, the likelihood and the gravity of harm determine the expected degree of diligence, the precautionary principle is not as revolutionary as it may seem. Both principles contributed to the crystallization of specific environmental duties. The precautionary approach, in particular, has considerably altered the knowledge criterion. Where full scientific evidence of an environmental risk is lacking, states are principally not expected to have or to acquire knowledge of it. Where, however, calamitous harm is looming, state practice and international jurisprudence require precautionary measures to be taken nonetheless, thereby lowering the knowledge threshold to a significant extent.[31] Besides, the complex nature of environmental risks has also raised awareness for the importance of actively collecting information so as to increase knowledge of environmental risks.

---

[27] Zander, "Precautionary Principle in Practice," pp. 14 ff.; de Sadeleer, "Precautionary Principle," p. 4; Sumudu Atapattu, *Emerging Principles of International Environmental Law* (Ardsley: Transnational Publishers, 2006), p. 211.

[28] Cosima Erben, *Das Vorsorgeprinzip im Völkerrecht* (Berlin: Duncker & Humblot, 2005), pp. 213 ff.

[29] Günther Handl, "Transboundary Impacts," in Daniel Bodansky et al. (eds.), *The Oxford Handbook of International Environmental Law* (Oxford: Oxford University Press, 2008), p. 539; Commission of the EC, Communication on the Precautionary Principle of 2 February 2000, COM(2000) 1, para. 6.2.

[30] Alan Randall, *Risk and Precaution* (Cambridge: Cambridge University Press, 2011), pp. 110 ff.

[31] Philippe Sands and Jacqueline Peel, *Principles of International Environmental Law* (Cambridge: Cambridge University Press, 3rd ed., 2012), p. 228; Ambrus, "Precautionary Principle," 261.

2. An Obligation to Acquire Knowledge: Environmental Impact Assessments

Substantiated by state practice and a wide range of judicial decisions, environmental due diligence obligations have become more and more concrete. Several of these obligations directly aim at the gathering of information on environmental risks and may be qualified as formal obligations to acquire knowledge.

As indicated already, environmental hazards are often difficult to deduce, which is why states could, in most scenarios, claim ignorance and deny an obligation to employ preventive means. It is against this background that standardized procedural obligations to acquire knowledge evolved on the international plane[32] – most notably, the duty to conduct an environmental impact assessment before engaging in hazardous activities. On several occasions, the ICJ confirmed that this duty – at least in scenarios in which significant transboundary harm could occur – enjoyed customary status.[33] If states are not properly informed about the relevant scientific facts, they cannot employ adequate measures of prevention.[34] Therefore, they are obliged to acquire knowledge of the risks involved in certain undertakings beforehand and to assess suitable preventive means accordingly,[35] not only with respect to official state activities but also when licensing private projects.

There is thus an international obligation to acquire the relevant and available knowledge of environmental risks before engaging in potentially harmful activities. It is important to notice, however, that this customary rule is merely an obligation to conduct an impact assessment at all. International law does not establish any detailed content requirements which are left to domestic law.[36] Nonetheless, diligence duties do not end once an environmental undertaking is licensed and put into

---

[32] Bratspies, "State Responsibility for Human-Induced Environmental Disasters," 195 f.
[33] ICJ, Pulp Mills, para. 204; ICJ, Construction of a Road in Costa Rica along the San Juan River (*Nicaragua* v. *Costa Rica*), Judgment of 16 December 2015, ICJ Reports 2015, 665, para. 104; see also: ITLOS, Activities in the Area Advisory Opinion, para. 145; and The Indus Water Kishenganga Arbitration (*Pakistan* v. *India*), Partial Arbitral Award of 18 February 2013, available online at: www.worldcourts.com/pca/eng/decisions/2013 .02.18_Pakistan_v_India.pdf, paras. 449 ff.
[34] Birnie et al., "International Law and the Environment," p. 169.
[35] In particular, ICJ, Road in Costa Rica, para. 161.
[36] ICJ, Pulp Mills, para. 205, but see, for instance, ICJ, Road in Costa Rica, Separate Opinion by Judge Bhandari suggesting a list of procedural and substantial requirements for EIAs; Minimum standards that should be fulfilled by an environmental impact assessment are also entailed in the Convention on Environmental Impact Assessment in

III. KNOWLEDGE 151

operation. States have an additional duty to employ adequate instruments of supervision and make the necessary adjustments in case of new or increased risks.[37] Moreover, even though key elements of an environmental impact assessment are left to the discretion of domestic law – such as the time frame, financing, and administrative procedures – the ICJ acknowledged that the assessment was subject to international review.[38] Notably, the Court also held that the burden of proof in showing that an adequate assessment had been carried out lied with the state undertaking an activity.[39] The strong emphasis on preventive obligations has thus rendered the knowledge criterion more approachable, in particular through standardized proceedings, including environmental impact assessments as formalized instruments to actively obtain knowledge.[40]

However, while risk assessment has become increasingly standardized, there is a flip side to such formalized procedures for obtaining knowledge: States could easily claim to have carried out an impact assessment that did not reveal any environmental hazards. Since international law does not impose any strict requirement as to the content of such assessments, states could use low domestic standards as a pretext to circumvent their preventive obligations.[41] To a certain extent, however, this risk is mitigated by subjecting domestic standards to international review so that an assessment could still fall short of international standards if important facts are neglected. In spite of this potential for abuse, the standardized approach of environmental impact assessments thus renders the constructive knowledge threshold easier to handle.

Most importantly, this is due to the fact that the obligation to carry out environmental impact assessments is recognized as an independent procedural obligation forcing states to actively obtain knowledge. If states do not conduct an assessment, they do not meet the standard of care expected in international environmental law.[42] Failure to

a Transboundary Context (Espoo Convention), signed on 25 February 1991, entered into force on 10 September 1997, 1989 UNTS 309.

[37] ICJ, Pulp Mills, paras. 197 and 205; and also ITLOS, Activities in the Area Advisory Opinion, paras. 142 ff.
[38] ICJ, Road in Costa Rica, paras. 155 ff.
[39] Ibid., para. 154.
[40] Neil Craik, *The International Law of Environmental Impact Assessment* (Cambridge: Cambridge University Press, 2008), pp. 64 ff.
[41] For a fundamentally critical view of procedural obligations based on this concern, see Editorial Board of the Harvard Law Review, "International Environmental Law" (1991) 104 *Harvard Law Review* 1484–1639 at 1513.
[42] ICJ, Pulp Mills, para. 204.

exercise due diligence in the planning phase of a project may thus engage state responsibility, even in the absence of any material damage to another state.[43] The ICJ's Pulp Mills judgment – though dealing with specific bilateral treaty obligations, still a decision of general character – found that compliance with substantive obligations would not absolve states from their procedural obligations,[44] which they had to "answer for ... separately."[45] There is thus grounds for state responsibility, even where significant harm does not materialize but a state failed to carry out its procedural obligation to conduct an assessment. In emphasizing the separate existence of such procedural obligations, the Court clearly strengthened the preventive potential of environmental due diligence. If preventive proceedings are recognized as forming an independent obligation, coercive steps to sanction noncompliance could be taken already at an early stage before damage is done.[46] Evidentiary difficulties as well would be easier to overcome. Instead of laboriously proving significant harm and its causation by another state, victim states could easily establish failure to fulfill procedural requirements.

Despite these clear advantages, however, the ICJ's approach in its recent Road in Costa Rica decision was more ambiguous. While the Court found that Costa Rica had failed to discharge its obligation to undertake an assessment,[47] it found no failure to comply with the substantive obligation not to cause significant transboundary harm.[48] Since Nicaragua could not establish any harm resulting from Costa Rica's construction work, the Court neither granted compensation nor an order to cease.[49] With no effective way to enforce preventive obligations, potential victim states are yet left with little assistance so that Judges felt urged to add clarifying remarks in their separate opinions striving for stricter preventive obligations.[50] The Court's majority – though less progressive on enforcement matters – at least considered the separate existence of procedural obligations to be qualified as an independent wrongful act, even in the absence of actual

---

[43] ICJ, Road in Costa Rica, Separate Opinion of Judge Cançado Trindade, para. 9.
[44] ICJ, Pulp Mills, para. 78.
[45] Ibid., para. 79.
[46] Craik, "Environmental Impact Assessment," p. 66.
[47] ICJ, Road in Costa Rica, para. 162.
[48] Ibid., para. 217.
[49] Ibid., para. 224.
[50] Ibid., Separate Opinion by Judge ad hoc Dugard, para. 10, and Separate Opinion by Judge Donoghue, para. 9.

damage. Moreover, it was not ruled out by the Court that in case of *significant* harm, it might be sufficient for the injured state to show that no adequate impact assessment had been carried out to establish insufficient diligence without the need to produce further evidence on the foreseeability of harm. Taken together and despite a still rather law-enforcement record, the development of an independent procedural obligation to carry out environmental impact assessments has thus corroborated an obligation to actively obtain knowledge of environmental risks.

3. An Obligation to Share Knowledge? Duties to Cooperate

Next to duties of investigating and assessing, most environmental treaties also entail duties of consultation and cooperation,[51] which the ICJ derived from "general and well-recognized principles" such as "elementary considerations of humanity."[52] Such duty to notify and consult with other affected states is also linked to the assumption that environmental problems are of common concern[53] and beyond individual solutions.[54] States should notify potentially affected states of environmental projects to give them an opportunity to voice their concerns.[55] Neighbor states will be given enough information to evaluate potential risks and take preventive measures on their own.[56] In general, the field of environmental protection has thus provided for several formalized procedures that will enable states to better assess environmental risks and adjust their measures accordingly.

---

[51] See, for instance, Art. 2 (IV) Espoo Convention (fn. 36); Art. 12 UN Convention on Non-navigational Uses of International Watercourses, signed on 21 May 1997, entered into force 17 August 2014, 36 ILM 700; Arts. 9(III), 10 (II) Convention on the Transboundary Effects of Industrial Accidents, signed on 17 March 1992, entered into force on 19 April 2000, 2105 UNTS 457; Art. 2 Basel Convention on the Control of Transboundary Movements of Hazardous Wastes and Their Disposal, signed on 22 March 1989, entered into force on 5 May 1992, 1673 UNTS 57.

[52] ICJ, Corfu Channel, p. 22.

[53] Durner, "Common Goods," pp. 234 ff.

[54] Edith Brown Weiss, "The Contribution of International Environmental Law to International Law" (2011) 54 *Japanese Yearbook of International Law* 1–27 at 5; Birnie et al., "International Law and the Environment," p. 130; Yoshiro Matsui, "Some Aspects of the Principle of Common but Differentiated Responsibilities" (2002) 2 *International Environmental Agreements* 151–171 at 153.

[55] ICJ, Road in Costa Rica, para. 104.

[56] Sands and Peel, "Principles of International Environmental Law," p. 624.

IV. Capacities

As the general part has already indicated, however, it is particularly the question of diverging capacities that has shaped the field of environmental law. Effective prevention usually requires a certain level of technical expertise and the costs of preventive measures and undoing environmental damage may well reach colossal amounts. It comes as little surprise that several environmental treaties expressly address the capacity problem. Article 194 (I) UNCLOS, for instance, states that "States will take ... all measures ... that are necessary to prevent, reduce and control pollution of the marine environment from any source, using for this purpose the best practical means at their disposal and in accordance with their capabilities." In the Pulp Mills case, the ICJ used similar terms when stating that a state had to use "all means at its disposal,"[57] though no further clarification was added by the Court as to what consequences diverging capacities could have for the due diligence standard.

The commentaries to the Draft Articles on Prevention of Transboundary Harm discuss diverging state capacities in a more detailed manner. With the costs of environmental technology steadily increasing, they explicitly acknowledge that the economic capacity of states may play an important role in determining adequate standards of care: "It is ... understood that the degree of care expected of a State with a well-developed economy and human and material resources and with highly evolved systems and structures of governance is different from States which are not so well placed."[58] Similar concerns are mirrored in those treaties which include best available technology standards and usually refer to the economic feasibility of preventive measures as an important parameter.[59] Notwithstanding, the ILC commentary asserts that lacking capacities cannot discharge states of their due diligence obligations altogether: "The economic level of States is one of the factors to be taken into account in determining whether a State has complied with its obligation of due diligence. But

---

[57] ICJ, Pulp Mills, para. 101.
[58] ILC Draft Articles on Prevention of Transboundary Harm, Commentary to Article 3, para. 17.
[59] For instance, Annex I, Helsinki Convention on the Protection and Use of Transboundary Watercourses and International Lakes, signed on 17 March 1992, entered into force 6 October 1996, 1936 UNTS 269; Annex I, Convention for the Protection of the Marine Environment of the North-East Atlantic, signed on 22 September 1992, entered into force 25 March 1998, 2354 UNTS 67.

IV. CAPACITIES

a State's economic level cannot be used to dispense the State from its obligation."[60]

Yet again, a distinction is drawn between institutional and economic capacities. Whereas the latter may be taken into account, insufficient legal or institutional capacities do not absolve states from their obligations as the Draft Articles underline: "It [the government] should possess a legal system and sufficient resources to maintain an adequate administration apparatus to control and monitor the activities." Even in the case of less-developed states, "vigilance, employment of infrastructure and monitoring of hazardous activities ... are expected."[61] The conclusion reached in the general part is thus confirmed by environmental provisions. A lack of institutional capacities does not lower the degree of diligence whereas technical and financial capacities play a more important role. Against this background, several strategies have been developed to mitigate the issue of capacities in the environmental context. Two concepts in particular call for further investigation: first, whether there is an obligation to employ the best available technologies and, second, the concept of common but differentiated responsibilities.

1. Best Available Technologies

The controversially disputed question of whether there is a duty to employ the best available technologies is closely intertwined with environmental impact assessments. As part of their assessments, states should inform themselves about available technical options and employ the technology that best serves environmental interests.[62] An explicit obligation to use the best available technologies is entailed in several international treaties.[63] Such explicit provisions have tempted several authors to argue that the duty to employ best available technologies forms part of environmental due diligence, with the result that a state not applying the utmost technological expertise fails to act in a sufficiently diligent

---

[60] ILC Draft Articles on Prevention of Transboundary Harm, Commentary to Article 3, para. 13.
[61] Ibid.
[62] Tanaka, "Obligations and Liability of Sponsoring States," 162.
[63] See, for instance, Art. 3 Convention for the Protection of the Marine Environment of the North-East Atlantic, signed on 22 September 1992, entered into force 25 March 1998, 2354 UNTS 67; Art. 6 I Convention on the Protection of the Marine Environment of the Baltic Sea Area, signed on 9 April 1992, entered into force 17 January 2000, 1507 UNTS 167.

manner.[64] At least for the member states to treaties explicitly prescribing a best technology standard, applying a heightened standard of care indeed seems justified.[65] From the standpoint of customary international law, however, there remain several questions to discuss. It is clear that, under the no-harm rule, states have a duty to employ adequate measures to prevent transboundary harm. This logically implies an obligation to explore what options are generally available and best serve the environmental interests at stake.[66] How far such an obligation extends, however, remains unsettled. Its scope becomes particularly relevant where states neither have adequate technology nor the financial means to purchase it. Notably, even treaties with best technology standards mention "economic feasibility" as a relevant parameter in that regard.[67] Since adequate environmental protection often depends on specific technologies, it is vigorously discussed whether capacity-lacking states are under an obligation to seek technical assistance and whether states with sufficient capacities are under a corresponding obligation to transfer it. This controversy lies at the core of the concept of common but differentiated responsibilities.

2. Common but Differentiated Responsibilities

The principle of common but differentiated responsibilities evolved in the context of international climate change negotiations.[68] It is based on a twofold assumption: Climate change affects every state resulting in a common responsibility to confront it. Responsibility for fighting climate change is yet differentiated in that industrial states have made a significantly higher contribution to climatic problems and therefore should bear greater burdens when it comes to their solution – all the more as they have better means to afford expensive strategies.[69]

---

[64] Tanaka, "Obligations and Liability of Sponsoring States," 162 f.
[65] Ibid., p. 165.
[66] Atapattu, "Emerging Principles," p. 307.
[67] Art. 3 of the Helsinki Convention on the Protection and Use of Transboundary Watercourses and International Lakes, signed on 17 March 1992, entered into force 6 October 1996, 1936 UNTS 269.
[68] For a comprehensive analysis, see Tuula Honkonen, *The Common but Differentiated Responsibility Principle in Multilateral Environmental Agreements* (The Hague: Kluwer Law, 2009).
[69] Philippe Cullet, "Differential Treatment in Environmental Law" (2016) 5 *Transnational Environmental Law* 305–328 at 308; Sands and Peel, "Principles of International Environmental Law," p. 233; Rachel Boyte, "Common but Differentiated

Elements of differential treatment based on the development status of states were indeed included in various treaties and declarations.[70] The field of environmental law is thus the first area of international law in which a conceptual basis was developed for imposing differentiated obligations upon states in relation to their respective capacities. Two purposes are served by the concept of common but differentiated responsibilities: First, it supports the argument that the degree of diligence should be determined in accordance with a state's capacities. Second, it calls upon industrial states to actively engage in cooperation efforts and to technically and financially support less-developed states. However, while the concept is considered an equitable way of fostering overall environmental protection,[71] it is also criticized for being too vague and unsubstantiated to trigger legally binding obligations. The lack of reference to differentiated responsibilities outside of the climate framework further cautions against a too broad acceptance of varying degrees of diligence in environmental law.[72]

This comes as little surprise when considering that – at a practical level – the principle mainly comes into play when differentiated responsibilities and technology transfer are at stake. Article 4 II of the UNFCCC, for instance, imposes an obligation to reduce greenhouse gas emissions on developed states only,[73] whereas UNCLOS Article 144 prescribes that states should initiate and support the transfer of expertise and technology. No treaty, however, clearly defines common but differentiated responsibilities and the precise legal duties it encompasses. Article 3.1 of the UNFCCC merely declares that states will be guided by the principle when implementing their environmental policies, which suggests that it is not in itself a strict legal obligation but

---

Responsibilities" (2010) 14 *New Zealand Journal of Environmental Law* 63–101 at 66; Laurence Boisson de Chazournes, "Technical and Financial Assistance," in Daniel Bodansky et al. (eds.), *The Oxford Handbook of International Environmental Law* (Oxford: Oxford University Press, 2008), p. 970.

[70] For instance, Rio Declaration on Environment and Development, Principle 7.
[71] Cullet, "Differential Treatment in Environmental Law," 327; Boyte, "Common but Differentiated Responsibilities," 64.
[72] Sands and Peel, "Principles of International Environmental Law," p. 236; Christopher Stone, "Common but Differentiated Responsibilities in International Law" (2004) 98 *AJIL* 276–301 at 300.
[73] UN Framework Convention on Climate Change, signed on 9 May 1992, entered into force 21 March 1994, 1771 UNTS 107; see also Art. 5 I of the Montreal Protocol on Substances that Deplete the Ozone Layer, signed on 16 September 1987, entered into force 1 January 1989, 1522 UNTS 3.

rather serves as point of reference when designing environmental measures.[74]

Reluctance to further concretize the principle also stems from practical difficulties that apply not only to environmental protection but also to other areas of international law. First, even though several guidelines and indicators exist,[75] there is no general and accepted definition of what constitutes a developing state.[76] Thus it is not entirely clear when countries should be eligible to lower diligence duties.[77] Second, and more importantly, the recognition of varied degrees of diligence involves the risk of a regulatory down-to-the-bottom race.[78] Different environmental provisions could well be an incentive for private actors to move their activities to countries with low standards so as to avoid strict supervision.[79]

With such criticism frequently raised, a clarifying remark is yet required. The concept of common but differentiated responsibilities expects different results of less developed states without specifying whether this entails lesser diligence or merely relates to lower results in absolute terms. The same efforts employed with fewer resources automatically produce a lower outcome. Actually, states are thus required to exercise equal diligence. The quality of efforts might vary, but states are still expected to make their best respective efforts.[80] Notwithstanding, different absolute results are achieved with respect to the regulatory aim in question, potentially endangering the overall outcome.[81] In any event, however, environmental law has raised awareness for this general problem of international law[82] and pioneered the development of strategies to address varying economic and technical capacities, which is further mirrored in the notion of reasonableness.

---

[74] Thomas Deleuil, "The Common but Differentiated Responsibilities Principle" (2012) 21 *Review of European Community & International Environmental Law* 271–281 at 275.

[75] See, for instance, UN, Department of Economic and Social Affairs, Criteria for the Identification of Least Developed Countries, available online at: www.un.org/development/desa/dpad/least-developed-country-category/ldc-criteria.html.

[76] Boyte, "Common but Differentiated Responsibilities," 85; Lavanya Rajamani, *Differential Treatment in International Environmental Law* (Oxford: Oxford University Press, 2006), pp. 165 ff.

[77] Cullet, "Differential Treatment in Environmental Law," 317 f.

[78] See also Chapter 4, III, 2, b.

[79] Matsui, "Common but Differentiated Responsibilities," 158.

[80] ILA Study Group on Due Diligence, Second Report of July 2016, available online at www.ila-hq.org/index.php/study-groups, p. 22.

[81] Tanaka, "Obligations and Liability of Sponsoring States," 164.

[82] Atapattu, "Emerging Principles," p. 431; Rajamani, "Differential Treatment," p. 160.

V. Reasonableness

As we have seen previously, several factors commonly determine the standard of care in the environmental sphere: most notably, the likelihood of environmental damage but also its potential scope and nature, including its effects on particularly sensitive rights such as the right to life and health. Next to these general factors, the environmental standard of reasonableness has several further characteristics, among which its inherent flexibility and the notion of sustainability will be considered before the issue of objective versus subjective standards and the burden of proof will be assessed.

1. Technological Development

As mentioned previously, the standard of care in the environmental sphere is context specific and has to be adjusted if changed circumstances so require. Environmental protection is inextricably linked to scientific and technological developments, which constantly change the perception of environmental risks and the means to address them. Thus states need to constantly supervise their activities and make factual and legal adjustments where necessary.[83] The expected standard of care thus changes if new scientific evidence arises or if new technologies allow for improved environmental protection.[84] A first conclusion to be drawn is thus that the standard of reasonableness is a flexible and evolving one and that preventive obligations do not seize with the initial licensing process. An important part of a reasonable approach toward environmental risks is to constantly monitor environmental undertakings.

2. Sustainability

Other peculiarities of environmental protection have further shaped the reasonableness test. Most notably, this can be said of the principle of sustainability, which the ICJ first called a "concept"[85] and later an "objective"[86] of environmental law. The notion of sustainability

---

[83] Iron Rhine Railway Arbitration, para. 59; ILC Draft Articles on Prevention of Transboundary Harm, Commentary to Article 3, para. 11; ITLOS, Activities in the Area Advisory Opinion, para. 117.
[84] ICJ, Gabčíkovo-Nagymaros Project, para. 140.
[85] Ibid.
[86] ICJ, Pulp Mills, para. 177.

combines several normative concepts that have in common their emphasis on the potential long-term effects of environmental undertakings.[87] While the principle's legal status remains unclear, its underlying assumptions can be integrated into environmental reasonableness tests.[88] The sustainable use of resources should be taken into account when designing measures that potentially affect the environment,[89] though it is but one among several parameters that determine the reasonableness of an environmental approach.

3. Objective versus Subjective Standards of Care

The decisive role that research and new technologies play in the field of environmental law also has an impact on the debate on whether objective standards of care or *diligentia quam in suis* should apply. The commentaries to the Draft Articles on Prevention of Transboundary Harm favor an objective approach stating that "the standard of due diligence ... is that which is *generally* considered to be appropriate and proportional to the degree of risk ... in the particular case."[90] A notable development fostering objective environmental standards is the adoption of guidelines and minimum requirements, which are developed by international organizations such as the IMO and the IAEA or even included in Annexes to international treaties such as the MARPOL Convention. Where such minimum standards are agreed upon, states do not act diligently if they fail to apply even those basic requirements. As the term "minimum standard" suggests, however, they contain but the smallest consensus. This is particularly problematic if they fall significantly short of the best available

---

[87] Marie-Claire Cordonier Segger, "Commitments to Sustainable Development Through International Law and Policy," in Marie-Claire Cordonier Segger and Christopher Weeramantry (eds.), *Sustainable Developments Principles in the Decisions of International Courts and Tribunals* (London: Routledge, 2017), p. 30; Virginie Barral,"Sustainable Development in International Law" (2012) 23 *EJIL* 377–400 at 380; Sands and Peel, "Principles of International Environmental Law," p. 207; Atapattu, "Emerging Principles," p. 127.

[88] In a similar manner, see Daniel Barstow Magraw and Lisa Hawke, "Sustainable Development," in Daniel Bodansky et al. (eds.), *The Oxford Handbook of International Environmental Law* (Oxford: Oxford University Press, 2008), p. 631.

[89] Vaughan Lowe, "Sustainable Development and Unsustainable Arguments," in Alan Boyle and David Freestone (eds.), *International Law and Sustainable Development* (Oxford: Oxford University Press, 1999), pp. 31 ff.

[90] ILC Draft Articles on Prevention of Transboundary Harm, Commentary to Article 3, para. 11, emphasis added.

technology standard[91] or, due to changed circumstances, are no longer sufficient but could not be adjusted in a timely manner. Therefore – though minimum standards serve as the baseline of environmental due diligence – preventive obligations go beyond them. Under the due diligence standard, states may well be required to do more than the minimum standard entails. Notwithstanding, the mere fact that common parameters are included into treaties or determined by specialized agencies is a strong indicator that environmental law favors an objective approach toward the standard of care. What constitutes a reasonable response is evaluated in light of common expertise and objective guidelines. Scientific difficulties are mitigated even further through specialized compliance systems including observing committees that are established by several treaties.[92] These committees monitor the activities of states, issue statements and advice, and may also provide for dispute settlement mechanisms. How this has influenced evidentiary standards in environmental proceedings will be considered next.

4. Burden of Proof

As with any form of due diligence obligations, producing evidence is relatively difficult in the field of environmental law.[93] Generally, an applicant has to prove all aspects of his claim, and in the context of environmental law, two major obstacles may stand in his way. First, the previously mentioned scientific uncertainties naturally have a significant impact on the ability to collect evidence. Complex causal relationships are just as difficult to establish as the gravity and urgency of environmental risks[94] – all the more so where environmental damage results from numerous sources with individual contributions that are impossible to assess. Second, it is equally difficult to produce evidence on the adequateness of certain measures and to show that the measures actually

---

[91] Birnie et al., "International Law and the Environment," p. 150.
[92] Art. 12 of the Montreal Protocol; Art 8 of the UNFCCC and Art. 14 of the Kyoto Protocol to the UNFCCC, signed on 11 December 1997, entered into force on 16 February 2005, 2303 UNTS 162.
[93] Knox, "Transboundary Impact Assessment," 294.
[94] Markus Benzing, *Das Beweisrecht vor internationalen Gerichten und Schiedsgerichten in zwischenstaatlichen Streitigkeiten* (Heidelberg: Springer, 2010), pp. 704 f.; Lothar Gündling, "Verantwortlichkeit der Staaten für grenzüberschreitende Umweltbeeinträchtigungen" (1985) 45 *ZaöRV* 265-292 at 285.

applied were insufficient.[95] Some authors thus argue that it is indispensable to shift the burden of proof in order to ensure effective environmental protection. Already in the Nuclear Test case in 1995, Judge Weeramantry held in his dissenting opinion that "the law cannot function in protection of the environment unless a legal principle is evolved to meet this evidentiary difficulty."[96] It should be sufficient to provide prima facie evidence for the causation of environmental harm, following which it would be for the respondent state to prove that its measures had been diligent enough.[97] Of particular evidentiary difficulty are constellations in which the respondent state did employ preventive measures, but those measures are seen as insufficient by the applicant. Such were the facts the ICJ was confronted with in the Pulp Mills case. Even though the case dealt with a specific treaty between Argentine and Uruguay, environmental due diligence obligations were contained in that treaty, which is why more general assumptions can be derived from the Court's reasoning. Uruguay issued a license for a pulp mill, prior to which it had conducted an impact assessment and notified state officials and the affected public in Argentine. Argentine, however, claimed that those steps had not adequately addressed the concrete risks. Before the Court, both parties supported their claims by scientific studies and calculations, though those greatly differed in their conclusions. In its judgment, the Court first made clear that the peculiarities of environmental law did not allow for generally shifting the burden of proof[98] and found the evidence produced by Argentine insufficient to establish that Uruguay had breached its due diligence obligations. The case thus illustrates how difficult it can be to produce compelling evidence of a breach of due diligence obligations, in particular where the risk evaluation undertaken by different parties produces diverging results.

The difficulties of proving causal links between certain activities and negative impacts on the environment and human health have also become relevant in the field of human rights law. Here as well, it is principally the applicant which has to establish that a certain activity

---

[95] Tanaka, "Obligations and Liability of Sponsoring States," 165; Gündling, "Grenzüberschreitende Umweltbeeinträchtigungen," 290.
[96] ICJ, Request for an Examination of the Situation in Accordance with Paragraph 63 of the Court's Judgment of 20 December 1974 in the Nuclear Tests Case (*New Zealand v. France*), Order of 22 September 1995, ICJ Reports 1995, 288; Dissenting Opinion of Judge Weeramantry, p. 342.
[97] Ambrus, "Precautionary Principle," 266.
[98] ICJ Pulp Mills, para. 162.

caused harm, with the European Court of Human Rights rejecting a general shift of the burden of proof. In its *Dubestka* v. *Ukraine* decision, however, the Court did acknowledge that even if the damage could not be fully accounted for, living in a region heavily affected by air pollution might amount to a violation of Article 8 of the Convention.[99] In a similar manner, the IAComHR adopted "precautionary measures" and ordered Peru to carry out an impact assessment with regard to the human rights risks related to the removal of intoxicated sludge.[100] At least where fundamental rights are severely affected, a more reluctant approach to the burden of proof is thus considered and the precautionary principle finds wider acceptance.

Despite an increasingly standardized understanding of appropriate environmental diligence, the assessment of scientific evidence still meets with difficulties in international proceedings. Against this background, greater emphasis is generally laid on the procedural obligations of states – such as the duty to carry out impact assessments. In contrast to proving complicated causal links, it is easier to show whether states adhered to their procedural duties.[101] Acknowledging that states which did not abide by those duties thereby failed to act with due diligence is thus a major step toward tackling the great evidentiary difficulties inherent in environmental disputes.

VI. Summary

In sum, several important conclusions can be drawn from the development of due diligence in environmental law and other aspects deserve some concluding remarks as well. Stemming from the fundamental no-harm rule, environmental obligations of diligent conduct are well-established. The fact that environmental damage might be calamitous and irreversible has fostered the development of environmental due diligence obligations to a significant extent. A strong emphasis is laid on preventive obligations, particularly through independent procedural obligations requesting states to acquire knowledge of environmental risks

---

[99] ECtHR, *Dubetska and Others* v. *Ukraine*, Judgment of 10 February 2011, Application No. 30499/03, paras. 106 ff.
[100] IAComHR, *Community of San Mateo de Huanchor and its Members* v. *Peru*, Decision of 15 October 2004 (Admissibility), Report No. 69/40, para. 12.
[101] Jutta Brunnée, "Procedure and Substance in International Environmental Law" (2016) 5 *ESIL Reflections* at 7; René Lefeber, *Transboundary Environmental Interference and the Origin of State Liability* (The Hague: Kluwer Law, 1996), p. 319.

and share such knowledge with potentially affected other states before such risks even materialize. The knowledge threshold is lowered even further through the growing acceptance of precautionary obligations. Moreover, the duty to assess is one of ongoing supervision. It does not end with the licensing of a specific undertaking but requires the state to constantly monitor potentially harmful activities and intervene where necessary. All of these procedural obligations have contributed to a more standardized approach toward preventive obligations and lowered the procedural hurdles in environmental proceedings.[102]

However, while the recognition of procedural duties has made claims of state responsibility for environmental harm significantly easier, often enough even massive environmental catastrophes did not lead to legal proceedings at the international level.[103] Even in the case of devastating environmental incidents – such as the nuclear accident of Chernobyl – the affected states abstained from claiming compensation and rather focused on negotiating new international conventions that should help prevent similar incidents in the future.[104] Obviously, a state that, in one case, enforces environmental obligations against another state "might find itself the defendant in the next"[105] with high amounts of reparations looming. Given the various procedurals hurdles yet persisting and the great political reluctance to enforce state responsibility, environmental law has moved toward managing compliance through less intrusive means, such as reporting, monitoring, and capacity building.[106] Though while these cooperative efforts improve preventive mechanisms and the exchange of information between states parties, they are not likely to provide for full compensation in case of severe transboundary damage. Against this backdrop, an exclusive focus on state

---

[102] Brunée, "Procedure and Substance in International Environmental Law," 6.
[103] Alexandre Kiss, "Tchernobâle ou la Pollution Accidentelle du Rhin par des Produits Chimiques" (1987) 33 *Annuaire Français de Droit International* 719–727 at 724; Daniel Bodansky, "Implementation of International Environmental Law" (2011) 54 *Japanese Yearbook of International Law* 62–96 at 91; Handl, "Transboundary Impacts," 545.
[104] Notably the 1986 Convention on Early Notification of a Nuclear Accident, 1439 UNTS 275, and the 1986 Convention of Assistance in the Case of a Nuclear Accident or Radiological Emergency, 1457 UNTS 133.
[105] Bratspies, "State Responsibility for Human-Induced Environmental Disasters," 209.
[106] Mark Drumbl, "Trail Smelter and the ILC's Work on State Responsibility for Internationally Wrongful Acts and State Liability," in Rebecca Bratspies and Russell Miller (eds.), *Transboundary Harm in International Law* (Cambridge: Cambridge University Press, 2006), p. 94; Dinah Shelton, "Righting Wrongs: Reparations in the Articles on State Responsibility" (2002) 96 *AJIL* 833–856 at 854.

VI. SUMMARY

responsibility is increasingly considered insufficient to address environmental risks – in particular, where states failed to implement adequate domestic regulations of private activities.[107] Similar to the field of human rights protection,[108] some authors shift their emphasis from the regulatory obligations of states to international liability on the part of private operators.[109] Though as we have seen already, overemphasizing individual responsibility may have certain disadvantages, which equally applies in the environmental context. Focusing on individual wrongful conduct could easily disguise general shortcomings of a state's regulatory framework to systematically prevent and sanction environmentally harmful conduct.

Effective environmental protection, however, not only presupposes adequate compensation but also general preventive measures[110] – an aspect that is well-illustrated by the Deepwater Horizon incident, which was directly caused by the negligent behavior of BP and its partners. What enabled these companies to commence their activities in the first place, however, was the lax US regulation on offshore drilling. Holding BP and its partners accountable would change nothing about these inadequate domestic regulations. It might well have a deterrent effect on other companies, but similar offshore operations remain an option as long as the United States refrains from adopting more rigorous domestic regulations. State responsibility, therefore, is a much stronger incentive to solve structural problems that are beyond the reach of non-state actors.[111] There are thus good reasons to rely on state responsibility with regard to preventive measures, and even where compensation schemes are concerned, it would be in the interests of the victims of environmental disasters to have recourse to state compensation. Domestic civil law usually knows upper limits and equity standards, which may lead to an insufficient cover of damages in particular in cases of unexceptionally extensive harm. In case of large-scale environmental disasters, private companies might even lack the necessary financial funds to adequately compensate all affected victims.[112]

---

[107] Bodansky, "Implementation of International Environmental Law," 78.
[108] See Chapter 1, I.
[109] Thomas Gehring and Markus Jachtenfuchs, "Liability for Transboundary Environmental Damage" (1993) 4 EJIL 92–106 at 106.
[110] Birnie et al., "International Law and the Environment," p. 211.
[111] Bratspies, "State Responsibility for Human-Induced Environmental Disasters," 214.
[112] Gehring and Jachtenfuchs, "Liability for Transboundary Environmental Damage," 105.

Summarizing the previously considered developments, environmental law certainly is among the areas of international law that contain the most specific diligence duties. Most notably, its preventive orientation led to independent procedural obligations standardizing the content of obligations of diligent conduct and thereby facilitate their judicial enforcement. While states still show great reluctance to actually enforce state responsibility for environmental harm, obligations of diligent conduct are formalized even further through cooperative efforts between states and treaty committees both promoting a more objective and predictable standard of care in the field of environmental protection.

Next to the field of environmental protection, due diligence standards have been applied in the context of counterterrorism efforts. The substantial threats imposed by non-state terrorist actors have triggered an animated debate on how an adequate duty to diligently prevent harmful terrorist activities could be conceptualized. In particular, the issue of capacities and the inability of many states to successfully combat terrorist actors operating on their territory have given rise to new concepts and developments. How this has altered the general understanding of due diligence in international law will be considered next, in order to assess what lessons might be derived therefrom for the further development of human rights due diligence.

5.2

Due Diligence Obligations to Curb Terrorist Activities

I. Introductory Remarks

After the 9/11 attacks, the challenges imposed by powerful terrorist groups on the international legal order have triggered an ardent debate about state responsibility for the activities of terrorist non-state actors. State involvement in terrorist activities takes on various forms, ranging from effectively controlling and guiding terrorist actors to financial or logistical support to simply tolerating the territorial presence of terrorist groups. With the high threshold for attribution under the effective control standard often not met, preventive duties have become all the more relevant, particularly in two constellations: in a transboundary context, if states tolerate terrorist groups using their territory for the preparation of attacks that are later carried out on another state's territory; and in a domestic context, if terrorist groups conduct violent acts against individuals. As for the latter constellation, a rich vein of precedents has been created by the Claims Commissions' early jurisprudence. In particular, their decisions on mob violence and revolutionary insurgents provide guidance for the rules on state responsibility applicable to non-state terrorist groups and the harm they cause to individuals within a state's territory. Today, international human rights law entails further obligations for states to protect individuals within their jurisdiction from harmful terrorist activities.[113]

When transferring the corpus of international law as developed by the Claims Commissions, it seems relatively straightforward that states have

---

[113] François Dubuisson, "Vers un Renforcement des Obligations de Diligence en Matière de Lutte Contre le Terrorisme?," in Karine Christakis-Bannelier et al. (eds.), *Le Droit International Face au Terrorisme* (Paris: Pedone, 2002), p. 145.

a duty to diligently prevent terrorist activities on their territory. A breach of this duty would arise if states have notice that their territory is being used by terrorist groups and fail to take reasonable steps to curb these activities. Moreover, the duty to diligently prosecute and punish offenders if attacks occur in spite of preventive measures also applies to terrorist activities. A first obstacle yet appears when conceptualizing due diligence obligations in the fight against terrorist activities: terrorism takes various forms, and there have been countless efforts to reach a single comprehensive definition in international law.[114] Finding consensus on a definition of terrorism has been particularly difficult, since any such definition necessarily judges the moral validity of the activities in question,[115] with states being inclined to abuse "terrorism" as a subjective and derogatory label.[116] Notwithstanding, several working definitions might serve as a basis for analyzing attribution and state responsibility with regard to terrorist activities. Generally, terrorism means that a non-state actor "unlawfully and intentionally causes death or serious injury to any person, or serious damage to property, when the purpose of the conduct, by its nature or context, is to intimidate a population, or to compel a Government or an international organization to do or abstain from doing any act."[117] A range of treaties and UN documents have further specified the duty of due diligence in the context of terrorist activities. Starting with the obligation to prosecute or extradite terrorist suspects recognized already in the League of Nations 1937 Convention,[118] several treaties and Security Council Resolutions have provided for catalogs of more concrete obligations. Initially, terrorism had mostly been treated as a matter of criminal law. Several international

---

[114] For an overview on definition efforts, see Commission on Human Rights, Report of 27 June 2001 by Special Rapporteur Kalliopi Koufa on Terrorism and Human Rights, UN Doc. E/CN.4/Sub.2/2001/31, para. 24, fn. 15, referring to 109 different definitions of the term "terrorism"; and also Christian Walter, "Defining Terrorism in National and International Law," in Christian Walter et al. (eds.), *Terrorism as a Challenge for National and International Law* (Heidelberg: Springer, 2004), pp. 23–44.

[115] Pierre-Marie Dupuy and Cristina Hoss, "Trail Smelter and Terrorism: International Mechanisms to Combat Transboundary Harm," in Rebecca Bratspies and Russell Miller (eds.), *Transboundary Harm in International Law* (Cambridge: Cambridge University Press, 2006), p. 231.

[116] Anthony Richards, *Conceptualizing Terrorism* (Oxford: Oxford University Press, 2015), pp. 25 f.

[117] Tal Becker, *Terrorism and the State: Rethinking the Rules of State Responsibility* (Oxford: Hart, 2006), p. 117; Walter, "Defining Terrorism," 42 f.

[118] Convention for the Prevention and Punishment of Terrorism, 16 November 1937, 19 League of Nations OJ 23 (1938); the Convention never entered into force.

I. INTRODUCTORY REMARKS 169

Conventions and Security Council Resolutions require states to criminalize terrorist activities in their domestic penal codes and to ensure that individuals responsible for terrorist activities are prosecuted or extradited.[119]

In the aftermath of 9/11, the scope of counterterrorism obligations yet became significantly broader. Security Council Resolution 1373, most notably, entails detailed obligations concretizing the counterterrorism efforts expected of all states.[120] To a considerable extent, these expansions clarified an international due diligence standard to fight terrorism, and the international community has become more strongly involved in qualifying terrorist activities ever since.

Most of the recently ratified treaties on counterterrorism operate within a due diligence framework, requiring states to take reasonable measures. This includes both preventive due diligence obligations as well as due diligence obligations in the aftermath of an incident. Article 15 (I) of the International Convention for the Suppression of Terrorist Bombings,[121] for instance, requires state parties to take "all practicable measures to prevent and counter preparations [of terrorist activities] in their respective territories," whereas article 7 (I) contains the obligation to take the necessary steps to investigate terrorist offenses.

The Security Council also addressed terrorist attacks by non-state actors in numerous Resolutions.[122] On account of particular terrorist incidents, broader international frameworks for the suppression of terrorist activities were put in place. For example, Resolution 1267 – though primarily addressing the Taliban regime – establishes a Committee to surveil the counterterrorism efforts of all states and requests reports to the Committee on a regular basis.[123] The general due diligence

---

[119] See, for instance, UN Security Council, Resolution No. 1189 of 13 August 1998, UN Doc. S/RES/1189, and various instruments on certain terrorist activities, such as Convention for the Suppression of Unlawful Seizure of Aircraft, signed on 16 December 1970, entered into force on 14 October 1971, 860 UNTS 105; and International Convention against the Taking of Hostages, signed on 18 December 1979, entered into force 3 June 1983, 1316 UNTS 205.

[120] UN Security Council, Resolution No. 1373 of 28 September 2001, UN Doc. S/RES/1373, para. 2 e.

[121] International Convention for the Suppression of Terrorist Bombings, signed on 15 December 1997, entered into force 23 May 2001, 2149 UNTS 256; see also Art. 8 (I) of the International Convention for the Suppression of the Financing of Terrorism, signed on 9 December 1999, entered into force on 10 April 2002, 2178 UNTS 197.

[122] See, for instance, UN Security Council, Resolution No. 1267 of 15 October 1999, UN Doc. S/RES/1267.

[123] Ibid., paras. 6 ff.

obligations of states were further clarified by Resolution 1373 imposing on states an obligation to "take the necessary steps to prevent the commission of terrorist acts" and to ensure that their territory is not misused as a "safe haven" by terrorist actors. Several concrete steps are identified by the Resolution – such as the strengthening of border controls and the implementation of suitable screening mechanisms in asylum procedures – which states are expected to take in order to comply with their obligation to prevent terrorist activities.[124] By Resolution 1540, the Council further obliged states to diligently prevent non-state actors from acquiring nuclear, chemical, or biological weapons and installed another Committee to monitor compliance.[125]

Two important elements can be derived even from this very short overview of international counterterrorism efforts: first, the very broad obligation to diligently prevent terrorist activities was concretized through the formulation of specific duties. For the first time, the Security Council itself contributed to narrowing down what international law precisely expects of states. And second, the formulation of those duties was accompanied by the establishment of international Committees that would support and monitor compliance with the respective provisions. Thereby, the discretion once enjoyed by states in deciding on what preventive measures to employ was effectively limited.[126]

As we have seen in the general part, the lack of precise parameters for assessing reasonable measures is among the central practical concerns of international due diligence obligations. In the counterterrorism context, however, international monitoring mechanisms and detailed lists of concrete measures have rendered the reasonableness standard much more tangible.[127] While the international community still has to arrive at a universal definition of what terrorism consists of, it has succeeded in jointly addressing terrorist activities through corresponding preventive and punitive obligations.[128] At the same time, cooperation mechanisms and increased international awareness have significantly limited the

---

[124] UN Security Council, Resolution No. 1373 of 28 September 2001, UN Doc. S/RES/1373.
[125] UN Security Council, Resolution No. 1540 of 28 April 2004, UN Doc. S/RES/1540.
[126] Kimberley Trapp, *State Responsibility for International Terrorism* (Oxford: Oxford University Press, 2011), p. 79.
[127] Marja Letho, *Indirect Responsibility for Terrorist Acts* (Leiden: Brill, 2009), p. 383.
[128] Alan Greene, "Defining Terrorism: One Size Fits All?" (2017) 66 *ICLQ* 411–440 at 415; Helen Duffy, *The "War on Terror" and the Framework of International Law* (Cambridge: Cambridge University Press, 2nd ed., 2015), p. 70.

margin of appreciation states used to enjoy when assessing reasonable responses to threats emanating from their territory. The following section will thus address how this affects the main elements of international due diligence – knowledge and diverging capacities.

II. Knowledge

The knowledge requirement was not fundamentally altered by the phenomenon of terrorism. As with most other areas of international law, positive knowledge is difficult to establish, which is why recourse is mostly taken to the constructive knowledge standard. Some characteristics of terrorist actors make it difficult to meet the constructive knowledge threshold. With non-state terrorist groups being inherently secretive, gathering evidence on terrorist activities is a complicated task. Discerning the cellular structure of terrorist groups, their financial networks, and their communication channels through new technologies proves particularly difficult. Besides, individuals may radicalize outside of organized terrorist groups and commit harmful attacks without sophisticated planning or significant resources.

It is important to notice, however, that the duty to take preventive steps does not presuppose knowledge of a specific terrorist attack being planned. It is triggered already by knowledge of the presence of active terrorist groups on a state's territory or a heightened risk of attacks.[129] The post 9/11 efforts and the establishment of enhanced cooperation mechanisms have considerably limited a state's ability to deny knowledge of terrorist threats. The reporting system established pursuant to the mentioned Security Council Resolutions forces states to collect information on suspicious activities and ensures greater international awareness of potential threats. With the international community allocating increasingly more intelligence resources toward the detection of terrorist activities, it becomes far more difficult for states to claim ignorance of such activities – either because they access information following their own reporting duties or because they are informed by other states and international organizations. In particular, where the international community or specialized international agencies had issued warnings on

---

[129] Paulina Starski, "Right to Self-Defense, Attribution and the Non-State Actor" (2015) 75 ZaöRV 455–501 at 479.

specific terrorist threats, constructive knowledge on behalf of the respective states is likely to be assumed.[130]

III. Capacity

Much more difficult to address is the question of how to handle scenarios in which a terrorist threat is well-known but the state in question is incapable of an adequate response. An effective strategy against terrorist groups requires intelligence resources as well as significant financial and military capacities. Post 9/11 developments, in particular, have triggered an animated debate on this matter. Most notably, the emergence of the "unable or unwilling" standard has altered the approach toward lacking capacities.

1. Institutional Capacities

As the introductory remarks have already indicated, the phenomenon of terrorism has not changed the way in which institutional capacities are addressed. The standard of due diligence requires states to use their available capacities to effectively prevent and sanction terrorist activities. From an institutional perspective, states are thus required to implement domestic provisions preventing and criminalizing terrorist activities. They are also required to diligently enforce those provisions by prosecuting and sanctioning responsible individuals and entities. Insofar, the standard of care expected of states with regard to terrorist threats is not substantially different from the standard of care generally expected with regard to harmful activities emanating from their territory. What has changed, however, is the fact that international conventions and resolutions have concretized the form those domestic provisions should take. Especially with regard to institutional capacities, state practice tends to apply a rather strict approach, given the institutional capacity-building activities of the United Nations and related international agencies.[131] Just as much as the margin of appreciation of states has been limited when it comes to assessing terrorist threats on their territory, it has been limited with respect to adequate criminal provisions and enforcement mechanisms.

---

[130] See already Richard Lillich and John Paxman, "State Responsibility for Injuries to Aliens Occasioned by Terrorist Activities" (1977) 26 *American University Law Review* 217– 313 at 244.

[131] Trapp, "State Responsibility for International Terrorism," p. 71.

2. Financial and Territorial Capacities

In contrast, the issue of financial and territorial capacities underwent quite significant changes in the counterterrorism context. Both financial and territorial resources play a crucial role in a state's ability to effectively prevent terrorist activities on its territory. It thus comes as little surprise that the problem of lacking resources was soon acknowledged by the Committees monitoring the Security Council Resolutions mentioned herein. Even with regard to very basic obligations – such as the duty to regularly report to the Committees – capacity issues have become relevant. The Monitoring Group established in pursuance with Resolution 1267, for instance, stated in its first assessment that many states failed to produce the required reports. Not only would they lack "the human resources necessary to produce reports but also the national supervisory and coordination mechanisms needed to gather the information required."[132] If capacity issues already hamper the implementation of reporting duties, quite evidently, they are an even greater hindrance to preventive obligations. Effective counterterrorism strategies depend on significant financial capacities and require military expertise as terrorist groups tend to operate secretly in areas that are remote or even impassable[133] – a further challenge to a state's territorial capacities that cautions against a lenient approach toward insufficient capacities so as not to create an incentive for terrorist groups to operate in countries with limited capacities where they are shielded against international action.[134] It is this concern, above all, that considerably altered due diligence standards in the terrorism context. A vigorous controversy evolved as to whether the international community or other states should be allowed to combat terrorist actors on the territory of states that are incapable of curbing such activities themselves. Initially focusing on a potential right to self-defense against non-state terrorist actors, the debate soon took a more general character on how to deal with states that prove "unwilling" or "unable" to actively engage in counterterrorist efforts.

a. Self-Defense against Non-State Actors?

Following 9/11, the applicability of Article 51 of the UN Charter became a thoroughly contested issue. Whether terrorist attacks amount to an

---

[132] Letter from the Chairman of the Security Council Committee established pursuant to Resolution 1267, UN Doc. S/2004/679 (2004), para. 78.
[133] Kimberley Trapp, "Shared Responsibility and Non-State Terrorist Actors" (2015) 62 NILR 141–160 at 153.
[134] Trapp, "State Responsibility for International Terrorism," p. 70.

armed attack and thereby trigger the right to self-defense was subject to a particularly animated controversy; as was the question of whether ongoing terrorist activities would allow other states to take preemptive steps where those states in which terrorist groups are present were not able to effectively prevent terrorist attacks.

Some authors argue that self-defense could only be legitimately inferred where a state was directly responsible for terrorist activities. Any other approach would unduly infringe upon the principle of territorial integrity.[135] An attack carried out by a non-state actor, so they argued, had to be attributable to a state under the "effective control" standard for Article 51 rights to be invoked. Those in favor of a broader interpretation, in contrast, accentuate the wording of Article 51 as opposed to Article 2 (IV) of the Charter. Whereas the latter explicitly speaks of a use of force by one member state against another, such language is not repeated in Article 51, leaving room for an understanding of armed attacks that includes harmful acts by non-state actors.[136] Terrorist attacks, they further explain, can be of such scale and effect that they would unquestionably be classified as an armed attack, had they been carried out by the regular armed forces of a state. Any unlawful use of force under the pretense of self-defense would still be subject to an ex post control by the Security Council and the international community, limiting the potential for abuse.[137] Support for this opinion is often derived from Security Council Resolution 1368, which characterized the 9/11 attacks as a "threat to international peace and security" and simultaneously reaffirmed the "inherent right of ... self-defence."[138] It should not be overlooked, however, that the United States – while blaming Al-Qaeda for the attacks – were still convinced they had "been made possible by the decision of the Taliban regime." Consequently, its self-

---

[135] Jordan Paust, "Use of Armed Force against Terrorists in Iraq, Afghanistan and Beyond" (2002) 35 *Cornell International Law Journal* 533–557 at 540.

[136] ICJ, Legal Consequences of the Construction of a Wall in the Occupied Palestinian Territory, Advisory Opinion of 9 July 2004, ICJ Reports 2004, 135, Separate Opinion by Judge Higgins, p. 33; Niaz Shah, "Self-Defence, Anticipatory Self-Defence and Pre-emption" (2007) 12 *Journal of Conflict & Security Law* 95–126 at 104 f.; Noam Lubell, *Extraterritorial Use of Force against Non-State Actors* (Oxford: Oxford University Press, 2010), p. 31.

[137] Ashley Deeks, "Unwilling or Unable: toward a Normative Framework for Extraterritorial Self-Defense" (2012) 52 *Virginia Journal of International Law* 483–550 at 496; Thomas Franck, "Terrorism and the Right of Self-Defense" (2001) 95 *AJIL* 839–842 at 840.

[138] UN Security Council, Resolution No. 1368 of 12 September 2001, UN Doc. S/RES/1368.

defense response was not limited to Al-Qaeda bases but also targeted the Taliban as the official Afghan government at the time. A right to exercise self-defense exclusively against non-state actors was therefore not invoked in the aftermath of 9/11.

For several reasons, a cautionary approach toward expanding the right to self-defense is indispensable.[139] What should not be dismissed too easily is that any use of force carried out on another state's territory without that state's explicit consent constitutes an infringement upon the fundamental principle of territorial integrity, even where terrorist groups are the declared military target. Remarkably, the ICJ has so far refused to explicitly pronounce itself on the matter of self-defense against non-state actors. In its Wall Advisory Opinion, the Court briefly considered whether Israel's construction of the wall amounted to a legitimate exercise of Article 51 rights. An armed attack "imputable to a foreign State" would always trigger the right to self-defense, the Court found. The threat that Israel considered to justify the wall's construction, however, originated within and not outside the territory controlled by Israel, leaving no room to appeal to the international right to self-defense.[140]

Set in the peculiar context of the Palestinian territories, the Wall Advisory Opinion is yet of limited authority.[141] Shortly after, however, the Court once more refrained from voicing an express opinion, even though the *DRC v. Uganda* case dealt with attacks against Uganda, which were prepared and carried out by armed groups operating on DRC territory. Those activities the Court did not attribute to the DRC, which is why Uganda could not forcibly respond in self-defense against the DRC as such. Not explicitly engaged by the Court, though, was the question of whether Uganda could have used force in self-defense, had its forcible response exclusively targeted the responsible non-state actors and their bases.[142] While it is thus clear that states cannot use force against entire states in response to unattributable terrorist acts, whether forcible self-defense would be justified if the response was strictly limited to attacking terrorist actors remains open to debate.

---

[139] I. M. Lobo de Souza, "Revisiting the Right of Self-Defence against Non-State Armed Entities" (2015) 53 *Canadian Yearbook of International Law* 202–243 at 233; Becker, "Terrorism and the State," p. 150.

[140] ICJ, Wall Advisory Opinion, para. 139.

[141] Kimberley Trapp, "Back to Basics: Necessity, Proportionality, and the Right to Self-Defence against Non-State Terrorist Actors" (2007) 56 *ICLQ* 141–156 at 144.

[142] ICJ, Armed Activities on the Territory of the Congo (*DR Congo v. Uganda*), Judgment of 19 December 2005, ICJ Reports 2005, 168, paras. 146 f.

Such substantial yet limited broadening of Article 51 found the support of many scholars, in particular when considering the difficulties of satisfying the criteria for attribution.[143] As we have seen, the threshold for attributing non-state conduct to a state is not met by a general situation of dependence and support.[144] Even a more lenient standard of overall control would still require a substantial link between the state and a terrorist group. Mere tolerance is not enough to attract attribution, and active state support for terrorist organizations will often enough be difficult to establish, in particular where the state was not involved in a specific attack.[145] It thus comes as little surprise that affected states and scholars have looked for alternative paths to justify forcible self-defense, even where terrorist attacks could not be attributed. Occasionally, even a strict liability approach has been suggested, automatically providing for state responsibility in case of non-state terrorist activities on a state's territory.[146] Though the latter approach did not find wide-spread support, alternatives to the traditional requirements of attribution have become increasingly popular. Interestingly, it is the failure to meet due diligence standards that turned out to be a major problem. In fact, the most prominent suggestion made so far takes a state's failure to diligently prevent terrorist attacks from being prepared on its territory as justification for affected third states to conduct defensive operations on that territory.[147] Purely private

[143] Among others, see Jasper Finke, "Selbstverteidigungsrecht gegen nichtstaatliche Akteure" (2017) 55 *AVR* 1–42 at 35; Christian Henderson, "Non-State Actors and the Use of Force," in Mart Noortmann et al. (eds.), *Non-State Actors in International Law* (Oxford: Hart, 2015), p. 96; Daniel Bethlehem, "Self-Defense against an Imminent or Actual Armed Attack by Non-State Actors" (2012) 106 *AJIL* 770–777; Deeks, "Unwilling or Unable," 489; Shah, "Self-Defence, Anticipatory Self-Defence and Pre-emption," 111; Thomas Franck, *Recourse to Force: State Action against Threats and Armed Attacks* (Cambridge: Cambridge University Press, 2002), p. 54.
[144] ICJ, Military and Paramilitary Activities in and against Nicaragua (*Nicaragua* v. *USA*), Judgment of 27 June 1986, ICJ Reports1986, 14, para. 115.
[145] Federica Paddeu, "Use of Force against Non-State Actors and the Circumstances Precluding Wrongfulness of Self-Defence" (2017) 30 LJIL, 93–115 at 96.
[146] See, for instance, Vincent-Joël Proulx, "Babysitting Terrorists: Should States Be Strictly Liable for Failing to Prevent Transborder Attacks" (2005) 23 *Berkeley Journal of International Law* 615–668 at 655 ff.
[147] Among many others, see Human Rights Council, Report of the Special Rapporteur on Extrajudicial, Summary or Arbitrary Executions Philip Alston of 28 May 2010, UN Doc. A/HRC/14/24/Add.6, para. 35; Michael Schmitt, "Preemptive Strategies in International Law" (2002) 24 MJIL 513–548 at 542 f.; Dubuisson, "Obligations de Diligence en Matière de Lutte Contre le Terrorisme," 149; Deeks, "Unwilling or Unable," 489; and Lobo de Souza, "Revisiting the Right to Self-Defence," 243.

acts – if grave enough – could then trigger the right to self-defense if retaliation is strictly limited to the responsible non-state actors and their bases within the host state, which proves unwilling or unable to curb terrorist activities itself.[148] Attribution to the state would only be necessary where the forcible response should be extended against the host state itself.[149] This has come to be known as "safe haven" doctrine – in the terms of the Security Council[150] – or as the "unable or unwilling" standard. While failure to exercise due diligence in preventing terrorist attacks is not equated with actually committing such an attack,[151] terrorist threats are considered to be of such fundamental concern as to justify infringing upon the territorial integrity of those states that are either unwilling or unable to ensure that their territory is not misused by terrorist groups – a doctrine that is not without its problems and gave rise to much controversy.

b. The Unwilling or Unable-Standard

In the heated debate on terrorist threats, it was repeatedly argued that states which prove unwilling to combat terrorism on their territory could be held accountable for being complicit in these activities.[152] General international jurisprudence indeed suggests that the unwillingness of a state to take preventive steps in spite of a positively known risk could justify accusing that state of complicity based on acquiescence if sufficient means had been available which it refused to employ.[153] Though, as we have seen, it is difficult enough already to determine when a state's unwillingness is so persistent that it amounts to complicity.[154] What has complicated matters even further is that responsibility based on acquiescence has also been assumed, where

---

[148] Finke, "Selbstverteidigungsrecht gegen nichtstaatliche Akteure," p. 35.
[149] Henderson, "Non-State Actors and the Use of Force," 94.
[150] UN Security Council, Resolution 1373 of 28 September 2001, UN Doc. S/RES/1373, p. 2.
[151] Duffy, "The War on Terror," p. 90; Vincent-Joël Proulx, *Transnational Terrorism and State Accountability* (Oxford: Hart Publishing, 2012), p. 58.
[152] Christian Tams, "The Use of Force against Terrorists" (2009) 20 *EJIL* 359–397 at 385; Derek Jinks, "State Responsibility for the Acts of Private Armed Groups" (2003) 4 *Chicago Journal of International Law* 83–95 at 90; Davis Brown, "Use of Force against Terrorism after September 11th" (2003) 11 *Cardozo Journal of International and Comparative Law* 1–53 at 30 f.
[153] See Chapter 3, V, 5.
[154] Robert Barnidge, *Non-State Actors and Terrorism* (The Hague: TMC Asser, 2008), p. 216; Kristina Bautze, "Die 'Unwilling or Unable'-Doktrin" (2016) 49 *Kritische Justiz* 535–548 at 545.

states proved merely unable to curb terrorist activities.[155] A lack of capacities, we have seen in the general part, is a relevant factor in determining the standard of care states are expected to perform in order to comply with their due diligence obligations. Failure to combat terrorist activities due to insufficient resources yet lacks any element of support or approval and could hardly be equated with willful state acquiescence.[156] It is at this point exactly where counterterrorism efforts have blurred the line between the standard of due diligence and the concept of complicity based on acquiescence. Two legal consequences following from a state's inability to combat terrorist activities are particularly vigorously discussed: whether states should be obliged to enhance their capacities in order to better respond to terrorist threats and whether the international community and/or other states should have a right to step in if states still neglect their obligations.

aa. Is There an Obligation to Enhance Capacities?

With various international treaties and the Security Council insistently addressing the issue, the fight against terrorism has become an international priority of outstanding importance. For this reason, so it is often argued, states should assign sufficient resources toward counterterrorism efforts, even if this necessitates cutting other expenses[157] and seeking international assistance if necessary. Support for this position can indeed be found in Security Council Resolution 1617, requiring states "to allocate sufficient resources, including through international partnership" to effectively fight terrorist threats.[158] Notwithstanding, it seems doubtful whether states could really be required to allocate disproportionate amounts of their budgets to counterterrorism efforts if this means they would no longer be able to ensure, for instance, the protection of core human rights obligations.[159] The debate surrounding the legal consequences of a state's inability to combat terrorist threats has yet gone even further.

---

[155] See already Quincy Wright, "The Prevention of Aggression" (1956) 50 *AJIL* 514–532 at 527; Manuel García-Mora, *International Responsibility for Hostile Acts of Private Persons against Foreign States* (The Hague: Martinus Nijhoff, 1962), p. 30.
[156] Henderson, "Non-State Actors and the Use of Force," 94.
[157] Barnidge, "Non-State Actors and Terrorism," pp. 211 f.
[158] UN Security Council, Resolution No. 1617 of 29 July 2005, UN Doc. S/RES/1617.
[159] Ahmed Dawood, "Defending Weak States against the Unwilling or Unable Doctrine of Self-Defense" (2013) 9 *Journal of International Law and International Relations* 1–37 at 9.

bb. **Does Inability Justify a Forceful Response by Other States?** States that are unable to effectively combat the activities of terrorist groups on their territory, several authors went on to argue, would be required to not only seek international assistance but also authorize coercive means, should the need arise.[160] Dogmatically, this argument is derived from a broadened understanding of complicity: if a state is not able to effectively combat terrorist groups on its territory, yet persistently rejects reasonable plans of action by other states, it becomes a complicit harboring state.[161] State practice, however, remains ambiguous on this issue. After Israeli citizens were killed in Cyprus in 1985, for instance, Israel attacked the PLO headquarter located in Tunisia. Having invoked the right to self-defense, Israel claimed that Tunisia – even though it knew of the terrorists' plans and could have stopped them – failed to show even "an inkling of a desire or an intention to prevent the PLO from planning and initiating terrorist activities from its soil."[162] The Security Council[163] yet condemned Israel's attack as being in flagrant violation international law.[164] In 1995, Turkey took military action against the PKK on Iraqi territory, which it justified with Iraq's inability to "exercise its authority over the northern part of its country." Its operations were thus "legitimate measures" safeguarding Turkey's security and could not "be regarded as a violation of Iraq's sovereignty"[165] – a claim unanimously rejected as illegitimate by several governments.[166] In 1998, however, the United States referred to the very same arguments after US embassies had been targeted in Kenia and Tanzania, and it responded by bombing Al-Qaeda training camps in Sudan and Afghanistan. The American statement assured the attacks were carried out "only after repeated efforts to convince the Government of the Sudan and the Taliban regime in Afghanistan to shut these terrorist activities down."[167] This time, there

---

[160] Becker, "Terrorism and the State," p. 162; Jochen Frowein, "Der Terrorismus als Herausforderung für das Völkerrecht" (2002) 62 *ZaöRV* 879–905 at 884.
[161] Bethlehem, "Self-Defense," 776; Lubell, "Extraterritorial Use of Force," p. 41; Trapp, "Back to Basics," 147.
[162] Record of the Meeting of the Security Council on 2 October 1985, UN Doc. S/PV.2611, Statement by the Israeli representative Netanyahu, in particular paras. 59, 65, and 69.
[163] Notably with the United States abstaining.
[164] UN Security Council, Resolution No. 573 of 4 October 1985, UN Doc. S/RES/573.
[165] Letter from the Charge d'Affaires of the Permanent Mission of Turkey to the UN, UN Doc S/1995/605 (1995), p. 1.
[166] See, for instance, UN Doc S/1995/566; UN Doc S/1997/461.
[167] Letter from the Permanent Representative of the USA to the UN, UN Doc. S/1998/780 (1998), p. 1.

was little condemnation at all, the Security Council decided to remain seized of the matter[168] and later imposed sanctions against the Taliban regime for harboring terrorists on Afghan territory.[169] Meanwhile, there is a long list of further incidents in which states forcibly responded to violent attacks by non-state actors on the territory of third states: Israel's attacks against Hezbollah in Lebanon 2006, Russia's use of force against alleged Chechen rebels in Georgia 2002, or Colombia's attacks against FARC members in Ecuador in 2008.[170] Most recently, the United States have claimed its air campaign launched against terrorist groups operating in Syria would be justified as "the Syrian regime has shown that it cannot and will not confront these safe havens effectively itself."[171] In all of these cases, reference was made not only to the unwillingness of the respective states (though this was particularly emphasized) but also to a lack of adequate means on behalf of the host state.

Even though these incidents do not convey solid consistent state practice, they have let many authors conclude that the inability of states to curb terrorist activities could justify a forcible reaction on their territory, as long as such reaction exclusively targets non-state terrorist groups.[172] Though given the substantial interference with the sovereign rights of the affected states, much skepticism remains,[173] and rightly so. The obligation to prevent terrorist activities is an obligation of due diligence and not an obligation of result. The occurrence of terrorist attacks triggers state responsibility only where states failed to employ preventive due diligence. Acknowledging the "unwilling or unable" standard would yet necessarily imply that it would not take more than a state's insufficient capacities to justify forceful reactions by other states. Even where states had done everything in their power to combat terrorist threats but failed to prevent a particular attack from occurring, other

---

[168] UN Security Council Resolution No. 1189 of 13 August 1998, UN Doc. S/RES/1189, p. 2.
[169] UN Security Council Resolution No. 1267 of 15 October 1999, UN Doc. S/RES/1267, p. 2 f.
[170] Examples taken from: Henderson, "Non-State Actors and the Use of Force," 93.
[171] Letter dated 23 September 2014 from the Permanent Representative of the US to the UN, UN Doc. S/2014/695.
[172] Finke, "Selbstverteidigungsrecht gegen nichtstaatliche Akteure," p. 35; Elizabeth Wilmshurst and Michael Wood, "Self-Defense against Nonstate Actors: Reflections on the Bethlehem Principles" (2013) 107 *AJIL* 390–395 at 393; Deeks, "Unwilling or Unable," 486; Bethlehem, "Self-Defense," 776.
[173] Olivier Corten, "The 'Unwilling or Unable' Test: Has It Been, and Could It Be Accepted?" (2016) 29 *LJIL* 777–799; Bautze, "Die Unwilling or Unable-Doktrin"; Vincent-Joël Proulx, *Institutionalizing State Responsibility* (Oxford: Oxford University Press, 2016), p. 339.

states could resort to military action without that state's consent.[174] Inevitably, this would considerably affect our understanding of the prohibition of the use of force as a pillar of general international law which calls for caution.[175]

Widening the scope of permitted forceful actions is a particularly dubious undertaking wherein the incapability of states is not determined by independent institutions but by those states which supposedly act in self-defense.[176] Though even if independent institutions were in charge of such determination, it would still be difficult to assess whether a state could actually have done more, especially since capacities might evolve or decline over time. Moreover, it is not clear whether only those states should be found "unable" that entirely lack any capacity to curb terrorist activities or if states that did employ preventive means but still failed to prevent particular attacks would also fall in that category. Equally uncertain is whether inability would manifest itself already by the occurrence of a single terrorist attack or whether inability could only be established after ongoing terrorist activities over a significant period of time. It does not take more than these few questions to show how much ambiguity the "unwilling or unable" doctrine entails, rendering the standard susceptible of arbitrary application and abuse. Not surprisingly, the standard encountered much opposition, in particular by those states that are a likely target of forceful reactions.[177] In spite of some relevant state practice, therefore, the "unwilling or unable" standard has not achieved customary status. Unwillingness to engage in counterterrorist efforts could well amount to complicity based on acquiescence. Insufficient counterterrorism efforts due to lacking capacities are yet an inherently different matter. To assume that inability alone could justify forceful responses would turn the duty to diligently prevent harmful terrorist activities into strict liability. While this seems to be going too far, the problem of lacking resources has nonetheless altered due diligence obligations to a considerable extent.

cc. **Broadening the Scope of Reasonable Efforts** With terrorist activities being a substantial security threat to all states, the international

---

[174] Theodore Christakis, "Challenging the 'Unwilling or Unable' Test" (2017) 77 *ZaöRV* 19–22 at 20.
[175] Corten, "The Unwilling or Unable Test," 793.
[176] Lubell, "Extraterritorial Use of Force," p. 79.
[177] For an overview of relevant state practice, see Corten, "The Unwilling or Unable Test," 785 ff.

community seeks to thwart the efforts of terrorist groups that exploit the inability of some states to effectively monitor and control their territory. While such inability should not justify forceful responses on a state's territory without its consent, there is growing consensus that capacity-lacking states are at least expected to seek the assistance of international organizations and other states. Some authors even go so far as to suggest that they should be obliged to allow other states to perform security operations on their territory if necessary.[178] When considering our due diligence framework and its components, we will see that a lack of capacities indeed modifies the type and scope of counterterrorist measures that can be reasonably expected of states.

We have concluded already that a lack of capacities, while being a relevant parameter when assessing due diligence standards, may never entirely absolve a state from its international duties. States are still expected to employ all reasonable means at their disposal, among which seeking international help and assistance is an easily available option. Even those states with the lowest resources are able to ask for military assistance and other forms of support.[179] Therefore, it seems all but reasonable to expect them to seek international assistance if they know of terrorist threats on their territory. What this quest for assistance should look like depends on the circumstances. In extreme cases where a terrorist threat is substantial and imminent, allowing the international community to take active measures could well be the only reasonable option.

Acknowledging an obligation to seek international assistance broadens the scope of reasonable measures under the due diligence standard. States are no longer expected to merely employ all reasonable measures available within their territory but to also ask for international help.[180] Including cooperative obligations in the due diligence framework clarifies under which circumstances states may be held responsible for a failure to prevent terrorist attacks. If they can be reasonably expected to seek assistance, failure to do so would amount to a breach of the obligation to diligently prevent terrorist harm. Even if such failure could not justify a forceful response, it would still attract international

---

[178] See, for instance, Frowein, "Terrorismus als Herausforderung," 884.
[179] Britta Sjöstedt, "Applying the Unable/Unwilling State Doctrine – Can a State Be Unable to Take Action?" (2017) 77 ZaöRV 39–42 at 42.
[180] Sjöstedt, "Applying the Unable/Unwilling State Doctrine," 42; Trapp, "Back to Basics," 147; Becker, "Terrorism and the State," pp. 144 f.; Frowein, "Terrorismus als Herausforderung," 884.

responsibility on behalf of the undiligent state, eventually including an obligation to make reparations and allowing for countermeasures, as provided by the customary rules on state responsibility.

IV. Summary

Summing up the developments and changes the concept of due diligence underwent in the counterterrorism context, several concluding remarks should be made. An increased sensitiveness of states toward the threats posed by terrorist groups has generated deep concerns about noncompliance and led to intensified international efforts to jointly combat terrorism[181] – a development that clearly left its mark on the due diligence standard. By laying out increasingly more specific measures – even including individualized sanctions – the margin of appreciation for evaluating reasonable counterterrorism options was perceptibly limited. An increasing number of conventions and resolutions now describe what states are expected to do when fighting terrorist threats. The vague and flexible standard of due diligence has thus become ever more precise as the international community is actively involved in expanding what constitutes diligent efforts to combat terrorist actors.

Moreover and more importantly, the debate on insufficient capacities has been altered to an unprecedented extent. With terrorist attacks potentially having devastating effects for other states, the "unwilling or unable" standard emerged as a tool to justify international intervention. It is not a substantially new assumption that states acquiesce in private harm, where they know of a risk but are not willing to confront it. Such willful acquiescence could give ground for state responsibility and justify international reactions. Post-9/11 state practice, however, has added inability to the range of justifications. As we have seen, there are indeed several incidents that support the assumption that capacity-lacking states are required to either enhance their capacities or seek international assistance. Considering the fundamental importance of the prohibition of the use of force, the "unwilling or unable" standard should not be read as to justify military action on a state's territory without its consent. Notwithstanding, refusal to employ reasonable means – including quests for assistance – may well amount to

---

[181] Becker, "Terrorism and the State," p. 130.

a failure to diligently prevent terrorist harm, which is an internationally wrongful act allowing other states to react accordingly.

The section on due diligence obligations in the human rights context will recall these developments, in particular when analyzing whether insufficient human rights capacities could alter due diligence standards in a similar manner.

5.3

Due Diligence Obligations in the Cybersphere

I. Introductory Remarks

Another field of international law in which due diligence obligations have gained importance is the realm of cyberspace. With the dependence on computer systems ever increasing, cybersecurity has become one of the most controversially and intensively discussed topics of international law. Cyber devices, while easily and anonymously used, may cause a wide range of harmful consequences. Even from remote locations abroad, they can trigger physical destruction and interfere with critical infrastructure, including hospitals, energy and water supply companies, the banking sector, transportation systems, and military bases. Cyber devices can also be used to manipulate data and information, possibly influencing political decision-making processes or elections. Such a vast amount of potentially devastating consequences clashes with enormous technical difficulties in preventing harmful cyber activities. In contrast to conventional attacks, access to electronic devices is as easy as tracing back malicious cyber conduct is difficult.[182]

It comes as little surprise that these technical peculiarities have called many core concepts of international law into question, including the law on state responsibility. International law as it stands today, so several authors argued, was ill equipped to effectively deal with such new threats.[183] Cyberspace was "not a physical place," defying "measurement

---

[182] Christian Walter, "Cyber Security als Herausforderung für das Völkerrecht" (2015) 70 *Juristen-Zeitung* 685–736 at 688.

[183] Scott Shackelford and Richard Andres, "State Responsibility for Cyber Attacks" (2010) 42 *Georgetown Journal of International Law* 971–1016 at 999; Philippe Lagrange,

in any physical dimension or time space continuum."[184] Despite all peculiarities, however, cyberspace requires physical infrastructure located on a state's territory, which provides for a jurisdictional link.[185] States have already used their power to regulate and enforce cyber-related issues on various occasions.[186] The group of experts that published the Tallinn Manual – the first comprehensive attempt to identify the general rules of international law applicable to cyberspace – consequently concluded that though cyberspace in its entirety was beyond the control of single states, they could exercise sovereign rights over cyberinfrastructure located on their respective territory.[187] There is thus no need for "reinventing the wheel," and general international law remains applicable to cyber-related activities.[188] Notwithstanding, the characteristics of cyberspace have confronted general norms of international law with severe challenges, including the rules on state responsibility. A first significant problem to be addressed is that the requirements for attributing conduct to a state are particularly hard to establish for cyber-related activities (II.). At first glance, this could entail an even more important role for the due diligence standard. As we will see, however, proving a state's failure to fulfill its cyber due diligence obligations faces just as many challenges (III.).

II. The Problem of Attribution in the Cybersphere

It is subject to a particularly intense debate what constitutes use of force in the cyber realm and how cyber activities can be attributed to a state. It is beyond the scope of this book to delve deeply into those discussions.[189]

"Internet et l'Évolution Normative du Droit International," in Société Française pour le Droit International (ed.), *Internet et le Droit International* (Paris: Pedone, 2014), p. 84.

[184] Thomas Wingfield, *The Law of Information Conflict* (Falls Church: Aegis, 2000), p. 17.

[185] Anders Henriksen, "Lawful State Responses to Low-Level Cyber-Attacks" (2015) 84 *Nordic Journal of International Law* 323–351 at 332.

[186] Wolff Heintschel von Heinegg, "Cyberspace – Ein völkerrechtliches Niemandsland?," in Roman Schmidt-Radefeldt and Christine Meissler (eds.), *Automatisierung und Digitalisierung des Krieges* (Baden-Baden: Nomos, 2012), p. 169; Sean Kanuck, "Sovereign Discourse on Cyber Conflict under International Law" (2009) 88 *Texas Law Review* 1571–1597 at 1573.

[187] Michael Schmitt (ed.), *Tallinn Manual on the International Law Applicable to Cyber Warfare* (Cambridge: Cambridge University Press, 2013), Rule 1, pp. 15 f.

[188] UN General Assembly, Report of the Group of Governmental Experts on Developments in the Field of Information and Telecommunications in the Context of International Security, UN Doc. A/68/98 (2013), p. 8.

[189] On armed attacks in the cyber context, see Peter Stockburger, "Known Unknowns: State Cyber Operations, Cyber Warfare, and the Jus ad Bellum" (2016) 31 *American University*

II. THE PROBLEM OF ATTRIBUTION IN THE CYBERSPHERE

For our purpose, it is sufficient to summarize the central difficulties related to matters of attributing harmful conduct as they become relevant to the role of non-state actors. Identifying the actual source of a cyberattack is a technically demanding and often impossible undertaking. Whereas tracing back the physical location of a computer device is not extensively difficult, the mere proof of physical location is not enough for attributing an activity to a state.[190] Control over territory in itself does not allow for the conclusion that a state knew or ought to have known "of any unlawful act perpetrated therein."[191] Any other assumption would necessarily entail absolute state liability, which is not (and probably will not be) supported by state practice. In most cases, there is no conclusive evidence on which person actually used the device involved in a certain attack. Whether the devices were effectively controlled by a state, therefore, is often beyond the provable – all the more as they are not necessarily located on the territory of a single state. It is estimated that the 2007 attack on Estonia, for instance, involved about 85.000 computers from 178 countries.[192]

Against this background, a rather cautious approach is followed by the Tallinn Manual, which states in its Rule 7 that even the fact of government infrastructure having been used in a cyber operation does not allow for attributing the harmful conduct but merely indicates that state's involvement.[193] Several scholars criticized this view for relying too heavily on the protection of the source state. While acknowledging that government infrastructure can be hacked by non-state actors without authorization, it is still the source state, so they argue, which is best equipped to monitor and detect unauthorized activities in its networks. Thus, it should also be the source state that bears the costs of compliance creating an important incentive for constantly updating cybersecurity infrastructure.[194] Several scholars even suggested a complete revision of

---

International Law Review 545–592; Nicholas Tsagourias, "Cyber Attacks, Self-Defence and the Problem of Attribution" (2012) 17 *Journal of Conflict and Security Law* 229–244.

[190] Shackelford and Andres, "State Responsibility for Cyber Attacks," 984.

[191] ICJ, The Corfu Channel Case (*UK v. Albania*), Judgment of 9 April 1949, ICJ Reports 1949, 4, 18.

[192] Numbers taken from Eneken Tikk et al., *International Cyber Incidents: Legal Considerations* (Tallinn: CCD COE Publication, 2010), pp. 20, 23.

[193] Tallinn Manual 2013, Rule 7, pp. 34 ff.; reemphasized by Michael Schmitt (ed.), *Tallinn Manual 2.0 on the International Law Applicable to Cyber Operations* (Cambridge: Cambridge University Press, 2017), Commentary to Rule 15, para. 12.

[194] Peter Margulies, "Sovereignty and Cyber Attacks: Technology's Challenge to the Law of State Responsibility" (2013) 14 *Melbourne Journal of International Law* 496–519 at 511 f.

the rules of attribution insofar as overall rather than effective control should be the standard of attribution for cybersecurity threats by private actors.[195] Thus far, however, such progressive approaches have not found any support in state practice. Neither for the large-scale attacks against Estonia nor those against Iran was state responsibility even invoked, despite several clues that third states were involved in initiating the attacks. Due to technical difficulties, the threshold for attribution is even higher in the cybersphere than it already is in general international law.

Therefore, alternative approaches toward state responsibility become all the more important. Without an adequate responsibility scheme, states might well begin to unilaterally interpret the legal consequences of cyber incidents and stretch the limits of self-defense due to the potentially enormous harm such incidents could bring about.[196] And with cyber infrastructure in many states owned and operated by private companies, the role of due diligence obligations is once again crucial.[197] The next section will thus examine what the standard of due diligence entails for cybersecurity and which specific problems could arise.

III. Due Diligence in the Cybersphere

In the cybersphere, the contours of due diligence are far from clear. State practice is still evolving, and comprehensive case law more or less absent. There are hardly any specific norms of international law governing cyberspace. Among the few exceptions is the Convention on Cybercrime adopted by the Council of Europe in 2001. It requires member states to adopt legislative and other measures to introduce criminal offenses under domestic law in cyber-related matters and contains a duty for states to cooperate in investigating and prosecuting criminal cyber offenses.[198] Other than that, however, substantial approaches to concretize the cyber obligations of states are still missing.

---

[195] Matthias Herdegen, "Possible Legal Framework and Regulatory Models for Cyberspace" (2015) 58 *GYIL* 169–185 at 184 f.; Shackelford and Andres, "State Responsibility for Cyber Attacks," 992.

[196] Joanna Kulesza, "State Responsibility for Cyber-Attacks on International Peace and Security" (2009) 29 *Polish Yearbook of International Law* 139–151 at 151.

[197] Michael Schmitt, "In Defense of Due Diligence in Cyberspace" (2015) 125 *Yale Law Journal Forum* 68–81 at 74; Mary Ellen O'Connell, "Cyber Security without Cyber War" (2012) 17 *Journal of Conflict and Security Law* 187–209 at 207.

[198] Budapest Convention on Cybercrime, signed on 23 November 2001, entered into force on 1 July 2004, ETS No. 185.

The authors of the Tallinn Manuals could not reach consensus on the peacetime cyber obligations of states, and the Manuals remain confined to general remarks. They do acknowledge that states have cyber due diligence obligations and that failure to comply with these obligations might allow affected states to resort to remedies such as self-defense or countermeasures.[199] The exact parameters of those due diligence obligations, however, are not detailed any further.

Nevertheless, some contours of those duties can be drawn already. Obviously, technical questions of practical feasibility have to be taken into consideration when defining the standard of care in international cyber law,[200] and as with all areas of international law, preventive and punitive due diligence obligations have to be distinguished. Since due diligence obligations in the aftermath of an incident are relatively straightforward, somewhat unchronologically, they will be addressed first (1.), whereas the unresolved issue of preventive obligations will be considered later on (2.).

1. Due Diligence Obligations in the Aftermath of a Cyber Incident

Once cyber incidents have occurred, a diligent reaction is expected of the source state.[201] In the aftermath of a harmful event, states are under an obligation to show their best efforts in identifying the perpetrators of an attack and to prosecute them. They should inform and cooperate with other potentially affected states and with non-state actors who may be able to render effective assistance, such as service providers and internet experts. Whether it is mutual assistance or a 24/7 support network, duties to cooperate and to communicate also lie at the core of the Convention on Cybercrime.

At least some elements of a cyber due diligence standard can thus be identified: the domestic implementation of criminal laws and the establishment of investigative cyber capabilities enabling government authorities to identify and combat the sources of cyberattacks.[202] And

---

[199] Tallinn Manual 2013, Rule 5, pp. 26 ff.; Rule 9, pp. 36 ff., and Rule 13, pp. 54 ff. reemphasized by Tallinn Manual 2017, Rule 6, p. 30.
[200] Kanuck, "Discourse on Cyber Conflict," 1592; Dieter Fleck, "Searching for International Rules Applicable to Cyber Warfare" (2013) 18 *Journal of Conflict and Security Law* 331–351 at 338.
[201] David Graham, "Cyber Threats and the Law of War" (2010) 4 *Journal of National Security Law & Policy* 87–102 at 93 f.
[202] Matthew Sklerov, "Solving the Dilemma of State Response to Cyberattacks" (2009) 201 *Military Law Review* 1–85 at 12.

evidently, it is not only the enactment of such legislation that forms part of the required standard of care but also sufficiently diligent and effective enforcement. Recognized and established duties of cooperation and information are thus applicable to the cybersphere.[203]

2. Preventive Due Diligence Obligations in the Cybersphere

It is less clear though whether states are also under an obligation to take preventive cyber measures. The Tallinn Manual asserts in its Rule 5 that a state "shall not knowingly allow the cyber infrastructure located in its territory or under its exclusive governmental control to be used for acts that adversely affect other States,"[204] thereby seemingly acknowledging the existence of preventive duties. The Advisory Group on Cross-border Internet of the Council of Europe used similar language in that states should "prevent, manage and respond" to transboundary internet incidents.[205] Analyzing the individual components of due diligence obligations in the cybersphere will yet reveal that when it comes to preventive obligations, the knowledge threshold is particularly hard to overcome, and it is difficult to determine what constitutes reasonable cyber measures.

a. Knowledge: The Foreseeability of Harmful Cyber Incidents

As we have seen, a key element triggering international due diligence obligations is the foreseeability of harmful events. Obviously, states that positively know of harmful cyber activities on their territory are under an obligation to take preventive measures[206] at least encompassing a warning to potentially affected other states. Principally, this also applies where states should have known of harmful activities. The peculiarities of the cybersphere, however, challenge the constructive knowledge threshold to a considerable extent.

Cyberattacks can be carried out much faster than harmful undertakings in the "real world," leaving states less time to react and evaluate the most suitable reaction. A crucial point for the ICJ's Corfu Channel

---

[203] Christian Walter, "Obligations of States before, during, and after a Cyber Security Incident" (2015) 58 GYIL 67–86 at 81.
[204] Tallinn Manual 2013, Rule 5, p. 26.
[205] CoE, Ad-hoc Advisory Group on Cross-border Internet, Interim Report on the Media and New Communication Services, International and Multi-stakeholder Cooperation on Cross-border Internet, 2010, para. 64.
[206] Tallinn Manual 2.0. 2017, Commentary to Rule 6, para. 37, p. 40.

III. DUE DILIGENCE IN THE CYBERSPHERE

decision had been that Albania knew of the existence of the mines "in sufficient time" before they eventually harmed British ships.[207] Even where a threat is well-known, however, most cyber activities are carried out too quickly to react preventively. Besides, the circumstances under which constructive knowledge can be assumed are far more difficult to determine. Outside of the cybersphere, claiming ignorance of long-term threats is difficult, as such threats are often preceded by objective indications or even warnings by other states and international organizations. Cyber activists, however, often employ new and unknown malware.

Certainly, this calls into question the applicability of the constructive-knowledge threshold for the entire cybersphere. Notwithstanding, some conceptual parallels can be detected with respect to environmental law.[208] As mentioned previously, scientific uncertainties in many cases defy the adequate assessment of environmental projects, making it difficult to assume constructive knowledge. In the cybersphere, identifying potential risks and impacts can be just as onerous a task. Both fields are shaped by scientific uncertainty and technological complexity. As for environmental law, this motivated the precautionary approach requiring preventive measures, even where comprehensive evidence is missing but harm would be particularly devastating.[209] With the harmful consequences of cyber activities just as far-reaching and enormous as those of ecological disasters, similar approaches seem to suggest themselves. Nevertheless, factual differences between both fields have to be taken into account. Whereas high environmental risks can usually be linked to specific undertakings, cyber risks evolve from myriad sources. Risks for the environment can usually be traced back to single projects or at least certain types of activities that can be regulated and controlled even if their harmful potential is not fully established. In contrast, the signs of harmful cyber conduct are difficult to identify in advance: Cyberattacks might be initiated from a vast amount of different sources. Theoretically, any citizen using a mobile device could trigger harmful attacks without any further material resources. Cyber activities can be routed through many different systems, which may easily lead to the misidentification of the

---

[207] ICJ, Corfu Channel Case, p. 22.
[208] See, for a more detailed analysis, Thilo Marauhn, "Customary Rules of International Environmental Law – Can They Provide Guidance for Developing a Peacetime Regime for Cyberspace?," in Katharina Ziolkowski (ed.), *Peacetime Regime for State Activities in Cyberspace* (Tallinn: NATO CCD COE Publications, 2013), 465–484.
[209] See Chapter 5.1, III, 1.

attack source.[210] Attacks may even consist of many different sets that – though not significantly harmful on their own – cause far-reaching harm as a coordinated attack. As mentioned earlier, many cyberattacks are also of an unprecedented character using new technologies or methods making them even harder to predict.[211] In environmental law, states usually know at least the source of potential harm and are obliged to weigh the probability of harm against its potential scope. As for cyber threats, not even the sources of potential harm can be easily identified, let alone the likelihood of harmful incidents or their potential scope.

Some authors thus argue that knowledge in the cybersphere could only be established upon notification by affected victim states,[212] and there was no obligation to actively gather information.[213] Constructive knowledge as a concept would not fit for the cybersphere at all. In fact, the authors of the first Tallinn Manual could not agree on this matter either. While not denying its applicability per se, they found the constructive knowledge threshold difficult to overcome, mainly due to the challenges of effectively policing cyber activities, tracing back sources, and identifying separate sets of a coordinated attack.[214] In the second Manual, however, the authors explicitly confirmed that the concept of constructive knowledge was germane to the cybersphere and should merely be adjusted so as to meet the peculiarities of net activities. The Commentary suggests that constructive knowledge could be assumed where government cyber infrastructure was used during an attack or where previously known malware and vulnerabilities were employed. While still cautioning against an expanded understanding of constructive knowledge in light of the unprecedented and complex nature of cyberattacks, the Manual requires states to surveil such cyber infrastructure as they control and operate and to keep security systems up-to-date.[215] Notably, however, the Manual denies any obligation to generally monitor cyber activities on a state's territory,[216] which also means that, according to the Manual, states are not obliged to actively obtain knowledge of private cyber activities on their territory.

[210] Graham, "Cyber Threats," 102.
[211] Tallinn Manual 2013, Commentary to Rule 5, para. 4.
[212] Constantine Antonopoulos, "State Responsibility in Cyberspace," in Nicholas Tsagourias and Russell Buchan (eds.), *Research Handbook on International Law and Cyberspace* (Cheltenham: Edward Elgar, 2015), p. 69.
[213] Schmitt, "In Defense of Due Diligence in Cyberspace," 75.
[214] Tallinn Manual 2013, Commentary to Rule 5, para. 11, p. 28.
[215] Tallinn Manual 2.0 2017, Commentary to Rule 6, paras. 40 f., p. 41.
[216] Ibid., Commentary to Rule 7, para. 10, p. 45.

As far as the foreseeability of risks is concerned, similar problems arise for the preventive obligations of so-called transit states. Some authors suggest that cyber-related due diligence obligations should not only apply to the state from which harmful cyber activities emanate but also to neutral transit states through which such activities are mounted.[217] If a state knew or should know that its territory was being crossed by another state or a private group with the aim of attacking a third state, preventive measures are required – at least in the form of warnings.[218] This view deserves support insofar as the source of potential harm is not relevant to preventive due diligence obligations. As soon as states obtain knowledge of harmful conduct and have the means to stop it, they should become preventive no matter where this harmful conduct stems from. The concerns with constructive knowledge in the cybersphere yet equally apply to transit states. The Tallinn Manual's authors could not reach substantial consensus but stated that insofar as preventive obligation were applicable at all, they would require transit states to take reasonable preventive steps.[219] This takes us to the next controversially discussed issue, and that is the question of what would even constitute reasonable measures to prevent harmful cyber incidents.

b. Reasonable Measures of Prevention

Technical difficulties in the cybersphere not only call the foreseeability of harm into question; they also complicate the identification of reasonable preventive concepts. As mentioned before, the standard of due diligence is usually described as what a "good government" should have done under the circumstances at hand. Above all, this implies that states are to take preventive measures only within the framework of their legal obligations.[220]

As for cyber activities, however, effective prevention has the potential of clashing substantially with other international obligations, most notably in the field of human rights protection.[221] The due diligence standard generally requires states to control and regulate potentially harmful

---

[217] See, for instance, Schmitt, "In Defense of Due Diligence in Cyberspace," 73.
[218] Benedikt Pirker, "Territorial Sovereignty and Integrity and the Challenges of Cyberspace," in Katharina Ziolkowski (ed.), *Peacetime Regime for State Activities in Cyberspace* (Tallinn: NATO CCD COE Publications, 2013), p. 209; Karine Bannelier-Christakis, "Cyber Diligence: A Low-Intensity Due Diligence Principle for Low-Intensity Cyber Operations" (2014) 14 *Baltic Yearbook of International Law* 23–40 at 27.
[219] Tallinn Manual 2013, Commentary to Rule 8, para. 2, p. 36.
[220] See also Chapter 4, IV, 1, c.
[221] Walter, "Obligations of States before, during and after a Cyber-Incident," 76.

private conduct. As we have seen, though, the preparation of malicious cyber activities is rather difficult to detect. With harmful cyber conduct theoretically stemming from anywhere, widespread surveillance would seem the only way to identify harmful activities beforehand. The obligation to regulate private conduct is yet limited, where the conduct in question is protected by human rights guarantees,[222] and in the field of cyber activities, freedom of expression and the right to privacy are most likely to be adversely affected. Complete preventive surveillance of private cyber activities would contravene these human rights guarantees and cannot be a reasonable preventive concept. This becomes all the more important when taking into account that some states might well take advantage of cyber-prevention strategies to justify extensive surveillance legislation under the pretense of fulfilling due diligence obligations.

Prevention in the cybersphere is further complicated by the limited options states have for addressing cyber threats even after they have been identified. To initiate all-comprising surveillance or block countrywide online access seems excessive and too burdensome an intervention, depending on the scale of potential harm. Obstructing individual devices or accounts, however, seems ineffective, as they could easily be reactivated. The experts involved in drafting the first Tallinn Manual thus had difficulties in determining whether there were any effective preventive measures at all.[223] Whereas several experts argued in favor of a general duty to take reasonable measures of prevention, others denied any such obligation, given the difficulties of identifying and defending against all possible threats.[224]

For now, this leaves us with the somewhat dissatisfying conclusion that concrete due diligence obligations can only be assumed in the aftermath of a cyberattack with preparatory activities being still too speculative to give rise to a duty to act. The core concept of due diligence obligations, however, is not only to punish wrongful behavior but also – and maybe more importantly – to prevent it from even occurring. Several authors thus suggest readjustments to render international rules on cyber matters more effective. Thus far, the most prominent approach in this regard is to alter the evidentiary requirements in international proceedings.[225]

---

[222] Oliver Dörr, "Obligations of the State of Origin of a Cyber Security Incident" (2015) 58 GYIL 87–99 at 95.
[223] Tallinn Manual 2013, Commentary to Rule 5, para. 4, p. 27.
[224] Tallinn Manual 2013, Commentary to Rule 5, para. 7, p. 27.
[225] Pirker, "Territorial Sovereignty," 206; Herbert Lin, "Responding to Sub-Threshold Cyber Intrusions" (2010) 11 Georgetown Journal of International Affairs 127–135 at

c. Shifting the Burden of Proof?

State responsibility for cyber incidents, so it is argued, should not be based on knowledge of a specific cyberattack but rather on a state's actions to generally prevent such attacks. A state could then be found in violation of its due diligence obligations, where it failed to enact and enforce adequate cyber-regulating legislation.[226] While this would significantly simplify the production of evidence for victim states, assuming state responsibility based merely on the absence of cyber-related legislation seems to go too far. Knowledge always has to be linked to concrete incidents and circumstances. The mere failure to enact cyber-specific legislation is not sufficient to hold the state responsible for any harmful cyber conduct stemming from its territory.[227] This would come close to strict liability, for which there is no indication of any supporting state practice, and it is doubtful how consensus could even be reached on which domestic legislation would be sophisticated and efficient enough. Vice versa, it would be just as inadequate to assume that a state that enacted cyber-related legislation would thereby alone fulfill its due diligence obligations. As was repeated various times, endorsing legislation falls short of the due diligence standard if it is not implemented and enforced in an effective manner.

Next to this rather extreme position of de facto strict liability, several authors support a moderate but revised approach to the burden of proof in cyber-related proceedings.[228] They argue that victim states should merely be required to show that another state's cyber infrastructure was used for harmful activities.[229] It would then be for the respondent state to prove that its infrastructure was misused or manipulated without the government's knowledge.[230] While the proof of physical location was not

---

131; Daniel Ryan et al., "International Cyberlaw: A Normative Approach" (2010) 42 *Georgetown Journal of International Law* 1161–1197 at 1188 f.; Sklerov, "State Response to Cyberattacks," 71.

[226] Sklerov, "State Response to Cyberattacks," 71.

[227] Sven-Hendrik Schulze, *Cyber-"War" – Testfall der Staatenverantwortlichkeit* (Tübingen: Mohr Siebeck, 2015), p. 121.

[228] Pirker, "Territorial Sovereignty," 206; Wolff Heintschel von Heinegg, "Legal Implications of Territorial Sovereignty in Cyberspace," in Christian Czosseck et al. (eds.), *Fourth International Conference on Cyber Conflict* (Tallinn: NATO CCD COE Publications, 2012), p. 17; Lin, "Sub-Threshold Cyber Intrusions," 131; Ryan et al., "International Cyberlaw," 1188 f.

[229] Heintschel von Heinegg, "Territorial Sovereignty in Cyberspace," 17; Ryan et al., "International Cyberlaw," 1188 f.

[230] Pirker, "Territorial Sovereignty," 206; Kriangsak Kittichaisaree, *Public International Law of Cyberspace* (Cham: Springer, 2017), p. 42.

necessarily sufficient, evidence of government cyber infrastructure being used in mounting an attack would trigger a "rebuttable presumption" that the respective state should have known of the activity in question. Though not automatically allowing for attribution, it would indicate a failure to comply with cyber-related due diligence obligations if the state was not able to show its infrastructure had been usurped.[231] Such responsibility would also serve as an important incentive for states to invest in effective cybersecurity infrastructure protecting against intrusions and tracing back potential attack sources.[232] This is insofar in line with international jurisprudence as international human rights bodies – namely the European Court of Human Rights – reversed the burden of proof in the event of exclusive state control over an institution or incident. In *Salman* v. *Turkey*, the Court held that it would usually adhere to the standard of proof beyond reasonable doubt. Where, however, "the events in issue lie wholly, or in large part, within the exclusive knowledge of the authorities ... the burden of proof may be regarded as resting on the authorities to provide a satisfactory and convincing explanation."[233] Applied to the cybersphere, this could mean that a state whose government cyber infrastructure had been used during an attack should convincingly explain that it was not involved.

The ICJ, in contrast, has been more reluctant to derive a shift of evidentiary burdens from the mere fact of control over territory.[234] Not even the precautionary approach in environmental law was seen as operating as reversal of the burden of proof.[235] Against this background, exclusive control of cyber infrastructure should not automatically allow for shifting the burden of proof.[236] Such reversal would entail the significant risk of false assumptions and may inflict an undue burden upon states that lack the capacity to show their cyber infrastructure had been hacked,[237] even though the standard of proof primarily exists to protect the respondent against erroneous attributions and not to disadvantage

---

[231] Heintschel von Heinegg, "Territorial Sovereignty in Cyberspace," 17.
[232] Margulies, "Sovereignty and Cyber Attacks," 515.
[233] ECtHR, *Salman* v. *Turkey*, Grand Chamber Judgment of 27 June 2000, Application No. 21986/93, para. 100.
[234] See already ICJ, Corfu Channel Case, p. 18.
[235] ICJ, Case Concerning Pulp Mills on the River Uruguay (*Argentina* v. *Uruguay*), Judgment of 20 April 2010, ICJ Reports 2010, 14, para. 164.
[236] See also Marco Roscini, "Evidentiary Issues in International Disputes Related to State Responsibility for Cyber Operations" (2015) 50 *Texas International Law Journal* 233–273 at 246.
[237] Ibid., p. 248.

the applicant.[238] This is all the more true when considering the potential consequences of lowering the evidentiary thresholds for attribution. If a cyberattack is considered to amount to an armed attack and trigger the right to self-defense, forceful counter-reactions would be justified, and as Judge *Higgins* rightly pointed out in the Oil Platforms case, "the graver the charge the more confidence must there be in the evidence relied on"[239] – a position confirmed by the ICJ in the Genocide Convention case when it stated that for charges of "exceptional gravity," actions and attribution had to be established by "fully conclusive" evidence.[240]

In particular, where states are confronted with grave charges, caution is thus called for before shifting the burden of proof. Notwithstanding, an adjusted approach to the standard of proof in cyber law could still be applied when it comes to establishing failure to comply with the preventive obligations of diligent conduct. Taking into consideration the ICJ's differentiated approach in its Genocide Convention case, it is worth recalling that with due diligence obligations, there might be room for a more lenient approach, as the high thresholds of establishing positive knowledge and/or intent do not have to be met.[241]

However, when summarizing these suggestions, it is important to notice that so far, there are no inter-state proceedings on transboundary cyber harm. The debate on shifting the burden of proof, therefore, is not backed up by state practice or international case law and rather reflects normative arguments on how evidence issues should be handled in the future. Notwithstanding, these arguments hint already that the issue of capacities is once again crucial since states with insufficient capacities might not be able to absolve themselves from accusations that their infrastructure had been hacked. How to handle diverging capacities is thus controversially discussed also in the cyber context.

d. Capacities in the Cybersphere

Comparable with environmental law, cyber activities are a field of rapid changes. Keeping up with technological developments is as cost-intensive

---

[238] Ibid., p. 251.
[239] ICJ, Case Concerning Oil Platforms (*Iran* v. *USA*), Judgment of 6 November 2003, ICJ Reports 2003, 161, Separate Opinion by Judge Higgins, para. 33.
[240] ICJ, Case Concerning the Application of the Convention on the Prevention and Punishment of the Crime of Genocide (*Bosnia and Herzegovina* v. *Serbia and Montenegro*), Judgment of 26 February 2007, ICJ Reports 2007, 43, para. 209.
[241] ICJ, Genocide Convention Case, para. 432.

as it is complex.[242] Therefore, limited capacities play a most significant role also with regard to cyber diligence obligations, with many authors supporting varying standards of care.[243] The Advisory Group of the Council of Europe confirmed that the standard of care in the cybersphere "should be subject to capabilities of the states concerned."[244] As with lower degrees of care in environmental or counterterrorism law,[245] however, there is a significant risk that cyber activists deliberately choose low-capacity states and exploit their inability to effectively prevent and sanction harmful activities.

This takes us back to a range of problems already addressed in the context of terrorist activities by non-state actors operating on remote parts of the territory of weak governance states.[246] Due diligence obligations are crucial in order to determine if and when third states may take remedial measures once a state has proved unwilling or unable to fight harmful private conduct, which becomes highly relevant in the cybersphere as well.[247] When recalling the debate on counterterrorism efforts, it is no stretch to assume that – at least where cyber incidents reach the scale of forcible attacks – weak states are under an obligation to either take active steps to enhance their capacities or tolerate that other states engage in responses on their territory.[248] In fact, the second Tallinn Manual emphasizes that states which lack the technical expertise to tackle cyber threats could be reasonably expected to seek help, including that of private companies.[249] When compared to the field of counterterrorism, where responses usually amount to forcible action on the respective state's territory, fighting cyber threats even seems less intrusive, as it does not require physical counter-efforts.

The legality of remedial measures once a state permanently fails to keep up with its due diligence obligations, however, has been heavily

---

[242] Oren Gross, "Cyber Responsibility to Protect: Legal Obligations of States Directly Affected by Cyber-Incidents" (2015) 48 *Cornell International Law Journal* 481–512 at 503.
[243] Dörr, "Obligations of the State of Origin," 95; Schmitt, "In Defense of Due Diligence in Cyberspace," 74; Bannelier-Christakis, "Cyber Diligence," 37.
[244] CoE, Ad-hoc Advisory Group on Cross-border Internet, Interim Report on the Media and New Communication Services, International and Multi-stakeholder Cooperation on Cross-border Internet, 2010, para. 77.
[245] See Chapter 5.1, IV and Chapter 5.2, III.
[246] See Chapter 5.2, III, 2, b.
[247] Robert Kolb, "Reflections on Due Diligence Duties and Cyberspace" (2015) 58 GYIL 113–128 at 125; Fleck, "International Rules Applicable to Cyber Warfare," 339.
[248] Gross, "Cyber Responsibility to Protect," 497.
[249] Tallinn Manual 2.0 2017, Commentary to Rule 7, para. 17, p. 47.

criticized already in the terrorism context. And in spite of a lower level of potential intrusion, there are good reasons for an equally cautious approach in the cybersphere. Even if the safe harbor concept is deemed part of customary international law allowing for self-defense measures against non-state actors on the territory of an unwilling or unable third state, it is hard to see how the "unable or unwilling" threshold could be usefully applied in the cybersphere.[250] Unwillingness could only be assumed where non-state actors use state cyber infrastructure on a regular and systematic basis, without any state intervention.[251] As we have seen, however, the preparation of cyberattacks is even more difficult to monitor than the preparation of terrorist activities. Theoretically, cyberattacks can be carried out anywhere and by anyone with no need for intense preparation. New technological options can develop quickly and unpredictably. The safe-haven concept in the counterterrorism context, in contrast, was relied on where states showed an unwillingness or inability to combat terrorist groups on their territory when the presence of the latter was positively known to that state. International reporting duties and enhanced international intelligence efforts have significantly facilitated the detection of terrorist bases. Here, the difference to cyber threats becomes obvious. The knowledge of the threat itself is the greatest hurdle to overcome, whereas in the counterterrorism context, the threat is known and "merely" the states' unwillingness or inability hinders an effective response. State complicity in cyberattacks based on acquiescence is thus conceivable only where states have positive knowledge of cyber threats (for instance, due to an explicit warning) but fail to react. And even though remedial cyber measures are usually less intrusive, they still have the potential of causing devastating effects, which is why recourse to unilateral reactions should be just as narrowly tailored as in the counterterrorism context.

IV. Summary: Is There Room for Preventive Cyber Obligations?

At first glance, analyzing cyber due diligence thus produces rather dissatisfying results. Whereas a diligent response is unequivocally expected as soon as cyber incidents have actually occurred, preventive concepts are less clear. Notwithstanding, several authors (and government experts)

---

[250] Laurie Blank, "International Law and Cyber Threats from Non-State Actors" (2013) 89 *International Law Studies* 406–437 at 416.
[251] Graham, "Cyber Threats," 94 f.

are optimistic about the future role of due diligence standards for international cyber regulations. Technological changes have always required the adjustment of international rules and principles, so they argue, and the cyber domain is not so different as to justify the complete abandonment of established international standards.[252] Moreover, it is precisely the inherently flexible nature of due diligence that makes it the most suitable tool to tackle new challenges. The mere fact that the peculiarities of cyber law make the determination of adequate international standards more difficult does not allow for the conclusion that such determination is virtually impossible.[253]

While the technical distinctiveness of cyberspace hinders states from detecting the entire range of potential sources of harm, there still is room for preventive measures. Even though states cannot be required to obtain knowledge of any individual cyberattack, it can reasonably be expected that they are generally aware of the fact that their cyber infrastructure is susceptible to attacks. Knowledge of this broad and general risk should trigger preventive obligations. Naturally, these preventive obligations are not overly specific, but the fact that any cyber system is vulnerable to attacks at least calls for general prevention. In this context, some inspiration may be drawn from the ILC's recent work on the protection of persons in the event of disasters that resulted in a set of draft articles launched in 2016.[254] Similar to the unpredictable character of cyber incidents, disasters are difficult to anticipate but cause large-scale and devastating effects. With this in mind, the ILC's work focused on enhancing risk mitigation and developing effective methods of disaster relief. The Articles acknowledge the difficulties in predicting disasters, given that they are usually the result of a complex set of causes,[255] and thus address preventive obligations of a rather general character. A strong emphasis is laid on the collection of information and its early exchange, as well as the development of relief strategies.[256] In particular, effective prevention requires states to adopt preparatory strategies on how to react in case of disasters, which includes preparing the potentially affected population, establishing international cooperation mechanisms, and

---

[252] Brandon Valeriano and Ryan Maness, *Cyber War versus Cyber Realities* (Oxford: Oxford University Press, 2015), pp. 196 f.
[253] Schulze, "Cyber-War," p. 121; Bannelier-Christakis, "Cyber Diligence," 39.
[254] ILC, Draft Articles on the Protection of Persons in the Event of Disasters with Commentaries, ILC Yearbook 2016, Volume II, Part II.
[255] Ibid., Commentary to Article 3, para. 4.
[256] Ibid., Commentary to Article 9, para. 6.

IV. SUMMARY

evaluating how harm might be mitigated in the most effective manner. Such a general and broad preventive approach could be fruitfully applied to the cyber context as well. While it would be incompatible with international human rights law to introduce widespread surveillance measures for the identification of cyber risks, several preventive measures could be reasonably employed. To name but a few, this might include implementing a domestic duty upon private actors that operate sensitive infrastructure to keep up with technological developments and update their security system.[257] It could further include the installation of a mandatory reporting system for cyber incidents in order to develop adequate counter-strategies.[258] As indicated in the second Tallinn Manual, reporting systems and enhanced information sharing mechanisms could also form part of a preventive concept[259] that fosters the identification of risks and improves cyber resilience. Finally, developing relief strategies for emergency situations form a distinct element of prevention. Such strategies should include ways to protect critical infrastructure and institutions minimizing harm potentially caused by cyber incidents.

In sum, there is thus a range of general preventive measures that could be reasonably expected of states to prevent and mitigate harmful cyber incidents. While limited in its reach, it would thus be going too far to assume that preventive obligations in the cybersphere are inconceivable from the start.

---

[257] Scott Shackelford et al., "Toward a Global Cybersecurity Standard of Care?" (2015) 50 *Texas International Law Journal* 305–355.

[258] Katharina Ziolkowski, "General Principles of International Law as Applicable in Cyberspace," in Katharina Ziolkowski (ed.), *Peacetime Regime for State Activities in Cyberspace* (Tallinn: NATO CCD COE Publications, 2013), pp. 185 f.

[259] Tallinn Manual 2.0 2017, Commentary to Rule 7, para. 12; see also Gross, "Cyber Responsibility to Protect," 496.

5.4

Summary

Analyzing how due diligence obligations are applied in various fields of international law has provided further insights into how the different components of the due diligence standard might be adjusted so as to meet specific challenges. Several concepts and strategies evolved in each of the analyzed fields, tailored to address its unique characteristics. With the field of human rights protection facing similar challenges – at least to a certain extent – these concepts and strategies afford guidance on how due diligence standards could promote global human rights protection.

When assessing the potential of human rights due diligence obligations in the following chapters, the transferability of these concepts will be further discussed and evaluated. With regard to the field of environmental protection, this mostly concerns the attempt to establish standardized procedural obligations such as mandatory impact assessments but also to address the issue of diverging capacities through the concept of common but differentiated responsibilities. The problem that many states lack the ability to diligently prevent harmful activities on their territory is also what lies at the core of the "unwilling or unable" standard, as developed in the context of counterterrorism efforts. In contrast, the field of cybersecurity is confronted with severe difficulties in monitoring risks, speaking for a rather broad and general approach toward preventive measures. How some or all of these strategies can be fruitfully applied to the field of human rights protection will be considered next.

With this in mind, the following section will analyze how the general framework of due diligence can be transferred to the human rights context. As we have seen, human rights protection shows several peculiarities when compared with other areas of international law, especially

IV. SUMMARY

when considering its focus on individual complaint mechanisms outside the reciprocal framework of state responsibility.

Notwithstanding, there are good reasons to focus on the rules on state responsibility and exploit their full potential in order to advance human rights protection.[260] As for the broad notion of positive obligations, distinguishing between different forms of such obligations based on the conduct that is expected of states could improve compliance with international human rights law. As mentioned previously, most cases in which state responsibility for human rights violations is at stake involve a failure on behalf of the state to exercise sufficient diligence. It is against this background that the following chapter will analyze international human rights jurisprudence, with a focus on how the broad and general notion of due diligence can be better conceptualized.

---

[260] See Chapter 1, V.

6

Applying the Due Diligence Framework to the Field of Human Rights Protection

I. Introductory Remarks

In order to explore both the potential of the due diligence concept in the field of human rights protection as well as the problems related thereto, the following chapter will analyze in greater detail the different elements of due diligence with respect to international human rights obligations. While paying due regard to the peculiarities of human rights protection, it will address if and to what extent the due diligence concepts developed in other areas of international law can be meaningfully applied to a human rights context. Along the three components introduced previously,[1] it will first be analyzed how knowledge of human rights risks might be established. Second, the issue of diverging capacities deserves consideration when evaluating how resource gaps can be taken into account in determining the expected standard of care. Finally, what constitutes reasonable measures in the human rights sphere will be discussed, taking into account the distinct problems the reasonableness standard can produce when it comes to human rights protection.

II. Knowledge

As with any other area of law, due diligence obligations to prevent human rights violations only arise where states know or should know of a specific human rights risk. States are not required to guarantee the prevention of any harmful conduct and strictly control the relationships between individual citizens. Generally, human rights bodies thus assume that

---

[1] See Chapter 4.

for obligations of diligent conduct to arise, states must have knowledge of a concrete risk affecting an individual person or an identifiable group of persons.[2] They are "conditional on its awareness of a situation of real and imminent danger for a specific individual or group of individuals."[3] Therefore, at least three preconditions have to be fulfilled in order to assume state knowledge of a human rights risk: the danger of human rights violations has to be real and imminent, and it has to affect an identifiable group of individuals. Obligations of diligent conduct thus presuppose positive or constructive knowledge of both the potential victims in need of protection and the source of potential harm.[4] The following section will analyze when these preconditions are fulfilled and which particular problems with the knowledge criterion arise in the human rights context.

First of all, it is important to notice that human rights risks might stem from a myriad of different sources. Whereas environmental risks generally relate to certain types of activities – and we have seen that obtaining such knowledge is rather difficult already – human rights risks cannot be limited to certain sources or activities. This makes it significantly harder to assess which conduct requires diligent measures of prevention. The Strasbourg Court regularly refers to the "unpredictability of human conduct" and the "difficulties involved in policing modern societies" when it comes to establishing knowledge on behalf of a state.[5] On the other hand, however, it is not necessary to establish that state authorities "had specific prior knowledge" of a human rights risk. Foreseeability is sufficient to trigger an obligation to prevent, which recognizes the constructive knowledge standard, despite all difficulties in obtaining knowledge of human rights risks.[6] Similar to the field of cybersecurity[7] however, there is an inherent risk related to the foreseeability standard.

---

[2] Linos-Alexander Sicilianos, "Preventing Violations of the Right to Life: Positive Obligations under Article 2 of the ECHR" (2014) 3 *Cyprus Human Rights Law Review* 117–129 at 119; Benedetto Conforti, "Reflections on State Responsibility for the Breach of Positive Obligations" (2003) 13 *Italian Yearbook of International Law* 3–10 at 6.

[3] IACtHR, *González et al. (Cotton Field)* v. *Mexico*, Judgment of 16 November 2009, Series C, No. 205, para. 280.

[4] Walter Kälin and Jörg Künzli, *Universeller Menschenrechtsschutz* (Basel: Helbing Lichtenhahn, 3rd ed., 2013), para. 302; Dimitris Xenos, *The Positive Obligations of the State under the ECHR* (London: Routledge, 2012), p. 76.

[5] Among many others, see ECtHR, *Osman* v. *UK*, Grand Chamber Judgment of 28 October 1998, Application No. 23452/94, para. 116.

[6] IACtHR, *Case of the Pueblo Bello Massacre* v. *Colombia*, Judgment of 31 January 2006, Series C, No. 140, paras. 135 ff.

[7] See Chapter 5.3, III, 2, a.

Given the fact that practically any conduct could entail the risk of human rights infringements, imposing obligations upon states to obtain knowledge of potential human rights risks might lead to excessive surveillance and control.

1. Obtaining Knowledge: The Risk of Excessive Surveillance and Control

As we have seen, it was recognized already at an early stage that imputing to a state every fault committed by its citizens would be improper. An absolute form of responsibility would logically entail absolute state control over any private conduct.[8] Such all-comprising oversight would be incompatible with the classical negative dimension of human rights. Some authors have therefore criticized that ever extending the preventive and protective obligations of states would force individuals under the increasing control of an omnipresent state inevitably resulting in "a far-reaching accumulation of power in hands of public authorities" and potentially endangering the bottom-up approach undergirding democracy itself.[9] With this in mind, the Inter-American Court stressed that there "are individual domains that are beyond the reach of the State or to which the State has but limited access. Thus, the protection of human rights must necessarily comprise the concept of the restriction of the exercise of state power."[10] Likewise, the ILC stated that not to attribute any private conduct to the state recognized "the autonomy of persons acting on their own account,"[11] and the European Commission on Human Rights found that the "right to respect for private life is of such a scope as to secure to the individual a sphere within which he can freely pursue the development and fulfilment of his personality"[12] without

---

[8] Olivier de Schutter, *International Human Rights Law* (Cambridge: Cambridge University Press, 2nd ed., 2014), pp. 486 f.; Kälin and Künzli, "Universeller Menschenrechtsschutz," para. 300; Thomas Koenen, *Wirtschaft und Menschenrechte* (Berlin: Duncker & Humblot, 2012), p. 212.

[9] Christian Tomuschat, *Human Rights: Between Idealism and Realism* (Oxford: Oxford University Press, 3rd ed., 2014), pp. 8 ff.; Olha Cherednychenko, "Toward the Control of Private Acts by the European Court of Human Rights" (2006) 13 *Maastricht Journal of European and Comparative Law* 195–218.

[10] IACtHR, The Word "Laws" in Article 30 of the ACHR, Advisory Opinion of 9 May 1986, Series A, No. 6, OC-6/86, para. 21.

[11] ILC, Responsibility of States for Internationally Wrongful Acts with Commentaries, ILC Yearbook 2001, Volume II, Chapter II, para. 2.

[12] EComHR, *Brüggemann and Scheuten v. Germany*, Report of the Commission adopted on 12 July 1977, Application No. 6959/75, para. 55, p. 18.

undue state interference. Employing too wide protection bears the risk of "unacceptable paternalism and occasion an inadmissible interference by the State with the individual's right[s]."[13] Any state obligation to prevent and to protect against human rights violations thus has to be balanced with individual freedom and autonomy.[14]

This is underlined even further by the fact that most human rights instruments now explicitly recognize the right to privacy as a distinct human right. The ECtHR held that the notion of private life as employed in Article 8 of the Convention would protect "a right to personal development" and considered with regard to its role within the Convention "that the notion of personal autonomy is an important principle underlying the interpretation of its guarantees."[15] Even the concept of positive obligations as such has been criticized by some authors arguing that human rights bodies would not "take seriously the considerations of ... the preservation of private autonomy" by expanding the reach of the human rights instruments "into the sphere of the relations between private parties, including the most sacred spheres protected by private law."[16]

Some authors have further criticized due diligence as "a weak standard," the application of which could only bring disadvantages to human rights protection. It would allow for too broad a margin of appreciation and merely required states to employ reasonable efforts which would often enough result in states escaping their responsibility.[17] When considering the fundamental importance of personal freedom and independence, however, the flexibility of the due diligence standard, yet again, stands out as an important feature. Any other concept of state responsibility would necessarily entail substantial infringements by the state into the private autonomous sphere of its citizens. States could and should not be held responsible for any harmful non-state conduct stemming from their territory, as

---

[13] Argument by the Dutch government in ECtHR, *X and Y v. Netherlands*, Judgment of 26 March 1985, Application No. 8978/80, para. 25.
[14] See also de Schutter, "International Human Rights Law," p. 487; Tomuschat, "Human Rights," p. 8; Richard Lillich et al., *International Human Rights* (New York: Aspen, 4th ed., 2006), p. 364.
[15] ECtHR, *Pretty v. UK*, Judgment of 29 April 2002, Application No. 2346/02, para. 61.
[16] Cherednychenko, "Control of Private Acts," 218; see also Menno Kamminga, "Due Diligence Mania: The Misguided Introduction of an Extraneous Concept into Human Rights Discourse" (2011) Maastricht Faculty of Law Working Paper No. 7; Heike Krieger, "Positive Verpflichtungen unter der EMRK" (2014) 74 ZaöRV 187–213.
[17] Kamminga, "Due Diligence Mania," 6.

this would require complete control, which is inherently incompatible with the notions of individual autonomy and privacy.

In order to achieve both an adequate protection of individuals against human rights threats posed by non-state actors and an adequate protection of individual autonomy, a suitable balance has to be found for the foreseeability standard in human rights law. Comparable to the field of cybersecurity, the knowledge threshold is less of a problem when assessing punitive obligations, since the human rights violation that requires a diligent reaction has already occurred. It is only with regard to preventive obligations that an adequate balance between necessary prevention and undue interference has to be found. In contrast to the cybersphere, however, in which threats are particularly difficult to assess beforehand, risks in the human rights context are somewhat easier to predict. Often enough, cyber threats are of an unprecedented nature and leave little time to react as they are usually not announced by any signs or symptoms.[18] While any method of obtaining knowledge of human rights risks has to avoid an undue interference with privacy rights as well, at least some human rights risks are assessable through objective indicators. In fact, human rights jurisprudence reveals several categories of cases in which human rights risks are considered to be foreseeable. Even though the exact threshold for the constructive knowledge standard cannot be defined for each individual case, those categories provide substantial guidance on how the standard operates with regard to human rights risks.

2. *The Knowledge Standard in Human Rights Jurisprudence*

At least three instances can be identified in which knowledge of human rights risks can be positively established or assumed. The first and rather evident category comprises situations in which potential victims inform states of looming human rights risk or such information is made available by experts or government institutions (a.). In such scenarios, information might either be substantial and detailed enough to even establish positive knowledge or at least require the state to carry out further investigations. Next to this, foreseeability can be assumed if states themselves engage in or allow activities that bear the potential of human rights infringements (b.). Even if such activities are ultimately carried out by non-state actors, states still contribute to

---

[18] See Chapter 5.3, III, 2, a.

the existence of related human rights risks. Finally, there is room for constructive knowledge in case of consistent patterns of human rights violations in a particular region or toward a particular group of individuals (c.).

a. Information of Human Rights Risks

It is rather evident that states that had been informed of certain human rights risks are generally assumed to also have positive knowledge or at least constructive knowledge where information about such risks is available and easily accessible.[19]

There are various sources from which information on potential human rights violations can be gathered. If potentially affected individuals inform state organs of such risks, the latter are under an obligation to at least investigate those allegations.[20] The same holds true in case of "early warning signs" on behalf of potential perpetrators.[21] Not every individual allegation, however, automatically amounts to knowledge on behalf of the state. In its *Osman* decision, the ECtHR found no violation of the preventive obligations under Article 2, even though the victims had previously reported several incidents and the perpetrator communicated its murderous intentions to the police.[22] Notwithstanding, the information obtained by the competent state organs had not been precise enough for the Court to assume that they knew of an imminent risk. Knowledge, therefore, can only be established if the information given is substantial and well-founded. Where these preconditions are fulfilled, though, states are assumed to have knowledge the moment they are informed by the affected individuals.[23] Besides, if individuals or experts report in detail about threats of severe human rights violations, states are at least under an obligation to undertake reasonable investigations, even if the initial

---

[19] Hélène Tran, *Les Obligations de Vigilance des États Parties à la Convention Européenne des Droits de l'Homme* (Brussels: Bruylant, 2013), p. 45; Xenos, "Positive Obligations," p. 87.

[20] This is a separate form of obligations when compared to the duty to carry out investigations introduced in Chapter 2. While states are under an obligation to carry out investigations of alleged human rights violations that have already occurred, the obligation at hand is an obligation to investigate whether there is a risk of future human rights violations that should be prevented.

[21] See, for instance, AfComHPR, *Association of Victims of Post Electoral Violence and Interights v. Cameroon*, Decision of 25 November 2009, Com 272/2003, para. 117.

[22] ECtHR, *Osman v. UK*, Grand Chamber Judgment of 28 October 1998, Application No. 23452/94, paras. 119 f.

[23] Xenos, "Positive Obligations," p. 83.

information is not precise enough.[24] Such duty to investigate has been recognized by the courts for various constellations, including reports on incidents of domestic violence,[25] health risks resulting from the unsafe operation of industrial plants,[26] infringements upon the protection of the home stemming from insupportable noise,[27] or limitations to the right to assemble and express one's opinion due to counterdemonstrations.[28] If states fail to reasonably investigate such complaints and human rights risks eventually materialize, constructive knowledge will usually be assumed.

This might even be the case where human rights risks are not reported by individual complaints but publicly known.[29] In particular, for refoulement cases in which states have to assess whether the expulsion of individuals is compatible with human rights, the Strasbourg Court has attached great importance to the evaluations of independent human rights associations. Before rendering extradition decisions, states are required to actively collect the relevant material.[30] Where information on the situation in a particular country is "well known and easy to verify on the basis of multiple sources," states are assumed to know of the inherent human rights risks.[31] As for consistent patterns of human rights violations that do not affect particular individuals but certain regions or groups of individuals, it is thus for the state to independently assess human rights in peril.

Later on, the ECtHR picked up this reasoning when it instructed states to obtain knowledge of human rights risks that are not created by third parties but stem from external sources, such as natural disasters. In the *Budayeva* case, for instance, the Court found that Russia was expected to

---

[24] Tran, "Obligations de Vigilance," p. 45; Alastair Mowbray, *The Development of Positive Obligations under the ECHR by the European Court of Human Rights* (Oxford: Hart, 2004), pp. 37 ff.
[25] ECtHR, *Opuz* v. *Turkey*, Judgment of 9 June 2009, Application No. 33401/02, paras. 147, 173–174.
[26] ECtHR, *Öneryildiz* v. *Turkey*, Grand Chamber Judgment of 30 November 2004, Application No. 48939/99, para. 98.
[27] ECtHR, *Moreno Gomez* v. *Spain*, Judgment of 16 November 2004, Application No. 4143/02, para. 59.
[28] ECtHR, *Plattform "Ärzte für das Leben"* v. *Austria*, Judgment of 21 June 1988, Application No. 10126/82, para. 10.
[29] Xenos, "Positive Obligations," p. 84.
[30] See, for instance, German Federal Constitutional Court, Decision of 18 December 2017, 2 BvR 2259/17, para. 18.
[31] See, among others, ECtHR, *Hirsi Jamaa and Others* v. *Italy*, Grand Chamber Judgment of 23 February 2012, Application No. 27765/09, para. 131.

take diligent preventive measures in view of an imminent "natural hazard that had been clearly identifiable."[32] Obligations to assess the human rights risks of natural disasters even apply where scientific certainty cannot be fully achieved. The ECtHR's Tătar case dealt with health problems that the applicants claimed to result from the operations of a gold mine close to their homes. Even though the Court found the applicant had not succeeded in proving a causal link between the exposure to cyanide and his aggravated asthma disease, it still held that "malgré l'absence d'une probabilité causale en l'espèce, l'existence d'un risque sérieux et substantiel pour la santé et pour le bien-être des requérants faisait peser sur l'État l'obligation positive d'adopter des mesures raisonnables et adéquates capables à protéger les droits des intéressés aus respect de leur vie privée et leur domicile." Romania should have conducted further assessments of the environmental and health risks related to gold mining and its impacts on the local population.[33] Endorsing this reasoning, the Inter-American Court found in its 2017 Advisory Opinion on Environment and Human Rights that the customary obligation to conduct environmental impact assessments formed part of a state's human rights obligation to protect the life and physical integrity of individuals: "Con el propósito de respetar y garantizar los derechos a la vida e integridad de las personas bajo su jurisdicción, los Estados tienen la obligación de prevenir daños ambientales significativos, dentro o fuera de su territorio, para lo cual deben ... realizar estudios de impacto ambiental."[34] This illustrates another important aspect of the knowledge criterion – namely the relevance of international practice and awareness raised by international legal documents or reports. "Information of human rights risks" thus not only comprises instances in which explicit complaints are raised but also information that is publicly available, including through exchange and cooperation with other states and international organizations.[35]

---

[32] ECtHR, *Budayeva and Others* v. *Russia*, Judgment of 20 March 2008, Application Nos. 15339/02 a.o., para. 137.
[33] ECtHR, *Tătar* v. *Romania*, Judgment of 27 January 2009, Application No. 67021/01, paras. 107 ff.
[34] IACtHR, Advisory Opinion No. OC-23/17 of 15 November 2017, Medio Ambiente y Derechos Humanos, Series A, No. 23 (in Spanish only), p. 97, para. 5, which reads: "In order to comply with their obligation to respect and guarantee the right to life and physical integrity of persons within their jurisdiction, states are obliged to prevent significant environmental harm within and outside of their territory and to that end, they must ... carry out environmental impact assessments" (translation by author).
[35] Xenos, "Positive Obligations," p. 84.

Next to those constellations in which information of human rights risks is either brought to the state's attention or readily available, there are other constellations in which states are assumed to have at least constructive knowledge, in particular where states have themselves created human rights risks or helped bring them about.

b. Constellations in Which States Create or Contribute to the Creation of Human Rights Risks

Obligations to take diligent preventive and protective measures arise where state support is rendered to private conduct that later results in human rights contradictions or where states actively create situations that bear the risk of human rights contradictions.

aa. Licensing Procedures This does not necessarily mean that state authorities actively and purposely support human rights contraventions by private actors (which would rather open up questions of attribution) but rather an obligation to assess human rights risk stemming from private conduct which states license or support.[36] Among others, this is underlined by the ECtHR's *López Ostra* case, involving a privately operated waste-treatment plant causing nuisance and health problems in the surrounding areas. Even though "the Spanish authorities ... were theoretically not directly responsible for the emissions in question," the Court held, "the town allowed the plant to be built on its land and the State subsidised the plant's construction," triggering an obligation to assess human rights risks emanating from the plant's operation.[37] Later on, the Court repeated in various instances that wherever dangerous activities entailed the risk of human rights infringements, states were under an obligation to "govern the licensing, setting up, operation, security and supervision of the activity and must make it compulsory for all those concerned to take practical measures to ensure the effective protection of citizens."[38] They are expected to assess potential human rights risks, to diligently supervise ongoing operations and take adequate preventive measures. This applies both in cases involving particular licensing procedures for individual undertakings and general provisions allowing for potentially harmful private activities.

---

[36] See also Mowbray, "Positive Obligations," p. 14.
[37] ECtHR, *López Ostra* v. *Spain*, Judgment of 9 December 1994, Application No. 16798/90, para. 52.
[38] ECtHR, *Öneryildiz* v. *Turkey*, Grand Chamber Judgment of 30 November 2004, Application No. 48939/99, para. 90.

bb. Creation of Risks Next to this, states are required to perform a heightened standard of care if they have themselves created situations that bear the risk of human rights contradictions.[39] An illustrative example is to be found in the ECtHR's *Neyet Günay* case, in which a prisoner was supposed to assist security authorities during a secret operation. The Court held that "le cas de l'espèce se distingue radicalement des cas où la source du danger pour la vie est une tierce personne, où le fardeau qui pèse sur les autorités en vertu des obligations positives qui découlent de l'article 2 de la Convention est plus modéré,"[40] indicating that where state organs have created a particular human rights risk, they are obliged to apply even wider and stricter measures of prevention. Even where harmful conduct is ultimately carried out by private actors without active state support, states are therefore expected to acquire knowledge wherever they create a situation in which such conduct could occur. In such scenarios, identifying the potential victims individually is not even necessary. If states create a generally dangerous situation, they are obliged to take adequate measures of general protection.

This becomes even clearer in the ECtHR's *Mastromatteo* case, which involved risks to the right to life stemming from convicted criminals who were released or day-released and later committed homicide. While potential victims could not be identified beforehand, the Court still held that states were generally required to employ preventive due diligence when deciding on the premature release of prisoners whose conduct might harm other individuals. Preventive measures are thus not only required where states have knowledge of the risk of individual human rights violations, but states should also take preventive steps to "afford general protection to society,"[41] if they create situations with the potential of human rights contradictions.[42] The IACtHR has confirmed this position when arguing that Colombia, in encouraging the formation of self-defense groups "objectively created a dangerous situation for its inhabitants" and thus was under "special

---

[39] Kälin and Künzli, "Universeller Menschenrechtsschutz," para. 303; Tran, "Obligations de Vigilance," pp. 62 f.; Xenos, "Positive Obligations," pp. 86 f.

[40] ECtHR, *Nehyet Günay* v. *Turkey*, Judgment of 21 October 2008, Application No. 51210/99, para. 79.

[41] ECtHR, *Mastromatteo* v. *Italy*, Grand Chamber Judgment of 24 October 2002, Application No. 37703/97, para. 69; ECtHR, Tagayeva and Others v. Russia, Judgment of 13 April 2017, Application No. 26562/07 a.o., para. 482.

[42] See also Tran, "Obligations de Vigilance," p. 64.

obligations of prevention and protection in the zones where the paramilitary groups were present."[43]

Similar considerations were applied where human rights infringements occurred while individuals were in state custody. Whenever an individual is under state control, protective obligations apply.[44] In its *Salman* case, the Strasbourg Court instructed states to adequately guard persons in custody from harm.[45] The *Keenan* case[46] confirmed that persons in custody were in such a vulnerable position that states were expected to explain how injuries or death could occur during custody in particular, since the events in issue were usually within the exclusive knowledge of the authorities. Even the burden of proof might be shifted, insofar as it may "be regarded as resting on the authorities to provide a satisfactory and convincing explanation," indicating that failure to do so would allow for an assumption of state responsibility, even if it could not be established beyond a reasonable doubt that state organs had caused the injuries in question.[47] It can thus be summarized that state involvement in the creation of human rights risks – be it through licensing procedures, financial support, or the creation of dangerous situations – triggers an obligation on behalf of the state to obtain knowledge of the related human rights risks, even if the potential victims cannot be individually identified beforehand.

Similar considerations apply with respect to consistent patterns of human rights violations.

c. Consistent Patterns of Human Rights Violations

When it comes to determining whether a human rights violation had been predictable or not, another important factor is the regularity with which specific forms of human rights violation occur. It is more difficult for states to claim ignorance of human rights contraventions that occur frequently within a certain region or in relation to a particular group of

---

[43] IACtHR, *Case of the Pueblo Bello Massacre v. Colombia*, Judgment of 31 January 2006, Series C, No. 140, para. 126.
[44] Sicilianos, "Preventing Violations of the Right to Life," 125; Tran, "Obligations de Vigilance," p. 46.
[45] ECtHR, *Salman v. Turkey*, Grand Chamber Judgment of 27 June 2000, Application No. 21986/93, para. 99.
[46] ECtHR, *Keenan v. UK*, Judgment of 3 April 2001, Application No. 27229/95, para. 91.
[47] ECtHR, *Salman v. Turkey*, Grand Chamber Judgment of 27 June 2000, Application No. 21986/93, para. 100.

non-state actors.[48] In such cases, states are usually expected to know of these human rights risks, which have been classified as "empirical knowledge by context."[49]

aa. Frequency of Human Rights Contraventions in the Past

In its *Osman* case, the Strasbourg Court stated that "in assessing the level of knowledge which can be imputed to the police at the relevant time, the Court has also had close regard to the series of acts of vandalism."[50] Likewise, it found in the *Özgür Gündem* decision that Turkey failed to live up to its positive obligations since a newspaper and its staff had been subject "to a series of violent acts."[51] In its *Hajduova* decision, the Court referred to the perpetrator's prior convictions and his criminal antecedents to find that Slovakia "should have exercised an even greater degree of vigilance."[52] The frequency of threats and harmful incidents is thus an important parameter when assessing whether a particular human rights violation was foreseeable.[53] In a similar manner, the African Commission rejected claims of unforeseeability where there had been frequent occurrences of human rights violations in the past. In a decision involving violent incidents in the aftermath of an election, the Commission rejected Cameroon's claims that the events were of an unpredictable character as "disturbances of public law and order existed in the country since May 1990 and specifically during the holding of the elections,"[54] thereby confirming that prior incidents of violence are strong indicators for the constructive knowledge-threshold to be met.

bb. Frequent Human Rights Violations in a Particular Region

The frequency of harmful incidents might not only indicate a heightened risk for particular individuals but could also exist within a particular region.

---

[48] AfComHPR, *Zimbabwe Human Rights NGO Forum v. Zimbabwe*, Decision of 15 May 2006, Communication No. 245/2002, 21st Activity Report of the Commission, EX.CL/322 (X), para. 158.
[49] Xenos, "Positive Obligations," p. 80.
[50] ECtHR, *Osman v. UK*, Grand Chamber Judgment of 28 October 1998, Application No. 23452/94, para. 119.
[51] ECtHR, *Özgür Gündem v. Turkey*, Judgment of 16 March 2000, Application No. 23144/93, paras. 44 f.
[52] ECtHR, *Hajduova v. Slovakia*, Judgment of 30 November 2010, Application No. 2660/03, para. 50.
[53] Xenos, "Positive Obligations," pp. 84 f.
[54] AfComHPR, *Association of Victims of Post Electoral Violence and Interights v. Cameroon*, Decision of 25 November 2009, Com 272/2003, para. 117.

An illustrative example is the ECtHR's recent *Tagayeva* decision. It involved an attack in North Ossetia where a terrorist group laid siege to a school, holding pupils, teachers, and parents hostage for several days. When discussing Russia's preventive obligations under Article 2, the Court found that the circumstances were such that Russia should have known of a heightened risk for which it failed to apply adequate preventive measures. Several terrorist attacks with similar patterns had been committed before all of which involved civilian targets. The attack took place on the so-called Day of Knowledge, a day on which schools in the region traditionally celebrate the beginning of the academic year with ceremonial acts. Since several government agencies had issued warnings of a heightened terrorist threat in the region, Russia should have considered a real and imminent risk of terrorist attacks on that particular day.[55] Explicitly, the Court contrasted the judgment with its holding in the *Finogenov* case on the hostage situation at the Dubrovka theatre in Moscow. Since the Dubrovka attack was not predated by similar incidents, the Court found the authorities did not have any "specific information about the hostage-taking being prepared."[56] If certain regions are subject to violent conflicts or terrorist threats, states are therefore assumed to know of a heightened risk of human rights violations and have to adjust their preventive measures accordingly. The Court has further confirmed on several occasions that the sensitive position of civilians had to be given due regard in conflict areas and during the planning and carrying out of security operations.[57]

In sum, the consistency of certain human rights violations in the past or in certain regions is thus an important factor that could trigger positive obligations of diligent conduct. In this context, not only is the frequency of prior human rights violations important but also the character of harmful conduct and the status and identity of its victims.

cc. **Particular Risks for Certain Groups of Individuals** Knowledge of a particular human rights risk may also arise through the membership of affected individuals to a particular group – be it their religion, ethnic

---

[55] ECtHR, *Tagayeva and Others v. Russia*, Judgment of 13 April 2017, Application No. 26562/07 a.o., para. 486.
[56] ECtHR, *Finogenov and Others v. Russia*, Decision on Admissibility of 18 March 2010, Application No. 18299/03 a.o., para. 173.
[57] See, for instance, ECtHR, *Isayeva and Others v. Russia*, Judgment of 24 February 2005, Application No. 57950/00, para. 191.

origin, profession, or political affiliation.[58] In its *Kaya* case, for instance, the ECtHR found Turkey under an obligation to provide shelter to a "doctor suspected of aiding and abetting the PKK [who] was at that time at particular risk of falling victim to an unlawful attack."[59] Likewise, the Court confirmed in the *Akkoç* case that a teacher and active trade union member of Kurdish origin was at particular risk of being unlawfully attacked.[60] The *Gongdaze* judgment further emphasized that the authorities "ought to have been aware of the vulnerable position in which a journalist who covered politically sensitive topics placed himself."[61] The IACtHR confirmed this approach by requiring special safeguards for human rights defenders[62] or for the particularly vulnerable members of indigenous groups.[63] Applying the same logic, a special duty of care toward children has been recognized by the Courts.[64] Taken together, these examples illustrate that states are under an obligation to obtain knowledge of human rights risks for particular social groups – all the more if those groups are vulnerable and in need of special protection.[65]

d. Summary

It can therefore be summarized that while states are not expected to know of each particular human rights risk, they should actively acquire knowledge under certain circumstances. International human rights bodies have developed several such categories, including situations in which states are informed of human rights in peril, situations in which states

---

[58] Tran, "Obligations de Vigilance," p. 57; see, in greater detail, Francesca Ippolito and Sara Iglesias Sánchez, *Protecting Vulnerable Groups* (Oxford: Hart, 2015).
[59] ECtHR, *Mahmut Kaya v. Turkey*, Judgment of 28 March 2000, Application No. 22535/93, para. 89.
[60] ECtHR, *Akkoç v. Turkey*, Judgment of 10 October 2000, Application No. 22947/93 a.o., paras. 80 f.
[61] ECtHR, *Gongadze v. Ukraine*, Judgment of 8 November 2005, Application No. 34056/02, para. 168.
[62] IACtHR, *Valle Jaramillo et al. v. Colombia*, Judgment of 27 November 2008, Series C, No. 192, para. 81; see also HRC, *Hernandez v. Philippines*, Decision of 26 July 2010, Communication No. 1559/2007, UN Doc. CCPR/C/99/D/1599/2007.
[63] IACtHR, *Sawhoyamaxa Indigenous Community v. Paraguay*, Judgment of 29 March 2006, Series C, No. 146, para. 157.
[64] See, for instance, ECtHR, *A v. UK*, Judgment of 23 September 1998, Application No. 25599/94, para. 22; IAComHR, *Jessica Lenahan Gonzalez et al. v. United States of America*, Case. 12.626, Report No. 80/11 of 21 July 2011, para. 129.
[65] Laurens Lavrysen, "Positive Obligations in the Jurisprudence of the Inter-American Court of Human Rights" (2014) 7 *Inter-American and European Human Rights Journal* 94–115 at 112 f.; Sicilianos, "Preventing Violations of the Right to Life," 125; Kälin and Künzli, "Universeller Menschenrechtsschutz," para. 303.

contribute to the creation of human rights risks, and consistent patterns of human rights violations. In all of these constellations, the constructive knowledge threshold is usually met. Obviously, however, human rights risks can arise outside of those rather narrow categories and in a great many other circumstances. In general, the knowledge threshold still is difficult to overcome. Expressing dissatisfaction with the fact that states are often able to claim ignorance of human rights risk, several scholars thus call for a general obligation to conduct human rights impact assessments.

3. Human Rights Impact Assessments

Against this background, it is suggested that the tool of impact assessments as developed for environmental law should be transferred to the field of human rights protection.[66] In particular, the Maastricht Principles take a proactive stance when stating in Principle 13 that uncertainty about potential harmful impacts of state conduct "does not constitute justification," thereby introducing the precautionary approach to the field of human rights protection.[67] Principle 14 then introduces a general obligation to conduct impact assessments in the human rights sphere by urging states to systematically assess the human rights risks of their laws, policies, and practices. In fact, human rights impact assessments are becoming more popular, at least with regard to the protection of economic, social, and cultural rights. Most notably, they are increasingly carried out to evaluate the effects of development projects, trade agreements, and investments.[68]

Social and economic rights, however, are generally more suitable for impact assessments due to their programmatic character. As we have seen earlier, they mostly require states to develop overall policy

---

[66] James Harrison and Alessa Goller, "Trade and Human Rights: What Does 'Impact Assessment' Have to Offer?" (2008) 8 HRLR 587–615 at 611; Malayna Raftopoulos, "REDD+ and Human Rights: Addressing the Urgent Need for a Full Community-Based Human Rights Impact Assessment" (2016) 20 *The International Journal of Human Rights* 1–22 at 13.

[67] Olivier de Schutter et al., "Commentary to the Maastricht Principles on Extraterritorial Obligations of States in the Area of Economic, Social and Cultural Rights" (2012) 34 HRQ 1084–1169 at 1115, Commentary to Principle 13.

[68] See, with further state practice examples, Simon Walker, "Human Rights Impact Assessments. Emerging Practice and Challenges," in Eibe Riedel et al. (eds.), *Economic, Social, and Cultural Rights in International Law* (Oxford: Oxford University Press, 2014), pp. 393 ff.; Harrison and Goller, "Trade and Human Rights," 603 ff.

strategies.[69] It yet seems doubtful how a general obligation to conduct impact assessments could be practically implemented for all human rights provisions and what additional value such an instrument would have. Already in the field of environmental protection – where a customary duty to carry out impact assessments is broadly recognized – their practical reach is limited, as the concrete content and form of such assessments are determined by domestic law, with few international minimum requirements. As states are merely required to carry out any form of assessment, it can become even harder for potential victims to establish that states had or should have had knowledge of a certain risk.[70] An assessment undertaken prior to an incident can serve as a strong indicator that certain violations were not foreseeable, even if domestic regulations on impact assessments are rather lenient.[71] With this in mind, it is debatable whether introducing an obligation to carry out human rights impact assessments would actually foster more effective human rights protection – all the more so, as there are even more fundamental problems to be considered. As we have seen earlier, human rights risks may stem from myriads of different sources. In contrast to the field of environmental protection, in which it is relatively clear which types of activities bear the risk of environmental harm, assessing human rights risks cannot be limited to certain forms of conduct. Requiring states to supervise any form of private conduct with regard to its human rights impact would be disproportionate.

The only instances in which a human rights impact assessment are feasible and appropriate thus are constellations in which states license or support private conduct or in which they contribute to the creation of human rights risks. For these constellations, however, international human rights bodies assume a heightened standard of care anyway, which also includes the adequate assessment of risks.[72] In fact, human rights impact assessments are already frequently applied by states to assess the impacts of their domestic legislation or with regard to development programs and trade agreements.[73]

---

[69] See Chapter 2, III, 3.
[70] See Chapter 5.1, III, 2.
[71] Harrison and Goller, "Trade and Human Rights," 613.
[72] Andreas Papp, *Extraterritoriale Schutzpflichten* (Berlin: Duncker & Humblot, 2013), p. 310.
[73] Various human rights bodies have called upon states to assess the human rights impact of their own activities. See, for instance, Committee on the Elimination of Discrimination against Women, Concluding Observations on the Philippines of 25 August 2006, UN Doc. CEDAW/C/PHI/CO/6, para. 26; CESCR, Concluding Observations on Ecuador of 7 June 2004, UN Doc. E/C.12/1/Add.100, para. 56.

In sum, however, human rights impact assessments – while an attractive solution at first glance – do meet with practical difficulties: First of all, they bring about higher procedural hurdles for human rights victims. Moreover, it seems hardly possible to define the scope of activities for which human rights impacts should be assessed as theoretically any type of private conduct could lead to human rights contraventions. Against this background, human rights impact assessments have only evolved in constellations that are similar to the field of environmental protection – namely where states license private activities that bear the risk of causing adverse impacts. In these scenarios, human rights risks are assessable with regard to concrete activities and early assessments could indeed contribute to a more standardized and predictable approach toward harmful private conduct. Principally, however, it does not seem adequate to recognize human rights impact assessments as general obligations under international human rights law. The range of potential sources for human rights risks is too broad to define with regard to which activities formalized assessments could be meaningfully introduced for. When enacting legislation, developing policy strategies, or participating in international agreements, states are already obliged to evaluate the human rights risks related to such undertakings. The only field in which standardized impact assessment thus seems to be a suitable option are scenarios in which states license potentially harmful activities by private actors. In particular, with regard to business activities, there is growing practice to impose upon business entities an obligation to carry out human rights related assessments and document the results. While some developments thus point toward a more standardized assessment of human rights risks, the problem of finding an adequate balance between acquiring knowledge of human rights risks and protecting personal autonomy remains important.

Next to these limitations, when it comes to obtaining knowledge, the issue of capacities is debated in the human rights sphere just as controversially as in other areas of international law.

III. Capacities

When it comes to obligations of diligent conduct in the human rights sphere, the issue of capacities is once again crucial.[74] While the negative

---

[74] Koen de Feyter, "The Common Interest in International Law: Implications for Human Rights," in Wouter Vandenhole (ed.), *Challenging Territoriality in Human Rights Law* (London: Routledge, 2015), pp. 164 ff.; Tran, "Obligations de Vigilance," pp. 69 ff.; Xenos,

obligation to refrain from violating human rights is not necessarily dependent on the availability of sufficient resources, the fulfillment of positive obligations requires them all the more, in particular the implementation of social and economic rights. It would be false to assume, however, that only social and economic rights required the broad allocation of means, even though much has been written on the difficulties of fulfilling such rights in times of resource constraints.[75] While it is clear that, in particular, the right to adequate living conditions is highly dependent on material resources, political and civil rights might just as well bind significant resources. Equipping an administrative and judicial apparatus involves the allocation of resources, as does the hiring of sufficient security personnel or the carrying out of licensing procedures, to provide but a few examples.

Most human rights bodies have therefore recognized that the standard of care in the field of human rights protection is to be determined with regard to a state's capacities. While the Strasbourg Court found a "presumption of competence" to apply to all parts of a state's territory,[76] it still acknowledged that positive obligations of diligent conduct should not be applied in a manner that would impose a disproportionate burden on member states. It repeatedly held that positive obligations of diligent conduct would merely arise if the authorities "retained a certain degree of control over the situation" and positive measures were "feasible in the circumstances."[77] "Due regard" had to be paid "to the resources of the community."[78] Likewise, the IACtHR argued the "obligation to adopt measures of prevention and protection for private individuals ... is conditional on ... the

---

"Positive Obligations," p. 105; Katja Wiesbrock, *Internationaler Schutz der Menschenrechte vor Verletzungen durch Private* (Berlin: Arno Spitz, 1999), pp. 170 f.

[75] Diane Desierto, "Austerity Measures and International Economic, Social, and Cultural Rights," in Evan Criddle (ed.), *Human Rights in Emergencies* (Cambridge: Cambridge University Press, 2016), 241–276; Sally-Anne Way et al., "Economic and Social Rights in the Great Recession," in Eibe Riedel et al. (eds.), *Economic, Social, and Cultural Rights in International Law* (Oxford: Oxford University Press, 2014), 86–110.

[76] ECtHR, *Assanidze v. Georgia*, Judgment of 8 April 2004, Application No. 71503/01, para. 139.

[77] ECtHR, *Osman v. UK*, Grand Chamber Judgment of 28 October 1998, Application No. 23452/94, para. 116; *Ergi v. Turkey*, Judgment of 28 July 1998, Application No. 23818/94, para. 79; *Finogenov and Others v. Russia*, Judgment of 20 December 2011, Application No. 18299/03 a.o., para. 209.

[78] ECtHR, *Johnston and Others v. Ireland*, Plenary Judgment of 18 December 1986, Application No. 9697/82, para. 55.

reasonable possibility of preventing or avoiding that danger"[79] and should not impose a "disproportionate burden"[80] on states. In general, all human rights bodies thus recognize that state capacities are relevant when determining an adequate standard of care. Again, however, a lack of resources cannot justify any failure to comply as "the whole point of the obligation is to require states to develop those measures" in the first place.[81] An adequate balance thus needs to be drawn. On the one hand, it seems counterproductive to hold states responsible for failure to fulfill cost-intensive human rights obligations for which their resources are simply insufficient.[82] On the other hand, it seems just as dangerous to allow states to escape their responsibility.[83] The issue of capacities has been addressed in various ways, particularly those involving developing countries, the protection of human rights in times of economic crisis, and conflict areas. A brief review of the jurisprudence on these subject matters will illustrate how insufficient resources might affect a state's ability to perform human rights obligations.

1. Human Rights Due Diligence Obligations of Developing Countries

As we have seen, one of the key controversies is whether countries with low capacities have to adhere to lower standards of care. Once again, the issue is whether lacking resources directly impact the standard of care, in that they alter the content of positive obligations, which has to be distinguished from the question of whether failure to comply with human rights obligations can be justified by invoking circumstances that preclude the wrongfulness of conduct.[84] Actually, states hardly ever claim necessity or other circumstances precluding wrongfulness as

---

[79] IACtHR, *González et al. (Cotton Field)* v. *Mexico*, Judgment of 16 November 2009, Series C, No. 205, para. 280.
[80] IACtHR, *Sawhoyamaxa Indigenous Community* v. *Paraguay*, Judgment of 29 March 2006, Series C, No. 146, para. 155.
[81] Xenos, "Positive Obligations," p. 106; Monica Hakimi, "State Bystander Responsibility" (2010) 21 EJIL 341–385 at 374.
[82] Kristen Boon, "Are Control Tests Fit for the Future? The Slippage Problem in Attribution Doctrines" (2014) 15 *Melbourne Journal of International Law* 330–377 at 367; Jan Arno Hessbruegge, "Human Rights Violations Arising from Conduct of Non-State Actors" (2005) 11 *Buffalo Human Rights Law Review* 21–88 at 85.
[83] Aaron Xavier Fellmeth, *Paradigms of International Human Rights Law* (Oxford: Oxford University Press, 2016), p. 261.
[84] See Chapter 3, III, 2, c.

an excuse for noncompliance with their human rights obligations anyway. This might be due to the fact that by invoking necessity, states would automatically confess the unlawfulness of their conduct with merely its wrongfulness possibly excluded.[85] Not surprisingly, invoking insufficient capacities as a limitation to the primary content of positive obligations is a more common phenomenon in international practice. It is yet important to recall that a lack of resources cannot justify any failure of a state to comply with its *negative* obligations to refrain from committing human rights violations.[86]

With regard to positive obligations, though, resource-related claims are indeed frequently raised.[87] On several occasions states, states claimed that they could not comply with their human rights obligation due to insufficient capacities. Cameroon, for instance, explicitly argued that detention conditions in its state prisons were a "factor of [its] underdevelopment."[88] An argument rejected by the Human Rights Committee stating that "certain minimum standards ... must be observed regardless of a State party's level of development ... even if economic or budgetary considerations may make compliance ... difficult."[89] In similar cases, both the IACtHR and the ECtHR supported the Committee's position asserting that "States cannot invoke economic hardships to justify imprisonment conditions that do not respect the inherent dignity of human beings"[90] and "lack of resources cannot in principle justify prison conditions which are so poor as to reach the threshold of treatment contrary to Article 3 of the Convention."[91] States were expected to ensure adequate prison conditions "regardless of financial or logistical difficulties."[92]

---

[85] In greater detail, see Cedric Ryngaert, "State Responsibility, Necessity and Human Rights" (2010) 41 NYIL 79–98 at 96 f.

[86] Eva Brems, "Human Rights: Minimum and Maximum Perspectives" (2009) 9 *HRLR* 349–372 at 365 f.

[87] See, with further state practice examples, Eva Brems, *Human Rights: Universality and Diversity* (The Hague: Martinus Nijhoff, 2001), pp. 346–349.

[88] HRC, *Womah Mukong* v. *Cameroon*, Decision of 21 July 1994, Communication No. 458/1991, para. 9.1.

[89] Ibid., para. 9.3; and also Consideration of Reports Submitted by State Parties, United Republic of Tanzania, UN Doc. CCPR/C/79/Add.12 (1992), para. 5.

[90] IACtHR, *Montero-Aranguren et al. (Detention Center of Catia)* v. *Venezuela*, Judgment of 5 July 2006, Series C, No. 150, para. 85.

[91] ECtHR, *Poltoratsky* v. *Ukraine*, Judgment of 29 April 2003, Application No. 38812/97, para. 148.

[92] ECtHR, *Mamedova* v. *Russia*, Judgment of 1 June 2006, Application No. 7064/05, para. 63; *Orchowski* v. *Poland*, Judgment of 22 October 2009, Application No. 17885/04, para. 153.

First developed with regard to detention conditions, this approach soon became a general feature of human rights law. Even states with low capacities were obliged to fulfill minimum requirements; if at all, responsibility could only be evaded where "no reasonable diligence could have prevented the event."[93] With regard to resource constraints imposed by unusual migration movements, for instance, the ECtHR emphasized that "problems with managing migratory flows cannot justify a State's having recourse to practices which are not compatible with its obligations under the Convention."[94] In the *Kiliç* decision, the Turkish government had also claimed it had not been in a position to provide effective protection to the victims. The Court rejected this argument, stating that "a wide range of preventive measures were available which would have assisted in minimising the risk."[95] Even "where the available resources are demonstrably inadequate," states are under an ongoing obligation to monitor human rights issues and to "devise strategies and programmes" for their promotion. An obligation that is "in no way eliminated as a result of resource constraints."[96] This is all the more relevant in countries suffering from corruption problems and governmental mismanagement, where insufficient resources should not be accepted as blank check justification for noncompliance. It is crucial that those states are at least obligated to account for their resource allocation and give substantial reasons for why they could not fulfill their duties.[97] Even for states with low capacities, there is an obligation to adopt substantial plans toward the realization of human rights, including access to information and accountability mechanisms so as to ensure transparency and participation.[98]

---

[93] AfComHPR, *Zimbabwe Human Rights NGO Forum v. Zimbabwe*, Decision of 15 May 2006, Communication No. 245/2002, EX.CL/322 (X), paras. 155 f.
[94] ECtHR, *Georgia v. Russia (I)*, Grand Chamber Judgment of 3 July 2014, Application No. 13255/07, para. 177.
[95] ECtHR, *Kiliç v. Turkey*, Judgment of 28 March 2000, Application No. 22492/93, para. 76.
[96] CESCR, General Comment No. 3 on the Nature of State Parties' Obligations under Article 2 (1) of the Covenant, UN Doc. E/1991/23 (1990), para. 11.
[97] Lilian Chenwi and Danwood Chirwa, "Direct Protection of Economic, Social and Cultural Rights in International Law," in Danwood Chirwa (ed.), *The Protection of Economic, Social and Cultural Rights in Africa* (Cambridge: Cambridge University Press, 2016), p. 54; Brian Griffey, "The 'Reasonableness' Test: Assessing Violations of State Obligations under the Optional Protocol to the ICESCR" (2011) 11 HRLR 275–327 at 323.
[98] Aoife Nolan and Mira Dutschke, "Article 2 (I) ICESCR and States Parties' Obligations: Whither the Budget?" (2010) 3 EHRLR 280–289 at 283.

Two initial conclusions may thus be drawn. First, insufficient resources are not generally accepted as an excuse not to comply with human rights provisions. Human rights bodies tend to apply a rather strict approach, requiring states to provide substantial reasons why resource constraints hampered their ability to comply. Second, there are minimum requirements and certain forms of obligations to be fulfilled even under difficult social and economic circumstances.[99] However, next to this very fundamental question of whether duties of care vary according to the development status of a state, there is an ongoing debate as to whether the expected standard of diligence has to be adjusted in times of crisis – in particular, where a decline in resources is due to exceptional events such as severe economic crises or military conflicts.

2. Human Rights Due Diligence Obligations in Times of Economic Crisis

The subject of insufficient resources becomes particularly relevant in times of economic crisis, which is well illustrated by the world economic crisis in 2008. It forced many states to enact austerity programs to bail out financial institutions and combat budgetary deficits, which had a serious impact on the enjoyment of human rights. Much of the debate has focused on social and economic rights, and it was discussed in a particularly vigorous manner whether retrogressive measures could be justified, which mainly concerns the obligations of progressive realization under the Covenant on Economic, Social and Cultural Rights.[100] As we have seen earlier,[101] duties of progressive realization instruct states to take steps toward the realization of certain human rights that might not be fully implemented immediately. It is controversial whether retrogressive measures, therefore, would per se violate the Covenant, since cutting back on obligations clearly undermines the aim of progressive realization. While it was argued during the crisis that states could not "use the economic damage caused by the crises to justify actions or

---

[99] See also sections III, 4.
[100] Among many others, see Desierto, "Austerity Measures," 247 ff.; Aldo Caliari, "Human Rights Law: How Has It Been Relevant to Austerity and Debt-Crises?" (2016) 110 *Proceedings of the ASIL Annual Meeting* 129–130; Ben Warwick, "Socioeconomic Rights during Economic Crises" (2016) 65 *ICLQ* 246–265; Andreas Fischer-Lescano, *Human Rights in Times of Austerity Policy* (Baden-Baden: Nomos, 2014), p. 72.
[101] See Chapter 2, III, 3.

omissions that amount to violations of basic human rights obligations,"[102] the particular challenges an economic recession presents to the protection of economic and social rights should not be overlooked, as in times of overall resource constraints, allocating resources to the protection of one right necessarily hampers the ability to protect others.

The Office of the High Commissioner on Human Rights published an in-depth report on human rights compliance criteria for the imposition of austerity measures.[103] It found that wherever states enacted retrogressive measures to fight an economic crisis, the burden of proof should be shifted, forcing the state to provide justification for its policies. Even a "presumption of incompatibility" has been suggested, which states could rebut by demonstrating their programs were necessary and adequate.[104] Retrogressive measures, therefore, are compatible with the Covenant, only where they are tailored to help economic recovery and foster general welfare.[105] While the crisis thereby sparked a debate on how human rights considerations could be generally integrated into economic and fiscal policy,[106] the Committee was yet reluctant to actually contend that austerity programs were impermissible under the Covenant.[107]

While focusing on the impact on social and economic rights, however, it is easily overlooked that resource constraints just as adversely affect civil and political rights.[108] In fact, the Strasbourg Court was confronted with several applications lodged in reaction to domestic austerity

---

[102] Human Rights Council, Report on the Question of Human Rights and Extreme Poverty, Magdalena Sepúlveda Carmona, UN Doc. A/HRC/17/34 (17 March 2011), para. 12.

[103] Office of the High Commissioner on Human Rights, Report on Austerity Measures and Economic and Social Rights, Geneva 2013, available at: www.ohchr.org/Documents/Issues/Development/RightsCrisis/E-2013-82_en.pdf.

[104] Markus Krajewski, "Human Rights and Austerity Programmes," in Thomas Cottier et al. (eds.), *The Rule of Law in Monetary Affairs* (Cambridge: Cambridge University Press, 2014), p. 517.

[105] Amrei Müller, "Limitations to and Derogations from Economic, Social and Cultural Rights" (2009) 9 *HRLR* 557–601 at 587.

[106] Caliari, "Human Rights Law," 129–130; Warwick, "Socioeconomic Rights during Economic Crises," 262 f.; Krajewski, "Human Rights and Austerity Programmes," 515 f.

[107] See, for a broader analysis of the Committee's position, Aoife Nolan et al., "Two Steps Forward, No Steps Back? Evolving Criteria on the Prohibition of Retrogression in Economic and Social Rights," in Aoife Nolan (ed.), *Economic and Social Rights after the Global Financial Crisis* (Cambridge: Cambridge University Press, 2014), p. 127.

[108] Linos-Alexandre Sicilianos, *The European Court of Human Rights at a Time of Crisis in Europe*, SEDI/ESIL Lecture of 16 October 2015, pp. 2 f., available at www.esil-sedi.eu/sites/default/files/Sicilianos_speech_Translation.pdf; Matthias Goldmann, "Human Rights and Sovereign Debt Workouts," in Juan Pablo Bohoslavsky and Jernej Letnar

programs and cutbacks in social expenditure during the recent crisis. The Court expressly acknowledged the difficulties imposed by "the existence of an exceptional crisis without precedent," forcing states to implement austerity measures. The improvement of financial stability and future economic prospects were recognized as legitimate public interests, justifying cutbacks and restrictions.[109] In line with its general approach toward domestic budget decisions, the Court awarded great deference to how state authorities allocated their limited resources. Also with regard to civil and political rights, standard of care states can thus be adjusted if states suffer from unexceptional resource constraints, and a temporary lack of means is taken into consideration when assessing whether states have exercised sufficient diligence. Even in times of severe economic crises, however, states are not entirely discharged from their human rights obligations. On the contrary, in particular, the recent financial crisis has raised awareness of the importance of bringing human rights protection into an adequate balance with economic policy approaches.[110] While states principally enjoy a wide margin of appreciation in allocating their resources, they are still under an obligation to justify their policy choices, and as we will see later on,[111] several human rights obligations have to be fulfilled, regardless of ongoing or temporary constraints.

3. Human Rights Due Diligence Obligations in Conflict Situations

Next to economic resource constraints, issues of capacities have also been intensely debated with respect to conflict situations limiting a state's financial resources and its territorial capacities. All international human rights bodies have been confronted with conflict situations ranging from military activities in wartimes, to situations of military occupation, and clashes below the threshold of armed conflicts. According to their wording, international human rights treaties are unambiguously supposed to continuously apply at all times, which is most evident in the

---

Černič (eds.), *Making Sovereign Financing and Human Rights Work* (Oxford: Hart, 2014), 79–100; Brems, "Human Rights," 366.

[109] ECtHR, *Koufaki and Adedy v. Greece*, Decision of 7 May 2013, Applications Nos. 57665/12 and 57657/12, paras. 37–41.

[110] See, for instance, the recently adopted Guiding Principles on Foreign Debt and Human Rights, adopted by the Human Rights Council on 18 July 2012, UN Doc. A/HRC/RES/20/10.

[111] See sections III, 4.

derogation clauses contained in most treaties allowing for limited protection only for some rights and only in times of a public emergency.[112] The mere existence of said clauses shows that when drafting human rights treaties, states were well aware of the restraints imposed by conflicts and emergencies.[113] Yet, it is important to bear in mind that derogatory options under human rights treaties are limited to times of public emergency and even then do not allow for the derogation from core human rights provisions. They are of temporary character and only justified if strictly necessary under the given circumstances.[114]

Meanwhile, different conflict situations have come before international human rights courts. Most importantly, this concerns situations in which states have brought foreign territory under their control. Such constellations raise the question of whether military occupation triggers human rights obligations on behalf of the occupying state and vice versa whether occupied states are discharged from their obligations if they lost control over parts of their territory. In contrast to resource decline as a result of economic crises, which mainly affects a state's financial resources, conflict situations constrain territorial capacities as well. While ongoing conflict situations also have adverse impacts on a state's financial resources, they mainly bring about situations in which states are partly or entirely unable to control their territory.

With regard to the financial constraints resulting from conflicts, the same criteria as developed in the context of economic crises apply. Conflict situations and wars cause resource shortages, just as economic recession might temporarily limit a state's ability to fulfill its human rights obligations. Against this backdrop, the CESCR acknowledged how conflict situations may hamper a state's ability to fulfill its obligations under the Covenant,[115] yet again refrained from qualifying such constraints as justification for noncompliance. This is in line with the ECtHR's jurisprudence on security operations during armed hostilities. The Court was confronted with several cases in which individuals had been killed or injured during hostilities between security forces and

[112] Art. 4 of the ICCPR, Article 15 of the ECHR, Art. 27 of the ACHR.
[113] Gerald Neuman, "Constrained Derogation in Positive Human Rights Regimes," in Evan Criddle (ed.), *Human Rights in Emergencies* (Cambridge: Cambridge University Press, 2016), p. 28.
[114] de Schutter, "International Human Rights Law," pp. 587 ff.; Kälin and Künzli, "Universeller Menschenrechtsschutz," paras. 401 ff.
[115] See, for instance, CESCR, Concluding Observations on Armenia of 8 December 1999, UN Doc. E/C.12/1/Add.39, paras. 3 and 6; Concluding Observations on Guatemala of 12 December 2003, UN Doc. E/C.12/1/Add.93, para. 9.

irregular armed groups. While it was often impossible to reconstruct the exact course of events, the Court still established a range of positive obligations states were expected to fulfill. Despite all difficulties inherent in carrying out security operations in conflict areas states are under an ongoing obligation to employ protective means.[116] Even where it could not be established whether individuals were injured by security forces or by insurgents, the Court held states responsible if they failed to take diligent preventive measures,[117] an approach that finds support in the IACtHR's jurisprudence.[118] Again, a lack of resources might thus influence the standard of care but cannot absolve states from their human rights responsibilities.

What is less clear, however, is whether the same criteria apply if conflict situations affect the territorial capacities of a state. Not only do conflicts diminish the total amount of a state's resources; they might also affect a state's general ability to control its territory. As we have seen in the general part,[119] great importance has always been attached to territorial control. If and to what extent a temporary or permanent lack of territorial capacity alters the content of positive human rights obligations of diligent conduct is thus an interesting question to address. The Strasbourg Court dealt with several conflict situations – most notably, the conflict in Northern Ireland, the occupation of Northern Cyprus, the clashes between Kurdish activists and Turkish state organs, and violent incidents in the Transdniestrian Republic. While the Court's jurisprudence of conflict situations raises a great variety of controversial issues, the only relevant aspect for our analysis is whether it can be derived from the Court's holdings that the content of positive obligations of diligent conduct changes in the wake of conflict situations.

A first important conclusion to be drawn from the Court's approach toward conflict situations is that if states have brought areas outside their

---

[116] See, for instance, ECtHR, *Isayeva and Others* v. *Russia*, Judgment of 24 February 2005, Application No. 57947/00 a.o., paras. 178 ff.; HRC, *Pedro Pablo Camargo* v. *Colombia*, Decision of 31 March 1982, Communication No. R.11/45, UN Doc. A/37/40 (1982), paras. 13.2 ff.; IACtHR, *Victor Neitra-Alegria, Edga Zenteno-Escobar and William Zenteno-Escobar* v. *Peru*, Judgment of 19 January 1995, Series C, No. 20, paras. 74 ff.

[117] See, for instance, ECtHR, *Ergi* v. *Turkey*, Judgment of 28 July 1998, Application No. 23818/94, para. 81; *Ahmet Özkan and Others* v. *Turkey*, Judgment of 6 April 2004, Application No. 21689/93, para. 308.

[118] IACtHR, *Case of the Pueblo Bello Massacre* v. *Colombia*, Judgment of 31 January 2006, Series C, No. 140, para. 140; *Case of the Ituango Massacres* v. *Colombia*, Judgement of 1 July 2006, Series C, No. 148, para. 134.

[119] See Chapter 4, III, 2, a.

national territory under their effective control, they are obliged "to secure, in such an area, the rights and freedoms set out in the Convention."[120] By referring to "obligations to secure," the Court expressly acknowledges that effective control over foreign territory obliges states to fulfill the obligations of the Convention in their entirety, including positive obligations of diligent conduct. On the other hand, however, the Court was hesitant to acknowledge that states were no longer bound by human rights provisions once they lost control of parts of their territory. In the *Assanidze* decision, which involved the Ajarian Autonomous Republic refusing to comply with orders by the central Georgian government, the Court found that the "Ajarian Autonomous Republic is indisputably an integral part of the territory of Georgia and subject to its competence and control."[121] The Court found a presumption of competence to apply within the entire territory of a state, which could not be easily rebutted, as the Convention contained only limited options for territorial exclusions.[122] In general, it rejected the idea that the Convention's applicability could be selectively restricted to only parts of a territory and seemed to accept an exclusion of responsibility only where another state exercised *exclusive* control over the respective area.[123] In its *Ilaşcu* judgment, the Court took this strict approach even further, arguing that where a state was prevented from exercising control over a part of its territory, that part was not removed from its jurisdiction and an obligation to take positive steps toward remedying the situation still applied.[124] The majority opinion explained this by pointing out that the factual situation would reduce the scope of Moldovia's jurisdiction.[125] In this regard, however, the holding is somewhat unclear, as states either have jurisdiction or they do not, leaving no room for different shades of jurisdiction. Judge Ress, in his partly dissenting opinion, thus rightly pointed out that it was not Moldovia's jurisdiction that was reduced but rather the scope of responsibility.[126]

---

[120] ECtHR, *Loizidou v. Turkey*, Grand Chamber Judgment of 23 March 1995 (Preliminary Objections), Application No. 15318/89, para. 62.
[121] ECtHR, *Assanidze v. Georgia*, Grand Chamber Judgment of 8 April 2004, Application No. 71503/01, para. 139.
[122] See Arts. 56 and 57 of the Convention.
[123] ECtHR, *Assanidze v. Georgia*, Grand Chamber Judgment of 8 April 2004, Application No. 71503/01, paras. 140–142.
[124] ECtHR, *Ilaşcu and Others v. Moldova and Russia*, Grand Chamber Judgment of 8 July 2004, Application No. 48787/99, paras. 331–333.
[125] Ibid., para. 333.
[126] Ibid., Partly Dissenting Opinion of Judge Ress, para. 1.

Regardless of the difficult situation in the Transdniestrian Republic, Moldovia was still obliged to employ any reasonable means at its disposal to comply with its human rights duties under the Convention. Limited access and control over certain areas may thus be taken into account when determining the standard of care states are expected to abide by. Even effective control by another state, however, does not absolve states from making maximum efforts to protect human rights in the areas concerned.[127]

The African Commission was equally hesitant to acknowledge that conflict situations would absolve states from their human rights obligations, all the more so since the African Charter does not contain a derogation clause. It explicitly held that "even a civil war ... cannot be used as an excuse by the State violating or permitting violations of rights in the African Charter."[128] When Sudan rejected allegations of human rights violations by referring to a difficult security situation, the Commission emphasized that "limitations on the rights and freedoms enshrined in the Charter cannot be justified by emergencies or special circumstances."[129] Generally, there thus seems to be a consensus among international human rights bodies that conflict situations, while severely affecting a state's financial and territorial capacities, do not absolve states from their human rights obligations.[130] Moreover, the next section will reveal that there are several forms of obligations that need to be fulfilled at all times, irrespective of a state's individual capacities.

4. Human Rights Obligations Not Dependent on Capacities

All human rights bodies that have dealt with the issue of diverging capacities have acknowledged that while a lack of capacities is to be taken into account when determining the expected standard of care, it cannot excuse complete failure to comply with human rights obligations. When analyzing international jurisprudence on this matter, several forms of obligations can be identified that may never be discharged.

---

[127] Kälin and Künzli, "Universeller Menschenrechtsschutz," para. 363; Ioana Petculescu, "Droit International de la Responsabilité et Droits de l'Homme" (2005) 109 RGDIP 581–607 at 593 f.

[128] AfComHPR, *Commission Nationale des Droits de l'Homme et de Liberté v. Chad*, Decision of 2–11 October 1995, Communication No. 74/92, para. 21.

[129] AfComHPR, *Sudan Human Rights Organisation and Centre on Housing Rights and Evictions v. Sudan*, Decision of 27 May 2009, Communication Nos. 279/03, 296/05, paras. 139 and 165.

[130] Tran, "Obligations de Vigilance," p. 81.

Even under the most extreme circumstances, states can neither justify violations of these obligations nor claim that an adjusted standard of care should apply. Most importantly, these capacity-independent obligations are obligations of nondiscrimination, obligation to provide access to relevant information and issue warnings, and finally duties of cooperation and consultation.

a. Nondiscrimination

With nondiscrimination being among the most fundamental principles undergirding human rights law, it is often argued that even states with low capacities are at least obliged to allocate their limited resources in a nondiscriminatory manner.[131] The Human Rights Committee has defined discrimination as "any distinction, exclusion, restriction or preference which is based on any ground ... and which has the purpose or effect of nullifying or impairing the recognition, enjoyment or exercise by all persons, on an equal footing, of all rights and freedoms."[132] Not any form of differentiation thus amounts to discrimination, and different treatment can be justified if it objectively and reasonably pursues a legitimate aim.[133] The Committee's definition yet strongly underlines that universal human rights do not exclude particular groups. All major human rights treaties, therefore, contain clauses expressly prohibiting discrimination,[134] and most derogation clauses prescribe that any derogation must not lead to discriminatory patterns,[135] underlining that nondiscrimination is an aspect of human rights protection independent of capacities. In fact, the principle of nondiscrimination is of particular importance to positive human rights obligations. Especially where resources are allocated or protective schemes established, it is vital that such steps do not discriminate against certain social groups to the exclusive benefit of others. Even if states suffer from unexceptional

---

[131] Stijn Smet, *Resolving Conflicts between Human Rights* (London: Routledge, 2017), p. 149; Manisuli Ssenyonjo, *Economic, Social and Cultural Rights in International Law* (Oxford: Hart, 2nd ed., 2016), p. 155; Sicilianos, "The ECtHR at a Time of Crisis," 5; Hessbruegge, "Human Rights Violations," 85; Stephanie Farrior, "State-Responsibility for Human Rights Abuses by Non-State Actors" (1998) 92 *ASIL Proceedings of the Annual Meeting* 299–303 at 303.

[132] HRC, General Comment No. 18 of 10 November 1989, UN Doc. HRI/GEN/1/Rev.6, para. 7.

[133] Ibid., para. 13.

[134] See Art. 14 ECHR, Art. 1 ACHR, Art. of the African Charter, Art. 2 (I) ICCPR, and prominently Art. 2 (II) ICESCR.

[135] See Art. 27 ACHR, Art. 4 (I) of the ICCPR.

resource constraints, they are thus under an obligation to allocate the remaining resources in a nondiscriminatory manner, in particular since adhering to nondiscrimination does not require many resources in itself.[136]

That the prohibition of discrimination is an obligation independent of the availability of resources became obvious during the recent financial crisis. When considering the criteria for human rights compliance, the High Commissioner of Human Rights, recalling Article 2 II of the ICSECR, firmly insisted that austerity measures should not be implemented in a discriminatory manner.[137] Against this backdrop, it has been suggested that many austerity measures applied during the recent crisis have actually been contrary to important human rights provisions, as they had discriminatory effects to the disadvantage of particularly vulnerable groups.[138] The case of *N.K.M. v. Hungary* is, in fact among the few instances in which the Strasbourg Court found domestic austerity measures incompatible with the Convention. Importantly, the Court's decision focused on the disproportionate burden the measures in question imposed on a particular group of civil servants compared to other civil servants in similar circumstances.[139]

To summarize, nondiscrimination is a fundamental aspect of international human rights law in general and of positive obligations in particular. Whenever states employ active protective means, they have to do so in a nondiscriminatory manner. Discriminatory patterns may never be justified by a lack of resources, and even in times of severe resource constraints, states are required to carry out their due diligence obligations in a nondiscriminating way.

b. Duties to Monitor and to Inform

Next to the obligation not to discriminate, even states with limited resources are under an obligation to monitor human rights developments within their jurisdiction and adequately inform their population

---

[136] CESCR, An Evaluation of the Obligations to Take Steps to the "Maximum of Available Resources" under an Optional Protocol to the Covenant, UN Doc. E/C.12/2007/1 (2007), para. 7.

[137] Office of the High Commissioner on Human Rights, Report on Austerity Measures and Economic and Social Rights, Geneva 2013, available at www.ohchr.org/Documents/Issues/Development/RightsCrisis/E-2013-82_en.pdf (11.05.2017), p. 13.

[138] See, for instance, Fischer-Lescano, "Human Rights in Times of Austerity Policy," p. 78.

[139] ECtHR, *N.K.M. v. Hungary*, Judgment of 14 May 2013, Application No. 66529/11, para. 71.

about relevant human rights risks.[140] This mainly entails an obligation to surveil the realization of human rights and to develop strategies for how to best ensure their further promotion.[141] Moreover, the duty to inform includes transparency in the decision-making process and access to relevant information.[142] In its *Taşkin* case, the Strasbourg Court stressed "the importance of public access to ... information which would enable members of the public to assess the danger to which they are exposed."[143] In order to make autonomous decisions, it is crucial for individuals to possess all relevant information. Especially where states find themselves unable to provide sufficient protection, it is even more important to at least issue warnings and provide information so that potentially affected individuals might be able to adjust their own behavior. Again, the issuing of warnings is not cost intensive for the state itself, which is why lacking resources could not justify failure to comply with informative duties.

Several decisions by international human rights bodies have emphasized the importance of proper access to information. In the *Guerra* case, for instance, the ECtHR found Italy responsible for a failure to provide relevant information that would have enabled a family to adequately assess the risk of living near an industrial plant and being exposed to its emissions.[144] The African Commission held that even states that are unable to assess and monitor human rights risks themselves are at least required to permit independent scientific monitoring, provide individuals with the necessary information, and grant them meaningful access to decision-making processes[145] – all the more where states have exclusive access to the most relevant information.[146] Against this background, the ECtHR also established that – as a matter of human rights law – states were obliged to make environmental impact assessments publicly

---

[140] See, for instance, Desierto, "Austerity Measures," 246.
[141] Ssenyonjo, "Economic, Social and Cultural Rights," p. 108.
[142] Way et al., "Economic and Social Rights in the Great Recession," 96 ff.; Benedict Kingsbury et al., "The Emergence of Global Administrative Law" (2005) 68 *Law and Contemporary Problems* 15–61 at 38.
[143] ECtHR, *Taşkin and Others* v. *Turkey*, Judgment of 10 November 2004, Application No. 46117/99, para. 119; see also Sicilianos, "Preventing Violations of the Right to Life," 127.
[144] ECtHR, *Guerra and Others* v. *Italy*, Grand Chamber Judgment of 19 February 1998, Application No. 14967/89, para. 60.
[145] AfComHPR, *Social and Economic Rights Action Center and Center for Economic and Social Rights* v. *Nigeria*, Decision of 27 October 2001, Communication No. 155/96, para. 53.
[146] Robert Robertson, "Measuring State Compliance with the Obligation to Devote the 'Maximum of Available Resources' to Realizing Economic, Social and Cultural Rights" (1994) 16 HRQ 693–714 at 696.

available before licensing industrial activities.[147] While this obligation has prominently developed in the context of health risks resulting from industrial activities, it has found further support in relation to other risks.

The Strasbourg Court confirmed a duty to inform potentially affected individuals in conflict areas where security operations eventually involved lethal force. While states are not expected to prevent any conflict-related human rights violation, they are obliged to at least inform the local population as adequately as possible.[148] The Court has recently underlined this with respect to several terrorist attacks in the North Ossetia region. The *Tagayeva* judgment found a failure to comply with preventive obligations inter alia due to the fact that the authorities did not issue warnings to the affected population.[149] Furthermore, duties to inform were recognized for human rights risks resulting from natural disasters. The *Budayeva* judgment, for instance, found an obligation to adequately inform the potentially affected population and to make advance arrangements for an evacuation of areas at risk of being impaired by a natural disaster.[150] While such duties to inform are mainly of preventive character in that they should enable individuals to assess human rights risk in time, they also entail an obligation to provide information on potential human rights violations in the past. In its *McGinley and Egan* case, the ECtHR found an obligation to inform army members that had been exposed to nuclear material about the circumstances of the exposure and related health risks.[151] Even where human rights risks have already materialized, there is thus still an obligation to ensure access to relevant information.

Taking these examples together, states are under a general obligation to inform potentially affected individuals as adequately as possible.[152] As ensuring access to relevant information is "extraordinarily

---

[147] ECtHR, *Tătar v. Romania*, Judgment of 27 January 2009, Application No. 67021/01, para. 115.
[148] See, for instance, ECtHR, *Isayeva and Others v. Russia*, Judgment of 24 February 2005, Application No. 57950/00, para. 189.
[149] ECtHR, *Tagayeva v. Russia*, Judgment of 13 April 2017, Application No. 26562/07, para. 489.
[150] ECtHR, *Budayeva and Others v. Russia*, Judgment of 20 March 2008, Application No. 15339/02 a.o., paras. 152 f.
[151] ECtHR, *McGinley and Egan v. UK*, Judgment of 9 June 1998, Application Nos. 21825/93 and 23414/94, para. 101.
[152] Dinah Shelton and Ariel Gould, "Positive and Negative Obligations," in Dinah Shelton (ed.), *The Oxford Handbook on International Human Rights Law* (Oxford: Oxford University Press, 2013), p. 572.

inexpensive,"[153] states are required to perform them even in times of resource constraints.

c. Duties of Cooperation

Finally, the issue of insufficient capacities gives reason to discuss whether there are any obligations of cooperation and assistance under international human rights law and whether states are obliged to enhance their capacities if they find themselves incapable of fulfilling their obligations. This has been particularly vigorously debated for social and economic rights[154] as Article 2 (I) of the ICESCR establishes that states are obliged to employ the maximum of their available resources, individually *and* through international cooperation. What constitutes the "maximum of available resources" and whether such maximum encompasses an obligation to seek and render assistance in case some states lack the resources to independently comply with their obligations have been controversial ever since.

Already during the Covenant's drafting process had the definition of the "maximum of available resources" been disputed. The Lebanese representative, for instance, underlined that "available resources" should refer to the "real resources of the country and not to budgetary appropriation."[155] The French representative, in contrast, suggested reading the provision broadly so as to include "budgetary appropriations and also technical assistance, international cooperation and other elements."[156] Today, the clause is usually understood as imposing an obligation to actively engage in cooperation. Most prominently, the CESCR found the phrase to refer to both "the resources existing within a State and those available from the international community through international cooperation and assistance."[157] In like manner, the Committee on the Rights of the Child stated that the obligation to employ the maximum extent of available resources included seeking international cooperation.[158]

---

[153] Robertson, "Measuring State Compliance," 697; Xenos, "Positive Obligations," p. 106.
[154] See, with further references, Philip Alston and Gerard Quinn, "The Nature and Scope of States Parties' Obligations under the ICESCR" (1987) 9 *HRQ* 156–229 at 188 f.; de Schutter, "International Human Rights Law," pp. 198 ff.; Ssenyonjo, "Economic, Social and Cultural Rights," pp. 118 ff.
[155] UN Commission on Human Rights, Summary Record of the Eighth Session, 271st Meeting, UN Doc. E/CN.4/SR.271 (1952), p. 5.
[156] Ibid., p. 6.
[157] CESCR General Comment No. 3, adopted at the Fifth Session of the Committee on 14 December 1990, UN Doc. E/1991/23, para. 13.
[158] Committee on the Rights of the Child, General Comment No. 5 on General Measures of Implementation, UN Doc. CRC/GC/2003/5 (2003), para. 21.

This takes us to the question of whether states are under a binding obligation to seek assistance when they find themselves incapable of fulfilling their human rights obligations and whether other states are under a corresponding obligation to render such assistance if they have ample resources at their disposal. Logically, such obligations would continue to apply in times of crises or economic recession that trigger resource constraints in the first place.[159] Much of the legal debate on this subject matter has so far exclusively focused on social and economic rights and the relatively clear cooperative duties entailed in the respective international instruments. How cooperative duties are handled for social and economic rights thus will be addressed first. In a second step, it will then be analyzed whether any conclusions drawn from those specific human rights instruments could be transferred to other human rights regimes in order to assess whether there are general obligations to assist and to cooperate in international human rights law.

aa. **Obligations to Seek Assistance** As indicated previously, there now seems to be a consensus that "the maximum of available resources" is not limited to the resources within a state's territory. If states do not possess sufficient resources to comply with their obligation to ensure social and economic rights, they cannot be excused for not taking any measures at all. Instead, they are expected to actively seek assistance and employ such resources as are available through cooperation and assistance.[160] At least with regard to human rights treaties that contain similar clauses, there is thus a recognized legal obligation on behalf of resource-lacking states to actively engage in cooperation.[161] Whenever support could have been achieved through international channels, lacking capacities should not affect the standard of care states are expected to adhere to.

On the other hand, however, states cannot justify noncompliance merely by pointing to the fact that they could not get any assistance. The existence of cooperative obligations on behalf of other states, so the Commentary to the Maastricht Principles points out, does in no way

---

[159] Desierto, "Austerity Measures," 258.
[160] Chenwi and Chirwa, "Direct Protection," 53; Takhmina Karimova, "The Nature and Meaning of 'International Assistance and Cooperation' under the ICESCR," in Eibe Riedel et al. (eds.), *Economic, Social, and Cultural Rights in International Law* (Oxford: Oxford University Press, 2014), pp. 163–192; Robertson, "Measuring State Compliance," 700.
[161] Ssenyonjo, "Economic, Social and Cultural Rights," p. 108.

imply that less developed states could discharge their own obligations by invoking a failure of other states to cooperate and assist.[162] They remain under an ongoing obligation to work toward overall compliance and fulfill those obligations which are not dependent on the availability of resources. The CESCR further stressed that "mismanagement of international cooperation aid and unbalanced budgetary allocation constitute serious breaches in the obligations of the State party under article 2.1 of the Covenant."[163] Rather evidently, states that gain international assistance are thus under an additional obligation to employ those means as effectively as possible toward the realization of those human rights which they could not fulfill independently.[164] This allows for the conclusion that states which lack sufficient resources are indeed under an obligation to seek assistance in order to improve their human rights compliance where human rights instruments contain a cooperative clause.[165]

Not all human rights treaties, however, contain express cooperative clauses, making it necessary to discuss whether such obligations could equally apply to other human rights provisions. Indeed, there are good reasons to assume that seeking assistance falls within the range of measures that can reasonably be expected of states, in particular where international assistance is readily available and has a real prospect of improving the human rights situation at stake. As we have now seen on various occasions, insufficient capacities can never fully discharge a state of complying with its international obligations. Resource-lacking states are still expected to employ reasonable measures, among which seeking assistance is an option that can be pursued even by states with the lowest capacities.

As for state practice, support for such obligations can be found in the counterterrorism context where similar suggestions have already been made – in particular, that states with insufficient capacities are instructed to seek international assistance and failure to do so could be equated with failure to comply with the obligation to diligently prevent terrorist activities.[166] An obligation to seek assistance has also been included in the ILC's recent Draft Articles on the Protection of Persons in the Event of Disasters, which contain in their Article 11 an explicit duty on behalf of

---

[162] Commentary to the Maastricht Principles 2012, p. 1096, Principle 4.
[163] CESCR, Concluding Observations on the Combined Second to Fourth Periodic Reports of the Democratic Republic of the Congo, UN Doc. E/C.12/COD/CO/4 (2009), paras. 16 and 29.
[164] Ssenyonjo, "Economic, Social and Cultural Rights," p. 125.
[165] See, in particular, CESCR General Comment No. 3, UN Doc. E/1991/23, para. 13.
[166] See Chapter 5.2, III, 2, b.

affected states to seek international assistance if disaster relief manifestly exceeds their capacities.[167] While so far, such obligations have not been raised in any international proceedings, there are thus growing signs of acceptance for a general obligation to seek assistance on behalf of those states that lack sufficient resources to comply with their human rights obligations. In particular, in scenarios that bear the potential of grave and fundamental human rights violations – such as terrorist attacks or natural disasters – it could be reasonably expected even of resource-lacking states to seek international assistance – all the more so if it is readily available. What is more difficult to answer, however, is whether better-equipped states are under a corresponding obligation to provide aid and assistance to resource-lacking states.

bb. Obligations to Render Assistance: Drawing Inspiration from the "Common but Differentiated Responsibilities" Approach Whether an obligation to provide assistance can be construed under international human rights law is indeed a more challenging question to address. As we have seen, the "maximum of available resources" is not limited to financial measures.[168] It could thus be argued that if states are capable of effectively improving human rights situations abroad, this would fall under the maximum's scope. In fact, the Committee on the Rights of the Child expressly held that all states ratifying the Convention "take upon themselves obligations not only to implement it within their jurisdiction, but also to contribute, through international cooperation, to global implementation."[169] With increasing frequency, progressive proposals are raised arguing in favor of an enhanced duty to render assistance.[170] Some argue that the UN-recommended target of 0.7 percent GDP being dedicated by developed states to international cooperation could be qualified as a clear and measurable obligation to render assistance.[171] Other proposals shift their focus from an exclusively

---

[167] ILC, Draft Articles on the Protection of Persons in the Event of Disasters with Commentaries of 2016, ILC Yearbook 2016, Volume II, Part II.
[168] Sigrun Skogly, "The Requirement of Using the 'Maximum of Available Resources' for Human Rights Realisation: A Question of Quality as well as Quantity?" (2012) 12 HRLR 393–420 at 413.
[169] Committee on the Rights of the Child, General Comment No. 5 on General Measures of Implementation, UN Doc. CRC/GC/2003/5 (2003), para. 5.
[170] See, for instance, Fellmeth, "Paradigms of International Human Rights Law," p. 262; Ssenyonjo, "Economic, Social and Cultural Rights," pp. 112 ff.
[171] The 0.7 percent target was first proposed by the Pearson Commission (see UN GA Resolution No. 2626/XXV, 24 October 1970, UN Doc. A/RES/2626, para. 43) and later

financial approach toward assistance as a broader concept encompassing administrative and structural assistance so as to foster more effective human rights protection in the recipient state.[172]

Occasionally, reference is now also made to the concept of common but differentiated responsibilities as developed in international environmental law by referring to the general historical responsibility of states when it comes to the capacities of former colonies.[173] Those who support the transfer of this approach to international human rights law point toward several similarities.[174] In particular, they argue that human rights protection is just as much a common concern as the protection of the environment.[175] All states should thus work jointly and cooperatively toward the implementation of basic human rights. Moreover, since positive obligations are just as resource intensive as environmental protection schemes, the concept of common but differentiated responsibilities could be adequately applied to the field of human rights protection. Not only would this entail that differing best efforts expectations should be applied with regard to human rights protection, but also that developed states would be under an obligation to render technical and financial assistance to states that are less capable. As we have seen earlier, however, the status of a common but differentiated responsibilities concept is disputed even within the context of environmental law.[176] It is not settled whether the concept is of a merely missionary character or actually entails concrete and legally binding obligations. Equally disputed is how the status of developing countries should be determined.[177] While

---

endorsed by the CESCR (see, for instance, the Concluding Observations on Italy referring to 0.7 percent as "the internationally agreed upon level," UN Doc. E/C.12/ITA/CO/5, 28 October 2015, para. 13) and the CRC Committee (General Comment No. 5 on General Measures of Implementation, UN Doc. CRC/GC/2003/5, 27 November 2003, para. 61).

[172] Skogly, "Requirement of Using the Maximum of Available Resources," 417 f.

[173] Ralph Wilde, "Dilemmas in Promoting Global Economic Justice through Human Rights Law," in Nehal Bhuta (ed.), *The Frontiers of Human Rights* (Oxford: Oxford University Press, 2016), p. 171; de Feyter, "Common Interest in International Law," 171 ff.; Margot Salomon, "Deprivation, Causation and the Law of International Cooperation," in Malcolm Langford et al. (eds.), *Global Justice, States Duties* (Cambridge: Cambridge University Press, 2013), p. 282.

[174] See, for instance, Statement by Thabo Mbeki, President of South Africa at the World Summit on Sustainable Development, 26 August–4 September 2002, record contained in UN Doc. A/CONF.199/20, p. 159.

[175] Rachel Boyte, "Common but Differentiated Responsibilities" (2010) 14 *New Zealand Journal of Environmental Law* 63–102 at 81.

[176] See Chapter 5.1, IV, 2.

[177] Boyte, "Common but Differentiated Responsibilities," 83 f.

the concept has been included in several international instruments, there is insufficient state action on how the concept should actually operate in practice.[178] Thus far, it would be too far a stretch to assume that it involves a measurable legal obligation that cautions against its transferability to other areas of international law.

Most authors, therefore, are rather hesitant, arguing that even though there might be an obligation to take positive steps with regard to severe human rights violations occurring abroad, there were no signs of a concrete international obligation to assist other states in developing the capacities necessary to prevent human rights contraventions.[179] If at all, the duty to render assistance was a broad and general duty to establish an international order in which human rights are realized.[180] This is in line with the ILC's recent Draft Articles on disaster relief, which do establish an obligation to seek assistance on behalf of resource-lacking states but merely state that other states will give "due consideration" to requests for assistance without providing for a legal obligation to actually render assistance.[181] While there is indeed wide state practice of voluntary cooperation, there are no indications for a legal obligation to render assistance upon request.[182] In fact, most countries have expressly rejected any legal entitlement to development assistance and referred to such assistance as a purely moral obligation.[183] Despite a growing awareness of the importance of cooperation in the human rights sphere, it has thus not crystallized into a legal obligation.

d. Core Obligations

Another element of human rights law that plays an important role for the problem of insufficient capacities is the assumption that some rights or

---

[178] Christopher Stone, "Common but Differentiated Responsibilities in International Law" (2004) 98 AJIL 276–301 at 281; Susan Biniaz, "Common but Differentiated Responsibility" (2002) 96 *ASIL Proceedings* 359–363 at 361.

[179] See, for instance, Karimova, "International Assistance and Corporation," 192; Luke Glanville, "The Responsibility to Protect Beyond Borders" (2012) 12 HRLR 1–32 at 32; Alston and Quinn, "State Obligations under the ICESCR," 192.

[180] Chenwi and Chirwa, "Direct Protection of Economic, Social and Cultural Rights," 59.

[181] Art. 12 of the ILC, Draft Articles on the Protection of Persons in the Event of Disasters with Commentaries of 2016, ILC Yearbook 2016, Volume II, Part II.

[182] de Feyter, "Common Interest in International Law," 170; Karimova, "International Assistance and Corporation," 192.

[183] See, for instance, the arguments raised by the representatives of the United Kingdom, the Czech Republic, Canada, France, and Portugal in Commission on Human Rights, Report of the open-ended working group to consider the elaboration of an optional protocol to the ICESCR, 10 February 2005, UN Doc. E/CN.4/2005, 52, para 76.

certain aspects of some rights are of such fundamental importance that resource constraints could not justify noncompliance. This general assumption is mainly reflected in two different categories: the status of nonderogable rights on the one hand (aa.) and the concept of minimum core obligations on the other (bb.).

aa. Nonderogable Rights Several human rights treaties contain clauses that allow for a temporary derogation from their provisions in times of emergencies but exclude certain rights from this option. While the concrete list of such nonderogable rights is different for each human rights treaty, all human rights instruments that generally allow for derogation exclude the right to life, the prohibition of torture and cruel or inhuman treatment, the prohibition of slavery, and the prohibition of retroactive criminal laws from the range of rights a state might derogate from.[184] The nonderogable character of these rights indicates that they are deemed so fundamental as to render their implementation indispensable, even in times of crisis or severe resource constraints. First of all, this implies that states could under no circumstances justify noncompliance with their negative obligation to refrain from violating these rights.[185] Moreover, the status of nonderogable rights also requires substantial positive measures at all times. The African Commission explicitly held that "for nonderogable human rights the positive obligations of States would go further than in other areas."[186] Even where the scope of positive obligations is generally limited due to an emergency, states are thus obliged to take active steps to protect the entire range of nonderogable rights. This applies all the more in scenarios that might cause severe resource constraints but do not meet the high threshold allowing for a temporary derogation.

bb. Minimum Core Obligations The concept of minimum core obligations has been developed within the ICESCR's context, and while it is beyond the scope of this thesis to reconstruct the scholarly debate in its entirety, the effects on the problem of insufficient capacities will briefly be summarized. In its General Comment No. 3, the CESCR explained that the Covenant entailed so-called minimum core obligations "to ensure the

---

[184] Art. 4 of the ICCPR, Art. 15 of the ECHR, Art. 27 of the ACHR.
[185] de Schutter, "International Human Rights Law," p. 624; Kälin and Künzli, "Universeller Menschenrechtsschutz," para. 405.
[186] AfComHPR, *Zimbabwe Human Rights NGO Forum v. Zimbabwe*, Decision of 15 May 2006, Communication No. 245/2002, EX.CL/322 (X), para. 155.

satisfaction of, at the very least, minimum essential levels of each of the rights" and that these core obligations had to be fulfilled even when taking resource constraints into account and even in times of economic recession.[187] Against this background, it is usually assumed that states are obliged to ensure the minimum core of each right regardless of their resources.[188] Defining this minimum core is not a static determination but rather takes scientific and technological advancements into account.[189] Soon, however, the concept of minimum core obligations was heavily criticized, especially as defining the concrete minimum core of each right seemed too difficult an undertaking. Moreover, it was rightly pointed out that even fulfilling but the minimum core could overburden states that are suffering from a heavy decline in resources.

Against this background, recognizing an immediate obligation to provide every individual with the minimum core of socioeconomic obligations seems to be going too far. The heightened standard of protection is better understood as to impose upon states a higher burden of justification if they fail to ensure even the minimum core.[190] When it comes to minimum core obligations, states may only justify their failure to comply with the Covenant provisions if they can show that "every effort has been made to use all resources that are at [their] disposition in an effort to satisfy, as a matter of priority, those minimum obligations." This also means that more intrusive means of acquiring resources might be justified when undertaken to guarantee the minimum core of socioeconomic obligations. When initiating domestic measures to achieve social and economic rights – such as imposing taxes or fees – states usually have to pay due regard to other interests and rights that might be negatively affected by those measures. Considering the outstanding importance of the minimum core, however, it could justify more intense infringements of less important interests.[191] Moreover, the Committee has published a range of general comments narrowing down the

---

[187] CESCR, General Comment No. 3 on the Nature of States Parties" Obligations, UN Doc. E/1991/23 (1990), para. 10.

[188] See, for instance, Commission on Human Rights, Second Progress Report by Special Rapporteur Danilo Türk on the Realization of Economic, Social and Cultural Rights, 18 July 1991, UN Doc. E/CN.4/Sub.2/1991/17, para. 52 d); Ssenyonjo, "Economic, Social and Cultural Rights," p. 105.

[189] Diane Desierto, "ICESCR Minimum Core Obligations and Investment" (2012) 44 *George Washington International Law Review* 473–520 at 488.

[190] Sandra Fredman, *Human Rights Transformed* (Oxford: Oxford University Press, 2008), p. 85.

[191] Robertson, "Measuring State Compliance," 702.

minimum core of several of the Covenant rights that serve as a benchmark for states to identify the threshold below which the amount of protection should not fall. In sum, the concept of minimum core obligations is thus well-recognized in the context of social and economic rights. While it has not been explicitly transferred to other human rights regimes, it is actually quite similar to the general assumption found previously: while insufficient resources of states are relevant when assessing whether they have complied with their due diligence obligations, they can never justify complete failure to take protective steps. The minimum core concept is thus a slight alteration of this general conclusion tailored to meet the characteristics of obligations of progressive realization.[192]

5. Summary

To conclude, capacities are yet again an important factor in determining the standard of care that is expected of states in the field of human rights protection. While international human rights bodies have shown judicial deference toward situations of resource constraints – such as internal conflicts or economic crises – they have not been willing to entirely discharge states of their human rights obligations. On the contrary, there are obligations that need to be fulfilled irrespective of a state's resources – the most important of which are the duty of nondiscrimination and the duty to inform in a meaningful manner. In addition to that, there is growing consensus that states are under a general obligation to seek international aid and assistance if they find themselves incapable of fulfilling their tasks, which further minimizes the danger that states will claim insufficient capacities in order to escape their responsibilities.

IV. Reasonableness

Finally, as with any other area of international law, due diligence obligations in the human rights sphere do not constitute absolute forms of obligations but merely require states to employ reasonable means.[193] As the Strasbourg Court put it: "a mere condition sine qua non does not suffice to engage the responsibility of the State under the Convention; it must be shown that ... [there was] a failure on the part of the national

---

[192] See Chapter 2, III, 3.
[193] Conforti, "Breach of Positive Obligations," 8.

authorities to do all that could *reasonably* be expected of them"[194] and that only failure "to take *reasonably* available measures which could have had a real prospect of altering the outcome or mitigating the harm is sufficient to engage the responsibility of the State."[195] The Human Rights Committee also has referred to the reasonableness standard,[196] as has the Inter-American Court of Human Rights.[197]

Given the fundamental importance of human rights, it is occasionally argued that a stricter standard of reasonableness should apply compared to other fields of international law, in particular where fundamental human rights are at stake or particularly grave human rights violations could occur.[198] Notwithstanding, while the seriousness of an expected violation is an important parameter in determining the reasonableness of an approach, it is also important to recall the differentiation drawn in the general part between the notions of reasonableness on the one hand and proportionality on the other. While the proportionality test is employed in order to determine whether an infringement upon a given human right by the state itself may be justified in the public interest,[199] reasonableness is a standard against which preventive and punitive steps to protect against human rights contravention by third parties are measured. What is hence assessed by the reasonable test is not whether a single human rights contravention can be justified but rather whether a state took adequate steps to prevent such contraventions or whether it took adequate investigative and punitive steps after such contraventions occurred.[200] While both tests rely on comparable criteria and often

---

[194] ECtHR, *Mastromatteo v. Italy*, Grand Chamber Judgment of 24 October 2002, Application No. 37703/97, para. 74, emphasis added.
[195] ECtHR, *E and Others v. UK*, Judgment of 26 November 2002, Application No. 33218/96, paras. 99 f., emphasis added.
[196] See, for instance, HRC, *William Eduardo Delgado Páez v. Colombia*, Decision of 4 July 1990, Communication No. 195/1985, UN Doc. CCPR/C/39/D/195/1985 (1990), para. 5.5; see also *Human Rights Chamber for Bosnia and Herzegovina, Ratko Grgić v. Republika Srpska*, Decision of 5 August 1997, Case No. CH/96/15, para. 17.
[197] IACtHR, *Velásquez Rodríguez v. Honduras*, Judgment of 29 July 1988, Series C, No. 4, para. 174.
[198] See, for instance, T. R. Hickman, "The Reasonableness Principle: Reassessing Its Place in the Public Sphere" (2004) 63 *Cambridge Law Journal* 166–198 at 186; Michael Krugmann, *Der Grundsatz der Verhältnismäßigkeit im Völkerrecht* (Berlin: Duncker & Humblot, 2004), pp. 68 f.
[199] See also IACtHR, *Case of the Pueblo Bello Massacre v. Colombia*, Judgment of 31 January 2006, Series C, No. 140, para. 133.
[200] See Chapter 4, IV, 1, d. For a general critique of applying balancing test to human rights protection, see: Francisco Urbina, *A Critique of Proportionality and Balancing* (Cambridge: Cambridge University Press, 2017).

yield similar results, the reasonableness test is less strict, as it does not require states to employ the least restrictive approach but merely to employ appropriate means. The Strasbourg Court explicitly stated that the notion of reasonableness was more flexible compared to the rather strict "necessary in a democratic society" test,[201] thus speaking in favor of a strict proportionality test for the active interference with human rights but a less strenuous reasonableness test when it comes to assessing protective obligations.[202] This approach is particularly obvious in its *Hatton* judgment, which dealt with the positive obligation to protect privacy rights. Whereas the Chamber had applied a strict proportionality test, arguing that states "were required to minimise, as far as possible, interference with Article 8 rights ... by generally seeking to achieve their aims in the least onerous way,"[203] the Grand Chamber held it would merely review whether the domestic authorities had struck "a fair balance" between competing rights and interests, thereby paraphrasing a less restraining reasonableness standard.[204] In general, the adequateness of preventive and punitive measures is thus subject to less-strict tests than the justification of a violation of negative obligations.[205]

In this context, it is also important to bear in mind that in preventive constellations a human rights violation has not yet materialized, and assessing the adequateness of any preventive attempt is necessarily an a priori evaluation, with the concrete consequences still unclear. Prevention aims at mitigating future risks, which – to a certain extent – are always speculative.[206] As we have seen earlier, positive human rights obligations bear the risk of inadequate surveillance and control, since human rights risk might theoretically stem from myriad different sources. When assessing the reasonableness of preventive measures, this inherent unpredictability has to be duly accounted for. Obviously, this is different for obligations of diligent conduct in the aftermath of a human rights violation, when the amount of damage is already clear. An assessment of the reasonableness of a state's human rights approach

---

[201] ECtHR, *Handyside* v. *UK*, Plenary Judgment of 7 December 1976, Application No. 5493/72, para. 48.
[202] Hickman, "The Reasonableness Principle," 189.
[203] ECtHR, *Hatton and Others* v. *UK*, Grand Chamber Judgment of 8 July 2003, Application No. 36022/97, para. 86.
[204] Ibid., para. 125.
[205] Samantha Besson, "Les Obligations de Protection des Droits Fondamentaux. Un Essai en Dogmatique Comparative" (2003) 1 *Revue de Droit Suisse* 49–96 at 91.
[206] Smet, "Resolving Conflicts between Human Rights," p. 55.

thus has to differentiate between obligations of diligent conduct before and after a human rights violation.

Given the fact that there are endless possible scenarios of human rights violations, international law is ill-equipped to define in detail the course of conduct that is expected of states under their human rights obligations of diligent conduct. On the other hand, states should not be awarded complete discretion in evaluating the reasonableness of their domestic policies. Even where states enjoy a wide margin of appreciation, this margin only comprises those measures, which can be considered reasonable under the circumstances at hand. Whenever domestic measures are deemed an unreasonable approach toward a given human rights risk, they do not fall within the pool of measures, among which states could take a pick in pursuance of the margin of appreciation concept. This is, for instance, clearly reflected in the ECtHR's *Lawless* case, in which the exercise of the derogation option on behalf of Ireland was tested before the Court. While a margin of appreciation was awarded to Ireland's assessment of whether there existed a state of emergency, the Court still reviewed this assessment and found it to be justified precisely because the existence of such emergency was "reasonably deduced by the Irish government from a combination of several factors,"[207] thereby indicating that an unreasonable assessment would have excluded the derogation. Limits to the margin of appreciation are further apparent in those decisions in which the Court found that, because states had not properly fulfilled their balancing task, their actions would fall outside the margin. In the *Kuck* case, for instance, the Court held that "no fair balance was struck between the interests. ... *In these circumstances*, the Court considers that the German authorities overstepped the margin of appreciation afforded to them."[208] In a similar manner, it emphasized in the *Broniowski* decision that no matter how wide the margin of appreciation might be, it would not entail "consequences at variance with Convention standards."[209] Even where states enjoyed significant discretion, their action could be tested against international human rights standards.

In general, state practice and international jurisprudence thus confirm that international law imposes certain constraints on the discretion of

---

[207] ECtHR, *Lawless* v. *Ireland* (No. 3), Judgment of 1 July 1961, Application No. 332/57, para. 28.

[208] ECtHR, *van Kuck* v. *Germany*, Judgment of 12 June 2003, Application No. 35968/97, paras. 84 f.; emphasis added.

[209] ECtHR, *Broniowski* v. *Poland*, Grand Chamber Judgment of 22 June 2004, Application No. 31443/96, para. 182.

individual states. While it is not possible to provide for a comprehensive definition of reasonable human rights protection, several overall conclusions and categories can be developed with respect to the factors and variables that determine the reasonableness of preventive and punitive approaches. Broadly, the elements of reasonableness as derived from international human rights jurisprudence can be categorized into elements determining the scope of measures and elements relating to their nature.

1. Scope of Measures

The scope of measures that states are expected to perform in order to fulfill their positive human rights obligations of diligent conduct depends on various different factors, at least some of which are relatively precisely described in human rights jurisprudence. For both preventive and punitive due diligence obligations, the status of the right that is to be protected in a given case is an important parameter. If fundamental human rights are at stake, a heightened standard of protection should apply. Next to this, the seriousness of the infringement that might occur or has occurred is an equally important factor. With regard to preventive obligations, the seriousness and imminence of a risk need to be balanced with the expected seriousness of a violation, while with regard to punitive obligations, it is merely the seriousness of the damage that determines the standard of care. The more serious a human rights violation has been, the more thorough investigatory and punitive efforts will need to be.

a. Status of the Right That Is to Be Protected

An important factor that needs to be taken into consideration is thus the status and character of the right in peril. While states should ensure all rights enshrined in international human rights instruments, there still is a hierarchy between those rights in that some rights are commonly considered absolute and more fundamental than others.[210] As we have already seen, this is illustrated by those clauses that allow for derogation from human rights obligations in times of necessity but explicitly exclude certain rights from the possibility of derogation underlying that

---

[210] Theo van Boven, "Categories of Rights," in Daniel Moeckli et al. (eds.), *International Human Rights Law* (Oxford: Oxford University Press, 2nd ed., 2014), pp. 150 ff.; Olivier de Schutter and Françoise Tulkens, "Rights in Conflict," in Eva Brems (ed.), *Conflicts between Fundamental Rights* (Antwerp: Intersentia, 2008), p. 179; Theodor Meron, "On a Hierarchy of International Human Rights" (1986) 80 *AJIL* 1–23.

nonderogable rights are so important that they should be guaranteed, even in case of an emergency,[211] and require more intense preventive and protective measures.[212]

Among the nonderogable rights are particularly those rights that concern the basic physical existence and well-being of individuals, such as the right to life, the protection against torture or inhuman treatment, and the prohibition of slavery. The importance of those rights is easily explained, given that they are the very precondition for the exercise of any other right. As for the right to life, the Inter-American Court described it as "the essential corollary for realizing the other rights."[213] Likewise, the Strasbourg Court emphasized that its case law "safeguards the right to life, without which enjoyment of any of the other rights and freedoms in the Convention is rendered nugatory,"[214] so that "the right to life is an inalienable attribute of human beings and forms the supreme value in the hierarchy of human rights."[215] Insofar, the heightened status of nonderogable rights shows similarities to the concept of minimum core obligations. The special protection that is awarded to the minimum core of social and economic rights is also based on the idea that at least the basic preconditions of an existence with dignity should be guaranteed.

When determining what constitutes reasonable measures, the status and hierarchical rank of rights is thus a relevant factor. It can even be important which aspect of a right is affected in a given scenario. In X and Y, the Strasbourg Court explained that "the nature of the State's obligation will depend on the particular aspect of private life that is at issue,"[216] thereby indicating that the adequacy of a state's response to a certain human rights risk depends on whether the essence of human rights is affected. While some infringements may affect the very core of a particular human right, others may merely touch upon its peripheral aspects. Among other examples, this is illustrated by the wide protection of political speech under the freedom of expression – which is inextricably linked with freedom of expression as an important precondition for

---

[211] Art. 4 of the ICCPR, Art. 15 of the ECHR, Art. 27 of the ACHR.
[212] See section III, 4, d, aa.
[213] IACtHR, *Case of the Pueblo Bello Massacre* v. *Colombia*, Judgment of 31 January 2006, Series C, No. 140, para. 120.
[214] ECtHR, *Pretty* v. *UK*, Judgment of 29 April 2002, Application No. 2346/02, para. 37.
[215] ECtHR, *Streletz, Kessler and Krenz* v. *Germany*, Grand Chamber Judgment of 22 March 2001, Application Nos. 34044/96 a.o., para. 94.
[216] ECtHR, *X and Y* v. *The Netherlands*, Judgment of 26 March 1985, Application No. 8978/80, para. 24.

well-informed decision-making and political participation – as opposed to mere commercial speech that can be more easily restricted to protect other rights and interests.[217]

In sum, a heightened standard of care is to be expected, and less leeway will be granted to insufficient capacities with regard to the most fundamental rights and core obligations. When finding an adequate balance between conflicting rights and interests, the need of special protection for the most fundamental rights is to be duly accounted for.[218] The status of the respective human right is important with regard to a state's preventive obligations, as well as with regard to its obligation in the aftermath of a human rights violation. On the preventive side, states are expected to employ wider measures of protection and to take complaints of potential risks particularly seriously. Nonetheless, it is important to bear in mind that the special role of those fundamental rights should not mean that those rights automatically prevail over any other right or interest.[219] They merely require a special form of protection that pays due regard to their fundamental importance without neglecting other factors.

b. Preventive Obligations: Seriousness of Risk

With regard to preventive measures, the seriousness of a human rights risk is another important factor to determine whether a state's response was reasonable or not. While the imminence of a risk is decisive to assume whether states could even have knowledge of potential human rights violations, the scope and nature of that risk become relevant when assessing the reasonableness of concrete measures. The more probable the materialization of a given human rights risk, the more substantial a state's preventive approach is expected to be.

Again, however, the individual components of the due diligence standard are interlinked. The likelihood of an event determines its foreseeability as the threshold triggering due diligence obligations in the first

---

[217] See, for instance, ECtHR, *Biriuk v. Lithuania*, Judgment of 25 November 2008, Application No. 23373/03, para. 38.

[218] This is, for instance, underlined by the ECtHR's constant position that the Court will apply particularly thorough scrutiny with regard to violations of Articles 2 and 3 of the Convention, indicating that less discretion is paid to states with regard to their choice of means. See, among many others, ECtHR, *McKerr v. UK*, Judgment of 4 May 2001, Application No. 28883/95, para. 109; *van Colle v. UK*, Judgment of 13 November 2012, Application No. 7678/09, para. 93.

[219] Smet, "Resolving Conflicts between Human Rights," pp. 150 f.; de Schutter and Tulkens, "Rights in Conflict," 181; Cordula Dröge, *Positive Verpflichtungen der Staaten in der EMRK* (Heidelberg: Springer, 2003), p. 309.

IV. REASONABLENESS 251

place. Yet this threshold also influences whether a state's concrete measures can be considered reasonable. While the fundamental importance of a right might call for preventive measures, the fact that a risk is insufficiently substantiated can absolve the state from acting preventively.[220] The intensity of potential damage, however, is an additional factor in determining the standard of care, especially if such damage is eventually irreversible.[221] If particularly grave human rights violations are likely to occur, they might call for the application of wide protective means, even if it seems less probable that they might actually materialize.

c. Punitive Obligations: Seriousness of Violation

For obligations of diligent conduct in the aftermath of a human rights violation, it is especially the seriousness of that violation which determines what constitutes a reasonable state response. The ECtHR has repeated various times that the "gravity of the offence" is an important factor,[222] and breaches of the right to life should always be "repressed and punished,"[223] which is supported by the IACtHR.[224] Again, this underlines the twofold purpose of punitive obligations we have encountered earlier: on the one hand, they provide satisfaction and compensation for the victim. On the other hand, they will deter others from engaging in similar harmful conduct. In the case of particularly grave human rights violations, both aspects call for thorough and substantial investigations and adequate punishments.[225] In its *Öneryildiz* case, the ECtHR explicitly held that not to allow "life-endangering offences to go unpunished ... [was] essential for maintaining public confidence and ensuring adherence to the rule of law and for preventing any appearance of tolerance or of collusion in unlawful acts."[226] In a similar manner, the Basic Principles and Guidelines on the Right to a Remedy and Reparation for Victims of Gross Violations of International Human Rights Law, which the General

---

[220] Smet, "Resolving Conflicts between Human Rights," p. 151.
[221] Sandra Stahl, *Schutzpflichten im Völkerrecht* (Heidelber: Springer, 2012), p. 287.
[222] See, for instance, ECtHR, *Opuz v. Turkey*, Judgment of 9 June 2009, Application No. 33401/02, para. 170.
[223] ECtHR, *Giuliani and Gaggio v. Italy*, Grand Chamber Judgment of 24 March 2011, Application No. 23458/02, para. 298.
[224] IACtHR, *Case of the Pueblo Bello Massacre v. Colombia*, Judgment of 31 January 2006, Series C, No. 140, para. 143.
[225] van Boven, "Categories of Rights," 151.
[226] ECtHR, *Öneryildiz v. Turkey*, Grand Chamber Judgment of 30 November 2004, Application No. 48939/99, para. 96.

Assembly adopted in 2005,[227] calls upon states to guarantee access to justice and adequate reparations for the victims of gross human rights violations, thereby confirming the importance of ensuring effective remedies in case of the most-severe human rights contraventions. That the seriousness of violations is an important element in assessing the reasonableness of a state's punitive measures might also be derived from the ECtHR's differentiated approach toward the right to life. While the Court generally requires states to impose criminal sanctions for intentional killings, it explicitly held that where the right to life was infringed upon in a non-intentional manner, recourse to criminal sanctions was not mandatory and civil or administrative sanctions would be sufficient.[228] In sum, the seriousness of a human rights contravention is thus an important element shaping the standard of care states are expected to perform in order to comply with their punitive due diligence obligations.

d. Balancing with Other Human Rights and Public Interests

Another distinct feature of due diligence obligations in the field of human rights protection is the balancing of human rights with public interests and the human rights of other individuals.[229] In protecting one individual's rights against threats or invasions from another, it need not be neglected that this other individual enjoys human rights protection too.[230] As we have seen in the general part, the range of reasonable measures is exceeded where states infringe upon some international obligations to comply with others.[231] Reasonable measures to protect one human right, therefore, cannot consist in an undue infringement upon another.[232]

---

[227] UN General Assembly, Resolution No. 60/147, adopted on 16 December 2005, Basic Principles and Guidelines on the Right to a Remedy and Reparation for the Victims of Gross Violations of International Human Rights Law and Serious Violations of International Humanitarian Law, UN Doc. A/RES/60/147 (2006).
[228] ECtHR, *Zavoloka* v. *Latvia*, Judgment of 7 July 2009, Application No. 58447/00, para. 34.
[229] Fellmeth, "Paradigms of International Human Rights Law," p. 218; Hessbruegge, "Human Rights Violations," 66; Besson, "Obligations de Protection des Droits Fondamentaux," 93.
[230] de Schutter, "International Human Rights Law," p. 511; Kälin and Künzli, "Universeller Menschenrechtsschutz," para. 302; Fredman, "Human Rights Transformed," p. 73; Mowbray, "Positive Obligations," p. 17.
[231] See Chapter 4, IV, 1, c.
[232] See, among many others, ECtHR, *Appleby and Others* v. *UK*, Judgment of 6 May 2003, Application No. 44306/98, paras. 47 ff.; *Plattform "Ärzte für das Leben"* v. *Austria*,

Likewise, preventive and protective measures might come into conflict with general public interests. Most importantly, international human rights bodies were confronted with cases in which positive obligations to protect human rights were at odds with national security,[233] the economic well-being of a country,[234] or the protection of the environment,[235] all of which have been considered to present legitimate collective interests, which have to be accounted for in the balancing exercise. The same holds true where positive human rights obligations potentially clash with other international obligations incumbent upon the state. In particular, the Strasbourg Court had to decide several cases on domestic legislation that had been enacted by states with the intention to implement norms of international human rights law outside of the Convention. In the *Jersild* decision, for instance, the applicant challenged his conviction under a Danish provision on hate speech that Denmark had enacted in pursuance of the UN Convention for the Elimination of All Forms of Racial Discrimination. When assessing whether there was a violation of Article 10 of the Convention, the Court argued, Denmark's obligation under the Convention had to be "interpreted, to the extent possible, so as to be reconcilable with its obligations under the UN Convention."[236]

Any risk of a potential interference with other human rights thus has to be addressed by states when designing human rights policies and an adequate balance between conflicting rights and interests is indispensable.[237] While it is not possible to determine beforehand how such an adequate balance should look like in detail, some guidance can be derived from the case law of human rights bodies. It is with regard to this balancing exercise that the reasonableness standard most strikingly overlaps with the proportionality test. Even though the

Judgment of 21 June 1988, Application No. 10126/82, paras. 32 ff.; *Hannover* v. *Germany* (No. 1), Judgment of 24 June 2004, Application No. 59320/00, para. 57.

[233] ECtHR, *Chahal and Others* v. *UK*, Grand Chamber Judgment of 15 November 1996, Application No. 22414/93, para. 75; *Saadi* v. *Italy*, Grand Chamber Judgment of 28 February 2008, Application No. 37201/06, para. 137.

[234] ECtHR, *Powell and Rayner* v. *UK*, Judgment of 21 February 1990, Application No. 9310/81, para. 42; *López Ostra* v. *Spain*, Judgment of 9 December 1994, Application No. 16798/90, para. 58; *Fadeyeva* v. *Russia*, Judgment of 9 June 2005, Application No. 55723/00, para. 101.

[235] ECtHR, *Fredin* v. *Sweden* (No. 1), Judgment of 18 February 1991, Application No. 12033/86, para. 48.

[236] ECtHR, *Jersild* v. *Denmark*, Grand Chamber Judgment of 23 September 1994, Application No. 15890/89, para. 30.

[237] Dröge, "Positive Verpflichtungen," pp. 315 f.

standards are slightly different,[238] some common considerations apply. At the very least, the balancing exercise cannot lead to ensuring one right to the complete exclusion of another. This is underlined by the *Öllinger* case in which the Strasbourg Court held Austria responsible for failure to protect the freedom of assembly, as it did not consider any viable alternative for allowing two parallel assemblies and simply prohibited one assembly from protecting the other against any disturbances.[239] For some typical conflicts between human rights, international human rights jurisprudence has even developed rather clear and detailed categories along which the balancing of conflicting rights and interests can be assessed. Illustrative examples are the protection of freedom of expression and the right to privacy that often clash where press reports are published that affect the private lives of individuals. With regard to these typical conflicts of rights, the Strasbourg Court has promoted an entire list of factors that need to be taken into consideration in the balancing exercise.[240] Outside of these categorized conflicts, however, the balancing exercise will generally be dependent on the circumstances of each individual case. While this might seem dissatisfying insofar as it does not allow for a clear-cut definition of reasonableness, flexibility is an inherent characteristic of due diligence obligations and allows for their adjusted application to different cases and constellations.

Next to the scope and content of reasonable measures, international human rights jurisprudence provides further guidance on the nature of measures that states are expected to take.

2. Nature of Measures

As we have seen in the general part, the notion of reasonableness is also linked to the notion of rationality, which becomes clear in those cases in which states employed inapt measures or failed to live up to their own domestic standards. Most importantly, state policies were considered unreasonable if they did not really address the human rights risk at hand or were completely unsuitable to achieve protection. The ECtHR stressed that state measures, in general, have to effectively contribute to

---

[238] See Chapter 4, IV, 1, a.
[239] ECtHR, *Öllinger* v. *Austria*, Judgment of 29 June 2006, Application No. 76900/01, paras. 48 f.
[240] ECtHR, *Hannover* v. *Germany* (No. 2), Grand Chamber Judgment of 7 February 2012, Application No. 40660/08, paras. 108 ff.

the protection they are supposed to achieve.[241] Obligations of diligent conduct, so the Human Rights Committee confirmed, required states to take measures that were "specific and effective."[242] Any approach by a state that is unfit to actually contribute to the protection of human rights concerned can thus be considered unreasonable.

Furthermore, and rather evidently, states are under an obligation to effectively apply their own technical standards and security provisions, which is illustrated by the *Öneryildiz* decision that involved the death of several people caused by the explosion at a waste-treatment factory. As it had been known to the local authorities that the factory operated contrary to several security provisions, the Court found Turkey to be in clear violation of its preventive obligation as it failed to enforce even its own domestic standards.[243] Reports on the negative health effects of a waste-treatment plant had also been issued in the *López Ostra* case, which were not accounted for by the municipality in charge.[244] For the Court, this formed an important aspect to establish failure on behalf of Spain to comply with its positive obligations of diligent conduct. Whenever domestic measures do not even abide by national standards of security and protection, they can thus be considered unreasonable, too.

3. Conclusion

International human rights jurisprudence provides at least some guidance on how reasonable human rights measures can be defined. Once again, preventive and punitive obligations of diligent conduct have to be distinguished. While the status of a right is an important factor determining the reasonableness for both forms of obligations, it is the seriousness of a risk that influences preventive standards and the seriousness of a violation that shapes punitive standards. In addition to this, it is mainly the balancing of competing rights, interests, and obligations that frames the degree of diligence states are expected to perform in order to comply with their human rights obligations. Necessarily, this balancing approach

---

[241] ECtHR, *Opuz v. Turkey*, Judgment of 9 June 2009, Application No. 33401/02, para. 175.
[242] HRC, *Joaquín David Herrera Rubio et al. v. Colombia*, Decision of 2 November 1987, Communication No. 161/1983, UN Doc. CCPR/C/OP/2 (1990), para. 10.3; *Mojica v. Dominican Republic*, Decision of 15 July 1994, Communication No. 449/1991, UN Doc. CCPR/C/51/D/449/1991 (1994), para. 5.5.
[243] ECtHR, *Öneryilidz v. Turkey*, Grand Chamber Judgment of 30 November 2004, Application No. 48939/99, paras. 98 and 107.
[244] ECtHR, *López Ostra v. Spain*, Judgment of 9 December 1994, Application No. 16798/90, paras. 53. and 56.

is a flexible task, which escapes any precise and clear-cut definition. In sum, however, the balancing exercise still presents the most adequate instrument to bring competing rights and interests in concordance.

While sometimes criticized for being unforeseeable or even arbitrary, the flexibility of due diligence obligations and the reasonableness test is actually an advantage, as it ensures that the domestic peculiarities in each state are duly accounted for and also allows for the standard's adjustment to changed circumstances and new challenges. As human rights performance is inherently difficult to measure in a statistical manner, it is important to bear in mind that in spite of any categories and attempts of objective assessments, the substantial evaluation of each individual case is and remains important, especially when determining the reasonableness of human rights efforts.[245]

In fact, states may take recourse to a great variety of different tools in order to ensure compliance with their preventive and protective human rights due diligence obligations when it comes to the harmful conduct of private individuals.[246] There are regulatory approaches in each area of domestic law that ultimately seek to protect human rights against undue infringements by non-state actors and thus constitute reasonable measures of prevention. Human rights protection can be realized through criminal or civil liability that deters and sanctions harmful private conduct. Administrative tools such as licensing procedures and safety requirements may further help achieve higher standards of human rights protection, as do labor protection laws and commercial provisions.

V. Concluding Remarks

Even though the notion of due diligence is broad and flexible, human rights jurisprudence offers sufficient guidance on how to establish failure

---

[245] David McGrogan, "The Problem of Causality in International Human Rights Law" (2016) 65 ICLQ 615–644 at 641 ff.

[246] For a comprehensive overview, see Olivier de Schutter et al., Human Rights Due Diligence: The Role of States, Report of the International Corporate Accountability Roundtable, December 2012, available online at https://static1.squarespace.com/static/583f3fca725e25fcd45aa446/t/58671817d2b857fd0d141820/1483151386977/Human-Rights-Due-Diligence-The-Role-of-States.pdf. A more comprehensive review of domestic approaches is also contained in Jennifer Zerk, "Toward a Fairer and More Effective System of Domestic Law Remedies," Report prepared for the Office of the UN High Commissioner for Human Rights, February 2014, available online at www.ohchr.org/documents/issues/business/domesticlawremedies/studydomesticlawremedies.pdf.

V. CONCLUDING REMARKS

on behalf of states to diligently prevent or sanction human rights violations. Moreover, the standard can always be adjusted to individual circumstances without imposing disproportionate burdens upon states. As we have seen in the introductory chapter, the growing influence of non-state actors has nevertheless challenged the effectiveness of international human rights provisions, in particular due to the fact that powerful non-state actors operate in countries with insufficient capacities. While lacking capacities do not absolve states from fulfilling their positive human rights obligations and there are minimum requirements that states have to abide by even in times of crisis, compliance with those obligations remains low in many states. The human rights risks imposed by private actors are often so substantial that any effective counterstrategy exceeds the limited resources of weaker states.

It is against this background that directly binding obligations upon non-state actors have emerged as an alternative policy option.[247] With many states lacking the means to ensure sufficiently effective protection, the potential for private human rights contraventions has significantly increased. If powerful non-state actors such as business corporations or armed groups operate in states that are ill-equipped to diligently prevent and sanction human rights contradictions, substantial gaps of protection are an inevitable consequence. Given the fact that establishing direct human rights obligations yet meets with intense concerns,[248] the following section will analyze how the due diligence standard could be fruitfully applied to extraterritorial constellations in order to compensate for these shortcomings. As we will see, it is exactly the flexible character of due diligence obligations that allows for taking the peculiarities of extraterritorial constellations into account.

---

[247] See Chapter 1.
[248] See Chapter 1, IV.

7

A Case for Extraterritorial Due Diligence Obligations in the Human Rights Context

I. Introductory Remarks

The issue of diverging capacities is crucial for the due diligence standard, which merely requires states to employ best efforts with reasonably available means. While states with low capacities are still expected to do as much as they can, their best efforts will often fall short of what would be necessary to ensure effective protection. To solve this problem, several strategies have been developed in different areas of international law and especially where common goods or interests are concerned. Notable examples are the concept of common but differentiated responsibilities in environmental law and the "unwilling or unable" standard as advanced for counterterrorism efforts. As the entire international community is adversely affected by environmental degradation and terrorist threats, it comes as little surprise that states have sought to tackle the inability of low-capacity states in said areas. On the one hand, this led to enhanced cooperation mechanisms, including technical and financial support. On the other hand, it also prompted ideas and concepts that limit or even infringe upon the territorial sovereignty of low-capacity states, permitting other states to take the measures they were unable to perform themselves.

In the human rights context, however, the debate on lacking capacities has taken a slightly different direction. The protection of human rights directly concerns the manner in which states treat individuals within their jurisdiction – an area that used to lie at the core of a state's internal affairs.[1] While protective due diligence obligations were originally

---

[1] Walter Kälin and Jörg Künzli, *Universeller Menschenrechtsschutz* (Basel: Helbing Lichtenhahn, 3rd ed., 2013), pp. 5 ff.

developed for the purpose of alien protection, they remained an issue of diplomatic protection, with states invoking the infringement of their nationals' rights against other states. How states treated their own nationals yet remained a matter of domestic concern that only slowly started to change with the rise of international human rights regimes. Meanwhile, concepts such as that of *erga omnes* obligations and the responsibility to protect have cultivated an understanding that the protection of human rights is of concern to the entire international community and all states "have a legal interest in their protection."[2] The debate on lacking capacities has not remained unaffected by this development. In particular, the extraterritorial applicability of human rights provisions sparked questions about whether states have the right or even the obligation to diligently react to human rights risks outside of their own territory. For our purposes, it is most interesting how human rights due diligence obligations could operate in an extraterritorial context and advance human rights compliance. As we will see, there is indeed an underdeveloped potential for extraterritorial due diligence obligations that could foster the implementation of human rights to a significant extent.

When starting to analyze relevant jurisprudence, a rich vein of case law on the extraterritorial applicability of human rights unfortunately reveals both methodological inconsistencies and conceptual confusion. In essence, all cases revolve around whether states are accountable under international human rights law if they adversely affect human rights outside of their borders and whether – vice versa – they should improve human rights situations abroad. With this in mind, several extraterritorial "constellations" can be distinguished: first, states acting on foreign territory through their own state organs; second, states controlling third parties on foreign territory whose conduct is attributable; and third, actions and omissions of a state inside its own territory producing extraterritorial effects. These different constellations require different answers but often get entangled with one another. To explore the potential of extraterritorial due diligence obligations, it therefore seems helpful to take a step back and start with clarifying how the ideal of universal human rights relates to the principle of non-intervention – a tension that underlies the entire debate on extraterritorial human rights. As a second step, some general remarks on state responsibility for human rights

---

[2] ICJ, Case Concerning the Barcelona Traction, Light and Power Company, Limited (*Belgium* v. *Spain*), Judgment of 5 February 1970, ICJ Reports 1970, 3, para. 33.

violations in extraterritorial constellations will be made, with a focus on jurisdictional clauses to then assess the different extraterritorial application of negative and positive obligations. While extraterritorial positive obligations have met with particular skepticism, there are at least two scenarios in which such obligations could really foster human rights compliance, and the section closes with an outlook on how such obligations could operate in practice.

II. Between Universal Human Rights Protection and the Principle of Non-Intervention: The Tension Underlying Extraterritorial Human Rights Protection

A major point of critique commonly brought forward against a restrictive application of human rights is their universal character, implying that every state would ideally owe every human rights obligation to every individual, no matter when and where.[3] Human rights do not depend on citizenship, and "all human beings are born free and equal in dignity and rights."[4] Human rights protection is no longer seen as an exclusively domestic matter of states. There is an increasingly broad consensus that human rights violations are of concern to the entire international community,[5] which brings the focus back to diverging capacities. With the ability to ensure protection significantly varying among states, the level of human rights enjoyment shows just as many gaps that run counter to the ideal of universal application. A too-narrow interpretation could even pave the way for double standards, as it would tie states to high human rights standards at home while their conduct abroad was subject to much lower restrictions. Similar to other areas of international law, it is thus argued that states with sufficient capacities should actively contribute to enhanced

---

[3] Samantha Besson, "Sources of International Human Rights Law: How General Is General International Law?," in Samantha Besson et al. (eds.), *The Oxford Handbook on the Sources of International Law* (Oxford: Oxford University Press, 2017), p. 862; Mark Gibney, *International Human Rights Law: Returning to Universal Principles* (London: Rowman & Littlefield, 2nd ed., 2016), p. 2.

[4] Universal Declaration of Human Rights, GA Resolution of 10 December 1948, UN Doc. A/RES/217(III).

[5] Sigrun Skogly, "Regulatory Obligations in a Complex World," in Surya Deva and David Bilchitz (eds.), *Building a Treaty on Business and Human Rights* (Cambridge: Cambridge University Press, 2017), p. 327; Koen de Feyter, "The Common Interest in International Law: Implications for Human Rights," in Wouter Vandenhole (ed.), *Challenging Territoriality in Human Rights Law* (London: Routledge, 2015), p. 187.

II. HUMAN RIGHTS PROTECTION AND NON-INTERVENTION

human rights protection in low-capacity states.[6] Support for such an active stance is often derived from the collective character of human rights treaties. In contrast to traditional international treaties, they do not create reciprocal obligations but provide for individual rights and envisage an environment in which states parties cooperate to jointly ensure their protection. The Strasbourg Court, for instance, emphasized that "unlike international treaties of the classic kind, the Convention comprises more than mere reciprocal engagements. ... It creates over and above a network of mutual, bilateral undertakings,"[7] with its Preamble explicitly encouraging "collective enforcement."

Based on Articles 1 No. 3, 55 lit. (c) and 56 of the UN-Charter, proponents of the universalist approach further argue that international law generally requires cooperation on human rights matters, indicating that human rights protection as a common concern should not be limited to jurisdictional spheres.[8] Among others, the International Law Institute suggested that third states should respond to human rights violations in other states by taking diplomatic, economic, and other measures that would not amount to an unlawful intervention in that state's internal affairs.[9] Given the universal character of human rights, extraterritorial applicability should also be recognized on a broader basis,[10] most notably through a wider acceptance of universal jurisdiction.[11]

---

[6] See also Chapter 1, I.

[7] ECtHR, *Ireland v. UK*, Plenary Judgment of 19 January 1978, Application No. 5310/71, para. 239.

[8] Olivier de Schutter, *International Human Rights Law* (Cambridge: Cambridge University Press, 2nd ed., 2014), p. 190; Karen Weidmann, *Der Beitrag der OECD-Leitsätze für multinationale Unternehmen zum Schutz der Menschenrechte* (Berlin: Duncker & Humblot, 2014), p. 67; Michał Gondek, *The Reach of Human Rights in a Globalising World: Extraterritorial Application of Human Rights Treaties* (Antwerpen: Intersentia, 2009), pp. 317 ff.; Sigrun Skogly, *Beyond National Borders* (Antwerpen: Intersentia, 2006), pp. 74 ff.; Chris Jochnik, "Confronting the Impunity of Non-State Actors" (1999) 21 *HRQ* 56–79 at 73.

[9] International Law Institute, "The Protection of Human Rights and the Principle of Non-Intervention in Internal Affairs of States" (1989) 63 *Institut de Droit International Annuaire* at 338.

[10] Ibrahim Kanalan, "Extraterritorial State Obligations beyond the Concept of Jurisdiction" (2018) 19 *German Law Journal* 44–63 at 51; Skogly, "Regulatory Obligations," 334; Maarten de Heijer Rick and Lawson, "Extraterritorial Human Rights and the Concept of Jurisdiction," in Malcolm Langford et al. (eds.), *Global Justice, State Duties* (Cambridge: Cambridge University Press, 2013), p. 191; Surya Deva, "Acting Extraterritorially to Tame Multinational Corporations for Human Rights Violations" (2003) 5 *Melbourne Journal of International Law* 37–65.

[11] Constantin Köster, *Die völkerrechtliche Verantwortlichkeit privater (multinationaler) Unternehmen für Menschenrechtsverletzungen* (Berlin: Duncker & Humblot, 2010),

Other authors, however, call for caution so to avoid undue encroachments on the internal affairs of states. While recognizing deficiencies in international human rights protection, they doubt whether expansive extraterritorial obligations and the exercise of universal jurisdiction provide an adequate solution.[12] Extending universal jurisdiction is mostly denounced because of its inherent potential of abuse through selective and politically oriented application,[13] all the more as it would augment the extraterritorial reach of all judiciaries, including those that do not adhere to human rights and due process principles. It comes as little surprise, therefore, that states have been reluctant to widen the scope of universal jurisdiction.[14] Other expansions of extraterritorial obligations yet meet with equally intense concerns. Decried as "human rights imperialism," they are condemned for enforcing human rights standards in countries that are not members of the respective conventions and upholding a Western understanding of human rights without deference to other cultural traditions.[15] A state's sovereign decision not to ratify a particular human rights instrument could not simply be ignored, and no partisan conception of human rights should be enforced through extraterritorial measures,[16] lest they would infringe upon the sovereignty of those states.

---

p. 266; Moritz von Unger, Menschenrechte als transnationales Privatrecht (Berlin: Duncker & Humblot, 2008), p. 66; Donald Francis Donovan and Anthea Roberts, "The Emerging Recognition of Universal Civil Jurisdiction" (2006) 100 *AJIL* 142–163.

[12] Patrick Macklem, "Corporate Accountability under International Law: The Misguided Quest for Universal Jurisdiction" (2005) 7 *International Law Forum* 281–289; Eugene Kontorovich, "The Piracy Analogy: Modern Universal Jurisdiction's Hollow Foundation" (2004) 45 *Harvard International Law Journal* 183–237; Madeline Morris, "Universal Jurisdiction in a Divided World" (2001) 35 *New England Law Review* 337–361.

[13] Morris, "Universal Jurisdiction," 338.

[14] Lee McConnell, *Extracting Accountability from Non-State Actors in International Law* (London: Routledge, 2017), p. 103; Cedric Ryngaert, *Jurisdiction in International Law* (Oxford: Oxford University Press, 2nd ed., 2015), p. 130.

[15] See, in greater detail, de Feyter, "Common Interest in International Law," 184 f.; Josef Isensee, "Die heikle Weltherrschaft der Menschenrechte," in Marten Breuer et al. (eds.), *Der Staat im Recht* (Berlin: Duncker & Humblot, 2013), pp. 1105 f.; Ralph Wilde, "Compliance with Human Rights Norms Extraterritorially: 'Human Rights Imperialism'?," in Laurence Boisson de Chazournes and Marcelo Kohen (eds.), *International Law and the Quest for its Implementation* (Leiden: Brill, 2010), pp. 319–348, and with regard to the Responsibility to Protect, Philip Cunliffe, "A Dangerous Duty: Power, Paternalism and the Global Duty of Care," in Philip Cunliffe (ed.), *Critical Perspectives on the Responsibility to Protect* (London: Routledge, 2011), pp. 51–70.

[16] Emmanuelle Jouannet, "Universalism and Imperialism: The True-False Paradox of International Law?" (2007) 18 *EJIL* 379–407 at 389.

In sum, the debate on extraterritorial human rights is thus driven by two legitimate yet often irreconcilable aims: the universal character of human rights speaking for their broadest possible application on the one hand and the fear of human rights imperialism on the other. As we will see, it is this tension that shaped the legal debate on extraterritorial human rights, including the development and interpretation of jurisdictional clauses.

III. Jurisdictional Clauses in International Human Rights Regimes

Much of the confusion surrounding cases with extraterritorial elements stems from the jurisdictional clauses that are contained in most human rights treaties[17] and instruct states parties to ensure the rights enshrined in the respective instrument to everyone within their jurisdiction. Jurisdiction, however, is not a uniform concept in international law and has been employed to describe different phenomena. The Strasbourg Court reads Article 1 of the Convention as reflecting the notion of jurisdiction commonly employed in international law, which would mean that "the jurisdictional competence of a State is primarily territorial"[18] and other forms of jurisdiction required "special justification in the particular circumstances of each case."[19]

Though whereas the Convention's jurisdictional clause defines under which circumstances states are responsible to implement the Convention, the notion of territorial jurisdiction has traditionally been used in a slightly different context. As international law is built on the assumption of equal states with exclusive control over their respective territories, the exercise of jurisdiction by states over activities outside of their territories has always been deemed a potential infringement

---

[17] Art. 1 ECHR, Art. 1 ACHR, Art. 2 (I) ICCPR, as well as Art. 7 of the International Convention on the Protection of the Rights of All Migrant Workers and Members of Their Families, signed 18 December 1990, entered into force 1 July 2003, 2220 UNTS 2; Arts. 3 and 6 of the Convention on the Elimination of All Forms of Racial Discrimination, signed on 7 March 1966, entered into force 4 January 1969, 660 UNTS 195; or Arts. 2, 5, 7, 11, 12, 13, 16, and 22 of the Convention against Torture and Other Cruel, Inhuman or Degrading Treatment or Punishment, signed on 10 December 1984, entered into force on 26 June 1987, 1465 UNTS.

[18] ECtHR, *Banković and Others* v. *Belgium and Others*, Grand Chamber Judgment of 12 December 2001, Application No. 52207/99, para. 59.

[19] Ibid., para. 61.

upon the sovereignty of other states.[20] In this context, jurisdiction used to describe "the extent of each state's right to regulate conduct and the consequences of events."[21] From a historical and conceptual basis, the notion of jurisdiction is thus inextricably linked to the principle of non-intervention: while each state is supreme in its internal affairs, it must not intervene in the jurisdictional spheres of others.[22] It described the authority of each state to apply and enforce its domestic legislation, which is why different forms of jurisdiction are commonly distinguished: prescriptive jurisdiction as the jurisdiction to enact domestic legislation, judicial jurisdiction as the trying of cases before domestic courts, and enforcement jurisdiction as the effective carrying out of judicial and police functions.[23]

While states are entitled to exercise all forms of jurisdiction on their territory, the exercise of extraterritorial jurisdiction has always been subject to restrictions as it potentially interferes with the territorial sovereignty of other states. Since enforcement jurisdiction is particularly intrusive, its extraterritorial exercise is commonly considered impermissible under general international law.[24] In contrast, the exercise of prescriptive and judicial jurisdiction is recognized in case of a sufficient nexus.[25] Indisputably recognized as such nexus is the active personality principle, according to which states may exercise prescriptive and judicial jurisdiction over the extraterritorial conduct of their own citizens. Somewhat more controversial are the protective and the passive personality approach, which provide for jurisdiction if important state interests are at stake or the victims of wrongful conduct are the citizens of the state that seeks to exercise jurisdiction. Even though both approaches have been referred to, their status under customary international law remains unsettled. In contrast, the concept of universal jurisdiction is recognized

---

[20] Malcolm Shaw, *International Law* (Cambridge: Cambridge University Press, 8th ed., 2017), p. 485; James Crawford, *Brownlie's Principles of Public International Law* (Cambridge: Cambridge University Press, 8th ed., 2012), p. 447.

[21] Robert Jennings and Arthur Watts, *Oppenheim's International Law* (London: Harlow, 9th ed., 1992), p. 456.

[22] Ryngaert, "Jurisdiction in International Law," p. 6.

[23] See, further, Michael Akehurst, "Jurisdiction in International Law" (1973) 46 *British Yearbook of International Law* 145–257.

[24] Ryngaert, "Jurisdiction in International Law," p. 9; Christian Walter, "Anwendung deutschen Rechts im Ausland und fremden Rechts in Deutschland," in Josef Isensee and Paul Kirchhof (eds.), *Handbuch des Staatsrechts*, vol. XI (Heidelberg: C.F. Müller, 3rd ed., 2013), p. 434.

[25] Walter, "Anwendung deutschen Rechts im Ausland," 433; Magdalena Jankowska-Gilberg, *Extraterritorialität der Menschenrechte* (Baden-Baden: Nomos, 2008), p. 31.

in criminal matters with regard to certain exceptionally grave international crimes. Based on this principle, any state may exercise prescriptive or judicial jurisdiction, irrespective of any personal or territorial nexus, because of the severe character of the crime. Most domestic legal orders recognize all or some of these jurisdictional principles.[26]

As even this brief overview has shown, the notion of jurisdiction was traditionally linked with permissive aspects – that is, under which circumstances the exercise of jurisdiction is compatible with international law. When it comes to human rights protection, though, it is less important whether the exercise of jurisdiction is permitted but rather whether states are bound by their international obligations if they act extraterritorially.[27] Fairly obviously, the notion of jurisdiction under general international law is different from the notion of jurisdiction in international human rights treaties.[28] In fact, the latter has become much more entangled in the notion of state responsibility.

IV. Jurisdictional Clauses and State Responsibility

Jurisdictional clauses are distinct features of human rights treaties in that they confine the obligations of member states to individuals within their jurisdiction. At first glance, this appears curious when considering the traditional understanding of state responsibility. The ILC Draft Articles, for instance, do not require any territorial nexus. Responsibility is established by an attributable breach of international law, no matter where and how that breach occurred. What needs to be explored, therefore, is whether jurisdictional clauses limit the primary responsibility of states to their jurisdictional sphere in a sense that responsibility may only be triggered where jurisdiction is exercised. At this point, it is worth

---

[26] For a comprehensive overview of these jurisdictional principles, see Shaw, "International Law," pp. 488 ff.; Ryngaert, "Jurisdiction in International Law," pp. 104 ff.

[27] Michael Duttwiler, "Authority, Control and Jurisdiction in the Extraterritorial Application of the ECHR" (2012) 30 *Netherlands Quarterly of Human Rights* 137–162 at 140; Anne Peters, "Die Anwendbarkeit der EMRK in Zeiten komplexer Hoheitsgewalt und das Prinzip der Grundrechtstoleranz" (2010) 48 AVR 1–57 at 6; Martin Scheinin, "Extraterritorial Effect of the ICCPR," in Fons Coomans and Menno Kamminga (eds.), *Extraterritorial Application of Human Rights Treaties* (Antwerpen: Intersentia, 2004), p. 79.

[28] Andreas Papp, *Extraterritoriale Schutzpflichten* (Berlin: Duncker & Humblot, 2013), pp. 69 ff.; Marko Milanovic, *Extraterritorial Application of Human Rights Treaties* (Oxford: Oxford University Press, 2011), pp. 26 ff; Olivier de Schutter, Globalization and Jurisdiction: Lessons from the ECHR, CRIDHO Working Paper 2005/04, pp. 6 f.

recalling how the notions of jurisdiction and state responsibility are commonly distinguished in general international law. As we have seen, jurisdiction relates to the power of states to make their laws applicable and to enforce them, whereas responsibility relates to the legal consequences if states breach their international obligations: "the law of jurisdiction is about entitlement to act, the law of state responsibility is about obligations incurred when a state does act."[29] In fact, state responsibility may be based exactly on a state's exercise of jurisdiction, where it does not have any jurisdictional entitlement. Traditionally, jurisdiction and state responsibility thus used to describe inherently different phenomena that the wording of jurisdictional clauses tied together. They have nothing to do with the question of when states are entitled to exercise jurisdiction but rather prescribe under which circumstances states they are required to ensure human rights protection[30] – that is, whether states are only bound by human rights provisions when acting on their own territory or whether extraterritorial conduct might also fall "within their jurisdiction."

Insofar, jurisdictional clauses are somewhat at odds with the classical structure of state responsibility, though as we have seen, human rights treaties do not match traditional reciprocal treaty structures either. With this in mind, jurisdictional clauses are not an instrument for states to flee their human rights obligations when operating abroad. As it cannot be reasonably expected of states to ensure the protection of human rights in all parts of the world,[31] they serve the legitimate aim of limiting human rights obligations to spheres in which they can be meaningfully implemented.[32] They should not be misread so as to remove any extraterritorial conduct from a state's jurisdiction,[33] and their nuanced

---

[29] Rosalyn Higgins, *Problems and Process: International Law and How We Use It* (Oxford: Clarendon, 1994), p. 146.

[30] Ryngaert, "Jurisdiction in International Law," p. 22.

[31] Claire Methven O'Brien, "The Home State Duty to Regulate the Human Rights Impacts of TNCs Abroad" (2018) 3 *Business and Human Rights Journal* 47–73 at 53 f.; Damira Kamchibekova, "State Responsibility for Extraterritorial Human Rights Violations" (2007) 13 *Buffalo Human Rights Law Review* 87–149 at 97 f.

[32] Milanovic, "Extraterritorial Application," p. 56; Guy Goodwin-Gill, "The Extra-Territorial Reach of Human Rights Obligations," in Laurence Boisson de Chazournes and Marcelo Kohen (eds.), *International Law and the Quest for its Implementation* (Leiden: Brill, 2010), p. 296.

[33] McConnell, "Extracting Accountability"; Karen da Costa, *The Extraterritorial Application of Selected Human Rights Treaties* (Leiden: Martinus Nijhoff, 2013); Milanovic, "Extraterritorial Application"; Gondek, "The Reach of Human Rights"; Jankowska-Gilberg, "Extraterritorialität der Menschenrechte"; Kamchibekova, "Extraterritorial

application becomes even clearer when considering the differences between negative and positive obligations.

V. Negative versus Positive Obligations in Extraterritorial Cases

It is commonly assumed that negative obligations apply at all times and states should refrain from violating human rights also when acting outside of their territory.[34] The Human Rights Committee held it "would be unconscionable to so interpret the responsibility under article 2 of the Covenant as to permit a State party to perpetrate violations of the Covenant on the territory of another State, which violations it could not perpetrate on its own territory,"[35] and the Inter-American Commission confirmed that where states "exercise power and authority over persons outside national territory, the state's obligation to respect human rights continues."[36] An adjusted approach, however, is suggested for failure to comply with positive obligations for which, so it is argued, states should only be held accountable if they had a sufficient degree of control over the situation concerned.[37]

The logic behind this distinction would seem to be as follows: Compliance with positive obligations requires actual capacity on behalf of the state.[38] Positive obligations presuppose state knowledge of human rights risks and sufficient means to address them – prerequisites that tend to be fulfilled only on a state's own territory.[39] Leeway to take protective

---

Human Rights Violations"; Skogly, "Beyond National Borders"; Fons Coomans and Menno Kamminga (eds.), *Extraterritorial Application of Human Rights Treaties* (Antwerpen: Intersentia, 2004).

[34] Milanovic, "Extraterritorial Application," p. 119; Rolf Künnemann, "Some Remarks on the Extraterritorial Application of the ICESCR," in Fons Coomans and Menno Kamminga (eds.), *Extraterritorial Application of Human Rights Treaties* (Antwerpen: Intersentia, 2004), pp. 216 f.

[35] HRC, *Lilian Celiberti de Casariego v. Uruguay*, Decision of 29 July 1981, Communication No. 56/1979, UN Doc. CCPR/C/13/D/56/1979, para. 10.3.

[36] IAComHR, *Armando Alejandre Jr. and Others v. Republica de Cuba*, Decision of 29 September 1999, Case 11.589, Report No. 86/99, OEA/Ser.L/V/II.106 Doc. 3 rev. at 586 (1999), para. 25.

[37] Gondek, "The Reach of Human Rights," p. 72.

[38] Peters, "Die Anwendbarkeit der EMRK," 53; Kamchibekova, "Extraterritorial Human Rights Violations," 97 f.; Erik Roxstrom et al., "The NATO Bombing Case and the Limits of Western Human Rights Protection" (2005) 23 *Boston University International Law Journal* 55–136 at 72 f.

[39] Daniel Augenstein and David Kinley, "Beyond the 100 Acre Wood: In Which International Human Rights Law Finds New Ways to Tame Global Corporate Power" (2014) *Sydney Law School Legal Studies* Research Paper No. 14/90, p. 8; Milanovic,

measures is equally restricted, as any act of enforcement on another state's territory potentially interferes with the latter's domestic affairs.[40] To ensure human rights, states have to regulate third-party conduct and take positive action, both of which infringe upon the sovereignty of other states when realized abroad.[41] In contrast, states can always control the conduct of their organs and to merely refrain from human rights violations does not interfere with the domestic affairs of another state either.[42] Whereas extraterritorial positive obligations are thus of inherently limited reach, negative obligations could easily be applied extraterritorially.

As we will see, however, the Strasbourg Court developed a distinct approach toward extraterritorial applicability, and while it has developed the most elaborate jurisprudence on these matters, its method was also criticized for being incoherent[43] and even arbitrary.[44]

1. The ECtHR's Perspective

The Strasbourg Court had to deal with several extraterritorial constellations, the first of which was the *Loizidou* case on the situation in Northern Cyprus that established the Court's effective control-standard. At stake were alleged human rights violations carried out by the Turkish Republic of Northern Cyprus, itself not a state party to the Convention. The Court, therefore, had to attribute the TRNC's perpetrations to Turkey in order to invoke the latter's responsibility, although the violations occurred outside of Turkey's territory. In this scenario, the question of attributing the TRNC's conduct to Turkey was inextricably linked to the Court's own jurisdiction. With the TRNC not being a signatory to the Convention and the proceedings brought against Turkey alone and not against Cyprus, the Court could not have exercised

---

"Extraterritorial Application," p. 210; Hugh King, "The Extraterritorial Human Rights Obligations of States" (2009) 9 *HRLR* 521–556 at 540 f.

[40] Methven O'Brien, "Home State Duty to Regulate," 56; Walter, "Anwendbarkeit deutschen Rechts im Ausland," 450 f.

[41] Jankowska-Gilberg, "Extraterritorialität der Menschenrechte," p. 174.

[42] See also Walter, "Anwendbarkeit deutschen Rechts im Ausland," 451.

[43] Kälin and Künzli, "Universeller Menschenrechtsschutz," para. 387; Milanovic, "Extraterritorial Application," p. 30; Sarah Miller, "Revisiting Extraterritorial Jurisdiction: A Territorial Justification for Extraterritorial Jurisdiction under the ECHR" (2009) 20 *EJIL* 1223–1246 at 1226 ff.; Roxstrom et al., "The NATO-Bombing Case," 61; Scheinin, "Extraterritorial Effect of the ICCPR," 80.

[44] Vassilis Tzevelekos, "Reconstructing the Effective Control Criterion in Extraterritorial Human Rights Breaches" (2014) 36 *MJIL* 129–178 at 141.

V. NEGATIVE VERSUS POSITIVE OBLIGATIONS

its jurisdiction had the conduct not been attributable. It is the central role of attribution for this case that explains how the standard of effective control became intertwined with the notion of jurisdiction. Ever since the ICJ's *Nicaragua* case, effective control had been a standard for state responsibility in relation to third-party conduct. The degree of state control over private actions and omissions determined whether they could be attributed.[45]

The *Loizidou* judgment, however, used effective control not to describe the relationship between the TRNC and Turkey but rather spoke of Turkey's control over Northern Cyprus as a territorial area.[46] Thereby linking the attribution of the TRNC's conduct to Turkey with the exercise of territorial jurisdiction over Northern Cyprus, the Court laid the groundwork for its assumption that effective control over a situation brought that situation within the jurisdiction of a state. It found the extent of Turkey's control over the TRNC so expansive that not only could its conduct be attributed to Turkey, but Northern Cyprus in general should be treated as Turkish territory. Against this background, it held that "Turkey's 'jurisdiction' must be considered to extent to securing *the entire range of substantive rights* set out in the Convention,"[47] underlining that Turkey was responsible not only for violations of negative obligations in Northern Cyprus but also for fulfilling the entire range of positive obligations. A first conclusion to be drawn is thus that territories under the effective control of states indisputably fall within their jurisdiction, where they are bound by the entire range of Convention obligations.

The next milestone of the ECtHR's jurisprudence on extraterritorial matters was the *Banković* decision on NATO's aerial bombing of Serbia, in which several Convention states participated. What the *Banković* case has in common with the *Loizidou* decision is that both cases deal with alleged violations that occurred outside the territory of the member states accused thereof. Though whereas the *Loizidou* case decided whether the TRNC's conduct could be attributed to Turkey, the *Banković* case dealt with the conduct of state organs that was unquestionably attributable.[48]

---

[45] ICJ, Military and Paramilitary Activities in and against Nicaragua (*Nicaragua* v. *USA*), Judgment of 27 June 1986, ICJ Reports 1986, 14, para. 115.

[46] ECtHR, *Loizidou* v. *Turkey*, Grand Chamber Judgment (Preliminary Objection) of 23 March 1995, Application No. 15318/89, para. 62.

[47] ECtHR, *Cyprus* v. *Turkey*, Grand Chamber Judgment of 10 May 2001, Application No. 25781/94, para. 77, emphasis added.

[48] The Court did not elaborate on the question of whether the fact that military action was coordinated by NATO excluded the attribution of harmful conduct to individual member states.

Still, the Court referred to the notion of effective control and thereby transformed the standard from one indicating control over third-party conduct to one marking control over territory. What has primarily mattered in extraterritorial cases ever since is not the attribution of harmful private conduct but rather the degree of control a state has over the situation in which the alleged violations took place. Only effective control in the latter sense attracted state responsibility, and since the air strikes did not lead to territorial control, the Court found them to fall outside the member states' jurisdiction.[49] While the applicants had explicitly suggested to at least apply negative obligations, the Court found the Convention's obligations could not be "divided and tailored in accordance with the particular circumstances of the extraterritorial act in question."[50] The judgment was widely and vigorously criticized, with many observers arguing that responsibility for the conduct of state organs could and should have been established, irrespective of where it took place. Any other solution would inevitably entail that states could commit human rights violations abroad that they were prohibited from at home.[51] Next to its distinct standard of effective control though, the Court developed an additional concept in the *Banković* decision by referring to the Convention as a European *espace juridique*, which spoke for its uniform application within the territory of all member states but not beyond. Explicitly, the Court distinguished the situation in Serbia from that in Cyprus, as the residents of the Cypriot north should not be deprived of the Convention's protection to which Cyprus and Turkey both were parties. As for Serbia, however, the Court held that

> the Convention was not designed to be applied throughout the world, *even in respect of the conduct of Contracting States.* Accordingly, the desirability of avoiding a gap or a vacuum in human rights' protection has so far been relied on by the Court in favour of establishing jurisdiction only when the territory in question was one that, but for the specific circumstances, would normally be covered by the Convention.[52]

---

[49] ECtHR, *Banković and Others v. Belgium and Others*, Grand Chamber Judgment of 12 December 2001, Application No. 52207/99, para. 82.
[50] Ibid., para. 75.
[51] Among many others, see Tzevelekos, "Reconstructing the Effective Control Criterion," 147; Duttwiler, "Authority, Control and Jurisdiction," 140; Roxstrom et al., "The NATO-Bombing Case," 62.
[52] ECtHR, *Banković and Others v. Belgium and Others*, Grand Chamber Judgment of 12 December 2001, Application No. 52207/99, para. 80, emphasis added.

An interpretation that basically allows member states to carry out substantive violations of the Convention on the territory of third-party states. Not surprisingly, it met with intense criticism[53] and soon became subject to qualifications by the Court itself.

The Court first lessened its restrictions in the *Issa* judgment that examined the conduct of Turkish state organs in northern Iraq. Next to situations of effective territorial control, so it held, states could also be accountable for violating the human rights of "persons who are in the territory of another State but who are found to be under the former State's authority and control through its agents operating – whether lawfully or unlawfully – in the latter."[54] In a range of cases, the Court later confirmed that it was not only effective territorial control that brought cases within the jurisdiction of states but also control over individuals,[55] which considerably widens the Convention's extraterritorial applicability.

Another notable exception to the control criterion was found in the *Ilaşcu* judgment on the Transdniestrian Republic. Officially a part of Moldovia, the Republic is under the effective control of Russia, which the Court found directly responsible for the human rights violations committed by Transdniestrian authorities.[56] In contrast to the *Loizidou* case, however, the victims had brought claims against both Russia and Moldovia, and the Court also found a failure on behalf of Moldovia to comply with its positive obligations.[57] Even if states have lost control over parts of their territory, they thus remain responsible under the Convention. While the judgment does not establish extraterritorial positive obligations in a general manner, as Transdniestria still formed part of Moldovia's territory, the Court's position is nonetheless important. While Russia was held responsible for directly causing human rights violations, Moldovia was held responsible for a failure to take adequate steps of prevention. The Court thereby acknowledged that several states

---

[53] Tzevelekos, "Reconstructing the Effective Control Criterion," 147; Milanovic, "Extraterritorial Application," p. 30; Roxstrom et al., "The NATO-Bombing Case," 61; Scheinin, "Extraterritorial Effect of the ICCPR," 80.

[54] ECtHR, *Issa and Others v. Turkey*, Judgment of 16 November 2004, Application No. 31821/96, paras. 70 f.

[55] See, for instance, ECtHR, *Öcalan v. Turkey*, Grand Chamber Judgment of 12 May 2005, Application No. 46221/99, para. 91; *Al-Skeini and Others v. UK*, Grand Chamber Judgment of 7 July 2011, Application No. 55721/07, paras. 149 f.

[56] ECtHR, *Ilaşcu and Others v. Moldovia and Russia*, Grand Chamber Judgment of 8 July 2004, Application No. 48787/99, paras. 393–394, 494.

[57] Ibid., paras. 352, 494.

may have simultaneous human rights obligations of varying degrees and concurrent responsibility could arise under the Convention.

2. The ICJ's Perspective

The International Court of Justice was also confronted with a range of cases involving the extraterritorial applicability of human rights instruments and developed a slightly different solution. Already in the Namibia Advisory Opinion had the Court confirmed that physical control over territory and not sovereignty or legitimacy of title formed the basis of state responsibility.[58] The first extraterritorial human rights situation to find its way before the ICJ was then the Advisory Opinion on the Legal Consequences of the Construction of a Wall in the Occupied Palestinian Territory.[59] Israel had denied the applicability of the two Covenants in the Palestinian territories as human rights law – in contrast to humanitarian law – was designed to "protect citizens *from their own governments* in time of peace."[60] Both arguments were rejected by the Court, which found human rights applicable in times of conflict and even where state agents acted abroad.[61] In a similar manner, it later held with regard to Uganda's activities in the Democratic Republic of Congo that international human rights instruments continued to apply "in respects of acts done by a State in the exercise of its jurisdiction outside of its own territory."[62] This is in line with the approach employed by the ECtHR: where the level of control over another state's territory is effective, state responsibility for human rights violations is to be determined as if the respective region formed part of the occupying state's territory, with positive and negative obligations fully applicable.[63]

---

[58] ICJ, Legal Consequences for States of the Continued Presence of South Africa in Namibia (South West Africa) Notwithstanding Security Council Resolution 276 (1970), Advisory Opinion of 21 June 1971, ICJ Reports 1971, 16, para. 118.

[59] ICJ, Legal Consequences of the Construction of a Wall in the Occupied Palestinian Territory, Advisory Opinion of 9 July 2004, ICJ Reports 2004, 136.

[60] Statement by the Israeli Government, quoted in the Wall Advisory Opinion, para. 102, emphasis added.

[61] ICJ, Wall Advisory Opinion, para. 109.

[62] ICJ, Case Concerning Armed Activities on the Territory of the Congo (*DR Congo v. Uganda*), Judgment of 19 December 2005, ICJ Reports 2005, 168, para. 216.

[63] da Costa, "Extraterritorial Application," 77 ff.; Ralph Wilde, "Human Rights beyond Borders at the World Court: The Significance of the ICJ's Jurisprudence on the Extraterritorial Application of International Human Rights Law Treaties" (2012) 12 *Chinese Journal of International Law* 639–677 at 673.

V. NEGATIVE VERSUS POSITIVE OBLIGATIONS

Later on, the ICJ's decision on the genocide in Bosnia and Herzegovina shed even further light on questions of extraterritorial applicability and drew a nuanced distinction between positive and negative obligations. At stake was whether Serbia had violated the Genocide Convention with regard to the actions the Republic of Srpska carried out on Bosnian territory. As the Court found the relationship between Serbia and the Srpska forces not close enough to meet the threshold of effective control, it could not find that Serbia had violated its negative obligation not to commit genocide either[64] and went on to discuss whether Serbia had perhaps violated its positive obligation to prevent genocide. As the Genocide Convention did not contain any territorial limitation akin to the jurisdiction clauses in other human rights treaties, the ICJ found the obligation to prevent genocide to apply extraterritorially.[65] It would arise wherever there was a foreseeable risk of genocidal acts and states had the "capacity to effectively influence" those persons that were likely to commit genocide. While dependent on geographical distance and political links, this capacity to influence is not limited to a state's territory[66] and presents a much lower threshold compared to the effective control standard.[67] In relation to their capacity, all states are thus obliged to take diligent preventive steps with regard to foreseeable risks of genocidal acts even outside of their territory.[68] Furthermore, this necessarily implies that several states will have preventive obligations of varying degrees that exist simultaneously and could lead to parallel state responsibility.[69]

Not surprisingly, an intense debate followed the Court's judgment. Several scholars suggested an expansion of the Court's approach toward extraterritorial positive obligations. Further support was derived from

---

[64] ICJ, Case Concerning the Application of the Convention on the Prevention and Punishment of the Crime of Genocide (*Bosnia and Herzegovina v. Serbia and Montenegro*), Judgment of 26 February 2007, ICJ Reports 2007, 43, para. 415.

[65] ICJ, Case Concerning the Application of the Convention on the Prevention and Punishment of the Crime of Genocide (*Bosnia and Herzegovina v. Yugoslavia*), Judgment of 11 July 1996 (Preliminary Objections), ICJ Reports 1996, 595, para. 31.

[66] ICJ, Genocide Convention Case, para. 430.

[67] Berglind Halldórsdóttir Birkland, "Reining in Non-State Actors: State Responsibility and Attribution in Cases of Genocide" (2009) 84 *NYU Law Review* 1623–165 5 at 1648.

[68] Marko Milanović, "State Responsibility for Genocide: A Follow-Up" (2007) 18 *EJIL* 669–694 at 685.

[69] Mark Gibney, "Litigating Transnational Human Rights Obligations," in Wouter Vandenhole (ed.), *Challenging Territoriality in Human Rights Law* (London: Routledge, 2015), p. 95; Luke Glanville, "The Responsibility to Protect Beyond Borders" (2012) 12 *HRLR* 1–32 at 18.

Articles 40 and 41 of the ILC's Draft Articles on State Responsibility, which instruct states to cooperate in ending serious violations of *ius cogens* norms.[70] At least with regard to *ius cogens* violations, states should therefore employ reasonable extraterritorial measures. Carrying these thoughts even further, some authors suggested that the Court's position should apply to all human rights treaties so that states were obliged to prevent human rights obligations extraterritorially whenever they have the ability to influence the course of events,[71] at least where particularly grave human rights violations were at stake.[72] It should not be overlooked, however, that the Court's judgment explicitly relied on the fact that the Genocide Convention did not contain any jurisdictional clauses and with genocide focused on a *ius cogens* violation as one of the gravest forms of human rights contravention, which speaks against its straightforward transferability to the entire range of international human rights obligations.

Notwithstanding, the Court's holding gives reason to explore the still underdeveloped potential of extraterritorial positive obligations in greater detail. The following section aims at exploring this potential while concentrating on positive obligations derived from core human rights provisions. Extraterritorial obligations in relation to international crimes and an expansion of universal jurisdiction, therefore, will not form part of the discussion. Focus will rather be laid on how extraterritorial obligations could be reasonably conceptualized so as to improve the level of human rights protection even in cases that do not meet the high threshold for universal jurisdiction or constitute violations of *ius cogens* obligations.

VI. The Underdeveloped Potential of Positive Obligations of Diligent Conduct in Extraterritorial Constellations

Extraterritorial positive obligations have always been accompanied by great skepticism.[73] Even among proponents of expansive human rights, it

---

[70] Annie Bird, "Third State Responsibility for Human Rights Violations" (2010) 21 *EJIL* 883–900 at 886 ff.; Giorgio Gaja, "Do States Have a Duty to Ensure Compliance with Obligations Erga Omnes by Other States?," in Maurizio Ragazzi (ed.), *International Responsibility Today* (Leiden: Martinus Nijhoff, 2005), 31–36.
[71] See, for instance, Mark Gibney, "Genocide and State Responsibility" (2007) 7 *HRLR* 760–773 at 769.
[72] Glanville, "Responsibility to Protect," p. 28.
[73] Among many others, see Methven O'Brien, "Home State Duty to Regulate"; Kälin and Künzli, "Universeller Menschenrechtsschutz," para. 389; Jankowska-Gilberg, "Extraterritorialität der Menschenrechte," p. 188.

VI. POTENTIAL OF POSITIVE OBLIGATIONS

is popular to support extraterritorial application only for negative but not for positive obligations.[74] As we have seen, the main reason for this is that due diligence obligations require active regulatory measures.[75] They presuppose significantly more control over a situation than merely refraining from violating negative human rights obligations. Preventive measures on foreign territory not only present a significant intrusion into another state's internal affairs;[76] states also lack the capacity to systematically screen human rights risks in other countries and engage in effective prevention.

At closer inspection, however, this seemingly clear-cut distinction between positive and negative extraterritorial obligations appears too rigid. Human rights obligations are always specified in a context which renders abstract distinctions between the prerequisites for negative and positive obligations unnecessarily uncompromising.[77] When considering that positive obligations of diligent conduct require states to employ all reasonable means at their disposal to mitigate foreseeable human rights risks, extraterritorial reactions could well be expected under certain circumstances.[78] Though due regard has to be paid to the principle of non-intervention, there are several extraterritorial constellations in which due diligence obligations could considerably enhance human rights protection. With this in mind, the following section explores how the components of the due diligence standard might operate in extraterritorial constellations. In a first step, it analyzes under what circumstances knowledge of extraterritorial human rights risks could be expected to discuss in a second step how a reasonable approach toward these risks might look like in extraterritorial cases.

1. When Knowledge Can Be Expected in Extraterritorial Constellations

We have seen already that the knowledge criterion in human rights law is difficult to establish, as human rights risks stem from myriad different sources and asking states to actively gather information could lead to

---

[74] Kamchibekova, "State Responsibility for Extraterritorial Human Rights Violations," 97 f.; Roxstrom et al., "The NATO-Bombing Case," 73.
[75] Skogly, "Regulatory Obligations," 327; Walter, "Anwendbarkeit deutschen Rechts im Ausland," 450 f.; Kamchibekova, "State Responsibility for Extraterritorial Human Rights Violations," 97.
[76] Methven O'Brien, "Home State Duty to Regulate," 56.
[77] Samantha Besson, "The Extraterritoriality of the ECHR: Why Human Rights Depend on Jurisdiction and What Jurisdiction Amounts To" (2012) 25 *LJIL* 857–884 at 880.
[78] da Costa, "Extraterritorial Application," 302.

inadequate surveillance and control.[79] Notwithstanding and despite the fact that acquiring knowledge is even more difficult with regard to human rights risks that exist outside of a state's territory, there are several constellations in which states could be expected to have knowledge of extraterritorial human rights risks. Some categories as developed in the general part on human rights due diligence obligations[80] equally apply to extraterritorial scenarios. Most importantly, this encompasses situations in which states contribute to the creation of human rights risks. Two subcategories are particularly relevant in an extraterritorial context: extradition cases and licensing procedures. While the former category deals with situations in which the potential victim of human rights violations is within a state's jurisdiction, the latter concerns situations in which the potential perpetrator is within a state's jurisdiction.

a. Due Diligence Obligations When the Victim is within a State's Jurisdictional Reach

Extradition cases are the first category for which positive obligations of diligent conduct with a nexus to human rights situations in other countries were recognized. Technically, extradition cases do not fall within the range of extraterritorial cases *stricto sensu*, as they concern decisions taken by states with regard to individuals on their territory and clearly within their jurisdiction.[81] Nonetheless, extradition decisions oblige states to take diligent measures with regard to human rights situations outside of their border[82] and may thus provide further guidance for extraterritorial positive obligations in general.

Extradition scenarios have long been recognized as triggering positive obligations on behalf of the extraditing state. In *Kindler* v. *Canada*,[83] the Human Rights Committee held that "if a State party extradites a person within its jurisdiction in circumstances such that as a result there is a real risk that his or her rights under the Covenant will be violated in another

---

[79] See Chapter 6, II, 1.
[80] See Chapter 6, II, 2.
[81] Miller, "Revisiting Extraterritorial Jurisdiction," 1234; Dominic McGoldrick, "Extraterritorial Application of the ICCPR," in Fons Coomans and Menno Kamminga (eds.), *Extraterritorial Application of Human Rights Treaties* (Antwerpen: Intersentia, 2004), p. 52.
[82] Helena de Vylder, "The Territorial Scope of the ACHR" (2014) 7 *Inter-American and European Human Rights Journal* 204–224 at 212; Kamchibekova, "State Responsibility for Extraterritorial Human Rights Violations," 93.
[83] HRC, *Kindler* v. *Canada*, Decision of 30 July 1993, Communication No. 470/1991, UN Doc. CCPR/C/48/D/470/1991.

VI. POTENTIAL OF POSITIVE OBLIGATIONS

jurisdiction, the State party itself may be in violation of the Covenant." Given the Covenant's jurisdictional clause, state parties would not "generally have responsibility under the Covenant for any violations of that person's rights that may later occur in the other jurisdiction." Though wherever they "take a decision relating to a person within its jurisdiction, and the necessary and foreseeable consequence is that that person's rights under the Covenant will be violated in another jurisdiction," they could be held responsible.[84] Similar obligations were recognized by the Strasbourg Court in its *Soering* judgment involving a German national the United Kingdom intended to extradite to the United States where a priorly imposed death penalty was awaiting him. Though the Court did not find an obligation to refrain from extraditions unless a member state was "satisfied that the conditions ... in the country of destination are in full accord with each of the safeguards of the Convention,"[85] extraditions could violate the Convention where severe human rights violations were foreseeable.

Before extraditing individuals, states are thus expected to assess human rights risks in the country of destination.[86] To that end, they are not only obliged to gather general information on the receiving country themselves but to also consult reports available from independent human rights protection associations.[87] Against this background, it will usually be assumed that states had at least constructive knowledge of potential human rights risks. Extradition cases are thus constellations in which states are expected to assess extraterritorial human rights threats and to diligently adjust their decisions accordingly.

b. Due Diligence Obligations When the Perpetrator is within a State's Jurisdictional Reach

In contrast, extraterritorial obligations have rarely been invoked with regard to potential perpetrators that are present within a state's

---

[84] Ibid., para. 6.2.
[85] ECtHR, *Soering v. UK*, Plenary Judgment of 7 July 1989, Application No. 14038/88, para. 86.
[86] Among many others, see IACtHR, *Familia Pacheco Tineo v. Bolivia*, Judgment of 25 November 2013, Series C, No. 227, paras. 203 ff.; ECtHR, *Jabari v. Turkey*, Judgment of 11 July 2000, Application No. 40035/98, para. 38; *Salah Sheekh v. The Netherlands*, Judgment of 11 January 2007, Application No. 1948/04, para. 135; and also da Costa, "Extraterritorial Application," 119 ff.; Jankowska-Gilberg, "Extraterritorialität der Menschenrechte," p. 78; Miller, "Revisiting Extraterritorial Jurisdiction," 1245; McGoldrick, "Extraterritorial Application of the ICCPR," 52 f.
[87] See, for instance, ECtHR, *Hirsi Jamaa and Others v. Italy*, Grand Chamber Judgment of 23 February 2012, Application No. 27765/09, paras. 118 ff.

jurisdiction. Notwithstanding, states could well be expected to know of such human rights risks. If they license activities that might contradict human rights extraterritorially, for instance, or if they are informed of extraterritorial human rights risks, the knowledge threshold is met with the consequence that states should at least assess related human rights risks.[88] As we have seen, it could reasonably be expected of states to acquire knowledge of human rights risks whenever they license activities that have the potential of human rights contradictions. Such obligations neither impose an undue burden upon states nor bear the risk of inadequate surveillance if the assessment is confined to concrete activities. It would produce inadequate double standards if states were merely obliged to assess the human rights risks that could materialize on their own territory.[89] Though while states already carry out impact assessments when licensing extraterritorial activities, they have not yet exploited the full potential of such instruments, as we will see later on.[90] Licensing procedures are thus among the constellations in which constructive knowledge can be assumed, even of human rights risks that exist outside of a state's own territory. Logically, the same holds true if states are informed of human rights risks either by affected individuals or by international organizations.

In summary, the knowledge threshold is not particularly hard to overcome for extraterritorial cases, even though states are not expected to actively monitor human rights risks outside of their territory. Especially where states license harmful activities or are informed of extraterritorial human rights risks, constructive knowledge can be assumed, which triggers an obligation to employ diligent measures. Once again, the exact content of such measures is determined by the reasonableness standard. How a reasonable approach toward extraterritorial human rights risks could be conceptualized will thus be considered next.

2. Reasonable Efforts in Extraterritorial Constellations: Reconciling Positive Obligations with the Principle of Non-Intervention

Just as domestic human rights risks do not attract strict state liability, extraterritorial human rights risks could merely require states to employ

---

[88] See also Chapter 6, II, 2.
[89] Deva, "Acting Extraterritorially," 48.
[90] See Section IX.

all reasonably available means. Even though the standard of reasonableness is inherently flexible and vague, several elements and characteristics can be derived from international jurisprudence,[91] at least some of which are equally important to extraterritorial human rights risks. As mentioned earlier, however, applying human rights standards extraterritorially always bears the risk of undue infringements upon the sovereignty of third states. A fundamental question to address first is thus whether the exercise of extraterritorial positive obligations is even permissible under international law.

The exercise of enforcement jurisdiction on another state's territory is commonly deemed contrary to general international law, whereas the exercise of prescriptive and judicial jurisdiction is legitimate if a sufficient jurisdictional nexus exists.[92] While states thus cannot be expected to let their state organs perform protective steps on foreign territory, they could exercise prescriptive and judicial jurisdiction with respect to such extraterritorial human rights risks they have a jurisdictional nexus to. Applying this assumption to the previously mentioned constellations, states could legitimately exercise their jurisdiction if the potential victim of human rights contraventions is present within their territory, as this would provide for territorial jurisdiction. The same holds true for licensing procedures that take place within a state's territory and thereby become subject to its territorial jurisdiction.[93] Somewhat more problematic are those cases in which states are informed of human rights risks abroad. For such scenarios, a case-by-case evaluation is necessary to decide whether there is a sufficient jurisdictional link, and positive action could be rightfully exercised. A much-discussed controversy involves the actions of citizens abroad and the question of whether it can be reasonably expected of states to regulate the extraterritorial conduct of their nationals if they learn of related human rights risks. This includes crimes and human rights contraventions committed by individuals, as well as the human rights impact of business activities by corporate nationals, for all of which a jurisdictional nexus can be derived from the active personality principle. As early as 1965, the European Commission on Human Rights confirmed that "the nationals of

---

[91] See Chapter 6, IV.
[92] Walter, "Anwendbarkeit deutschen Rechts im Ausland," 433; Crawford, "Brownlie's Principles," p. 478; Skogly, "Beyond National Borders," p. 46.
[93] Philipp Täger, *Der Schutz von Menschenrechten im internationalen Investitionsrecht* (Baden-Baden: Nomos, 2011), p. 246.

Contracting State are within its 'jurisdiction' even when domiciled or resident abroad."[94]

Even where the active personality principle provides for a jurisdictional basis, however, the exercise of jurisdiction is only insofar legitimate as it does not unduly interfere with the sovereignty of the state in which the harmful event took place.[95] Prescriptive jurisdiction, while being exercised exclusively on a state's territory, might still have a significant impact on other states. If states regulate extraterritorial conduct and enforce these regulations through sanctions upon a citizen's return or – with regard to corporate nationals – against parent companies even while subsidiaries still operate abroad, then these regulations will substantially shape the behavior of private actors abroad. They could even result in jurisdictional conflicts when one states permits conduct that another state declares impermissible.[96] In a human rights context, the risk for such jurisdictional conflicts is particularly high in two constellations: where states regulate the extraterritorial conduct of their citizens that operate in states which have not ratified international human rights treaties, and where states regulate the extraterritorial conduct of their citizens in states which have ratified human rights treaties but fail to fulfill them. Herein lies, once again, the fundamental tension in international human rights protection: extraterritorial regulations could advance universal protection but also amount to "human rights imperialism" if they are misused to undermine regional peculiarities and policy decisions.[97]

Given that almost all states have ratified at least some of the most fundamental human rights treaties,[98] that Article 1 III of the UN Charter[99] obliges all states parties to promote and encourage respect for

---

[94] EComHR, *X v. Germany*, Decision of 25 September 1965, Application No. 1611/62.
[95] Papp, "Extraterritoriale Schutzpflichten," p. 246; Kirsten Schmalenbach, "Multinationale Unternehmen und Menschenrechte" (2001) 39 AVR 57–81 at 72 ff.
[96] Augenstein and Kinley, "Beyond the 100 Acre Wood," 9.
[97] See also Halina Ward, "Securing Transnational Corporate Accountability Through National Courts" (2000) 24 *Hastings International and Comparative Law Review* 451–474 at 459 f., listing state practice of developing countries that have rejected foreign legal proceedings on corporate misconduct that occurred on their territory.
[98] See the list of ratifications in the UN Treaty Collection with 169 ratifications of the ICCPR (https://treaties.un.org/Pages/ViewDetails.aspx?src=TREATY&mtdsg_no=IV-4&chapter=4&clang=_en); 165 ratifications of the ICSECR (https://treaties.un.org/Pages/ViewDetails.aspx?src=TREATY&mtdsg_no=IV-3&chapter=4&clang=_en); and 162 ratifications of the Anti-Torture Convention (https://treaties.un.org/Pages/ViewDetails.aspx?src=TREATY&mtdsg_no=IV-9&chapter=4&clang=_en).
[99] Ratified by 193 states (https://treaties.un.org/Pages/ViewDetails.aspx?src=TREATY&mtdsg_no=I-1&chapter=1&clang=_en).

human rights, and that several human rights obligations are recognized as *ius cogens*, constellations in which one state regulates conduct in a state that is not bound by any human rights obligations at all are rather sparse. In the vast majority of cases, both states will be bound by human rights obligations. The actual level of human rights protection, however, greatly varies among states, and different rights and interests need to be considered. Diverging levels of human rights protection must not necessarily reflect malice or ideological antagonism. Just as well, they can be the result of a different conception of human rights or reflect economic necessities, in particular where states use low domestic standards to attract investors. Neither should it be neglected that when it comes to extraterritorial regulations, it is another state that enforces its very own understanding of human rights, which is not necessarily in line with that of other states. Even indirect effects stemming from the exercise of active personality jurisdiction thus bear a substantial risk for undue interference with another state's internal affairs. On the other hand, though, extraterritorial regulations based on the active personality principle merely regulate individual conduct. They do not impose upon foreign states an obligation to modify their human rights policy,[100] and they can always be adjusted so as to pay sufficient deference to the jurisdictional competences of other states.

An illustrative example is the extraterritorial reach of domestic criminal legislation. Many criminal law provisions ultimately aim at protecting human rights,[101] and their extension to extraterritorial constellations is the most common practical application of the active personality principle. Most domestic legal orders provide for the reach of their criminal law provisions to harmful conduct committed abroad, while some include limitations in deference to other states. In several states, criminal jurisdiction under the active personality principle is confined to situations in which the relevant conduct is also penalized under *lex loci*,[102] or to situations in which the victims or their government issue a request for prosecution.[103] Yet other states do not provide for any constraints, at least with regard to serious crimes,[104] and these do not seem to be

---

[100] Skogly, "Regulatory Obligations," 328; Uta Kohl, "Corporate Human Rights Accountability: The Objections of Western Governments to the Alien Tort Statute" (2014) 63 ICLQ 665–697 at 680 f.
[101] See Chapter 2, III, 1, a, aa.
[102] § 7 of the German Criminal Code; Section 12 III (c) of the Norwegian Criminal Code; Article 7 I of the Swiss Criminal Code.
[103] Article 113–8 of the French Criminal Code; Section 8 of the Finnish Criminal Code.
[104] Article 12 of the Russian Criminal Code; Section 5 of the Dutch Criminal Code; or § 64 of the Austrian Criminal Code and §§ 5, 6 of the German Criminal Code, containing a list

required by international law.[105] If, however, criminal jurisdiction under the active personality principle is not subject to compulsory restrictions derived from the principle of non-intervention, there are no compelling reasons to assume that civil jurisdiction should be. Civil jurisdiction is generally even less intrusive,[106] and one single incident may trigger criminal as well as civil liability anyway. Exercising active personality jurisdiction to protect against human rights contradictions, therefore, is not generally incompatible with international law. The broad recognition of extraterritorial penal laws based on the active personality principle can even be read to reflect an international consensus on the necessity to jointly protect fundamental human rights. As criminal law provisions sanction particularly grave human rights contradictions,[107] their extraterritorial reach indeed points toward a common conception at least of the most basic human rights, such as the right to life and physical integrity, including freedom from torture and inhuman or degrading treatment. With numerous UN bodies and international organizations concretizing fundamental human rights obligations and monitoring compliance, their protection is no longer an entirely domestic matter, which also makes it harder for states to argue that external legislation aiming at the implementation of basic human rights interferes with their internal affairs.[108]

Another concern easily dispelled upon closer inspection is that home states would make an improper evaluation of other states' human rights performance by adjusting their positive measures accordingly. Indisputably, this might trigger political tensions, and yet it already is a common phenomenon in any asylum or extradition case in which decisions are above all determined by the human rights situation in the receiving state. On several occasions, the Strasbourg Court itself openly

of crimes that will be subject to criminal proceedings, irrespective of whether the conduct is criminal under the *lex loci*.

[105] Ryngaert, "Jurisdiction in International Law," p. 105; Akehurst, "Jurisdiction in International Law," 156.
[106] With further references, Akehurst, "Jurisdiction in International Law," 170 ff.
[107] See Chapter 2, III, 1, a, aa.
[108] Skogly, "Regulatory Obligations," 328; Thomas Koenen, *Wirtschaft und Menschenrechte* (Berlin: Duncker & Humblot, 2012), p. 43; Jan Wouters and Cedric Ryngaert, "Litigation for Overseas Corporate Human Rights Abuses in the EU: The Challenge of Jurisdiction" (2009) 40 *George Washington International Law Review* 939–975; August Reinisch, "The Changing International Legal Framework for Dealing with Non-State Actors," in Philip Alston (ed.), *Non-State Actors and Human Rights* (Oxford: Oxford University Press, 2005), p. 60.

criticized the human rights situation in non-member countries.[109] States are expected to make the necessary assessments, and consequently, such evaluation does not amount to an unjustified interference in the affected state's internal affairs. Any potential for abuse is minimized even further by the fact that international human rights bodies and independent nongovernmental organizations constantly observe and evaluate the human rights situations in all countries. When drafting extraterritorial regulations, states can thus rely on neutral reports and expert opinions so as not to drift toward human rights imperialism.

In sum, the active personality principle thus serves as a recognized jurisdictional link based upon which states may regulate the extraterritorial conduct of their citizens.[110] If extraterritorial regulations aim at ensuring respect for fundamental human rights, other states may not claim undue interference with their internal affairs.[111] Such legislation can be adjusted so as to pay deference to the policy approaches of other states. Just as with criminal laws, it could be made a prerequisite for the exercise of jurisdiction that the other state is bound by international human rights provisions or that no parallel proceedings are initiated in the host state. Minimal interference would be guaranteed if states limited extraterritorial provisions to such human rights provisions that are broadly recognized and sufficiently concretized by international human rights bodies.[112] While the details of a reasonable approach can only be determined for individual cases, it can thus be stated that exercising prescriptive extraterritorial jurisdiction in order to respond to human rights risks does not breach international law per se, as long as states act upon an adequate jurisdictional link.[113]

---

[109] See, for instance, ECtHR, *Othman (Abu Qatada)* v. *UK*, Judgment of 17 January 2012, Application No. 8139/09, para. 191 in which the Court found the evidence "of torture in Jordanian prisons ... as consistent as it is disturbing" and ECtHR, *Hirsi Jamaa and Others* v. *Italy*, Grand Chamber Judgment of 23 February 2012, Application No. 27765/09, para. 123 in which the Court found a "disturbing picture" of the human rights situation for migrants in Libya.

[110] Olivier de Schutter, "Towards a New Treaty on Business and Human Rights" (2015) 1 *Business and Human Rights Journal* 41–67 at 47.

[111] Skogly, "Regulatory Obligations," 334; Täger, "Der Schutz von Menschenrechten," p. 250; Deva, "Acting Extraterritorially," 49; Schmalenbach, "Multinationale Unternehmen und Menschenrechte," 75.

[112] Wouters and Ryngaert, "Litigation for Overseas Corporate Human Rights Violations," 957.

[113] Sigrun Skogly, "Extraterritorial Obligations and the Obligation to Protect" (2016) 47 *NYIL* 217–244 at 241; Weidmann, "OECD-Leitsätze," p. 70; Kohl, "Corporate Human Rights Accountability," 695 ff.; Eric de Brabandare, "Human Rights and Transnational

3. *Capacities*

While states thus have the legal capacity to enact extraterritorial human rights regulations, institutional and financial capacities become relevant once again. Many states even lack the capacity to effectively comply with human rights obligations on their own territory and, obviously, extraterritorial obligations should not hamper a state's ability to protect its own population.[114] Nonetheless, all states should take those extraterritorial measures that do not entail disproportionate burdens.[115]

Most controversial is yet whether the apparent lack of capacities on behalf of some increases the positive obligations on behalf of other states that possess sufficient resources. Some guidance may be derived from social and economic rights, where the CESCR has long recognized that cooperative obligations were "particularly incumbent upon those States which are in a position to assist others."[116] With this in mind, the following section will reveal that it is particularly the problem of diverging capacities that speaks for acknowledging positive extraterritorial obligations.

VII. Can There Be an Obligation to Act Extraterritorially? Drawing Inspiration from the "Unwilling or Unable" Standard

As we have seen, there are several constellations in which states can be expected to know of human rights risks abroad and extraterritorial positive obligations are not generally incompatible with international law. As with any other form of due diligence obligations, however, the capacities of a state determine its ability to diligently react to human rights risks. Extraterritorial positive steps, therefore, are not expected of states that already lack the capacities to diligently mitigate human rights risks at home. Besides, undue infringements upon the principle of non-

---

Corporations" (2010) 4 *Human Rights & International Legal Discourse* 66–88 at 79; Olivier de Schutter, "The Accountability of Multinationals for Human Rights Violations in European Law," in Philip Alston (ed.), *Non-State Actors and Human Rights* (Oxford: Oxford University Press, 2005), p. 235.

[114] Ashfaq Khalfan, "Division of Responsibility amongst States," in Malcolm Langford et al. (eds.), *Global Justice, States Duties* (Cambridge: Cambridge University Press, 2013), p. 312.

[115] Margot Salomon, "Deprivation, Causation and the Law of International Cooperation," in Malcolm Langford et al. (eds.), *Global Justice, States Duties* (Cambridge: Cambridge University Press, 2013), p. 285.

[116] CESCR, General Comment on the Nature of States Obligations under Art. 2 (I) of the Covenant, 14 December 1990, UN Doc. E/1991/23, para. 14.

intervention can be accounted for by the reasonableness standard that limits a state's due diligence approach to measures that are compatible with norms of general international law.[117]

While there are thus no compelling reasons to deny an obligation to diligently react to extraterritorial human rights risks by employing reasonably available means,[118] there still is great reluctance to acknowledge the existence of such obligation. John Ruggie, the Special Representative on the issue of human rights and transnational corporations, was among the first to elaborate in greater detail on potential obligations to regulate extraterritorial conduct. While concluding that international law did not prohibit states from exercising their jurisdiction to regulate extraterritorial conduct, he found no explicit obligation to take diligent preventive steps toward extraterritorial human rights risks.[119] Support for this inference was derived from the questionnaire survey *Ruggie* had undertaken beforehand which revealed that the majority of states had not enacted any binding extraterritorial regulations and relied on voluntary guidelines at best.[120] There still seems to be a consensus that states are under no international obligation to control the activities of their citizens beyond the bounds of their territory.[121] While states could enact extraterritorial regulations under the active personality principle without coming into conflict with international law, failure to do so would not invoke responsibility under international human rights law.[122]

If one accepts, however, that states are obliged to diligently prevent and sanction human rights contraventions by private actors, then it seems implausible to limit this obligation to a state's territory where states have the capacity to effectively fulfill this obligation in an extraterritorial

---

[117] Daria Davitti, "On the Meanings of International Investment Law and International Human Rights Law: The Alternative Narrative of Due Diligence" (2012) 12 *HRLR* 421–453 at 450.

[118] Kanalan, "Extraterritorial State Obligations," 55; Gibney, "International Human Rights Law," pp. 10 f.

[119] John Ruggie, Business and Human Rights: Mapping International Standards of Responsibility and Accountability for Corporate Acts, UN Doc. A/HRC/4/035 (2007), para. 15.

[120] Ibid., para. 17.

[121] Weidmann, "OECD-Leitsätze," p. 108; Täger, "Der Schutz von Menschenrechten," pp. 234 f.; de Brabandare, "Human Rights and Transnational Corporations," 79; de Schutter, "Accountability of Multinationals," 237, and already Ian Brownlie, *System of the Law of Nations. Part I: State Responsibility* (Oxford: Clarendon, 1983), p. 165.

[122] Report of the Special Representative Ruggie, para. 15; Katarina Weilert, "Transnationale Unternehmen im rechtsfreien Raum?" (2009) 69 ZaöRV 883–917 at 891; de Schutter, "Globalization and Jurisdiction," 10.

context.[123] While linked to a particular situation, similar obligations have been acknowledged, in fact, by the Security Council. In light of the repressive measures taken by South African authorities in Namibia, the Council called upon all states "whose nationals and corporations are operating in Namibia ... to use all available means to ensure that such nationals and corporations conform ... to the basic provisions of the Universal Declaration of Human Rights."[124] In a recent Advisory Opinion, the IACtHR has now been the first major human rights organ to cautiously support such obligation. When examining whether states were – as a matter of human rights law – obliged to prevent transboundary environmental harm, the Court concluded that "el ejercicio de la jurisdicción surge cuando el Estado de origen ejerce un control efectivo sobre las actividades llevadas a cabo que causaron el daño y consecuente violación de derechos humanos,"[125] thereby confirming that potentially harmful extraterritorial activities would fall within the jurisdiction of those states able to control them. Based on these growing signs of recognition and certain similarities to the "unwilling or unable" standard, as developed in the context of counterterrorism efforts, the following section will look at the reasons that speak for generally expanding due diligence obligations to extraterritorial human rights risks.

1. Human Rights as a Common Concern and the Issue of Diverging Capacities

A first parallel to the "unwilling or unable" standard is that common international interests of fundamental importance are at stake. Just as the threat of terrorism concerns the entire international community, the protection of basic human rights is of fundamental interest to all states

---

[123] See, for similar arguments, Margot Salomon, "How to Keep Promises: Making Sense of the Duty among Multiple States to Fulfil Socio-Economic Rights in the World," in André Nollkaemper and Dov Jacobs (eds.), *Distribution of Responsibilities in International Law* (Cambridge: Cambridge University Press, 2015), p. 373; Tzevelekos, "Reconstructing the Effective Control Criterion," 174; Augenstein and Kinley, "Beyond the 100 Acre Wood," 15; Nigel White, "Due Diligence Obligations of Conduct: Developing a Responsibility Regime for PMSCs" (2012) 31 *Criminal Justice Ethics* 233–261 at 244; King, "Extraterritorial Human Rights Obligations," 556.

[124] UN Security Council Resolution No. 310 of 4 February 1972, UN Doc. S/RES/310.

[125] IACtHR, Advisory Opinion No. OC-23/17 of 15 November 2017, Medio Ambiente y Derechos Humanos, Series A, No. 23 (in Spanish only), para. 104 (h): "A state of origin exercises jurisdiction when it has effective control over those activities that cause [environmental] harm and consequently violate human rights." (translation by author).

VII. OBLIGATION TO ACT EXTRATERRITORIALLY?

as the recognition of *erga omnes* obligations[126] and the responsibility to protect concept[127] clearly illustrate. Yet, it is not surprising that the "unwilling or unable" standard found greater support as terrorist attacks threaten the territorial integrity of states, claim large numbers of individual victims, and possibly result in resource-intensive military engagements. In contrast, even large-scale human rights violations in other states are commonly deemed less urgent, as they rarely have direct transboundary effects. When acknowledging the inherent importance of human rights protection, however, this should not be a valid criterion to act extraterritorially with regard to terrorist activities but not in a human rights context. Moreover, low human rights standards and unbearable living situations in less developed countries do have a growing impact on other states, not only by sparking military conflicts but also by causing massive refugee flows. Enhancing global human rights protection, therefore, is not only a matter of appreciating human rights as a concept derived from dignity and mutual respect but also directly affects the economic and security interests of all states.

Similar to the counterterrorism context, the enormous gaps in human rights protection are caused by the inability of many states to maintain an effective human rights framework.[128] Compliance with positive obligations requires the allocation of sufficient resources, and the inadequate control of harmful private conduct imperils human rights protection. As we have seen, the activities of multinational corporations, in particular, give ground for concern when they contribute to large-scale human rights contradictions without being held responsible, due to lacking institutional and investigative capacities and for fear of deterring investors. While the inability of states has been intensely debated in the

---

[126] On the concept of erga omnes obligations in international human rights regimes, see Ilias Bantekas and Lutz Oette, *International Human Rights Law and Practice* (Cambridge: Cambridge University Press, 2nd ed., 2016), pp. 67 f.; de Schutter, "International Human Rights Law," pp. 113 ff.; Erika de Wet, "Jus Cogens and Obligations Erga Omnes," in Dinah Shelton (ed.), *The Oxford Handbook of International Human Rights Law* (Oxford: Oxford University Press, 2013), p. 554.

[127] Kishore Mahbubani, "Embedding R2P in a New Universal Declaration of Human Responsibilities," in Alex Bellamy and Tim Dunne (eds.), *The Oxford Handbook of the Responsibility to Protect* (Oxford: Oxford University Press, 2016), pp. 948–967; Christian Tomuschat, *Human Rights: Between Idealism and Realism* (Oxford: Oxford University Press, 3rd ed., 2014), pp. 322 ff.; Ramesh Thakur, "The Use of International Force to Prevent or Halt Atrocities," in Dinah Shelton (ed.), *The Oxford Handbook of International Human Rights Law* (Oxford: Oxford University Press, 2013), pp. 822 ff.

[128] Salomon, "Deprivation, Causation and the Law of International Cooperation," 279; and, in greater detail, Chapter 1, III.

counterterrorism context, though, it has received less attention where human rights are at stake. As we have seen earlier, the "unwilling or unable" standard found ample support in reaction to terrorist threats. Unable states are expected to seek international support and even allow for armed interventions on their territory.[129] Likewise, the "responsibility to protect" concept ultimately allows the use of force against states that fail to prevent mass human rights violations. Interestingly, the field of counterterrorism also witnessed the development of distinct obligations to establish jurisdiction, including an explicit obligation to exercise active personality jurisdiction over terrorist offences.[130] As for counterterrorism efforts, insufficient capacities have thus been identified as a substantial problem in need of joint protection strategies for common international interests. Against this background, it is astounding that far less intrusive means such as extraterritorial regulations meet with so little approval on behalf of the international community – all the more as they could prevent an escalation in the first place. The International Commission on Intervention and State Sovereignty rightly emphasized an urgent "need to do much better on prevention, and to exhaust prevention options before rushing to embrace intervention."[131]

It should, therefore, be thoroughly discussed how the issue of diverging capacities could be adequately addressed so as to ensure an enhanced level of global human rights protection, in particular with respect to the inability of less-developed states to cope with non-state human rights contradictions. If states know that the conduct of their nationals has the potential of causing human rights contradictions in capacity-lacking states, they should adjust the scope of positive measures accordingly. Regulating the extraterritorial conduct of one's own citizens is a legitimate exercise of active personality jurisdiction and could present a promising instrument to address insufficient human rights capacities in less-developed states.[132]

---

[129] See Chapter 5.2, III, 2, b.
[130] See, for instance, Article 6 I (c) of the International Convention for the Suppression of Terrorist Bombings, signed on 15 December 1997, entered into force 23 May 2001, 2149 UNTS 256; Article 7 I (c) of the International Convention for the Suppression of the Financing of Terrorism, signed on 9 December 1999, entered into force on 10 April 2002, 2178 UNTS 197.
[131] International Commission on Intervention and State Responsibility, *The Responsibility to Protect* (Ottawa: International Development Research Centre, 2001), p. 19.
[132] Nadia Bernaz, "Enhancing Corporate Accountability for Human Rights Violations: Is Extraterritoriality the Magic Potion?" (2013) 117 *Journal of Business Ethics* 493–511 at 511.

2. How Extraterritorial Regulations Based on the Active Personality Principle Could Improve Human Rights Protection

There are several reasons for which expanding the scope of extraterritorial regulations based on the active personality principle could add to human rights protection in capacity-lacking states. First, extraterritorial obligations to diligently prevent human rights violations have the advantage of being easily integrated in the existing human rights framework and hence would not require the adoption of new treaties and enforcement mechanisms.[133] As we have seen, the most prominent alternative – directly binding obligations for powerful non-state actors – not only faces serious objections but would also demand a long and complicated negotiation process and the establishment of corresponding enforcement mechanisms.[134] Extraterritorial due diligence obligations, in contrast, would give access to well-established judicial mechanisms, likely to ensure more effective protection than weak international enforcement machineries.[135]

Enacting regulation on the extraterritorial conduct of one's own citizens is broadly recognized and widely employed for domestic penal laws. It is thus hard to see why regulating extraterritorial conduct that potentially clashes with human rights provisions should not be subject to similar regulations. Any concern that this might lead to "human rights imperialism" and undue infringements upon the internal affairs of other states could be accounted for by reasonable assessments based on a common understanding of core human rights provisions as reflected in the work of international human rights bodies. Since those states that are able to guarantee high levels of human rights protection also possess capable institutional and judicial frameworks, making use of their jurisdictional links could actually improve human rights protection in capacity-lacking states. Explicit support for such an expanded approach is already found in the partly dissenting opinion of Judge Loucaides to the *Ilaşcu* judgment, in which he finds that jurisdiction under the Convention could be established by any "failure [on behalf of the state] to discharge its positive obligations in respect of any person if it was in

---

[133] Daniel Augenstein, "The Crisis of International Human Rights Law in the Global Market Economy" (2013) 44 *NYIL* 41–64 at 61 f.
[134] See Chapter 1, IV.
[135] See, in a similar manner for transnational litigation, von Unger, "Menschenrechte als transnationales Privatrecht," p. 248.

a position to exercise its authority directly or even indirectly over that person or over the territory where that person is."[136]

Evidently, this would not mean that all states would be responsible to react to any human rights risk no matter where it occurs.[137] Protective measures could reasonably be expected only of those states that have a legitimate jurisdictional link – though where such a link exists and human rights risks are foreseeable, states should be obliged to exercise their jurisdiction, particularly if they know that other affected states lack the capacity to effectively address contraventions.[138] Accepting such an obligation would not absolve capacity-lacking states from their responsibility to protect human rights, either. On the contrary, we have seen that human rights provisions entail a great variety of different obligations addressing different actors. There is no reason why next to the home state, the host state could not also be found in breach of its international commitments – each for its respective failure to act with due diligence.[139] Ideally, the responsibility of the host state and that of the home state would complement each other to the widest possible extent.[140] How international law could put such obligations to practice can be witnessed already in the context of social and economic rights.

VIII. First Steps in the Right Direction: Social and Economic Rights

The majority of international treaties protecting social and economic rights do not contain jurisdictional clauses, which is why acceptance for

[136] ECtHR, *Ilaşcu and Others* v. *Moldovia and Russia*, Grand Chamber Judgment of 8 July 2004, Application No. 48787/99, Partly Dissenting Opinion of Judge Loucaides.
[137] Gibney, "International Human Rights Law," p. 7; Daniel Augenstein and David Kinley, "When Human Rights 'Responsibilities' Become "Duties,"" in Surya Deva and David Bilchitz (eds.), *Human Rights Obligations of Business* (Cambridge: Cambridge University Press, 2013), p. 292.
[138] Kanalan, "Extraterritorial State Obligations," 61; Papp, "Extraterritoriale Schutzpflichten," p. 241; King, "Extraterritorial Human Rights Obligations," 556; Jan Arno Hessbruegge, "Human Rights Violations Arising from Conduct of Non-State Actors" (2005) 11 *Buffalo Human Rights Law Review* 21–88 at 83.
[139] Markos Karavias, "Shared Responsibility and Multinational Enterprises" (2015) 62 *NILR* 91–117 at 99; Gibney, "Litigating Transnational Human Rights Obligations," 110; Sigrun Skogly, "Causality and Extraterritorial Human Rights Obligations," in Malcom Langford et al. (eds.), *Global Justice, State Duties* (Cambridge: Cambridge University Press, 2013), p. 239; Davitti, "Alternative Narrative of Due Diligence," 452.
[140] Wouter Vandenhole, "Contextualising the State Duty to Protect Human Rights as Defined in the UN Guiding Principles on Business and Human Rights" (2012) 12 *Revista de Estudios Jurisdicos* 1–10 at 10.

an extraterritorial reach of their provisions has been broader from the start. The CESCR, for instance, consistently underlines that states do have an obligation to "prevent third parties from violating the right [to health] in other countries, if they are able to influence these third parties by way of political or legal means."[141] As business activities often have particularly adverse effects on the enjoyment of social and economic rights, the Committee also laid special emphasis on regulating extraterritorial corporate conduct. It urged states to "take steps to prevent human rights contraventions abroad by corporations that have their main seat under their jurisdiction, without infringing the sovereignty or diminishing the obligations of host states under the Covenant."[142] A comprehensive overview was later delivered by an expert group in the form of the Maastricht Principles.[143] Though not legally binding, the Principles provide substantial guidance into how extraterritorial positive obligations could operate. They suggest that capable states should actively regulate non-state conduct, so as to include "situations where such conduct may lead to violations of human rights in the territory of another state,"[144] and even in the absence of a jurisdictional link should try to influence harmful non-state conduct through diplomatic tools.

More recently, the CESCR further specified the duties to regulate extraterritorial business activities in case of a jurisdictional link. Relying on the cooperative obligations under the Covenant and the general obligation to jointly promote human rights in Articles 1 III and 55 of the UN Charter,[145] the Committee found an obligation on behalf of states to diligently react to human rights risks abroad, for instance by regulating the extraterritorial conduct of corporations domiciled under their jurisdiction.[146] Such obligation would even arise "if other causes have also contributed to the occurrence of the violation," stressing that several states could simultaneously be held responsible for human rights

---

[141] CESCR General Comment No. 14 on the Right to the Highest Attainable Standard of Health, 11 August 2000, UN Doc. E/C.12/2000/4, para. 39.

[142] CESCR, Statement on the Obligations of State Parties Regarding the Corporate Sector and Economic, Social and Cultural Rights, UN Doc. E/C.12/2011/1 (2011), para. 5; in a similar manner: Committee on the Elimination of Racial Discrimination, Concluding Observations on Canada, UN Doc. CERD/CAN/CO/19-20 (2012), p. 4.

[143] Reprinted in 34 HRQ 2012, 1084–1169.

[144] Ibid, Commentary to Principle 24.

[145] CESCR, General Comment No. 24 on State Obligations under the ICESCR in the Context of Business Activities, 10 August 2017, UN Doc. E/C.12/GC/24, para. 27.

[146] Ibid, paras. 28, 30.

violations of varying degrees.[147] While the ICESCR indeed has peculiarities – notably the absence of a jurisdictional clause and a strong emphasis on cooperative obligations – there are no reasons to limit this extraterritorial approach to social and economic rights.[148] In fact, the Committee did not confine its considerations to the Covenant but found its argument applicable to all core human rights treaties.[149] The recent IACtHR Advisory Opinion recognizes in like manner that states are obliged to diligently prevent transboundary environmental harm as a matter of human rights law and to regulate and monitor potentially hazardous extraterritorial activities.[150] While the Advisory Opinion is tailored to the peculiarities of environmental demands, the Court's approach still indicates further openness to a broader acceptance of due diligence obligations in extraterritorial constellations.

IX. Areas in Which Extraterritorial Due Diligence Obligations Could Be Applied

In order to illustrate the substantial potential such obligations have in the human rights context, the final part of this chapter will now discuss several concrete examples of how they could operate in practice. Most importantly, such obligations should apply to licensing procedures with an extraterritorial nexus and to the extraterritorial activities of business corporations.

1. Licensing Procedures

The first scenarios to which extraterritorial positive obligations can be adequately applied are the previously mentioned constellations in which states actively bring about the situation in which human rights contradictions ultimately occur. States are obliged to estimate and address human rights risks they have contributed to create.[151] This particularly applies where states support or license private conduct that might later

---

[147] Ibid, para. 32.
[148] Asfaq Khalfan and Ian Seiderman, "Extraterritorial Human Rights Obligations: Wider Implications of the Maastricht Principles and the Continuing Accountability Challenge," in Wouter Vandenhole (ed.), *Challenging Territoriality in Human Rights Law* (London: Routledge, 2015), p. 43.
[149] CESCR, General Comment No. 24, para. 27.
[150] IACtHR, Advisory Opinion No. OC-23/17 of 15 November 2017, Medio Ambiente y Derechos Humanos, Series A, No. 23, (in Spanish only), para. 104 h).
[151] See Chapter 6, II, 2, b.

result in harmful activities. Inevitably, it would impose improper double standards if states were merely required to assess the human rights risks toward their own population – in particular, if the licensing procedure concerns extraterritorial activities. Whenever states facilitate or support the extraterritorial conduct of their citizens, there should be an obligation to assess related human rights risks and take adequate preventive steps. Since it is beyond the scope of this book to identify each instance in which obligations of diligent conduct could be applied to extraterritorial scenarios, the potential for such obligations will be exemplified along two specific areas in which they most likely could significantly improve the level of human rights protection. The first one concerns licensing procedures and support in the context of foreign trade promotion and the second one the licensing of arms transfers. Both areas have in common a great potential of adversely affecting human rights in third countries and strong state involvement in enabling private conduct.

a. Foreign Trade Promotion: Drawing Inspiration from Procedural Obligations in Environmental Law

Most states actively support their companies engaging in foreign trade through a variety of means ranging from investment guarantees to export credits and licenses which speaks for the applicability of human rights due diligence obligations. When supporting foreign investments by their corporations, states bring them in a position where they can commit or contribute to human rights contradictions in other countries.[152] State support is, in fact, a decisive incentive for private actors to engage in a particular project,[153] with the consequence that states can be reasonably expected to mitigate foreseeable human rights risks.[154] With support usually given to individual projects, such assessments do not present a disproportionate burden either.

---

[152] Sara Seck, "Conceptualizing the Home State Duty to Protect," in Karin Buhmann et al. (eds.), *Corporate Social and Human Rights Responsibilities* (Basingstoke: Palgrave Macmillan, 2011), pp. 29 f.; Täger, "Der Schutz von Menschenrechten," p. 103.

[153] Papp, "Extraterritoriale Schutzpflichten," p. 303; Astrid Epiney, "Nachbarrechtliche Pflichten im internationalen Wasserrecht und Implikationen von Drittstaaten" (2001) 39 *AVR* 1–56 at 54.

[154] Nadia Bernaz, *Business and Human Rights* (London: Routledge, 2017), p. 250; Fons Coomans, "The Extraterritorial Scope of the ICESCR in the Work of the UN CESCR" (2011) 11 *HRLR* 1–35 at 30 f.; Robert McCorquodale and Penelope Simons, "Responsibility beyond Borders: State Responsibility for Extraterritorial Violations by Corporations of International Human Rights Law" (2007) 70 *Modern Law Review* 598–625 at 621.

Following this logic, Ruggie's Principles recognize a heightened duty of care for the harmful activities of such businesses that receive financial support by a state. The Commentary also suggests institutionalized human rights impact assessments before granting any form of support accompanied by additional due diligence obligations on behalf of corporations.[155] While several states indeed make instruments of foreign trade promotion dependent on human rights commitments by the receiving private actors, many states are still reluctant to abide by positive human rights obligations when promoting foreign investment. The CESCR has repeatedly criticized member states to the Covenant for shortcomings in their domestic licensing procedures.[156] Inspiration for the concrete implementation of such procedures could be drawn from the licensing of environmental projects. The procedural instruments, as developed with regard to environmentally hazardous activities, could well be transferred to foreign trade investments. What is at stake in both instances is the potentially harmful impact of a concrete undertaking, the effects of which could reasonably be overseen. Conducting human rights impact assessments thus seems an adequate tool that could be easily integrated into the practice of foreign trade promotion.

With regard to environmental protection, the concept of due diligence has developed a mainly procedural character.[157] This standardized approach toward assessing and monitoring the risks of concrete undertakings could be fruitful for the assessment of business-related human rights risks as well. Since the licensing or granting of support is always linked to a specific project, only a manageable number of risks would need to be assessed. States, therefore, should not grant any licenses unless an adequate impact assessment had been carried out. Private actors seeking state support for their extraterritorial activities should identify all foreseeable human rights risks and explain how they intend to prevent them from materializing. In this context, states should also take into account that they can exploit their full regulatory and punitive potential only as long as potential perpetrators are physically within their jurisdiction. Any measure the state might take after activities are initiated abroad will be significantly less effective. Even if extraterritorial human rights

---

[155] UN High Commissioner for Human Rights, Guiding Principles on Business and Human Rights, New York/Geneva 2011, HR/PUB/11/04, Commentary to Principle 4.
[156] Among others, CESCR, Concluding Observations on Germany of 12 July 2011, UN Doc. E/C.12/DEU/5, para. 10.
[157] See Chapter 5.1., III.

risks are not yet immediate, protective measures might thus be reasonable as the range of available means will be much smaller later on.[158]

In sum, making human rights impact assessments a mandatory prerequisite for any form of state support in the context of foreign trade and investment could help raise awareness for adverse impacts on human rights and develop adequate responses. Similar to the field of environmental protection, the duty to exercise due diligence would not end with granting a license. States were rather expected to monitor the activities and to intervene if human rights risks evolve at a later stage.[159] There are reasonable monitoring tools that could be applied so as to avoid any undue interference, even where activities are carried out abroad: Next to cooperation with other states, imposing complaint mechanisms and a duty upon the licensed private actors to regularly report would not present an intrusive course of action. Finally, states must also be willing to ultimately withdraw licenses or freeze financial support if private actors are continuously involved in extraterritorial human rights contradictions.[160] As many extraterritorial business activities depend upon state support, enforcing human rights compliance on behalf of the benefit-receiving private actors could make an actual difference.[161] There are thus good reasons to acknowledge an obligation to exercise human rights due diligence when engaging in foreign trade promotion.[162] While some states have already implemented human rights guidelines, the potential for further regulations is still substantial.[163] By granting licenses and support, states contribute to the creation of human rights risks abroad. With the licensing procedure entirely within their jurisdiction, states would impose improper double standards if they denied the applicability of human rights obligations solely on the fact that human rights risks would only occur abroad. If states do not take human rights risks into consideration when issuing export credits or investment guarantees, a violation of respective human rights provisions should thus be assumed.[164] As in the field of environmental protection, failure to carry out adequate assessments

---

[158] Papp, "Extraterritoriale Schutzpflichten," p. 197.
[159] Täger, "Der Schutz von Menschenrechten," p. 233.
[160] Papp, "Extraterritoriale Schutzpflichten," p. 317.
[161] Epiney, "Nachbarrechtliche Pflichten," 54.
[162] Markus Krajewski, "Menschenrechtliche Anforderungen an Investitionsgarantien der BRD," in Marten Breuer et al. (eds.), *Der Staat im Recht* (Berlin: Duncker & Humblot, 2013), p. 1126.
[163] Bernaz, "Enhancing Corporate Accountability," 502.
[164] Täger, "Der Schutz von Menschenrechten," p. 229.

should in itself amount to state responsibility under human rights law, so as to lower procedural and evidentiary hurdles.

Similar considerations apply in the context of arms transfers. Even though most states do not actively support and facilitate the transfer of arms, export procedures are subject to official controls and licenses. Again, there is thus a formal procedure carried out by state authorities in which the assessment of human rights risks outside of a state's territory should be integrated.

b. Applying the Due Diligence Standard to Arms Transfer Control

While the transfer of arms has long been considered an exclusive subject of distinct control regulations and humanitarian law, its human rights impact has now become a focus of international concern.[165] The use of arms within a state's jurisdiction undoubtedly falls within the ambit of human rights treaties and requires protective steps.[166] The sale and transfer of weapons to other countries, however, re-raises the question of whether extraterritorial due diligence obligations could mitigate related human rights risks.

As with foreign trade promotion, potential human rights violations would occur outside of the transferring state's territory following a domestic licensing decision. Obviously, it would surpass any state's capacity to control the use of arms once they have been transferred to another state. The licensing procedure, however, is entirely controlled by the transferring state and gives room for human rights considerations.[167] In order to determine an adequate due diligence standard though, it is first necessary to briefly recall which international norms regulate the sale and transfer of arms and to then evaluate how human rights assessments could be accounted for within this framework.

aa. International Norms Applicable to Arms Transfer "[T]here are no rules, other than such rules as may be accepted by the State concerned, by treaty or otherwise, whereby the level of armaments of a sovereign State can

---

[165] Susan Waltz, "Arms Transfers and the Human Rights Agenda," in George Andreopoulos and Zehra Kabasakal Arat (eds.), *The Uses and Misuses of Human Rights* (New York: Palgrave Macmillan, 2014), p. 147; Andrew McLean, "The EU Code of Conduct on Arms Exports," in Michael Addo (ed.), *Human Rights Standards and the Responsibility of Transnational Corporations*, (The Hague: Kluwer Law, 1999), p. 117.

[166] See Section bb.

[167] Francesco Francioni, "The Role of the Home State in Ensuring Compliance with Human Rights by Private Military Contractors," in Francesco Francioni and Natalino Ronzitti (eds.), *War by Contract* (Oxford: Oxford University Press, 2011), p. 105.

be limited,"[168] so the ICJ ruled in its 1986 *Nicaragua* judgment. The General Assembly later confirmed "the right of all States to manufacture, import, export, transfer and retain conventional arms for self-defence and security needs, and in order to participate in peace support operations."[169] While there is no general arms treaty, several international agreements restrict the production and transfer of certain types of weapons, such as the Biological Weapons Convention,[170] the Chemical Weapons Convention,[171] the Convention on Certain Conventional Weapons,[172] and the Convention on Cluster Munitions.[173] Embargoes on the transfer of arms to certain countries are a common reaction of the Security Council to conflict situations, and the Wassenaar Agreement[174] establishes a multilateral regime on arms exports that is voluntary in nature but ensures the ongoing exchange of information and best practices. Finally, the 2013 Arms Trade Treaty is the first attempt to provide for general international obligations on most conventional weapons.[175] Its Article 6 explicitly prohibits the transfer of arms, where they will be used in violation of *ius cogens* norms or Security Council embargos. If not generally prohibited under this provision, states are still obliged to assess the impact of any transfer prior to its authorization. As part of this assessment, they should identify human rights risks[176] and mitigate potential harm. Outside of those treaty regimes, however, the production and sale of many weapons are not subject to any international constraints. Yet further restrictions upon the production and transfer of arms might be derived from international human rights provisions.

bb. Human Rights Law and Arms Transfer As arms are often used to commit serious and large-scale human rights violations,[177] it comes as

---

[168] ICJ, Case concerning Military and Paramilitary Activities in and against Nicaragua (*Nicaragua* v. *USA*), Judgment of 27 June 1986, ICJ Reports 1986, 14, para. 269.
[169] UN GA, Resolution adopted on 6 December 2006, UN Doc. A/RES/61/89, p. 1.
[170] Signed on 10 April 1972, entered into force 26 March 1975, 1015 UNTS 163.
[171] Signed on 3 September 1992, entered into force 29 April 1997, 1974 UNTS 45.
[172] Signed on 10 October 1980, entered into force 2 December 1983, 1342 UNTS 137.
[173] Signed on 30 May 2008, entered into force 1 August 2010, 2688 UNTS 39.
[174] Wassenaar Agreement on Export Controls for Conventional Arms and Dual-Use Goods and Technologies, signed on 12 May 1996; similar instruments were set up by the EU, see Council Regulation (EC) No. 428/2009 of 5 May 2009.
[175] Arms Trade Treaty, signed on 2 April 2013, entered into force on 24 December 2014, contained in UN Doc. A/CONF.217/2013/L.3 (2013) and Article 2 for the scope of application thereof.
[176] Art. 7 I (b) (ii) of the Arms Trade Treaty.
[177] An overview of statistical data is contained in UN High Commissioner for Human Rights, Impact of Arms Transfers on the Enjoyment of Human Rights, 3 May 2017, UN

little surprise that human rights bodies have recognized negative and positive obligations on arms control and regulations. Importantly, the right to life and the right to be free from torture and inhuman or degrading treatment – as the rights most likely affected by the illegal use of arms – are non-derogable rights, such that states have to abide by those provisions, even in times of public emergency. On the negative side, state organs themselves are prohibited from misusing weapons for human rights contraventions.[178] Resort to weapons has to be strictly proportionate to achieve a legitimate aim, and substantial precautionary measures are generally expected,[179] including proper trainings and instructions for security personnel.[180] An even higher degree of caution is required where security operations might affect civilian lives.[181] As for their positive obligations, states should regulate the sale and use of arms,[182] convict individuals in cases of illegitimate use, and provide compensation for the victims.[183] Harm should be diligently prevented through reasonable measures and access to relevant information. The ECtHR's *Albekov* case, for instance, found Russia responsible for a failure to adequately protect the right to life, as it did not seal off a mined area and failed to issue appropriate warnings.[184]

In sum, there is thus a broad range of negative and positive human rights obligations relating to the risks of arms possession and transfers.

Doc. HRC/35/88, paras. 14 ff., as well as in Shannon Lindsey Blanton, "Instruments of Security or Tools of Repression? Arms Imports and Human Rights Conditions in Developing Countries" (1999) 36 *Journal of Peace Research* 233–244.

[178] Among many others, see ECtHR, *McCann and Others* v. *UK*, Grand Chamber Judgment of 27 September 1995, Application No. 18984/91; IACtHR, *Case of the Santo Domingo Massacre* v. *Colombia*, Judgment of 30 November 2012, Series C, No. 259.

[179] IACtHR, *Case of the Santo Domingo Massacre* v. *Colombia*, Judgment of 30 November 2012, Series C, No. 259, paras. 216 ff.

[180] ECtHR, *McCann and Others* v. *UK*, Grand Chamber Judgment of 27 September 1995, Application No. 18984/91, para. 151.

[181] Among many others, see ECtHR, *Isayeva and Others* v. *Russia*, Judgment of 24 February 2005, Application Nos. 57947/00 a.o., paras. 171 ff.

[182] Alexandra Boivin et al., "International Law and Smalls Arms and Light Weapons Control" (2006) *Centre for Humanitarian Dialogue Briefing Paper*, pp. 3 f.; Barbara Frey, "The Question of the Trade, Carrying and Use of Small Arms and Light Weapons in the Context of Human Rights and Humanitarian Norms," Working Paper 2001/120 submitted to the Commission on Human Rights, UN Doc. E/CN.4/Sub.2/2002/39, para. 46.

[183] HRC, Concluding Observations on Israel of 18 August 1998, UN Doc. CCPR/C/79/Add.93, para. 17.

[184] ECtHR, *Albekov and Others* v. *Russia*, Judgment of 9 October 2008, Application No. 68216/01, paras. 85 ff.

All these considerations, however, only apply within a state's jurisdiction. The transfer of arms to other states where human rights contraventions might occur is generally considered to fall outside the ambit of human rights treaties. In contrast to the field of foreign trade promotion, however, state responsibility based on complicity is occasionally suggested with regard to arms transfers.

cc. Attribution, Complicity, and Aiding and Abetting in the Context of Arms Transfers When recalling the conclusions drawn in the general part,[185] transferring arms could indeed amount to a violation of international law where the preconditions for complicity are fulfilled. This would be the case if arms are employed to commit human rights violations (or violations of humanitarian law) and the exporting state has (at least) positive knowledge of these consequences or even intended them to occur. We have seen, though, that positive knowledge is difficult to establish and that complicity merely covers the transfer of arms between states. Where weapons are transferred to private actors, state responsibility for complicity would only arise for violations of international criminal law.[186] Arms transfers yet could fall under Article 41 II of the Draft Articles on State Responsibility, stipulating an obligation on behalf of states not to render aid or assistance in maintaining *ius cogens* violations. Besides, the provisions of special treaty regimes, such as the duty to prevent genocide or the prohibition of complicity therein, give additional grounds for state responsibility. The aiding and abetting standard in international criminal law also provides a valuable tool in sanctioning arms transfer where international crimes are committed.[187] However, its application is limited to the commission of recognized international crimes and *ius cogens* violations, and requires that subjective elements such as positive knowledge and intent can be established.

This leaves us with the unsatisfying conclusions previously reached in Chapter 3. The traditional tools of state responsibility do not cover the actions of the transferring state, even though there is state conduct that contributes to the commission of human rights violations abroad. Again,

---

[185] See Chapter 3, V, 5.

[186] Alexandra Boivin, "Complicity and Beyond: International Law and the Transfer of Small Arms and Light Weapons" (2005) 87 *International Review of the Red Cross* 467–496 at 474.

[187] Annyssa Bellal, "Arms Transfers and International Human Rights Law," in Stuart Casey. Maslen (ed.), *Weapons under International Human Rights Law* (Cambridge: Cambridge University Press, 2014), p. 470.

due diligence standards may thus prove fruitful in enhancing human rights protection.

dd. Due Diligence Obligations in the Context of Arms Transfers? As already indicated, there are good reasons speaking in favor of the application of human rights due diligence standards to the direct sale and transfer of arms or the licensing of such transfers by private actors. The reluctance to accept such obligations, however, is clearly mirrored in the *Tugar* case, so far the only decision in which an international human rights body decided on state responsibility for arms transfers.

(1) The Tugar *Decision* In 1995, an application was lodged before the European Commission of Human Rights alleging that Italy had violated its positive obligation to prevent human rights violations by failing to adequately regulate the trade of arms. According to the applicant, Italian mines were laid in Iraq, and state organs could have known of related human rights risks. Had Italy established an adequate domestic licensing system, the mines would not have been sold to a country that was knowingly involved in grave human rights violations, so the applicant argued. The Commission, however, rejected the application as inadmissible and found no "immediate relationship between the mere supply, even if not properly regulated, of weapons and the possible 'indiscriminate' use thereof in a third country." The adverse consequences of insufficient arms trade regulations were "too remote" to trigger Italy's responsibility.[188] In contrast to extradition decisions, so the Commission argued, which amounted to an exercise of jurisdiction, the relationship between arms trade and human rights violations was not close enough for state responsibility to arise.

Again, a distinction was thus drawn between constellations in which the potential victim of human rights violations and constellations in which the potential perpetrator or his means were within a state's jurisdiction. As we have seen earlier, states have indeed more effective options to protect individuals within their jurisdiction. Yet there are no plausible reasons why states should not do all within their power to prevent human rights violations if the perpetrator or the means of human rights violations are within their jurisdictional reach, as long as they do not wrongfully interfere with the internal affairs of other

---

[188] EComHR, *Tugar* v. *Italy*, Decision of 18 October 1995, Application No. 22869/93.

IX. EXTRATERRITORIAL DUE DILIGENCE OBLIGATIONS

states.[189] Even where the ultimate use of arms is not attributed to the transferring state, it could still be held responsible for insufficient preventive measures during the licensing process, without excluding the simultaneous responsibility of the importing state. With this in mind, the following section will apply the due diligence framework to arms-transfer procedures.

(2) Knowledge The standard of positive and constructive knowledge is not overly difficult to meet, as weapons evidently can be misused for human rights contraventions.[190] Information on the human rights situations in most countries is easily available through the assessments of United Nations organs and non-governmental organizations. If information on the potential misuse of arms is accessible, though, states should know of the potential consequences of arms transfers to the affected regions,[191] including not only the immediate risk of an illegitimate use of weapons by the purchasing actors but also the risk of weapons potentially being transferred to other actors. The Arms Trade Treaty even contains an obligation for the recipient state to provide access to relevant information in its Article 8, encouraging state parties to exchange and collect relevant information. Reliable knowledge from different sources can thus be easily obtained to assess the likelihood of arms-related human rights contraventions. That exported arms could be misused, therefore, is in most cases foreseeable, making it difficult for the exporting state to argue it was unaware of the related risks.

(3) Capacities More difficult to answer is whether and to what extent transferring states are even able to effectively protect against weapon-related human rights violations. Obviously, states are not in a position to regulate the use of weapons outside of their jurisdiction and only have the capacity to install licensing procedures and export limitations. The latter, however, mainly require omissive conduct: states should refrain from transfers in case of foreseeable human rights risk. Especially when

---

[189] Barbara Frey, "Obligations to Protect the Right to Life: Constructing a Rule of Transfer Regarding Small Arms and Light Weapons," in Mark Gibney and Sigrun Skogly (eds.), *Universal Human Rights and Extraterritorial Obligations* (Philadelphia: University of Pennsylvania Press, 2010), p. 53.

[190] Jamil Balga, "The New International Law of Arms Trade: A Critical Analysis of the Arms Trade Treaty from the Human Rights Perspective" (2016) 3 *Indonesian Journal of International and Comparative Law* 583–650 at 590.

[191] Balga, "The New International Law of Arms Trade," 616; Boivin, "Complicity and Beyond," 470.

compared to areas such as environmental or cybersecurity prevention, which depend on substantial financial and technical resources, the costs for implementing export controls are significantly lower. For exporting states, it is thus very difficult to claim they had not been capable of merely refraining from transferring arms.

The capacity issue, however, shows another interesting feature in the arms control context. The Arms Trade Treaty is among the few treaties that contain detailed provisions on international assistance. Article 16 calls upon states with insufficient capacities – for instance, in the field of stockpile management or disarmament programs – to seek international assistance. It also stipulates an obligation for each state party "in a position to do so" to provide such assistance upon request. States with low capacities, therefore, cannot use insufficient capacities as an excuse for not adhering to their obligations if they had not tried to obtain international assistance, and exporting states are obliged to render such assistance within the realm of their possibilities. Several provisions and commentaries further indicate that the capacities of the recipient state are a determining factor when assessing whether a particular transfer is in accordance with human rights requirements.[192] Here, again, states are thus obliged to exercise human rights due diligence with regard to events that take place outside of their jurisdiction but are connected to acts or omissions within their jurisdictional reach. The lower the capacities of the state in which human rights contraventions ultimately occur, the higher the degree of diligence expected of the state that sends its goods or nationals to that place, knowing that they might be involved in human rights contradictions.

(4) Reasonableness As we have seen earlier, most concerns with regard to extraterritorial preventive obligations can be made part of the reasonableness test, including necessary caution against improper interference with another state's internal affairs, as well as legitimate economic interests in fostering exports.[193] Whether it can be reasonably expected of states to take preventive measures with regard to human rights risks that materialize within another state's jurisdiction thus depends on the circumstances of each individual case. While the transfer of arms clearly enhances the ability of the recipient actors to commit human rights violations, the chain of causality necessary to establish the

---

[192] For instance, UN High Commissioner for Human Rights, Impact of Arms Transfers on the Enjoyment of Human Rights, 3 May 2017, UN Doc. HRC/35/88, para. 39.
[193] See Section VI.

responsibility of the transferring actor has often been considered too remote, as the final decision to employ weapons for human rights contraventions is taken by the recipient actor itself. In the context of arms transfers, however, it is even more apparent that while the commission of human rights violations ultimately occurs outside its jurisdiction, the exporting state could nonetheless take efficient steps within its jurisdiction to prevent human rights violations through the illegitimate use of weapons.[194] Denying the export of weapons may not halt any human rights violation, but it will deprive the perpetrators of important means to engage in such. While the exporting state is not the actor that ultimately carries out human rights violations, its conduct –the sale and transfer of arms – has an undisputed impact on the ability of actors in the importing state to carry out such violations. With the export and licensing regime, there is state conduct with a potentially adverse effect on human rights that clearly falls within the jurisdictional reach of the transferring state. If states have the capacity to shape the human rights outcome under such circumstances, it could and should be expected that they employ reasonable preventive means. Any licensing process for the export of arms should thus include considerations of foreseeable human rights risks. Comparable to the field of environmental law, preventive aspects can be easily integrated into mandatory impact assessments.

(5) Impact Assessments While establishing a sufficient causal nexus between transferring arms and the occurrence of human rights violations is often difficult, prior impact assessments could be modeled as an independent procedural obligation, the noncompliance with which would give rise to state responsibility, irrespective of actual harm, just as the failure to carry out an environmental impact assessment in itself amounts to a violation of international law.[195]

In fact, human rights impact assessments are increasingly made an integral part of arms transfer regulations. The Arms Trade Treaty contains an explicit obligation to take human rights concerns into consideration when issuing export licenses in Article 7 (I) lit. (b) (ii), which is not limited to "core rights" such as the right to life.[196] Critics yet pointed out

---

[194] See, with regard to the operation of private military companies, Nigel White, "Regulation of the Private Military and Security Sector" (2016) 16 *HRLR* 585-599 at 596.
[195] Nina Jørgensen, "State Responsibility for Aiding and Assisting International Crimes in the Context of the Arms Trade Treaty" (2014) 108 *AJIL* 722-749 at 729.
[196] Andrew Clapham, "Article 7," in Stuart Casey-Maslen et al. (eds.), *The Arms Trade Treaty: A Commentary* (Oxford: Oxford University Press, 2016), p.270.

that the Treaty prohibits the export of weapons only where there is an "overriding risk" that adverse effects would be produced, leaving the provisions' application to the discretion of state parties.[197] However, several states have declared upon ratification that they read the provision so as to contain an absolute prohibition of any transfer if the negative consequences are more likely to materialize than not.[198] The European Union even included the necessity of carrying out human rights impact assessments in its Common Position on the export of military technology and equipment,[199] calling upon member states to consider the respect for human rights in the recipient state and to deny any export license in case of a "clear risk" that weapons might be used "for internal repression." The risk of weapons being diverted from their stated end users and misused by other actors should receive consideration as well.[200] More recently, another due diligence framework was formulated by the United Nations.[201] Mandatory human rights risk assessment is required of UN entities before engaging in any form of technical, logistical, or financial support to other security forces. Information on potential human rights risks should be obtained from UN organs or other reliable sources, and support should be denied where the assessment reveals a real risk of human rights violations committed by the recipient security forces.[202] Consensus is thus growing that the inherent risk of arms being misused for particularly grave human rights violations calls for an obligation to carry out proper impact assessments before transferring arms. Such impact assessments could make a significant contribution to an enhanced human rights protection, as they not only raise awareness for potential human rights risks but also increase the transparency of the decision-

---

[197] Tom Coppen, "The Evolution of Arms Control Instruments and the Potential of the Arms Trade Treaty" (2016) 7 *Goettingen Journal of International Law* 353–382 at 366; Yasuhito Fukui, "The Arms Trade Treaty" (2015) 20 *Journal of Conflict and Security Law* 301–321 at 320.

[198] See the quotes contained in Stuart Casey-Maslen, "Article 7," in Stuart Casey-Maslen et al. (eds.), *The Arms Trade Treaty. A Commentary* (Oxford: Oxford University Press, 2016), p.275.

[199] Council Common Position 2008/944/CFSP of 8 December 2008 on defining common rules governing control of exports of military technology and equipment, Official Journal of the EU, L 335/99 of 13 December 2008.

[200] See Article 2 VII of the Common Position.

[201] Human Rights Due Diligence Policy on UN Support to Non-UN Security Forces, contained as Annex in UN Doc. A/67/775 (5 March 2013); endorsed by UN Security Council, Resolution No. 2149 of 10 April 2014, UN Doc. S/RES/2149 (2014), para. 39.

[202] Human Rights Due Diligence Policy on UN Support to Non-UN Security Forces, paras. 15–16.

making process, triggering legal responsibility as well as political pressure to adhere to better human rights standards in the context of arms transfers.

Though, when recalling the section on environmental law, procedural obligations like impact assessments also involve the risk of being misused as an all-too-easy excuse to justify failure to comply with preventive obligations, states can easily point toward an impact assessment carried out beforehand to show that they could not have known of a particular human rights risk or did all they could to prevent it. It is thus important to bear in mind that impact assessments should not absolve states from further preventive obligations. In contrast to environmental law, where the content of impact assessments is mostly left to the discretion of the assessing state's law, impact assessments in the context of arms transfers should be subject to international human rights standards. While stricter on content requirements, however, impact assessments related to arms transfers have so far not been recognized as independent procedural obligations – not even by the Arms Trade Treaty. Moreover, the obligations contained in the treaty are enforceable only between the respective member states so that compliance mechanisms are not likely to be initiated if human rights violations are committed within the recipient state. Neither the recipient nor the transferring state has an interest in pushing legal proceedings for a failure to carry out an adequate assessment.

Recognizing that failure to take preventive steps to control the transfer of arms is not only an issue under trade regulations but equally affects international human rights law would thus give affected victims an option to enforce compliance. Accepting human rights due diligence obligations on behalf of the exporting state could thus foster human rights protection to a considerable extent. When determining whether a state has complied with its preventive human rights obligations, the fact of whether it had carried out an impact assessment could serve as a strong indicator for compliance. On the other hand, it should not be neglected that states also have a verifiable interest in purchasing arms in order to ensure the security of their population and protect it against human rights violations.[203] An impact assessment should thus evaluate whether a state's resources are not disproportionately allocated for defense purposes to the disadvantage of human rights budgets.[204]

---

[203] Thyla Fontein, "Small Arms and Light Weapons: The Current Regime Is Insufficient and Ineffective: What Do We Need?" (2012) 25 *Humanitäres Völkerrecht* 92–102 at 98.
[204] UN Coordinating Action on Small Arms, *The Impact of Poorly Regulated Arms Transfers on the Work of the UN* (New York: UN Publications, 2013), p. 16.

ee. Summary Summarizing these considerations, human rights due diligence in the context of arms transfers could make a valuable contribution to enhanced human rights protection. Under human rights law, it is already recognized that states are obliged to regulate the use of weapons by state organs and private actors within their jurisdiction. As the analysis of international regulations on arms transfer revealed, consensus is now emerging that human rights considerations should also play a role when it comes to export procedures. Increasingly more arms transfer regulations contain an obligation to carry out impact assessments prior to licensing the export of arms, including an evaluation of related human rights risks. Acknowledging that such duty is not only an obligation in inter-state arms transfer regimes but also a human rights obligation would greatly enhance its enforcement, as potential victims were given a legal instrument to sanction noncompliance. Human rights obligations can be read as to restrict or even prohibit the transfer of arms if it is foreseeable that those arms will be used for contraventions.[205] Since many arms are still being transferred to states with poor human rights records,[206] enforcing existing obligations on transfer restrictions and emphasizing additional human rights due diligence obligations could advance the level of human rights protection in the affected countries.

c. Conclusion

Whenever states grant licenses or support the extraterritorial conduct of their nationals, human rights obligations should be fully applicable. The licensing procedure entirely falls within a state's jurisdiction, and with the potentially harmful situation being created by the licensing state, it is only appropriate that the full range of positive human rights obligations applies. Since licensing procedures always involve specific individual cases, the procedural elements of the due diligence standard as developed for environmental law can be adequately employed. States should carry out human rights impact assessments for the undertakings they license or support, monitor their development, and provide for sanctioning mechanisms in case of noncompliance, including the withdrawal of licenses and support.

---

[205] Frey, "The Question of the Trade, Carrying and Use of Small Arms and Light Weapons," para. 74.
[206] With detailed examples, see Jennifer Erickson, "Market Imperatives Meets Normative Power: Human Rights and European Arms Transfer Policy" (2011) 19 *European Journal of International Relations* 209–234; Lerna Yanik, "Guns and Human Rights" (2006) 28 *HRQ* 357–388.

2. Regulating Extraterritorial Corporate Conduct

a. Introductory Remarks

Another area in which extraterritorial due diligence obligations could be fruitfully applied is the regulation of private extraterritorial conduct based on the active personality principle, most notably the conduct of parent companies that are registered in industrial states and run subsidiaries abroad. In particular, where human rights situations are worsened by the insufficient capacities of host states, regulatory efforts on behalf of the home state could help ensure effective protection. As for the extraterritorial conduct of private individuals, such regulations already ensure that grave criminal misconduct is adequately sanctioned, and international efforts have further broadened their scope to certain forms of harmful conduct, such as the fight against child abuse or corruption.[207] After the general reasons speaking for an expansion of human rights due diligence obligations to the regulation of extraterritorial private conduct have already been laid out, the following section will now focus on the specific issue of extraterritorial corporate conduct and the contribution that home state regulations could make to more effective human rights protection.

It still seems to be a consensus that while not prohibited by international law, there is no obligation to regulate extraterritorial corporate conduct either.[208] Notwithstanding, corporate misconduct in capacity-lacking states presents a major obstacle to better human rights protection.[209] When acknowledging the many problems and concerns with directly binding international obligations for corporate actors, recognizing an obligation to exercise active personality jurisdiction with regard to extraterritorial corporate conduct could present a viable alternative. Such an obligation could be easily integrated into the existing human rights regime, and the flexibility of due diligence obligations

---

[207] A detailed analysis of regulations in these fields can be found in, for instance, Thorsten Müller, "Transnational Organised Crime and the Sale of Children, Child Prostitution, and Pornography," in Pierre Hauck and Sven Peterke (eds.), *International Law and Transnational Organised Crime* (Oxford: Oxford University Press, 2016), pp. 287–307; Sara Kaczmarek and Abraham Newman, "The Long Arm of the Law: Extraterritoriality and the National Implementation of Foreign Bribery Legislation" (2011) 65 *International Organization* 745–770.

[208] John Ruggie, Business and Human Rights: Mapping International Standards of Responsibility and Accountability for Corporate Acts, UN Doc. A/HRC/4/035 (2007), para. 15.

[209] See Chapter 1, III.

would ensure that no disproportionate requirements were imposed. When applying the different components of the due diligence standard to the issue of extraterritorial corporate conduct, it soon becomes clear that human rights risks related to such conduct are indeed foreseeable, and capable states would have reasonable protective means at their disposal.

Human rights risks resulting from corporate misconduct in capacity-lacking states are well-known and broadly documented.[210] A series of harmful incidents, several court proceedings, and reports by international organizations highlight the need for international efforts to mitigate the human rights risks of business activities. Against this background, the home states of sizeable corporations could hardly claim ignorance of these risks. That business activities in capacity-lacking states might cause human rights violations is all but unforeseeable. Consequently, home states should take such protective measures as could be reasonably expected. One reasonable means of action would consist of implementing domestic legislation that obliges corporate actors which are subject to a state's active personality jurisdiction to mitigate human rights risks related to their activities abroad. In contrast to direct international obligations for corporate actors, such domestic regulations would open the way to the home state's judicial system and allow court proceedings in a legal context where human rights are, in general, effectively implemented. Whereas an international agreement on direct obligations for non-state actors would probably be confined to broad and general obligations, domestic regulations are likely to be more precise and thereby ensure substantial enforcement. In doing so, and opposed to soft law instruments and voluntary initiatives, they would amount to an actual incentive for corporate actors to engage in preventive strategies, as the latter would risk being sued for damages in their domestic courts.

In light of these advantages, international human rights bodies do, in fact, become more explicit in their calls upon states to enact extraterritorial regulations to prevent business-related human rights contradictions. The Human Rights Committee, for instance, urged Germany to expand its regulation on extraterritorial corporate conduct,[211] and the CESCR recently appealed to the Covenant members for exploiting their

---

[210] McCorquodale and Simons, "Responsibility Beyond Borders," 619.
[211] HRC, Concluding Observations on Germany of 12 November 2012, UN Doc. CCPR/C/DEU/CO/6, para. 16.

IX. EXTRATERRITORIAL DUE DILIGENCE OBLIGATIONS

full regulatory potential, including the use of active personality jurisdiction.[212] As we have seen, one promising way of regulating the extraterritorial conduct of corporate nationals consists of imposing civil liability for human rights contradictions caused by corporate misconduct abroad. And in spite of all political reluctance, several recent instances of state practice that illustrate how such home state regulations could operate deserve closer consideration. Though the most frequently cited example is surely the US Alien Tort Statute, the statute contains several peculiarities speaking against its model character for other countries,[213] which is why the following section will rather focus on more recent domestic examples of how active personality regulation could be conceptualized.

b. The French Law on Duty of Care 2017

The first substantial effort to make use of the active personality principle's jurisdictional potential has recently been made by France. In February 2017, the French Parliament introduced a piece of domestic legislation specifically providing for a duty of care on behalf of French corporations operating abroad,[214] in an unprecedented attempt to regulate the extraterritorial conduct of business corporations. The law had been subject to an intense parliamentary debate since first proposed by the *Parti Socialiste* in 2013. After the Senate had rejected a previous draft claiming that unilateral regulations would lower France's competitive ability in an untenable manner,[215] the bill was eventually passed after lengthy negotiations. Integrated into the French Commercial Code, it provides for the civil liability of corporations to the exclusion of criminal liability. Though only applicable to corporations of a certain

---

[212] See Section VIII.
[213] Most notably, the Alien Tort Statute provides for tort liability in case of a violation of the laws of nations that created much uncertainty as to whether the Statute could be applied to conduct, which was not recognized as an international crime providing for individual responsibility as a matter of international law; for further details, see, among many others, Daniel Felz, *Das Alien Tort Statute* (Berlin: Duncker & Humblot, 2017); Nehal Bhuta, "The Ninth Life of the Alien Torts Statute" (2014) 12 *Journal of International Criminal Justice* 539–550; Michael Koebele, *Corporate Responsibility under the Alien Tort Statute* (Boston and Leiden: Nijhoff, 2009); Beth Stephens, *International Human Rights Litigation in US Courts* (Boston and Leiden: Nijhoff, 2008).
[214] Loi N° 2017–399 relative au devoir de vigilance des sociétés mères et des entreprises donneuses d'ordre, 27 March 2017, available online at www.legifrance.gouv.fr/eli/loi/2017/3/27/2017-399/jo/texte.
[215] See the summary of the debate in Sandra Cossart et al., "The French Law on Duty of Care" (2017) 2 *Business and Human Rights Journal* 317–323 at 318.

size,[216] the law binds around 120 French corporations. Their first and foremost duty under the new provisions is to publish and implement a so-called *plan de vigilance* that identifies environmental and human rights risks related to the corporation's activities and suggests suitable preventive measures. The assessment should extend to a corporation's subsidiaries and even to other corporations to which close business ties exist. It is accompanied by a further obligation to constantly monitor human rights risks and establish a warning system for potential victims in each part of the corporation.

If corporations fail to comply herewith, any person with a legitimate interest can bring a claim before the competent courts, which could order the corporation to perform the previously described measures, even before environmental or human rights risks have materialized. Originally, the bill even enabled the courts to impose a fine of up to 10 million Euros to enforce preventive compliance. This section was the only one rejected by the Conseil Constitutionnel when it reviewed the Act's constitutionality in March 2017,[217] as the provision was not precise enough to justify a fine with penal character.[218] In general, however, the Conseil Constitutionnel found the legislation in conformity with the Constitution and rejected claims of legal uncertainty and an unjustified infringement upon entrepreneurial freedoms.[219] Explicitly, the Conseil held that the relationship between parent companies and their dependencies was close enough to trigger legal responsibilities.[220]

In October 2019, Total was the first corporation to face claims of an insufficient *plan de vigilance* in relation to a project in Uganda.[221] So far, however, proceedings are pending, and the bill has not been tested further before the courts. It thus remains to be seen how they will interpret its provisions. Notwithstanding, it already is a remarkable example of how

---

[216] Article 1 prescribes that the duty of care applies to corporations having at least 5,000 employees in France or at least 10,000 employees in total (including subsidiaries abroad).
[217] France provides for preventive judicial review of the constitutionality of an Act; see Article 61 of the French Constitution.
[218] Conseil Constitutionnel, Decision of 23 March 2017, No. 2017-750 DC, para. 7.
[219] Ibid., paras. 15-19.
[220] Ibid., paras. 24-29. The opponents had argued that "ces dispositions instaurent, en violation du principe de responsabilité, une responsabilité du fait d'autrui," c.f. para. 25.
[221] See, further, *Le Monde* of 24 October 2019, available online at www.lemonde.fr/afrique/article/2019/10/24/le-groupe-total-assigne-en-justice-pour-ses-impacts-sociaux-et-environnementaux-en-ouganda_6016717_3212.html; and *Le Monde* of 13 December 2019, available online at www.lemonde.fr/afrique/article/2019/12/13/total-affirme-remplir-son-devoir-de-vigilance-a-l-egard-de-sa-filiale-ougandaise_6022780_3212.html.

IX. EXTRATERRITORIAL DUE DILIGENCE OBLIGATIONS

states may exercise their extraterritorial human rights due diligence obligations. In essence, the French bill imposes a duty upon French corporations to adequately surveil their subsidiaries and suppliers thereby preventing them from hiding behind the corporate veil. The bill establishes an independent duty of care on behalf of parent companies, which is mainly of a procedural character. Even though the parent company might not be involved in an actual human rights violation, it can still be held responsible if it failed to take adequate steps of prevention, to monitor the activities of its subsidiaries or suppliers, or to establish adequate warning and complaint mechanisms. By merely regulating French parent companies, France refrained from directly regulating foreign corporate nationals – such as subsidiaries or suppliers – thereby avoiding an undue interference with the internal affairs of other states. The conceptualization as an obligation of due diligence on behalf of the company also protects against imposing disproportionate burdens on corporations. A corporation that took all reasonable measures would not be liable under the provisions, even if harm ultimately occurs. The courts will have to decide on a case-by-case basis whether the measures employed by a company were satisfactory under the circumstances and whether the ties between a parent company and its subsidiary or supplier had been sufficiently close.

While the exact contours of such corporate due diligence obligations are not yet clear, the National Contact Points under the OECD Guidelines already provide guidance on how they can be reasonably applied. The National Contact Points, though not rendering legally binding judgments, provide alternative means of dispute settlement and handle complaints of adverse human rights impacts caused by multinational corporations.[222] Several of their proceedings indicate parameters that determine the degree of human rights diligence which corporations are expected to perform. In general, due diligence obligations are broader, the closer the business relation at hand. Corporations have to adhere to a higher standard of care with regard to their subsidiaries than with regard to their suppliers – though, in both cases, they have to monitor human rights compliance by sending independent inspectors and carry out unannounced assessments.[223] Moreover, they should negotiate contracts directly with their suppliers, ensuring that the

---

[222] For further information, see Markus Krajewski et al., "Menschenrechtliche Pflichten von multinationalen Unternehmen in den OECD-Leitsätzen" (2016) 76 ZaöRV 309–340 at 317 ff.
[223] German National Contact Point, Final Statement of 4 November 2014, Uwe Kekeritz against KiK Textilien and Non-Food GmbH, C&A Mode GmbH & Co., and Karl Rieker GmbH & Co. KG, available online at www.bmwi.de/Redaktion/EN/Downloads/oecd-ac-final-statement-kik.pdf?__blob=publicationFile&v=1, p. 7.

latter refrain from delegating tasks to other entities without adequate control.[224] Notwithstanding, the Contact Points also awarded deference to corporate decisions in difficult situations in host countries.[225] Even where human rights were in peril, they usually did not suggest withdrawing from business contracts altogether,[226] as long as corporations developed adequate strategies to address these risks.[227] Imposing human rights due diligence obligations upon corporations, therefore, does not necessarily overwhelm them with duties they cannot fulfill. While the National Contact Points have identified basic elements of corporate human rights due diligence, including areas in which improvement is necessary, they still paid due regard to business interests and the difficult circumstances under which some corporations operate. In sum, the French bill thus takes first steps toward the realization of the home state approach as suggested and could provide inspiration for other industrial states.[228] In fact, other European states are already assessing legally binding due diligence obligations for extraterritorial corporate conduct,[229] and the European Union has increased its regulatory efforts based on the active personality principle.

c. Proposals on Corporate Regulations within the European Union

Several suggestions and policy strategies have already been discussed at the European level. A first substantial approach was introduced by Directive No. 2014/95, providing for reporting duties of large corporations, and recently, the EU Flagship Initiative on the Garment Sector has taken an even more active stance.

---

[224] Ibid., pp. 6 f.
[225] Canadian National Contact Point, Final Statement of 25 May 2017, Banro Corporation and a Group of Former Employees, available online at www.international.gc.ca/trade-agreements-accords-commerciaux/ncp-pcn/statement-banro.aspx?lang=eng.
[226] UK National Contact Point, Final Statement of March 2015 on Lawyers for Palestinian Human Rights & G4S PLC, available online at www.gov.uk/government/uploads/system/uploads/attachment_data/file/431972/bis-15-306-lawyers-for-palestinian-human-rights-final-statement-after-examination-of-complaint-uk-national-contact-point-for-the-oecd-guidelines-for-multinational-enterprises-r1.pdf, pp. 14 ff.
[227] Swedish and Norwegian National Contact Point, Joint Final Statement of 9 February 2016, *Jijnjevaerie Saami Village v. Statkraft AS*, available online at http://nettsteder.regjeringen.no/ansvarlignaringsliv-en/files/2013/12/08022016_Final-statement_ENG.pdf, p. 16.
[228] Cossart et al., "The French Law on Duty of Care," 323.
[229] See below and also Ministero degli Affair Esteri e della Cooperazione Internazionale, Italian National Action Plan on Business and Human Rights 2016–2021, p. 17, available online at www.cidu.esteri.it/resource/2016/12/49109_f_NAPBHRENGFINALEDEC152016.pdf.

aa. EU Directive 2014/95/EU In 2014, the EU passed a directive on the disclosure policy of corporations on environmental matters, employer protection, and human rights risks.[230] It obliges member states to adopt national legislation providing for adequate reporting obligations on behalf of large corporations. As for human rights risks, the reporting duty should comprise an assessment of business-related human rights risks and the response policies a corporation has adopted. If relevant and proportionate, corporate reports should cover the activities of supply and subcontracting chains.[231] Though not providing for legal claims in case of harm, the Directive still raises awareness for potential human rights risks resulting from business activities in capacity-lacking states. It also prescribes that all persons and legal entities with a legitimate interest in such reports are brought in a position in which they can ensure respect for these obligations.[232] While reporting duties are of a rather broad character, the European Union has thus taken the first step toward independent procedural obligations in the human rights context.

bb. EU Flagship Initiative on the Garment Sector Further steps were taken by the European Parliament. In January 2017, the Committee on Development published its first draft report on the EU flagship initiative on the garment sector,[233] calling on the European Commission to present a legislative proposal that would impose binding due diligence obligations on corporations with regard to their subsidiaries and supply chains.[234] Corporations should abide by a mandatory reporting system with corporate liability encompassing the entire supply chain, including subcontractors in the formal and informal economy.[235] The EU, so the Committee argues, is best placed to provide for a comprehensive and harmonized strategy that would eliminate fears of adverse effects on the

---

[230] Directive 2014/95/EU of the European Parliament and the Council of 22 October 2014 amending Directive 2013/34/EU as regards disclosure of non-financial and diversity information by certain large undertakings and groups, Official Journal of the EU, 15 November 2014, L 330/1.

[231] Ibid., para. 6.

[232] Ibid., Recital 10.

[233] European Parliament, Committee on Development, Rapporteur Lola Sánchez Caldentey, Draft Report on the EU Flagship Initiative on the Garment Sector, 2016/2140 (INI), 12 January 2017.

[234] Ibid., p. 6, para. 4.

[235] Ibid., p. 7, para. 11. See also European Parliament, Committee on Employment and Social Affairs, Rapporteur Jean Lambert, Opinion on the EU Flagship Initiative on the Garment Sector, 2016/2140 (INI), 10 February 2017, p. 6, para. 22.

competitiveness of single states. In its statement to the report, the Committee on International Trade further suggested EU tariff preferences for those businesses that could demonstrate sustainable production through independent and strict certification systems.[236] Following these proposals, the European Parliament passed a resolution in April 2017, stressing that voluntary approaches have not succeeded in improving the human rights situation in states with poor resources and calling upon the Commission to create binding legislation requiring corporations to exercise human rights due diligence.[237] While it is far from clear whether the Parliament's proposal will find support within the Commission and among the representatives of the EU member states, the initiative is still worth mentioning, in particular when considering that an EU-wide approach could make an even more significant contribution compared with individual domestic efforts. If all member states regulate extraterritorial corporate conduct based on the active personality principle, competitive disadvantages among EU member states would fail to appear. It remains to be seen, though, whether consensus can be found within the EU to push forward more expansive regulatory efforts. Integrating such an approach in the EU's Agenda on Migration, which is inter alia designed to address the root causes of irregular migration, would present a political opportunity to regulate corporate conduct in order to enhance the living conditions in resource-lacking states.

Next to the EU initiatives and the broad regulation introduced in France, several states have enacted domestic legislation addressing specific human rights problems. Most notably are domestic provisions aimed at fighting human trafficking and modern slavery, which include regulations on extraterritorial corporate conduct.

d. The Californian Transparency in Supply Chains Act of 2010

In California, antislavery provisions were included in the Transparency Supply Chains Act of 2010.[238] Inter alia, it amended the disclosure

---

[236] European Parliament, Committee on International Trade, Rapporteur Sajjad Karim, Opinion on the EU Flagship Initiative on the Garment Sector, 2016/2140 (INI), 28 February 2017, p. 5, para. 8.

[237] European Parliament, Resolution of 27 April 2017 on the EU Flagship Initiative on the Garment Sector, No. 7, available online at www.europarl.europa.eu/sides/getDoc.do?pubRef=-//EP//NONSGML+TA+P8-TA-2017-0196+0+DOC+PDF+V0//EN.

[238] Transparency in Supply Chains Act of 2010, Senate Bill No. 657, Chapter 556, an act to add Section 1714.43 to the Civil Code, and to add Section 19547.5 to the Revenue and Taxation Code, relating to human trafficking. Filed with the Secretary of State on

obligations contained in Division 2 of the Revenue and Taxation Code by requiring corporations to disclose whether they engage in verification of their supply chains to assess risks of human trafficking and slavery by committing to independent surveys. Corporations, to this end, should indicate whether they audit their suppliers for compliance with antislavery efforts and whether such audits are carried out in an independent and unannounced manner. They should also enclose whether they provide their employees with training to raise awareness for slavery and human trafficking and have internal accountability mechanisms in place. Though not providing for tort liability on behalf of corporations, the Act enables consumers to take antislavery efforts into consideration when making their purchase decisions.

e. The UK Modern Slavery Act of 2015 Another recent domestic example is the UK Modern Slavery Act of 2015.[239] While the initial draft did not contain any provisions on corporate liability in supply chains, amendments on supply chain transparency were added in October 2015. For businesses of a certain size, there is now an obligation to publish annual statements either confirming that slavery and human trafficking are not taking place in any part of the business or in any supply chain or declaring that no measures have been taken in that area.[240] Following the Californian example, there are no penalties for noncompliance, but businesses are required to publish their statements, which is intended to facilitate the decisions of consumers or business partners that wish to adjust their behavior in accordance with a business's antislavery policy. By exclusively focusing on human trafficking and modern slavery, both acts deal with particularly grave forms of human rights contradictions but do not address other human rights risks created by corporate misconduct. Even though the Joint Committee on Human Rights had suggested regulatory options for the extraterritorial conduct of UK businesses as early as 2009,[241] no general legislative proposals have been introduced so far. In contrast, several other countries are starting

---

30 September 2010, available online at https://oag.ca.gov/sites/all/files/agweb/pdfs/cybersafety/sb_657_bill_ch556.pdf.
[239] Modern Slavery Act of 26 March 2015, 2015 Chapter 30, available online at www.legislation.gov.uk/ukpga/2015/30/pdfs/ukpga_20150030_en.pdf.
[240] Part 6, Section 54 of the Act.
[241] House of Lords/House of Commons, Joint Committee on Human Rights, "Any of Our Business? Human Rights and the UK Private Sector," 24 November 2009, available online at https://publications.parliament.uk/pa/jt200910/jtselect/jtrights/5/5i.pdf, volume I, para. 205.

to discuss broader legally binding regulations on extraterritorial corporate conduct following the French example.

f. Domestic Proposals on the Regulation of Extraterritorial Corporate Conduct While the French regulation is so far the only legally binding instrument, increasingly more proposals are submitted in other European countries advancing active personality regulations on extraterritorial corporate conduct.

aa. Proposal by the German Green Party of 2016 and Coalition Agreement of 2018 In Germany, the Green Party put forward a proposal in 2016, suggesting environmental and human rights due diligence obligations for corporations, accompanied by legal remedies for victims to claim damages before German courts.[242] As a member of various international human rights regimes, so the proposal argued, Germany was under an obligation to actively regulate the conduct of businesses incorporated in Germany whenever this conduct entailed the risk for human rights contraventions in Germany or abroad.[243] A mandatory reporting system was suggested, including independent reviews by administrative bodies. Noncompliance with reporting duties should be sanctionable in the form of an administrative offense (*Ordnungswidrigkeit*), even before human rights violations ultimately occur. In addition, victims should be given the opportunity to sue for damages in civil-law proceedings if harm actually materializes. Notably, the proposal also addresses a procedural problem that affects most European states. Article 4 (I) of the Rome II-Regulation[244] prescribes that in proceedings concerning noncontractual relations arising out of a tort/delict, the applicable law is the law of the country in which the damage occurred. This provision poses particular problems if harm occurs in a country with insufficient human rights resources. In most cases, there is not even a contractual relationship between the employees of a subsidiary and the parent company and almost certainly not between the latter and local communities. Claims based on alleged human rights contraventions by the parent corporation, therefore, are almost always

---

[242] Deutscher Bundestag, Antrag der Fraktion Bündnis 90/Die Grünen, Zukunftsfähige Unternehmensverantwortung – Menschenrechtliche Sorgfaltspflichten im deutschen Recht verankern, BT-Drucksache 18/10255, 9 November 2016.
[243] Ibid., p. 4.
[244] EC-Regulation No. 864/2007 of 11 July 2007 on the Law Applicable to Non-Contractual Obligations (Rome II), Official Journal of the EU, L 199/40 of 31 July 2007.

noncontractual in nature, which means that in accordance with Article 4 (I), the law of the country in which the contravention occurred would be applicable. Against this background, the Green Party proposed to explicitly render duties of care for parent companies, overriding mandatory provisions as enshrined in Article 16 of the Rome II Regulation, which would ensure the applicability of home-state regulations.[245]

While the Green Party's proposal was rejected, the German Parliament at least passed an amendment to the German Commercial Code, including an expanded obligation to report on environmental and human rights risks for businesses of a certain size,[246] following the EU directive just mentioned. According to the new section 289 c (II), businesses are obliged to include in their report the environmental risks of their undertakings, compliance with international labor law provisions, corruption risks, and explicitly in No. 4 the observance of human rights provisions. According to section 289 c (III) No. 4, the reporting duty comprises not only a corporation's own activities but also its business relationships. Giving wrongful information in such reports may be subject to criminal penalties pursuant to section 331 of the German Commercial Code. While there are thus no progressive regulations comparable to the French model, enforceable and sanctionable reporting duties present a first step toward raising awareness for human rights risks related to corporate activities.

Moreover, the Coalition Agreement of 2018 between the governing parties envisages a critical assessment of existing voluntary initiatives in the business and human rights sector, which is to be terminated in 2020. Should the investigation conclude that soft law instruments prove manifestly insufficient, a legislative proposal for a corporate duty of care would be drafted.[247] The Federal Ministry for Economic Cooperation and Development has already prepared a draft proposal akin to the French approach.[248]

---

[245] Deutscher Bundestag, Antrag der Fraktion Bündnis 90/Die Grünen, Zukunftsfähige Unternehmensverantwortung – Menschenrechtliche Sorgfaltspflichten im deutschen Recht verankern, BT-Drucksache 18/10255, 9 November 2016, p. 5.

[246] Deutscher Bundestag, Gesetz zur Stärkung der nichtfinanziellen Berichterstattung der Unternehmen in ihren Lage- und Konzernlageberichten (CSR-Richtlinie-Umsetzungsgesetz), BT-Drucksache 201/17, 10 March 2017.

[247] Coalition Agreement of 2018, Koalitionsvertrag für die 19. Legislaturperiode zwischen CDU, CSU und SPD, available online at www.bundesregierung.de/resource/blob/975226/847984/5b8bc23590d4cb2892b31c987ad672b7/2018-03-14-koalitionsvertrag-data.pdf?download=1, p. 156.

[248] See, further, Business and Human Rights Resource Centre, Report of 20 February 2019, available online at www.business-humanrights.org/en/will-germany-become-a-leader-in-the-drive-for-corporate-due-diligence-on-human-rights.

bb. **Switzerland:** *Konzerninitiative Verantwortung* The "*Konzerninitia -tive Verantwortung*" is another proposal drafted by several Swiss NGOs and petitioning for a referendum on environmental and human rights due diligence obligations for Swiss corporations.[249] In contrast to EU member states, Switzerland has not even implemented any rules on reporting duties so far. Following the proposal, corporations should now be obliged to assess environmental and human rights risks of their business activities; take adequate preventive steps and publicly report on their activities. Due diligence should not be limited to subsidiaries that are legally controlled by the parent company but extend to any business relationship in which human rights and environmental risks become relevant,[250] in particular to those subcorporations that are practically controlled by the parent company. Failure to comply with such duties should result in legal liability,[251] for which the proposal even contains a presumption. It is thus the corporation which has the burden of proving that it employed sufficient diligence. Similar to the proposal made by the German Green Party, the fundamental duties enshrined in the proposal should be subject to Swiss law, irrespective of which country's law would be applicable pursuant to the laws on conflict in private international law.[252]

The *Bundesrat* – Switzerland's federal executive council – yet decided not to support the proposal in January 2017. While expressing approval for its underlying motivation, the *Bundesrat* claimed the proposal would cause unreasonable disadvantages for Swiss corporations.[253] It rejected the initiative in its entirety without proposing any amendments or alternatives. Notwithstanding, polls indicate widespread support among the Swiss population, which is why the *Konzernverantwortungsinitiative* might still succeed in a referendum.[254] After the *Ständerat* accepted

---

[249] Eidgenössische Volksinitiative, "Für verantwortungsvolle Unternehmen – Zum Schutz von Mensch und Umwelt," text of the proposal handed in on 31 October 2015, published in Bundesblatt BBl (Swiss Federal Gazette) 2015, 3245; achieved quorum on 1 November 2016, see BBl 2016, 8107.

[250] Eidgenössische Volksinitiative, "Für verantwortungsvolle Unternehmen – Zum Schutz von Mensch und Umwelt," 31 October 2015, BBl 2015, 3245, para. b.

[251] Ibid., para. c.

[252] Ibid., para. d.

[253] Eidgenössisches Justiz- und Polizeidepartement (Swiss Federal Department of Justice), Bundesrat lehnt die Volksinitiative, "Für verantwortungsvolle Unternehmen – Zum Schutz von Mensch und Umwelt" ab, Press Release of 11 January 2017, available online at www.ejpd.admin.ch/ejpd/de/home/aktuell/news/2017/2017-01-112.html.

[254] See *Neue Zürcher Zeitung, Großer Zuspruch für Konzernverantwortungsinitiative*, 18 July 2016, available online at www.nzz.ch/schweiz/umfrage-in-der-schweizer-bevoelkerung-grosser-zuspruch-fuer-konzernverantwortungsinitiative-ld.106222.

a counterproposal to the initiative in December 2019, such a referendum might be scheduled for late 2020.[255]

Slow progress is thus made toward exploiting the jurisdictional potential to regulate extraterritorial corporate conduct based on the active personality principle. France is the first state to have imposed a legally binding duty upon its corporations to exercise due diligence with regard to their business activities abroad, and it remains to be seen how these provisions will operate in practice and whether other states will follow the French example and commit to an obligation to regulate extraterritorially.

g. Conclusion

In conclusion, an obligation of diligent conduct toward extraterritorial human rights risks could make a significant contribution to globally improving the level of human rights protection. When applying the due diligence framework to extraterritorial conduct, it becomes clear that extraterritorial human rights obligations could be reconciled with the principle of non-intervention and no disproportionate burden would be imposed upon states or businesses.

As we have seen in the general part, obligations of diligent conduct are triggered once states know or should know of human rights risks. Though the knowledge threshold is more difficult to meet in extraterritorial constellations, there are several instances in which states can be expected to know of extraterritorial human rights risks. The first category comprises those constellations in which states actively help bring about human rights risks abroad – in particular, if they license or support the extraterritorial conduct of their nationals. The second one comprises those constellations in which states are informed about harmful extraterritorial activities carried out by their nationals or information on such harmful conduct is readily available. In such cases, there is no reason why states should not be obliged to employ all reasonably available means to address these risks. Certainly, it would not be reasonable to violate other norms of international law in order to comply with positive human rights obligations. Any positive approach states chose to apply has to be in conformity with general international law – in particular, the principle of non-intervention. We have seen, though, that extraterritorial regulations that aim at the protection of internationally recognized human rights can be based on the active personality principle and hardly ever violate the

---

[255] See, further, *Neue Zürcher Zeitung* of 18 December 2019, available online at www.nzz.ch /schweiz/konzerninitiative-ld.1529345.

principle of non-intervention, especially if they focus on well-recognized core human rights provisions. Considering the fact that many host states are incapable of ensuring effective human rights protection themselves, the cooperative nature of human rights regimes requires states to employ their best efforts to enhance human rights protection, even outside of their own territories. In particular, if it is commonly known that human rights contradictions are caused by extraterritorial private conduct in capacity-lacking states, a heightened standard of care on behalf of those states that have sufficient capacities is indispensable. Though Ruggie still came to the conclusion that no obligation to regulate extraterritorially could be derived from international human rights law, the foregoing analysis revealed no plausible reason to deny them, especially when considering the object and purpose of human rights treaties that lie in the most effective protection of human rights, including adaption to changed circumstances and new forms of human rights risks. The substantial human rights risks caused by extraterritorial private conduct in general and corporate conduct in particular had not been envisaged during the drafting phase of international human rights regimes. Ensuring effective human rights protection yet requires states to react to new threats and adjust their protective measures accordingly.[256]

When compared to the creation of direct obligations of non-state actors, expanding the scope of human rights due diligence obligations to extraterritorial risks also has the advantage of being integrable in the existing human rights system and its enforcement mechanisms. In particular, it would allow handling corporate liability cases before domestic courts in those countries that already possess sophisticated human rights protection schemes. It thus comes as little surprise that states and international human rights bodies show increasing support for legally binding human rights obligation to regulate extraterritorial corporate conduct. The French legislation is a first substantial attempt to realize such regulation, and it remains to be seen whether other states will follow this example and whether human rights bodies will join the CESCR in its explicit recognition of an obligation to make use of jurisdictional links in order to mitigate extraterritorial human rights risks. Given the severe concerns related to the idea of direct international human rights obligations for non-state actors, such obligations seem to be the most promising way to address the problem of diverging human rights capacities. It would be for states, as the central duty-bearers under international

---

[256] Skogly, "Regulatory Obligations," 343.

human rights law, to establish legally binding obligations for their citizens and render them enforceable before domestic courts that operate within effective enforcement frameworks. As we have seen, any consensus on international direct obligations for non-state actors is likely to be a minimal consensus, which leaves many forms of corporate misconduct uncovered, and without corresponding enforcement mechanisms, this would not present a turn for the better. In contrast, regulatory efforts based on the active personality principle have the potential of making a substantial contribution to mitigating the harmful effects caused by states' diverging capacities to ensure effective human rights protection.

Summary and Outlook

The growing importance of non-state actors challenges the traditional inter-state order of public international law. In many respects, the reciprocal logic undergirding state responsibility is difficult to apply and high thresholds for attributing non-state conduct complicate matters even further, which stands in stark contrast to the increase in power on behalf of non-state actors, in particular where they operate in countries that lack the capacities to effectively regulate and control private actions. International law's traditional way to fill these accountability lacunae has been the recognition of due diligence obligations that require states to diligently prevent and sanction harmful private conduct. While failure to exercise due diligence does not render private conduct attributable, it gives rise to an independent ground for state responsibility. Due to its vague and broad character, however, the standard is often considered an inadequate tool in ensuring greater accountability, particularly in the field of human rights protection, with its focus on individual harm. It is against this background that a growing number of authors support the creation of directly binding human rights obligations for non-state actors.

Though greater accountability on behalf of non-state actors for human rights contraventions is certainly desirable, this analysis revealed serious concerns such direct obligations meet with, and it does not seem very likely that any international consensus could be reached in the foreseeable future either. Any agreement on direct obligations for private actors would have to precisely define these obligations and establish corresponding enforcement mechanisms for its provisions to be effective. Substantially, such a treaty could even be misused by non-state actors that engage in harmful activities that fall outside of its scope if states fail to agree but on the lowest common denominator. If some human rights duties would be regulated to the exclusion of others, it could become even harder to ensure far-reaching accountability. Besides, it is far from clear which categories of non-state actors should even be addressed and how their accountability relationship with states could be conceptualized. The most serious concern, however, would be to put non-state actors in a position they cannot adequately fulfill. Private actors neither have the legitimacy nor the resources to carry out the balancing of different rights and interests inherent in any system of human rights protection. Since direct human rights obligations for non-state actors, therefore, neither seem realistic nor politically desirable, focus should be shifted on exploiting the full potential of the rules on state responsibility.

So far, however, many attempts to describe and categorize human rights obligations do not provide any guidance on how to determine state responsibility for failure to prevent or sanction harmful private conduct. The traditional notion of positive obligations is too broad to describe the precise course of action that is expected of states. It is against this background that this book followed a more specific and conduct-based typology of positive human rights obligations which revealed that human rights treaties contain various different forms of obligations. On the active side, positive obligations of result requiring states to achieve an immediate result can be distinguished from positive obligations of diligent conduct and positive obligations of progressive realization. State responsibility may follow a violation of one of these types of obligations but also arise out of a combination of different forms and could even be shared between different states.

While positive obligations of result are relatively easy to establish – state responsibility is engaged as soon as a desired result is not achieved – responsibility for failure to exercise due diligence entails a greater procedural challenge. The standard of due diligence, while widely recognized among different areas of international law, is usually employed in a rather broad and general manner, with its actual content difficult to deduce. To explore its potential for the field of human rights protection, this book first retraced the origins of due diligence obligations as a historical instrument to establish state responsibility for harmful non-state conduct. Their flexibility ensured that responsibility standards adapted to changed circumstances and new challenges. While highly context-specific, such obligations still contain common components that can be conceptualized in an abstract manner. In brief, state responsibility may be established if a state knew or should have known of a particular risk and failed to employ reasonable preventive or punitive measures in spite of its capacity to do so.

With regard to human rights protection, two of these components become particularly problematic: First, it is difficult to determine under which circumstances human rights risks are foreseeable for states, as complete surveillance of private activities would in itself amount to a human rights contravention. Second, the due diligence standard merely requires states to employ reasonable means at their disposal. With the capacities of states greatly diverging, effective prevention is often lacking where it is most needed. In spite of all difficulties, however, the components of the due diligence standard have always undergone changes and amendments when applied to specific areas of international law. With this in mind, the application and development of due diligence obligations were analyzed in three areas of international law that face similar challenges to the field of human rights protection. How the standard has been adjusted to the peculiarities of each field provided guidance on how due diligence obligations could advance human rights protection.

In international environmental law, due diligence obligations have a strong preventive connotation. With environmental risks often causing long-term and irreversible damage, environmental due diligence standards place a strong emphasis on preventive strategies. Most importantly, this led to independent procedural obligations, such as the duty to carry out environmental impact assessments. An advantage of such standardized duties is that they resemble obligations of result, insofar as those states that suffered from transboundary harm may establish the source state's responsibility by proving the latter's failure to comply with independent procedural obligations, which is slightly easier than filling the broad reasonableness standard with content. Even though procedural obligations in the environmental context are still evolving and willingness to enforce them remains low, the idea of standardizing reasonable measures renders the broad and vague notion of due diligence more approachable. Most states now carry out at least some form of environmental impact assessments before engaging in hazardous activities, which certainly strengthens the preventive side of due diligence obligations. For human rights protection, preventive strategies are equally important making independent procedural obligations an option worth considering. Though whereas environmental hazards are often linked to certain types of activities, human rights risks stem from myriad sources, which is why general human rights impact assessments seem impractical. Unlike cybersecurity risks, however, which are even deemed inherently unforeseeable, knowledge of human rights risks can be established in a considerable number of constellations, and where human rights risks are clearly connected with certain undertakings, a standardized duty to assess related risks could strengthen preventive efforts and hinder states from claiming that certain hazards had not been foreseeable.

As for the problem of diverging capacities, environmental law witnessed the development of several concepts and strategies – most notably the approach of common but differentiated responsibilities. While closely linked to the climate change context, the concept still provides inspiration, insofar as it emphasizes the necessity of capable states assisting capacity-lacking states to strive for the realization of common goods. The problem of diverging capacities when common interests are at stake plays an equally crucial role in the context of counterterrorism efforts, where even more rigorous proposals on how to address shortcomings of capacity lacking have been introduced. At the same time, the most prominent and most controversial approach is the "unwilling or unable" standard, which suggests that the inability of states to effectively combat terrorist activities on their territory may allow other states or the international community to step in and take substitute measures, even including forceful operations. While resort to using force without the affected state's consent should not be thoughtlessly approved, the "unwilling or unable" standard still gives insights on how to handle the problem of lacking capacities. Most importantly, it has widened the understanding of what constitutes reasonable measures: When an important common interest is affected and cooperative mechanisms are readily available, it could be reasonably expected of capacity-lacking states to seek international assistance. When transferred to the field of human rights protection, it could thus be argued in a similar manner that capacity-lacking states are expected to exploit options of external assistance. Even more interesting, however, is what rights and duties states may have in reaction to a lack of resources on behalf of others. While a right to take forceful measures seems farfetched, it should be discussed whether resort to less intrusive means might not be justified where important goods and interests are at stake – most notably, whether positive human rights obligations toward harmful private conduct could be applied to extraterritorial human rights situations and thereby create not only rights but also duties to react toward extraterritorial human rights risk.

Accepting positive obligations on behalf of capable states could partially compensate for the inability of others and thereby eliminate the risk of powerful non-state actors enjoying impunity when operating in resource-lacking states. So far, such obligations have not been acknowledged on the international plane. While extraterritorial regulations are commonly considered legitimate when based on a sufficient jurisdictional link, their implementation is not mandatory. When considering a growing number of private human rights contraventions in capacity-lacking states on the one hand and the many problems with direct human rights obligations for private actors on the other, alternative options yet need to be explored. A strong case can be made in favor of expanding the reach of human rights due diligence obligations to extraterritorial risks. While due regard has to be paid to the principle of non-intervention, there are several constellations in which such obligations could be appropriately applied. In particular, where states are actively involved in bringing about potential human rights risks abroad – if they license extraterritorial activities or allow the export of potentially harmful goods – they should be obliged to assess related human rights risks and employ reasonable preventive means. The same holds true for constellations in which the potential perpetrators of human rights contraventions happen to be within a state's jurisdictional reach.

If it is foreseeable for a state that its nationals (including corporate nationals) engage in potentially harmful activities in other states, reasonable prevention can be expected. A standard as flexible as due diligence could ensure that states would not suffer disproportionate burdens, as the capacity-based approach acknowledges that states have limited regulatory and enforcement options outside of their territory. Most importantly, positive human rights obligations of diligent conduct in extraterritorial scenarios could easily be deduced from existing human rights provisions and would not require lengthy negotiations and new regulations. In sum, there are thus good reasons to apply the flexible standard of due diligence to extraterritorial human rights risks. Recognizing and enforcing such obligations would provide a valuable instrument in tackling the growing importance of non-state actors on the international plane.

INDEX

abuse of rights-clauses, 26
access to information, 39, 118, 153, 171, 224, 233, 298
access to the courts. *See* remedies
acquiescence, 107, 112, 113, 177, 183, 199
active personality jurisdiction. *See* jurisdiction
ad impossibilia nemo tenetur, 121
adequate living conditions, 74, 144, 148, 221, 287
administrative apparatus, 61, 71, 85, 221
Ago, Robert, 102, 105
aiding or abetting. *See* complicity
Alabama Arbitration, 83, 89, 91, 120, 122, 136
alien protection laws, 3, 77, **83**, 89, 124, 146, 259
Alien Tort Statute, 309
allocation of resources, 126, 178, 221, 224, 232, 243, 305
amnesty laws, 64
arbitrariness, 131, 135, 256, 268
Armed Activities on the Territory of the Congo case, 125, 272
armed attack, 174, 197, 198
armed conflict, 1, 9, 227, 287
armed forces. *See* security forces
Arms Trade Treaty, 297, 301, 303, 305
arms transfer, 296, 299, 300
asylum, 170, 282
attribution, 1, 24, 70, 79, 81, 82, 87, 92, 94, 95, 110, 111, 112, 140, 167, 174, 176, 186, 196, 212, 259, 265, 269, 270, 301
austerity programs, 225, 226, 233
autonomy, 40, 148, 206, 234

Banković case, 269
Basic Principles and Guidelines on the Right to a Remedy and Reparation for Victims of Gross Violations of International Human Rights Law, 251
best available technologies, 155
bilateral investment treaty, 27
British Claims in the Spanish Zone of Morocco case, 89, 136
burden of proof, 65, 117, 119, 120, 137, 151, 161, 195, 214, 226, 318
business relationships. *See* multinational corporations

capacities, 66, 117, 178, 267, 324
  financial capacities, 123, **126**, 155, 173, 284
  institutional capacities, 122, 137, 155, 172, 284
  of non-state actors, 35
  technical capacities, **126**
  territorial capacities, 123, **124**, 173, 227, 229
capacity-building, 164, 172
certification, 314
Charter of the United Nations, 19, 20, 173, 261, 280, 291
children. *See* vulnerable groups
circumstances precluding wrongfulness, 127, 222
circumstantial evidence, 120
citizens, 1, 24, 48, 80, 81, 82, 121, 179, 191, 204, 206, 207, 212, 260, 264, 272, 279, 283, 288, 293, 321
civil and political rights, 28, 49, 74, 221, 226
civil insurgencies, 88, 125, 167, 229
civil law. *See* domestic civil law

327

civil war, 48, 231
Claims Commissions, 83, **84**, 90, 106, 108, 123, 131, 136, 167
climate change, 156
codification, 90, 114, 138
collective responsibility, 79
commercial speech, 250
common but differentiated responsibilities, 156, 202, 240, 258, 325
common heritage of mankind, 47
compensation, 37, 47, 68, 72, 99, 164, 251, 298
competitive disadvantages, 34, 309, 314
compliance, 11, 35, 38, 42, 49, 56, 68, 71, 76, 99, 101, 105, 106, 133, 137, 152, 161, 164, 170, 183, 187, 267, 282, 287, 295, 303, 305, 306, 310, 311, 315
complicity, 38, 87, **106**, 108, 112, 120, 177, 199, 299
  in non-state conduct, 109
  in state conduct, 107
  in terrorist acts, 177, **179**
concurrent responsibility, 272, 273, 290, 292
conflict situations, 216, 225, 227, 228, 231, 235, 272, 297
consistent patterns of human rights violations, 210, 214
constructive knowledge. *See* foreseeability
Contact Points. *See* National Contact Points under the OECD Guidelines
Continued Presence of South Africa in Namibia advisory opinion, 20, 272
Convention of the Rights of the Child, 10
Convention on Cybercrime, 188, 189
cooperation
  in counter-terrorism efforts, 170
  in international environmental law, 153
  in international human rights law, 236, 261
  with regard to cyber risks, 189

core obligations, 56, 61, 69, 76, 178, 228, 241, 249, 250, 289, 303
Corfu Channel case, 96, 107, 111, 119, 120, 123, 145, 190
corporate nationals, 279, 309, 311, 326
corporate social responsibility. *See* multinational corporations
corporate veil, 311
corporations. *See* multinational corporations
corruption, 224
countermeasures, 103, 106, 152, 176, 183, 189, 197, 198
criminal law. *See* domestic criminal law
culpa. *See* fault
customary international law, 1, 14, 32, 106, 127, 145, 146, 148, 149, 156, 181, 199, 219, 264
cyberattacks
  attribution, 186
  source state, 187, 189
  sources, 191
cyberinfrastructure, 186, 187, 188, 192, 195, 199, 200
cybersecurity, 185, 196, 205, 208, 302, 324

de facto organ, 1
decision-making process, 32, 34, 39, 41, 118, 185, 234, 250, 305
Deepwater Horizon incident, 165
deference. *See* judicial deference
delegation, 15, 71, 312
democracy, 28, 49, 206
democratic legitimacy. *See* legitimacy
derogation clauses. *See* human rights treaties
detention conditions, 214, 223
deterrence, 72, 73, 165
developing states, 30, 122, 158, 222, 258, 261, 281
development aid, 238, 239, 241
differential treatment, 157, 232
dignity, 18, 74, 249, 260, 287
diligentia quam in suis, 136, 140, 160
diplomatic protection, 259

direct obligations for non-state actors, 2, 6, 10, **32**, 165, 257, 289, 307, 308, 320, 322
  in customary international law, 14
  in general principles of international law, 16
  in human rights treaties, 18
  in the African Charter on Human and People's Rights, 10
  in the Convention on the Rights of the Child, 10
  permissibility, 12
disaster relief, 200, 239, 241
disclosure obligations, 313, 315
discretion. *See* margin of appreciation
discrimination, 232
disproportionate burden. *See* undue burden
domaine réservé. *See* domestic affairs
domestic affairs, 126, 258, 260, 262, 264, 268, 275, 282, 289, 300, 302
domestic civil law, 14, 24, 52, 57, 72, 78, 100, 102, 165, 256, 309
domestic commercial code, 309, 317
domestic courts, 138, 308, 321
domestic criminal legislation, 14, 24, 52, 57, 58, 61, 67, 72, 168, 172, 188, 256, 281, 289, 307
domestic human rights legislation, 14, 24, 45, 56, 71, 73, 253
double standards, 260, 267, 270, 278, 293, 295
Draft Articles on Prevention of Transboundary Harm, 100, **101**, 134, 147, 154, 160
Draft Articles on State Responsibility for Internationally Wrongful Acts, 92, 94, 100, 105, 106, 109, 110, 111, 127, 265, 274, 299
Draft Articles on the Protection of Persons in the Event of Disasters, 200, 238, 241
Draft Norms on the Responsibilities of Transnational Corporations and Other Business Enterprises with Regard to Human Rights, 11
Draft Principles on the Allocation of Loss, 100

drafting process, 20, 32, 34, 45, 228, 236, 283, 320
drittwirkung, 23, 24
dynamic interpretation. *See* human rights treaties, living instruments

economic crisis, 225, 228, 233, 237, 243
economic, social, and cultural rights, 49, 73, 218, 221, 225, 236, 237, 242, 284, 290
effective control, 109, 167, 174, 187, 188, 230, 231, 269, 270, 271, 272
embargo, 297
empirical evidence. *See* scientific evidence
enforcement jurisdiction. *See* jurisdiction
enforcement mechanisms, 33, 39, 42, 44, 62, 63, 166, 289, 308, 320, 322
Environment and Human Rights advisory opinion, 211, 286, 292
environmental disasters, 144, 148, 164, 165, 210, 235
environmental impact assessment, 150, 155, 202, 211, 234, 294, 303, 324
environmental minimum standards, 160
environmental protection, 77, 142, 146, 153, 156, 157, 158, 159, 162, 165, 166, 202, 219, 220, 240, 295
equality of states, 1, 47, 263
equity. *See* reasonableness
erga omnes obligations, 47, 259, 287
espace juridique, 270
EU Agenda on Migration, 314
EU Directive No. 2014/95, 312
EU Flagship Initiative on the Garment Sector, 312
European Parliament, 313
European Union, 304, 312, 313
exclusive state control, 95, 118, 138, 139, 196, 214, 234
expert reports, 211, 277
extradition. *See* refoulement
Exxon Mobil case, 16

fault, 79, 80, 93, **94**
  intent, 95, 107
  negligence, 80, 81, 95, **96**, 97, 114

feasibility, 154, 156, 189, 221
financial assistance, 127
flexibility, 4, 83, 114, 115, 139, 140, 159, 183, 200, 207, 254, 256, 279, 307, 323, 326
force majeure, 127
forceful disappearance, 70
foreign citizens, 83, 84, 88, 90, 91, 136
foreign investment, 27, 218, 293
foreign trade promotion, 293, 294, 295, 296, 299
foreigners. *See* foreign citizens
foreseeability, 56, 71, 96, 113, 117, 128, 147, 190, 205, 250, 267, 275, 324
   availability of information, 172, 209, 277, 278, 301, 308
   impact assessments, 150
   objective criteria, 119
   of cyberattacks, 191, 192
   of human rights risks, 208
forfeiture, 28
freedom of assembly, 254
freedom of expression, 35, 194, 249, 254
French Law on Duty of Care, 309

Gabčíkovo-Nagymaros Project case, 104, 146
General Assembly, 252, 297
General Comment No. 24 on State Obligations under the ICESCR in the Context of Business Activities, 291
general principles of international law, 5, 16
genocide, 67, 104, 109, 113, 273, 274
Genocide Convention case, 104, 108, 109, 111, 112, 120, 124, 125, 140, 197, 273
globalization, 9
good governance, 49
Grotius, Hugo, 79
guilt. *See* fault

Hall, William Edward, 81
hazardous activities, 150, 155, 324
health, 162, 210, 211, 212, 235, 255
hierarchy of rights, 248

home state, 282, 290, 307, 308, 309, 312, 317
horizontal effect. *See* drittwirkung
host state, 86, 177, 283, 290, 291, 307, 320
human rights
   balancing of rights, 2, 75, 134, 250, 252
   common interest, 47, 259, 286
   domestic incorporation, 56, 67
   duty to sanction, 63, 72, 252
   investigation of violations, 63, 65, 72
   remedies, 64
   reparations for violations, 68
   respect, protect and fulfill-framework, 51
   sub-obligations, 50, 51, 62, 75, 290
   three generations, 49
   transboundary risks, 2, 48, 287
   universal character, 19, 232, 260, 261
Human Rights Council, 12, 31
   Working Group on an International Legally Binding Instrument on Transnational Corporations, 31
human rights impact assessments, 218, 278, 295, 303
human rights imperialism, 262, 280, 289
human rights risks
   foreseeability, 208
   of state actions, 213
   sources, 205, 220, 275
human rights treaties
   collective character, 261
   derogation clauses, 227, 232, 242, 247
   jurisdictional clauses, 277
   living instruments, 18, 22
   object and purpose, 18, 29, 320
   preparatory works, 28, 74
   reinterpretation, 17, 29
human trafficking, 315
humanitarian law, 296, 299

Ilaşcu case, 230, 271, 289
imminent threat, 71, 182, 205, 209, 216, 248, 250
independent procedural obligations, 151, 166, 296, 303, 324

INDEX 331

indigenous communities, 59, 217
individual criminal responsibility. *See* international criminal law
industrial states, 122, 127, 156, 307, 312
inhuman or degrading treatment. *See* prohibition of torture and inhuman or degrading treatment
intent. *See* fault
internal affairs. *See* domestic affairs
international assistance, 122, 156, 178, 237, 238, 239, 302, 325
international criminal law, 10, 14, 47, 109, 113, 265, 299
international jurisprudence, 55, 84, 89, 107, 119, 130, 136, 149, 177, 196, 231, 247, 279
International Law Commission, 5, 78, 84, 92, 96, 99, 101, 114, 200, 206
international organizations, 9, 20, 29, 34, 44, 160, 182, 278, 282, 308
  human rights obligations of, 14
  international treaties, 32
international proceedings, 118, 130, 139, 141, 163, 194, 239
international standards, 60, 62, 84, 121, 126, 127, 136, 137, 151, 200
internationally wrongful act, 47, 92, 94, 105, 109, 184, 223, 265
  temporal dimension, 103, 105
investigatory apparatus, 64
investigatory obligations, 209, 210, 245, 251
investment treaties, 30
ius cogens, 47, 274, 281, 297, 299

judicial apparatus, 63, 86, 221
judicial deference, 75, 86, 123, 126, 130, 134, 227, 244
judicial review, 75, 135, 151, 247
jurisdiction, 34, 230, 239, 258, 263, 276, 286, 288, 294, 303, 306
  active personality jurisdiction, 33, 264, 279, 281, 285, 288, 289, 307, 314, 319
  enforcement jurisdiction, 264, 268, 279
  extraterritorial jurisdiction, **264**, 268
  judicial jurisdiction, 264

jurisdictional clauses, 263, 265, 290, 292
jurisdictional conflicts, 280
jurisdictional link, 33, 186, 264, 279, 290
passive personality jurisdiction, 264
prescriptive jurisdiction, 264, 279
protective jurisdiction, 264
territorial jurisdiction, 33, 263, 269
universal jurisdiction, 15, 33, 261, 264

Kiobel case, 16
knowledge. *See* foreseeability
Konzerninitiative Verantwortung, 318

labor protection laws, 256
legal certainty, 4, 7, 22, 36, 37, 139
Legal Consequences of the Construction of a Wall in the Occupied Palestinian Territory advisory opinion, 68, 175, 272
legal remedies. *See* remedies
legitimacy, 15, 33, 39, 42, 45, 272, 323
legitimate aim, 39, 232, 266, 298. *See also* public interest
liability for acts not prohibited by international law, 99, 114
licensing procedures, 150, 212, 219, 221, 256, 278, 279, 292, 296, 301
likelihood of harm, 4, 119, 149, 159, 161, 250
living instrument. *See* human rights treaties
Loizidou case, 268, 269, 271
López Ostra case, 212, 255
lowest common denominator, 45, 141, 323

Maastricht Principles, 53, 218, 237, 291
malice. *See* fault
margin of appreciation, 56, 59, 66, 72, 75, 135, 137, 171, 172, 183, 207, 227, 247
maximum of available resources, 236, 239
migration. *See* refugees
militant democracy, 28

Military and Paramilitary Activities in and against Nicaragua case, 125, 269, 297
military occupation, 227, 228
minimum core obligations, 242, 249
minimum requirements of investigations, 66, 86
monitoring. *See* supervision
monitoring committees, 161, 169, 173
multinational corporations, 1, 9, 11, 30, 32, 34, 42, 44, 287, 291, 307
   active personality jurisdiction, 279, 307
   business relationships, 311, 317, 318
   corporate social responsibility, 40
   economic power, 30
   environmental harm, 144
   parent companies, 280, 307, 310, 316, 318
   political power, 30
   subsidiaries, 280, 307, 310, 313, 316, 318
   supply chains, 311, 313

National Contact Points under the OECD Guidelines, 311
necessary implication, 20, 23
necessary in a democratic society-test, 246
necessity, 127, 222
negative obligations, 3, 27, 38, 50, 52, 146, 206, 221, 223, 242, 267, 270
negligence. *See* fault
new technologies. *See* technological developments
no-harm rule, 145, 156, 163
non-compliance. *See* compliance
non-derogable rights, 242, 249, 298
non-discrimination. *See* discrimination
non-governmental organizations, 12, 283, 318
non-intervention, 7, 261, 264, 275, 280, 281, 285, 319
non-state actors
   capacities, 35
   categories, 34
   democratic legitimacy, 39, 40, 44
   dissolvement, 36
   human rights risks, 32
   international norm-setting, 15, 33
   positive obligations, 36, 42
   rights under international law, 30, 36, 39, 42
   self-defense against, 174
   shared accountability with states, 37, 41
non-state armed groups, 9, 29, 229

object and purpose. *See* human rights treaties
obligations of conduct. *See* obligations of diligent conduct
obligations of diligent conduct, 4, 55, 69, 76, 85, 94, **102**, 105, 138, 180, 229, 323
obligations of result, 4, 55, 56, 58, 62, 63, 65, 67, 68, 75, 76, 85, **102**, 105, 122, 138, 180, 323
obligations to fulfill, 51
obligations to protect, 51
obligations to respect, 51
OECD Guidelines on Multinational Enterprises, 311
omissions, 76, 79, 93, 96, 113, 114, 138
opinio juris, 14
Oppenheim, Lassa, 81, 144
ordinary meaning, 132
original intent, 12, 20, 29
Osman case, 62, 209, 215
overall control-test, 110, 176, 188

parallel responsibility. *See* concurrent responsibility
parent companies. *See* multinational corporations
participation, 28, 224, 250
policy choices, 75, 126, 133, 227
political speech, 249
positive knowledge, 107, 112, 114, 118, 120, 171, 190, 197, 199, 209, 299
positive obligations, 3, 23, 38, 49, 52, 54, 55, 146, 203, 207, 221, 222, 223, 240, 242, 267, 269, 275, 287, 298, 323
precautionary principle, 148, 163, 191, 196, 218
prescriptive jurisdiction. *See* jurisdiction

presumption of competence, 221, 230
presumption of incompatibility, 226
presumption of responsibility, 80
prevention, 56, 71, 84, 89, 101, 102, 105, 116, 126, 146, 167, 170, 190, 193, 199, 208, 245, 246, 250, 271, 288, 324
prima facie evidence, 139, 162, 196
primary norms, 92, 93, 94, 97, 101, 127
principle of non-intervention. *See* non-intervention
principle of prevention, 146
private actors. *See* non-state actors
private citizens. *See* citizens
private law. *See* domestic civil law
private property. *See* property
private security companies, 1
privatization, 9, 30, 62, 71
progressive realization, 54, 74, 76, 225, 323
prohibition of retroactive criminal laws, 242
prohibition of slavery, 22, 242, 249, 315
prohibition of torture and inhuman or degrading treatment, 242, 249, 282, 298
property, 84, 90, 168
proportionality, 39, 130, 245, 253
public emergency, 228, 231, 242, 247, 249, 298
public functions. *See* state functions
public interest, 38, 40, 135, 227, 245, 252, **253**, 302
Pufendorf, Samuel, 80
Pulp Mills case, 146, 152, 154, 162
punitive obligations, 52, 63, 65, 67, 72, 84, 89, 116, 168, 172, 194, 208, 245, 251

ratification, 33, 34, 44
rationality, 132, 254
reasonable doubt, 120, 138, 196, 214
reasonableness, 117, 128, **129**, 159, 245, 278, 285, 302
 balancing of interests, 134
 compliance with international law, 133, 193, 252
 historical development, 81
 negative definitions, 135, 139
 seeking assistance, 182, 198

subjectiveness, 129, 136
recession. *See* economic crisis
reciprocal nature of state responsibility, 2, 47, 203, 266, 322
refoulement, 210, 276, 282, 300
refugees, 48, 224, 287
regulatory aim, 130, 158
remedies, 64, 65, 69, 72, 189, 252, 316
reparation, 54, 68, 72, 87, 99, 112, 164, 183, 252
Reparations for Injuries Suffered in the Services of the United Nations advisory opinion, 19
reporting duties, 173, 199, 295, 313, 315, 317, 318
repressive obligations, 71, 84, 86
resources. *See* capacities
respect, protect and fulfill framework. *See* human rights
responsibility to protect, 47, 259, 287, 288
retrogressive measures, 225
right to a clean environment, 49
right to food, 50, 74
right to health. *See* health
right to life, 22, 24, 35, 43, 50, 59, 62, 63, 74, 159, 213, 242, 249, 251, 252, 282, 298, 303
right to privacy, 35, 194, 207, 249, 254
right to vote, 22
right to water, 27, 74
Rome II Regulation, 317
Ruggie, John, 11, 37, 285, 320
rule of law. *See* legal certainty

safe haven doctrine, 170, 177, 199
satisfaction. *See* compensation; reparations
scientific evidence, 133, 147, 159, 163, 191, 211
scientific uncertainties. *See* scientific evidence
secondary norms, 92, 96, 101, 111
Security Council, 168, 169, 171, 174, 177, 286, 297
Security Council Resolution 1368, 174
Security Council Resolution 1373, 169
security forces, 59, 125, 174, 213, 228, 298, 304

self-defense, 173, 181, 188, 189, 197, 199
seriousness of harm, 4, 119, 149, 245, 248, 250, 251
Shue, Henry, 51
slavery. *See* prohibition of slavery
social expenditure. *See* austerity programs
Soering case, 277
sovereignty. *See* territorial sovereignty
standard of care, 91, 121, 129, 136, 137, 154, 160, 198, 222
state functions, 9, 62
state organs, 1, 3, 39, 54, 61, 88, 89, 94, 95, 97, 110, 118, 209, 213, 268, 279
state practice, 7, 14, 16, 32, 83, 84, 90, 100, 112, 116, 119, 136, 140, 145, 149, 150, 172, 179, 180, 181, 183, 187, 188, 195, 238, 241, 247, 309
strict liability, 80, 83, 88, 89, 176, 187, 195, 206, 278
structural problems. *See* systemic deficiencies
subjects of international law, 35, 109
subsidiaries. *See* multinational corporations
supervision, 121, 151, 159, 164, 192, 212, 224, 234, 295, 310
supply chains. *See* multinational corporations
surveillance, 60, 194, 201, 206, 246, 276, 278, 324
sustainability, 159
systemic deficiencies, 64, 69, 97, 165

Tallinn Manual, 186, 190, 194, 198, 201
tariff preferences, 314
technological developments, 126, 159, 197, 199, 200, 243
technology transfer, 156, 157, 240
territorial control, 29, 95, 118, 121, 124, 138, 196, 228, 229, 230, 272
territorial exclusion, 230
territorial integrity, 1, 174, 175, 177, 287
territorial jurisdiction. *See* jurisdiction
territorial sovereignty, 4, 89, 118, 145, 180, 258, 262, 264, 268, 279
terrorism
    definition, 168
    domestic legislation, 172
    international cooperation, 171
    Security Council resolutions, 169
terrorist attacks
    foreseeability, 171
    scale, 174
The Hague Codification Conference, 87, 90
three generations. *See* human rights
torture. *See* prohibition of torture and inhuman or degrading treatment
trade agreements, 218, 219
Trail Smelter case, 144
transboundary harm, 1, 47, 89, 101, 144, 150, 164, 190, 324
transit states, 193
transparency, 39, 41, 224, 234, 304

UN Charter. *See* Charter of the United Nations
UN Guiding Principles on Business and Human Rights, 11, 53, 294
undue burden, 2, 7, 41, 196, 219, 221, 222, 233, 257, 278, 284, 293, 308, 311, 319
uniform implementation, 75, 121, 262, 281
United Nations, 11, 168, 172, 301, 304
Universal Declaration of Human Rights, 19, 286
universal jurisdiction. *See* jurisdiction
unwilling or unable-standard, 177, 181, 183, 198, 202, 258, 286, 325
Urbaser ICSID-Award, 26
use of force, 39, 174, 181, 183, 325

Vattel, Emmerich de, 80
Velásquez case, 69, 98, 245
vicarious responsibility, 82
vulnerable groups, 216, 232, 233
    children, 10, 217, 307
    indigenous communities, 217
    individuals in state custody, 214

Wassenaar Agreement, 297
Wipperman case, 85, 86
Wolff, Christian, 80

Printed in the United States
By Bookmasters